LOTUS
& CATERHAM
SEVEN
Gold Portfolio
1957-1989

Compiled by
R.M. Clarke

ISBN 1 85520 0007

Distributed by
Brooklands Book Distribution Ltd.
'Holmerise', Seven Hills Road,
Cobham, Surrey, England
Printed in Hong Kong

BROOKLANDS BOOKS SERIES

AC Ace & Aceca 1953-1983
AC Cobra 1962-1969
Alfa Romeo Alfasud 1972-1984
Alfa Romeo Alfetta Coupes GT.GTV.GTV6 1974-1987
Alfa Romeo Giulia Berlinas 1962-1976
Alfa Romeo Giulia Coupés 1963-1976
Alfa Romeo Spider 1966-1987
Allard Gold Portfolio 1937-1958
Alvis Gold Portfolio 1919-1967
Aston Martin Gold Portfolio 1972-1985
Austin Seven 1922-1982
Austin A30 & A35 1951-1962
Austin Healey 3000 1959-1967
Austin Healey 100 & 3000 Collection No. 1
Austin Healey 'Frogeye' Sprite Collection No. 1
Austin Healey Sprite 1958-1971
Avanti 1962-1983
BMW Six Cylinder Coupés 1969-1975
BMW 1600 Collection No. 1
BMW 2002 1968-1976
Bristol Cars Gold Portfolio 1946-1985
Buick Automobiles 1947-1960
Buick Riviera 1963-1978
Cadillac Automobiles 1949-1959
Cadillac Automobiles 1960-1969
Cadillac Eldorado 1967-1978
Camaro 1966-1970
Chevrolet Camaro & Z-28 1973-1981
High Performance Camaros 1982-1988
Chevrolet Camaro Collection No. 1
Chevrolet 1955-1957
Chevrolet Impala & SS 1958-1971
Chevelle & SS 1964-1972
Chevy II Nova & SS 1962-1973
High Performance Corvettes 1983-1989
Chrysler 300 1955-1970
Citroen Traction Avant 1934-1957
Citroen DS & ID 1955-1975
Citroen 2CV 1948-1988
Cobras & Replicas 1962-1983
Cortina 1600E & GT 1967-1970
Corvair 1959-1968
Daimler Dart & V-8 250 1959-1969
Datsun 240Z 1970-1973
Datsun 280Z & ZX 1975-1983
De Tomaso Collection No. 1
Dodge Charger 1966-1974
Excalibur Collection No. 1
Ferrari Cars 1946-1956
Ferrari Dino 1965-1974
Ferrari Dino 308 1974-1979
Ferrari 308 & Mondial 1980-1984
Ferrari Collection No. 1
Fiat-Bertone X1/9 1973-1988
Fiat Pininfarina 124+2000 Spider 1968-1985
Ford Automobiles 1949-1959
Ford Fairlane 1955-1970
Ford Falcon 1960-1970
Ford GT40 Gold Portfolio 1964-1987
Ford RS Escort 1968-1980
High Performance Capris Gold Portfolio 1969-1987
High Performance Escorts MkI 1968-1974
High Performance Escorts MkII 1975-1980
High Performance Mustangs 1982-1988
Honda CRX 1983-1987
Hudson & Railton Cars 1936-1940
Jaguar Cars 1957-1961
Jaguar Cars 1961-1964
Jaguar XK120 XK140 XK150 Gold Portfolio 1948-1960
Jaguar MK2 1959-1969
Jaguar E-Type Gold Portfolio 1961-1971
Jaguar E-Type 1966-1971
Jaguar E-Type V12 1971-1975
Jaguar XJ6 1968-1972
Jaguar XJ6 Series II 1973-1979
Jaguar XJ6 & XJ12 Series III 1979-1985
Jaguar XJ12 1972-1980
Jaguar XJS Gold Portfolio 1975-1988
Jensen Cars 1946-1967
Jensen Cars 1967-1979
Jensen Interceptor Gold Portfolio 1966-1986
Jensen Healey 1972-1976
Lamborghini Cars 1964-1970
Lamborghini Cars 1970-1975
Lamborghini Countach Collection No. 1
Lamborghini Countach & Urraco 1974-1980
Lamborghini Countach & Jalpa 1980-1985
Lancia Stratos 1972-1985
Land Rover 1948-1973
Land Rover Series II & IIa 1958-1971
Land Rover Series III 1971-1985
Land Rover 90 & 110 1983-1989
Lotus Cortina 1963-1970
Lotur Elan Gold Portfolio 1962-1974
Lotus Elan Collection No. 2
Lotus Elite 1957-1964
Lotus Elite & Eclat 1974-1981
Lotus Turbo Esprit 1980-1986
Lotus Europa 1966-1975
Lotus Europa Collection No. 1
Lotus & Caterham Seven Gold Portfolio 1957-1989
Lotus Seven Collection No. 1
Marcos Cars 1960-1988
Maserati 1965-1970
Maserati 1970-1975
Mazda RX-7 Collection No. 1
Mercedes 190 & 300SL 1954-1963
Mercedes 230/250/280SL 1963-1971
Mercedes 350/450SL & SLC 1971-1980
Mercedes Benz Cars 1949-1954
Mercedes Benz Cars 1954-1957
Mercedes Benz Cars 1957-1961

Mercedes Benz Competition Cars 1950-1957
Metropolitan 1954-1962
MG TC 1945-1949
MG TD 1949-1953
MG TF 1953-1955
MG Cars 1957-1959
MG Cars 1959-1962
MG Midget 1961-1980
MGA Collection No. 1
MGA Roadsters 1955-1962
MGB Roadsters 1962-1980
MGB GT 1965-1980
Mini Cooper 1961-1971
Morgan Cars 1960-1970
The Morgan 3-Wheeler Gold Portfolio 1910-1952
Morgan Cars Gold Portfolio 1968-1989
Morris Minor Collection No. 1
Oldsmobile Automobiles 1955-1963
Old's Cutlass & 4-4-2 1964-1972
Oldsmobile Toronado 1966-1978
Opel GT 1968-1973
Packard Gold Portfolio 1946-1958
Pantera Gold Portfolio 1970-1989
Pantera & Mangusta 1969-1974
Plymouth Barracuda 1964-1974
Pontiac Fiero 1984-1988
Pontiac GTO 1964-1970
Pontiac Firebird 1967-1973
Pontiac Firebird and Trans-Am 1973-1981
High Performance Firebirds 1982-1988
Pontiac Tempest & GTO 1961-1965
Porsche Cars 1960-1964
Porsche Cars 1964-1968
Porsche Cars 1968-1972
Porsche Cars in the Sixties
Porsche Cars 1972-1975
Porsche 356 1952-1965
Porsche 911 1965-1969
Porsche 911 1970-1972
Porsche 911 1973-1977
Porsche 911 Carrera 1973-1977
Porsche 911 SC 1978-1983
Porsche 911 Turbo 1975-1984
Porsche 914 Gold Portfolio 1969-1976
Porsche 914 Collection No. 1
Porsche 924 Gold Portfolio 1975-1988
Porsche 928 1977-1989
Porsche 944 1981-1985
Reliant Scimitar 1964-1986
Riley 1½ & 2½ Litre Gold Portfolio 1945-1955
Rolls Royce Silver Cloud 1955-1965
Rolls Royce Silver Shadow 1965-1980
Range Rover Gold Portfolio 1970-1988
Rover 3 & 3.5 Litre 1958-1973
Rover P4 1949-1959
Rover P4 1955-1964
Rover 2000 + 2200 1963-1977
Rover 3500 1968-1977
Rover 3500 & Vitesse 1976-1986
Saab Sonett Collection No. 1
Saab Turbo 1976-1983
Studebaker Gold Portfolio 1947-1966
Studebaker Hawks & Larks 1956-1963
Sunbeam Tiger and Alpine Gold Portfolio 1959-1967
Thunderbird 1955-1957
Thunderbird 1958-1963
Thunderbird 1964-1976
Toyota MR2 1984-1988
Triumph 2000-2.5-2500 1963-1977
Triumph Spitfire 1962-1980
Triumph Spitfire Collection No. 1
Triumph Stag 1970-1980
Triumph Stag Collection No. 1
Triumph TR2 & TR3 1952-1960
Triumph TR4.TR5.TR250 1961-1968
Triumph TR6 1969-1976
Triumph TR6 Collection No. 1
Triumph TR7 & TR8 1975-1982
Triumph GT6 1966-1974
Triumph Vitesse & Herald 1959-1971
TVR Gold Portfolio 1959-1988
Volkswagen Cars 1936-1956
VW Beetle 1956-1977
VW Beetle Collection No. 1
VW Golf GTi 1976-1986
VW Karmann Ghia 1955-1982
VW Scirocco 1974-1981
VW Bus-Camper-Van 1954-1967
VW Bus-Camper-Van 1979-1989
Volvo 1800 1960-1973
Volvo 120 Series 1956-1970

BROOKLANDS MUSCLE CARS SERIES

American Motors Muscle Cars 1966-1970
Buick Muscle Cars 1965-1970
Camaro Muscle Cars 1966-1972
Chevrolet Muscle Cars 1966-1972
Dodge Muscle Cars 1967-1970
Mercury Muscle Cars 1966-1971
Mini Muscle Cars 1961-1979
Mopar Muscle Cars 1964-1967
Mopar Muscle Cars 1968-1971
Mustang Muscle Cars 1967-1971
Shelby Mustang Muscle Cars 1965-1970
Oldsmobile Muscle Cars 1964-1970
Plymouth Muscle Cars 1966-1971
Pontiac Muscle Cars 1966-1972

BROOKLANDS ROAD & TRACK SERIES

Road & Track on Alfa Romeo 1949-1963
Road & Track on Alfa Romeo 1964-1970
Road & Track on Alfa Romeo 1971-1976
Road & Track on Alfa Romeo 1977-1989
Road & Track on Aston Martin 1962-1984

Road & Track on Auburn Cord & Duesenberg 1952-1984
Road & Track on Audi 1952-1980
Road & Track on Audi 1980-1986
Road & Track on Austin Healey 1953-1970
Road & Track on BMW Cars 1966-1974
Road & Track on BMW Cars 1975-1978
Road & Track on BMW Cars 1979-1983
Road & Track on Cobra, Shelby &
  Ford GT40 1962-1983
Road & Track on Corvette 1953-1967
Road & Track on Corvette 1968-1982
Road & Track on Corvette 1982-1986
Road & Track on Datsun Z 1970-1983
Road & Track on Ferrari 1950-1968
Road & Track on Ferrari 1968-1974
Road & Track on Ferrari 1975-1981
Road & Track on Ferrari 1981-1984
Road & Track on Fiat Sports Cars 1968-1987
Road & Track on Jaguar 1950-1960
Road & Track on Jaguar 1961-1968
Road & Track on Jaguar 1968-1974
Road & Track on Jaguar 1974-1982
Road & Track on Jaguar 1983-1989
Road & Track on Lamborghini 1964-1985
Road & Track on Lotus 1972-1981
Road & Track on Maserati 1952-1974
Road & Track on Maserati 1975-1983
Road & Track on Mazda RX7 1978-1986
Road & Track on Mercedes 1952-1962
Road & Track on Mercedes 1963-1970
Road & Track on Mercedes 1971-1979
Road & Track on Mercedes 1980-1987
Road & Track on MG Sports Cars 1949-1961
Road & Track on MG Sports Cars 1962-1980
Road & Track on Mustang 1964-1977
Road & Track on Peugeot 1955-1986
Road & Track on Pontiac 1960-1983
Road & Track on Porsche 1951-1967
Road & Track on Porsche 1968-1971
Road & Track on Porsche 1972-1975
Road & Track on Porsche 1975-1978
Road & Track on Porsche 1979-1982
Road & Track on Porsche 1982-1985
Road & Track on Porsche 1985-1988
Road & Track on Rolls Royce & Bentley 1950-1965
Road & Track on Rolls Royce & Bentley 1966-1984
Road & Track on Saab 1955-1985
Road & Track on Toyota Sports & G T Cars 1966-1986
Road & Track on Triumph Sports Cars 1953-1967
Road & Track on Triumph Sports Cars 1967-1974
Road & Track on Triumph Sports Cars 1974-1982
Road & Track on Volkswagen 1951-1968
Road & Track on Volkswagen 1968-1978
Road & Track on Volkswagen 1978-1985
Road & Track on Volvo 1957-1974
Road & Track on Volvo 1975-1985
Road & Track Henry Manney at Large & Abroad

BROOKLANDS CAR AND DRIVER SERIES

Car and Driver on BMW 1955-1977
Car and Driver on BMW 1977-1985
Car and Driver on Cobra, Shelby & Ford GT40
  1963-1984
Car and Driver on Datsun Z 1600 & 2000
  1966-1984
Car and Driver on Corvette 1956-1967
Car and Driver on Corvette 1968-1977
Car and Driver on Corvette 1978-1982
Car and Driver on Corvette 1983-1988
Car and Driver on Ferrari 1955-1962
Car and Driver on Ferrari 1963-1975
Car and Driver on Ferrari 1976-1983
Car and Driver on Mopar 1956-1967
Car and Driver on Mopar 1968-1975
Car and Driver on Mustang 1964-1972
Car and Driver on Pontiac 1961-1975
Car and Driver on Porsche 1955-1962
Car and Driver on Porsche 1963-1970
Car and Driver on Porsche 1970-1976
Car and Driver on Porsche 1977-1981
Car and Driver on Porsche 1982-1986
Car and Driver on Saab 1956-1985
Car and Driver on Volvo 1955-1986

BROOKLANDS MOTOR & THOROUGHBRED & CLASSIC CAR SERIES

Motor & T & CC on Ferrari 1966-1976
Motor & T & CC on Ferrari 1976-1984
Motor & T & CC on Lotus 1979-1983

BROOKLANDS PRACTICAL CLASSICS SERIES

Practical Classics on Austin A 40 Restoration
Practical Classics on Land Rover Restoration
Practical Classics on Metalworking in Restoration
Practical Classics on Midget/Sprite Restoration
Practical Classics on Mini Cooper Restoration
Practical Classics on MGB Restoration
Practical Classics on Morris Minor Restoration
Practical Classics on Triumph Herald/Vitesse
Practical Classics on Triumph Spitfire Restoration
Practical Classics on VW Beetle Restoration
Practical Classics on 1930S Car Restoration

BROOKLANDS MILITARY VEHICLES SERIES

Allied Military Vehicles Collection No. 1
Allied Military Vehicles Collection No. 2
Dodge Military Vehicles Collection No. 1
Military Jeeps 1941-1945
Off Road Jeeps 1944-1971
V W Kubelwagen 1940-1975

CONTENTS

BROOKLANDS BOOKS

ACKNOWLEDGEMENTS

There have been two Brooklands Books collections of articles on the Lotus Seven, *Lotus Seven 1957-1980* and *Lotus Seven Collection No. 1.* Yet so much has been published about this astonishing and charismatic car that we felt it deserved a new and more comprehensive treatment. Hence this new volume, in our Gold Portfolio series, which brings the Seven story right up to date.

Our aim has always been to make available to enthusiasts the articles that were current when their cars were new in the hope that these will assist in the appreciation and restoration of the cars themselves. The leading publishers of motoring journals have generously allowed reproduction of the articles used in this book, and I would like to extend my thanks to the publishers of *Australian Motor Sports, Autocar, Automobile Magazine, Autosport, Car and Driver, Classic and Sportscar, Fast Lane, Modern Motor, Motor, Motor Manual, Motor Sport, Performance Car, Practical Classics, Road Test, Road & Track, Sporting Motorist, Sports Cars Illustrated, Sports Car and Lotus Owner, Sports Car World and Thoroughbred and Classic Cars.*

R.M. Clarke

Thirty-three years young and still going strong: an enviable track record indeed and one which bears testimony to the excellence of Colin Chapman's original design for the Seven. This, the first road-going Lotus, was intended to build on the success enjoyed by Chapman's racing models in the early 1950s and to offer fast sporting motoring to the enthusiast at an affordable price.

It did precisely that. Deliberately spartan in order to save weight and cost but brooking no compromise on handling, road-holding, or performance, the Seven continued to excel from the moment of its introduction in 1957 through all the variants chronicled in the articles reproduced in this book. Today's Seven remains the cheapest way of purchasing supercar performance only available elsewhere in ultra-expensive exotic sporting machinery.

Lotus themselves, however, outgrew the Seven. By the early 1970s, the company was planning to move into the market for higher-priced sporting exotica with greater creature comforts, and the Seven did not fit this new image. So the manufacturing rights were sold in 1973 to Caterham Cars, who had been involved with marketing the car for several years and who continued to develop it in accordance with the spirit of the original. Today's Caterham Seven is instantly recognisable as a descendant of the 1957 Series I, but Cosworth-developed 16-valve Ford engines have replaced the trusty 1172cc sidevalve unit with which the car was first launched, and the car has kept pace with modern technology in other relevant areas as well.

This book provides a fascinating insight into the story of one of Britain's characteristically quirky sporting cars. Enthusiasts will find in it an entertaining selection of reading-matter about their favourite subject; the unconverted will find something in it to persuade them that they really ought to find out more about the Seven phenomenon; and there will be many motoring writers who, like me, will find it an invaluable reference source on a significant piece of motoring history.

Woodcote, Oxon.,
August 1989

James Taylor

Reasonable protection is provided by the lightweight hood, which is easy to erect. The cutaway body sides allow plenty of elbow room. The radiator cowling is quickly detachable

Lotus Seven

SPORTS cars today, apart from classes which have engine capacity as the main basis of classification, may be divided into three categories. There are the expensive continental hand-built models; there is a hard core of two-seaters made—mostly in Great Britain—in quantity by long-established manufacturers; and the remainder are the individually built sports cars of small manufacturers, from whose ranks come many entries for club race meetings in this country.

Many of the last-named have chassis of tubular ladder or space frame construction, and they use a variety of proprietary engines and transmissions. The Lotus comes under this heading, and the current aerodynamic models of 1½ litres and 1,100 c.c. have been outstandingly successful in international racing. Until last October the cheapest Lotus in production was the 1,172 c.c. club model which with purchase tax costs £1,511.

The model which established the reputation of Lotus was the Mark VI, as it was a very popular jumping-off point for the young enthusiast who wished to enter sports car racing without too much expenditure, and it could be used also as a normal road car, albeit with some degree of discomfort. It is two years since this model was produced, and the second-hand value has remained at a remarkably high figure.

To fill the gap caused by the discontinuance of this model, Lotus Engineering announced the Lotus Seven at the last Earls Court Show. Its object is the same as that of its predecessor, but it has a more up-to-date specification. When fitted with the four-cylinder side-valve Ford engine, it qualifies for the 1,172 c.c. formula in popular club events. The price with purchase tax of the basic model is £1,036; additional fittings are twin carburettors, special exhaust, hood and tonneau cover.

It is possible, however, to purchase frame, engine, gear box and other parts separately. If they are assembled by the purchaser with no professional help or facilities, purchase tax is not payable and the price is £526. The simple style of body of the Lotus Seven naturally helps to lower cost, as compared with the aerodynamic design of the other models.

The chassis frame of tubular construction is very similar to that of the more expensive streamlined models, and the front suspension is like that of the formula 2, with wishbones and coil springs. At the rear, a normal live axle is suspended on coil springs and located by radius arms. The body has no doors, but the cockpit sides are lowered so that they are easy to step over; entrance is a little more difficult with the hood erected. Without doors, the car cannot be used for International races, but it is not excluded from club meetings in this country. The front wheels are exposed, with separate

Left: With a height of 2ft 3½in to the top of the scuttle the Lotus Seven is a dwarf among other traffic. Right: The spare wheel rests in a tubular bracket and is secured by a leather strap. Brake stop lights and reflectors are incorporated in the rear lamps

mud deflectors, and they can be clearly seen when placing the car for a fast corner.

The car tested has a Ford Prefect engine, gear box (fitted with Buckler C-type gears to improve the ratio steps) and rear axle. The compression ratio is raised to 8.5 to 1, and twin S.U. carburettors and special exhaust manifold were fitted. There is available a wide choice of axle ratios, ranging from 3.73 to 1 to 5.375 to 1. The test car had 4.875 to 1 ratio.

An outstanding feature of the car is the road-holding and general stability. The suspension is, by normal saloon car standards, stiff, but not to the degree of the sports car of twenty years ago. The coil springs used to support the car at front and rear enclose piston-type dampers. At the front there is an anti-roll bar, which serves also as an arm of the upper wishbone.

Speed on corners seems to be limited only by visibility and/or the driver's experience. At first the Lotus gives the impression of wandering and lacking directional stability, but this disappears as soon as the steering wheel is allowed to float in the driver's hands. "Hands off," the car will maintain a straight course. The steering is sensitive but free from any vice, and there are no noticeable over or understeer characteristics.

Although the steering has only two turns from lock to lock, the effort at the wheel is very low; one can take quick corrective action if the back end should hop, which it tends to do on bumpy corners, probably because of the relatively high proportion of unsprung weight in such a light car. There is no reaction from the front wheels and in this respect the new wishbone suspension is a great improvement on the swing axle type of the Mark VI, which was subject to gyroscopic kick and tended to wander on the straight.

No seat adjustment is provided, and the car tested suited a driver with long legs better than a short person; such a car would normally have the driving position tailored to its usual occupant. The small two-spoked steering wheel is almost vertical and close to the facia; the outstretched position of the driver's arms is comfortable and gives full control. Cockpit space is limited and there is not much foot room around the pedals, though their angles are excellent and comfortable. Brake pedal and accelerator are set so that "heel and toe" changes become a natural manoeuvre. The handbrake lever, which has horizontal movement, pivots on the passenger's side of the cockpit; it is difficult to reach when needed for restarting on a steep hill.

When driving the Lotus Seven in reasonably traffic-free conditions one soon forgets minor discomforts in the exhilaration of its performance, and the manner of its achievement. The Prefect engine, mildly tuned in this case, gives an excellent power-weight ratio and, except for some reluctance to start when really cold, has no temperament.

The engine quickly reaches operating temperature (no fan or water pump is fitted) and it will then give full throttle response without hesitation. The exhaust note at high engine revolutions is noticeable, but the car can be driven quietly through built-up areas without attracting attention other than by its appearance. Acceleration in the open country is very good, and 35 m.p.h. on the high first gear is

Under-bonnet accessibility is not handicapped by the equipment usually seen in a road test illustration. The electric S.U. fuel pump is mounted close to the bulkhead, and plastic pipes are used for the fuel lines. The front mudguards are quickly detachable

reached very quickly with a hard snarl from the exhaust. Second gear ratio is close enough to top to give valuable hill-climbing performance. It provides a maximum speed of 70 m.p.h. and is very useful for overtaking at speeds in excess of 50 m.p.h.

Some saloon cars with not much larger engines, and capable of carrying four or more persons in greater comfort, have higher maximum speeds than the Lotus, but their occupants may never know the joy of driving such a car. It is a great pity that purchase tax prevents such cars as this, with especially high safety factors of road-holding, from reaching the hands of so many young enthusiasts who would benefit by the experience.

The maximum speed of 81 m.p.h. with two aboard is creditable. With a small racing screen and further tuning of the engine, 90 m.p.h. should be possible solo.

The light weight of the Lotus makes a three-speed gear box acceptable. No reverse stop is provided, so that sometimes reverse gear is "snicked" when coming out of first. Very quick, definite changes can be made, but some care and practice is required to engage bottom when changing down from second. The clutch pedal pressure appeared fairly high—indicative of stronger springs than standard. No clutch slip occurred during repeated standing start acceleration tests, and take-off was smooth once the short, stiff travel of the pedal had been mastered.

The fuel tank, strapped down by aero-elastic bands in the extreme rear with the small battery alongside it, adds valuable extra weight over the rear wheels and helps to balance the weight distribution.

Brakes of a size normally fitted to larger and heavier cars are used on the Lotus. There are two-leading shoes in the front units, and the system is smooth and progressive. These characteristics at first may not appear to be

Left: The handbrake lever moves in a horizontal plane on the left side of the compartment. The facia panel is fabric-covered to match the trim. Right: Tool kit and the jack are strapped in the luggage space. The fuel tank and battery can be reached by removing the plywood floor

Lotus Seven . . .

reconciled with the performance figures quoted in the data tables. The reason for the seemingly low efficiency is that at pedal pressures above 50 lb sq in, with two occupants aboard, the front wheels tend to lock at the 30 m.p.h. testing speed, indicating that the braking ratio on the front wheels is too high at present. This could be adjusted by varying the sizes of operating cylinders or, more economically, by having the same size brakes at front and rear. It is a rare occurrence for this journal to comment that the brakes are too powerful, but on the Lotus care was needed in applying them on wet roads to avoid locking the front wheels and losing adhesion for steering.

The driving lamps—a wide beam unit on the left and a long-range lamp on the right—are quickly detachable; the wiring used for the head lamp circuit appears to be unusually light. A switch on the facia incorporating the horn button cuts out the right-hand lamp for dipping purposes. The full width windscreen frame is secured by four bolts and can be removed easily. Twin wipers are fitted; the wiper motor is prominent and could be a danger to a passenger.

A hood and tonneau cover can be had; the hood affords reasonable protection, although as no rain was experienced during the test it could not be fully checked. Normally it is housed, with the light alloy hood sticks, in a small compartment behind the cockpit. A good quality tool kit and hydraulic jack are strapped in this compartment. The facia panel is fitted with the required minimum number of instruments. There is no fuel gauge, but a graduated dip stick is provided.

The hydraulic brake fluid reservoir is reasonably easy to reach for topping up purposes.

For the enthusiast with a desire for racing the Lotus Seven is a safe and sensible vehicle. Purchase tax makes it expensive, but those who can build it up themselves can avoid this burden. In its dual form of racer and road car it is particularly suitable for the young beginner; with diligence he can improve the standards of comfort for road use without detracting from its racing performance.

LOTUS SEVEN

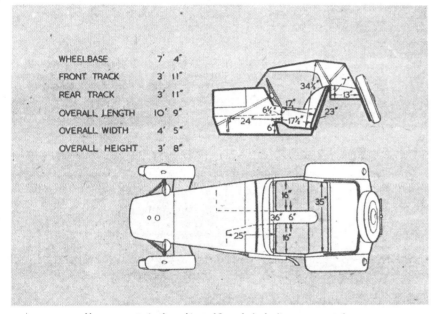

WHEELBASE	7' 4"
FRONT TRACK	3' 11"
REAR TRACK	3' 11"
OVERALL LENGTH	10' 9"
OVERALL WIDTH	4' 5"
OVERALL HEIGHT	3' 8"

Measurements in these ⅛in to 1ft scale body diagrams are taken with the driving seat in the central position of fore and aft adjustment and with the seat cushions uncompressed

PERFORMANCE

ACCELERATION: from constant speeds.
Speed Range, Gear Ratios and Time in sec.

		4.875 to 1	6.483 to 1	11.407 to 1
M.P.H.				
10—30	..	—	6.5	3.5
20—40	..	7.6	6.2	—
30—50	..	7.9	7.1	—
40—60	..	10.1	9.3	—
50—70	..	16.5	—	—

From rest through gears to:

M.P.H.			sec
30	..	..	4.7
50	..	..	11.7
60	..	..	17.8
70	..	..	30.7

Standing quarter mile, 20.8 sec.

SPEEDS ON GEARS:

Gear		M.P.H. (normal and max.)	K.P.H. (normal and max.)
Top ..	(mean)	76.3	122.8
	(best)	81.0	130.4
2nd ..	..	55—70	88—112
1st	....	25—40	40—64

TRACTIVE RESISTANCE: 17.5 lb per ton at 10 M.P.H.

TRACTIVE EFFORT:

			Pull (lb per ton)	Equivalent Gradient
Top ..	..	..	215	1 in 10.4
Second	..	..	310	1 in 7.1

BRAKES (in neutral at 30 m.p.h.)

Efficiency	Pedal Pressure (lb)
69 per cent	50
37 per cent	25
31 per cent	15

FUEL CONSUMPTION:

35.6 m.p.g. overall for 615 miles (7.9 litres per 100 km).
Approximate normal range 27—43 m.p.g. (10.4—6.5 litres per 100 km).
Fuel, premium grade.

WEATHER: Cloudy, slight head wind, dry.
Air temperature, 45–50 deg F.
Acceleration figures are the means of several runs in opposite directions.
Tractive effort and resistance obtained by Tapley meter.

DATA

PRICE (basic), with two-seater body, £690.
British purchase tax, £346 7s.
Total (in Great Britain), £1,036 7s.

ENGINE: Capacity: 1,172 c.c. (71.55 cu in).
Number of cylinders: 4.
Bore and stroke: 63.5 × 92.5 mm. (2.5 × 3.64in).
Valve gear: side valve.
Compression ratio: 8.5 to 1.
B.H.P.: 40 at 4,500 r.p.m. (B.H.P. per ton laden 65.9).
Torque: 58 lb ft at 2,600 r.p.m.
M.P.H. per 1,000 r.p.m. on top gear, 15.6.

WEIGHT: (with 5 gals fuel), 9 cwt (1,008 lb).
Weight distribution (per cent): F, 50; R, 50.
Laden as tested: 12 cwt (1,358 lb).
Lb per c.c. (laden): 1.2.

BRAKES: Type: Girling. 2 LS front, L and T rear.
Method of operation: hydraulic.
Drum dimensions: F, 9in diameter; 1¾in wide. R, 8in diameter; 1¼in wide.
Lining area: F, 61 sq in. R, 48 sq in (181 sq in per ton laden).

TYRES: 5.20—15in.
Pressures (lb sq in): F, 18; R, 22 (normal).

TANK CAPACITY: 7 Imperial gallons.
Oil sump, 4½ pints.
Cooling system, 12 pints.

TURNING CIRCLE: 32ft (L. and R).
Steering wheel turns (lock to lock): 2.

DIMENSIONS: Wheelbase: 7ft. 4in.
Track: F, 3ft 11in; R, 3ft 11in.
Length (overall): 10ft 9in.
Height: 2ft 3½in, to top of scuttle.
Width: 4ft 5in.
Ground clearance: 5in.
Frontal area: 10 sq ft (approximately).

ELECTRICAL SYSTEM: 12-volt; 34 ampère-hour battery.
Head lights: single dip; 36 watt bulbs.

SUSPENSION: Front, independent, coil springs and wishbones with anti-roll bar. Rear, coil springs, live axle with trailing links.

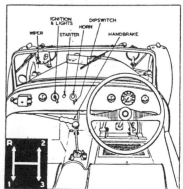

7

LOTUS SEVEN

Seen from above, the Lotus Seven is the starkest design available to-day. Yet everything about it is completely practical

UNDOUBTEDLY part of the Lotus legend or magic, is the fact that cynical motoring writers positively fight over the opportunity to subject a car of this make to a road test at the most unsuitable time of the year. During the spring and summer, when it would be sheer delight to drive any Lotus model, none are available, because the resources of the Lotus Engineering Co. Ltd., are stretched to the limit making and preparing cars for the ever growing number of people who want to go racing in Lotus cars. In the winter months however, almost every member of the staff of every motoring journal enjoys the opportunity of getting soaked to the skin.

The word "enjoys" is used advisedly, however, because there is no doubt that for sheer pleasure, a Lotus is very hard to beat. This is particularly true of the Seven, which is intended for sporting motoring rather than competition, although there is no doubt that as this model becomes more readily available it will become as familiar a feature

in club events all over this country as the Elevens are in International meetings, and probably just as successful.

Introduced at Motor Show time last year, the Seven is an interesting design. It offers the enthusiastic motorist the opportunity of buying at a comparatively reasonable price, an exceptionally lively, out-and-out sports car with none of the complication and expense involved in a car designed for the ultimate in high performance. Thus it uses basically the same frame and front suspension as the Le Mans winning Eleven, but in place of the costly overhead camshaft engine, four-speed gearbox, de Dion rear end, disc brakes and fully aerodynamic bodywork, it uses simpler, and hence less expensive items.

For example, the frame is a familiar Lotus multi-tubular structure comprising square and round steel tubes with the floor and propeller shaft tunnel forming part of the stressed whole. The frame is lighter than that of the Eleven because it does not have to carry the all-developing low drag body-

Without a background to give it scale, the Seven looks normal enough—a tribute to its good proportions. The screen could be wider

work, but its kinship with the frame of the Eleven is obvious. The front suspension consists of tubular lower wishbones and a forged upper arm triangulated with an anti-roll bar. Coil springs and telescopic shock absorbers are the suspension medium front and rear. At the rear a live axle is used controlled by a pair of parallel trailing arms at each side, and a Panhard rod. People new to the car are inclined to suggest that the springing is very hard, in the true vintage sports car fashion, but one can quickly demonstrate that in fact the springs are comparatively soft, while the shock absorbers are very firm. Thus the ride is surprisingly comfortable, leaving the driver and passenger untired even after journeying over rough roads; while the amount of roll is so small in cornering as to be almost undetectable.

Mounted almost completely rigidly in the frame is a Ford 100E engine of 1,172 c.c. capacity. The familiar Ford side valve four-cylinder unit can be obtained in various stages of tune, and as tested was equipped with two $1\frac{1}{4}$ in. S.U. carburetters, a compression ratio of 8.5 : 1, and a four-branch exhaust manifold leading into a single external silencer. Power output was reputed to be around 45 b.h.p. at 4,500 r.p.m., but the way the engine was able to run up to 6,000 r.p.m. without protest revealed that it had received some careful tuning. Nevertheless it idled smoothly, started readily and revealed no sign of temperament.

The normal Ford clutch is employed with a mechanical linkage, and is perfectly amenable to frequent stopping and starting in traffic, or to racing style gear changes. The only snag with the clutch concerns the pedal, which is somewhat cramped in the narrow end of the space frame, and it is necessary to operate it with the toe. A large man with wide shoes finds insufficient room for his left foot and care must be taken to insert the toe to ensure a clean disengagement.

The Ford three-speed gearbox is equipped with close ratio gears and a simple remote linkage. It is delightfully positive in operation and free from vices; it would however benefit by the addition of a stop to prevent accidental "snicking" of reverse gear when making a quick change from first to second. Every owner of a car with this gearbox will know all about this, which is made more likely in the Lotus because the short lever enables such quick, effortless changes to be made.

The rear axle is a B.M.C. unit, fitted as standard with a 4.875 : 1 final drive unit. Thus the emphasis is obviously on excellent acceleration, which as the test figures prove, is achieved without strain. The brakes are Girling hydraulic all round, the front drums being 9 in. in diameter and the shoes $1\frac{3}{4}$ in. wide, while at the rear the drums have a diameter of 8 in. and the linings are $1\frac{1}{4}$ in. wide. Very light pedal pressures produce all the retardation necessary, and in fact

it was found that violent application of the pedal resulted in the front wheels locking. As the weight distribution of the Seven is almost exactly 50/50 front and rear, this was considered surprising, and the obvious solution seems to be the radical one of putting smaller brakes on the front wheels— perhaps the same size as at the back. The situation on the car tested was that Tapley efficiencies of around 80 per cent could be obtained with the lightest pressures, but care is needed on ice or wet conditions to prevent difficulties.

Steering, by Burman worm and nut, is typically Lotus; quick, responsive, and extremely accurate. Only two turns are required from lock to lock, and the Seven makes history as the first Lotus with a respectable turning circle—to wit, 31 ft. between kerbs. It must however be admitted, that on full lock in either direction, the wheels rub the stays supporting the cycle-type mudguards and the headlights.

Some controversy arose during the tests on the Lotus Seven concerning the road holding and the general comportment of the car on the road. A gentle hand on the steering wheel is certainly best, and the car can be controlled with so little effort that after a while one wonders whether thought control rather than muscles are steering it. It neither under-steers nor over-steers, but it can be put off its line into a corner by bumps in the surface. After a while one becomes so used to its responsiveness, that quite fantastic things can be attempted and the Seven never fails, even if the driver's courage comes near to failing towards the end. In other words, the Seven possesses more than ordinary road-holding qualities. One thing which was considered important, was that the amount of throttle opening really had a minimum influence on the way the car cornered; obviously it is better to take a corner with the throttle open but the car can be cornered equally safely on a trailing throttle.

Much of the time during which the Lotus was in our hands, the roads were either wet or icy. Yet it was found that the Seven could be driven safely at cruising speeds around the 60–65 m.p.h. mark with bursts to higher speeds when overtaking was necessary. On one run, during which very heavy traffic was encountered on the way back to London along A40, it was found that the time taken from Denham to Shepherd's Bush was a mere 15 minutes. On ice, all four wheels tended to "go" together, but application of power and/or steering correction resulted in control being regained immediately.

Certain types of road surface resulted in a peculiar weaving motion, which may have been due entirely to the combination of load and tyre pressures at the time. On the other hand, the relation of spring rates front and rear could be improved; this would result in a more steady ride over this particular type of road surface, and would probably

With the hood up (protection against vertical rain), the Lotus Seven is only 3 ft. 9 in. high overall; it is 10 ft. 3 in. long overall, and 4 ft. 5 in. wide. The track is 3 ft. 11 in., and the wheelbase 7 ft. 4 in. Ground clearance is 5 in.

eliminate the side-to-side weaving experienced. Yet another contributory factor may have been the fact that the wheels on this particular car had either never been balanced or were in need of re-balancing.

Despite all this, every journey in the Seven was exhilarating. There is no sound-proofing, of course, and only a minimum of protection against wind and weather. After a while the driver's right ear takes on the same rosy tint as the passenger's left, and similarly, if it is wet, as it was most of the time *S.C.I.* had it, then the driver's right elbow and the passenger's left, became more and more wet.

The exhaust note is hearty, and as the engine speed rises towards its peak, takes on a shrill note which is most stirring; coming up behind slower cars on the open road, it was found that by dropping down into second gear at speeds up to the 65 m.p.h. region produced enough noise to alert the driver of the car immediately ahead. As the car is only 3 ft. 9 in. high overall, and only 2 ft. 3 in. up to the scuttle, this was valuable, because drivers of large vehicles were frequently seen scrutinizing the mirror in an effort to discover what it was they could hear behind them, but not see. The horn is reasonably efficient, but the exhaust note is often more effective.

passenger accompanying the driver, acceleration was slower by 2–3 sec. At no time during the test was it possible to obtain a maximum speed reading. The highest corrected speed attained was 86 m.p.h., but the car was still accelerating hard, and it seemed likely that 90 m.p.h. should be well within its range. Even so, this was by no means a drawback, and the car was driven safely at far higher speeds than most other cars on the roads. The tractive efficiency of the Seven, with its extremely low centre of gravity, is exceptional; its stability generally is of a high order.

Maximum speed in first gear was 42 m.p.h.—equivalent to 6,000 r.p.m. according to the markings on the speedometer —while second, when conditions permitted, would reach 74 m.p.h. The low weight of the Seven—9¼ cwt.—and the low axle ratio made it a real hill-climb car. In top gear, a gradient of 1 in 9 can be climbed without a change being necessary, while second will carry the car rapidly up 1 in 6.

With the 7 gallon fuel tank full, the Seven should be able to cover well over 200 miles; during our trials it averaged 28.4 m.p.g. Driving it quietly, with little use of the intermediate gears, over 40 m.p.g. should be possible.

Equipment is fairly comprehensive. There is a hood, but no side curtains, and the hood compartment is quite

Top bonnet panel is easily removed for access to engine and the nose cowl is equally easily removed. The picture shows this model with twin S.U. carburetters and four-branch exhaust system

There is ample leg room for an average adult in the Seven, but much of the available elbow room is external. The handbrake is particularly inconvenient in this model

The nearness of the outside exhaust pipe to the driver, and the relatively small capacity of the silencer, made gear-changing a particular delight, even bottom gear being available without undue difficulty, because it was so easy to adjust road and engine speeds before engaging this unsynchronized ratio. One snag (literally) concerning gear-changing was the fact that the bolt attaching the lever to the control rod protruded on the driver's side, and took small lumps out of the knees of taller drivers.

Not even this, it must be confessed, reduced the pleasure of driving the car. Acceleration is so good that one uses it at the slightest provocation. From a standstill, 30 m.p.h. is reached in 4 sec., and 50 m.p.h. is seen on the combined speedometer/rev. counter in 9.8 sec. This time, recorded with two people in the car, is the average of four runs. In another 4 sec., 60 m.p.h. is reached, and then a quick change into top gear, and 70 m.p.h. is recorded in 26 sec., from a standing start. Acceleration (driver only aboard) in second and third gears was surprisingly well sustained, as these figures show:—

			2nd gear	Top gear
20–40	..	..	7.2	5.8
30–50	..	..	9.2	5.4
40–60	..	..	9.4	8.8
50–70	..	..	11.8	—

At no time was a completely dry road available for these figures, which are thus all the more remarkable. With a

capacious. It is sensibly lined with Polyeurothene, so that the tools do not rattle about. There is no fuel gauge, but a misleading dip-stick gives a rough indication of the quantity of fuel remaining in the tank. The lighting is not ideal for long journeys at night; the lamps are a Lucas wide beam and a narrow long-range unit respectively, but as they are almost on the same level as the driver's eyes, their efficiency is somewhat wasted. Moreover, the light from them reflects from the chromium-plated backs and from the mudguard stays.

Carpet is fitted on the floor of the driving compartment, and the dash panel and internal panels are lined. The seats and squab could be a little thicker, and sealing between the various body panels would help eliminate the noise of the suspension working. But these are things the enthusiastic owner would probably undertake while assembling his Seven. When finished he would have a motor car which might lack in comfort but which makes up for it in amusement value a thousand times over; and, moreover, it would be a machine with a safety factor far higher than usual. As a means of learning how to handle a fast car, and at the same time appreciating what really goes on when a car is in motion, the Lotus Seven is hard to beat. Basic cost of the parts, ready for assembly, is £525, and it is possible to complete the assembly in some 75 hours. An assembled Seven costs £690 to which must be added purchase tax of £346 7s. which raises the total to £1,036 7s. ★

HOW TO BUILD A LOTUS SEVEN

By "Sports Car Fan"

ALTHOUGH there is nothing particularly complicated about assembling a Lotus Seven, many people who have built these cars feel that a guide to procedure would be useful. The set of parts is a little bewildering at first sight, and a great deal of work might be done twice over without a plan to follow. With this in mind I have listed the order of assembly together with the components required.

Before starting to put the car together it is best to take stock of the situation. Before delivery the chassis frame and body unit has been fitted with all the brake piping, brake and clutch master cylinders, dash panel and instruments, switches, regulator and fuse box, starter solenoid, stop lamp switch and wiring loom.

Inside the car are fitted the trim panels, while the rear houses the petrol tank and boot floor. The full width glass screen, body badge and rear lamps complete the external fittings.

You will seen then, that the more exacting jobs have already been done. The next step is to divide the components into their respective sections, and this I will do as we cover each stage of construction.

Having set the car at a working height, making sure that the trestles or beer crates are under a frame member and not merely an aluminium panel, remove the bonnet and nose cowling. Unscrew the boot floor and side trims, which are held with self tapping screws, and the tunnel top and body centre section, which are bolted.

Check that the tapped holes in the chassis are clean and then try the correct bolts for fit, making sure that you smear graphite grease on them first: Nuts, bolts and washers will be listed after the instructions for the fitting of each component. All threads used are U.N.F. unless otherwise stated.

FRONT SUSPENSION AND STEERING

Components

One pair of wishbones fitted with trunnions and kingposts.
One anti roll bar and mounting blocks.
One pair top arms.
Two suspension units.
Eight bonded rubber half bushes (long).
Two hubs, bearings and caps.
One pair steering arms.
One pair brake assemblies.
Two brake drums.
One rack and pinion and clamps.
Two ball joints.
One steering column and mountings.

1. Assemble each side as a unit, and fit the two-leading-shoe brakes to the kingposts. The bottom bolts screw into the steering arms which are fitted so that the track rod end is on top.

Bolts

Four bolts $\frac{3}{4}$" x $\frac{5}{16}$".
Two bolts $1\frac{1}{2}$" x $\frac{3}{8}$".
Two bolts $1\frac{1}{4}$" x $\frac{3}{8}$".
Two lock tabs.
Four $\frac{5}{16}$" spring washers.

2. Front hubs; make sure that these are perfectly clean. Pack the inside with grease, of the grade shown on the chassis tag, thumb grease well into the conical inner bearing and place in the hubs.

Tap oil seal retainer into position with the flange to the bearing. Note that the felt seal is squashed between the retainer and kingpost face. Slip hub on to stub pin, push in well greased outer cone bearing, D washer and slotted nuts.

When adjusting the bearings, turn the hub as you tighten the nut. When there is no play, back off the adjustment until the hub is quite free to rotate with the slightest rock. The ideal is .005-.020" at the wheel rim.

ON NO ACCOUNT LEAVE THE BEARINGS TIGHT.

Split pin the nuts and tap home the grease caps. Fit the suspension units to the wishbones making sure that the tubular spacers are pushed into the rubber eye bushes.

Bolts

Two bolts 2" x $\frac{1}{2}$".
Two Nyloc nuts.
Four flat washers.

3. Fit the wishbone assemblies using four of the bonded half bushes at the front pick ups.

Bolts

Two bolts 1" x $\frac{5}{16}$".
Two spring washers.
Two halfpenny washers.
Two bolts $3\frac{1}{2}$" x $\frac{1}{2}$".
Two Nyloc nuts.
Four flat washers.

4. Fit the top arms into the chassis brackets, and the suspension units to the front of the brackets.

Do not forget the tubular spacers in the rubber eye bushes.

Bolts

Two bolts $3\frac{1}{4}$" x $\frac{1}{2}$".
Two Nyloc nuts.
Four flat washers.

5. The anti-roll bar ends are cranked down 4 degrees. It is important that the bar is fitted the correct way up, so that the threaded ends are parallel to the ground when the car is at normal ride level.

Use the four remaining bonded half bushes (long) in the top arm eyes.

Bolts

Two Nyloc nuts $\frac{1}{2}$".
Two flat washers.

Next the split aluminium mounting blocks are bolted to the front of the chassis.

Bolts

Four bolts $1\frac{3}{4}$" x $\frac{5}{16}$".
Four spring washers.

LEFT: Method of Assembly for handbrake lever and cable. BELOW: The rear suspension unit mounting rubbers and caps fitted correctly, i.e., two caps and one rubber below, one cap and one rubber above.

Four flat washers.

Do not finally tighten bolts through rubber bushes until the car is on its wheels and at the correct ride level. This ensures that the bonded bushes are set at their neutral position and are not pre-stressed.

6. Connect brake hoses to bottom wheel cylinders, sealing with copper washers.

7. Fit the rack and pinion loosely with mounting clamps.

Bolts
Four bolts $2\frac{3}{4}$" x $\frac{1}{4}$".
Four Nyloc nuts.
Eight flat washers.

Adjust track roughly by eye, making sure that an equal amount of thread is used on both ends.

8. Fit the steering column so that the square bottom bearing is inside the footbox.

Fit the top bearing and, using the bottom bearing as a template, drill the footbox floor.

Fasten with:—
Four bolts $\frac{3}{4}$" x $\frac{3}{16}$".
Five Nyloc nuts.
Ten flat washers.
One bolt 2" x $\frac{3}{16}$".

Slip the splined end on to the pinion, noting that the pinch bolt in the universal joint has a particularly long shank.

Turn the rack and pinion up so that the centre universal joint touches the footbox floor; this ensures that the column will not slip off should the pinch bolt come out.

Do not fit the steering wheel until the car is on its wheels and has been tracked. Set the steering in the dead ahead position, check by wheeling the car back and forth, and then fit steering wheel.

This also applies should an alloy steering wheel be fitted, when the aluminium boss must be drilled, using the wheel as a template.
Six countersunk bolts $\frac{3}{4}$" x $\frac{3}{16}$".
Nyloc nuts.
Six flat washers.

REAR SUSPENSION

Components
One rear axle.
One pair top radius arms.
One L.H. bottom radius arm.
One 'A' bracket.
Six bonded rubber half bushes (short).
Two suspension units.

The rear axle must be fitted so that the pinion flange is on the centre line of the tunnel. Adjustment is provided by shim washers between the 'A' bracket and the axle bracket.

The top radius arms curve away from the suspension units and over the axle.

Fit the suspension units with one rubber and two caps below the chassis bracket, and

one rubber and one cap above.

Bolts
Two bolts 1" x $\frac{1}{2}$".
Two spring washers.
Two flat washers.
Do not tighten bolts until car is at ride level.

Bolts
Two bolts 2" x $\frac{1}{2}$".
Four bolts $4\frac{1}{2}$" x $\frac{1}{2}$".
Six Nyloc nuts.
Eight flat washers.
Two bolts $1\frac{3}{4}$" x $\frac{3}{8}$".
Two Nyloc nuts.
Four flat washers.
One bolt 1" x $\frac{5}{16}$".
One spring washer.
One halfpenny washer.

The front wishbones fitted with kingposts and trunnions, steering arms and two-leading-shoe brakes.

HANDBRAKE

Components
Handbrake lever.
Handbrake cable.
One barrel.
One Clevis pin.
One split pin.
Bolts
One bolt $2\frac{1}{4}$" x $\frac{1}{4}$".
One Nyloc nut.
Two flat washers.

The action is to push the outer cable with the lever.

Run the cable from the axle linkage through the triangular loop in the rear of the tunnel, the centre hole in tunnel gearbox mounting and a slot in the tunnel cover side. Pass the cable through the wire loop by the lever mounting.

With the handbrake lever in position and the slotted barrel placed in the end, run the inner cable through the barrel, which acts as the outer cable stop, and fit the cable and nipple into the square lug on the chassis.

Adjust the brakes by turning the square adjusters on the back plates clockwise until the drum will not turn, and then slacken off until it will revolve freely. Now adjust the handbrake cable.

FUEL LINE

Components
Hose.
Stems and nuts.
'O' clips.

This is run through the gearbox tunnel mounting left hand hole and the triangular loop at the rear. Clip to the undertray at intervals. The 'O' clips are tightened by squeezing each ear with pincers.

PEDALS

Components
One clutch pedal.
One brake pedal.
One throttle pedal.
Two hinges and nuts.

It is necessary to remove the master cylinder mounting bracket to enable the throttle pedal to enter the footbox. The brake and clutch pedals are quite straightforward; use in clevis ends.
Bolts
Two bolts 1" x $\frac{5}{16}$".
Two Nyloc nuts.
Four flat washers.

BRAKES

Fit the front drums and wheels. Adjust the front brakes; each shoe has an adjuster which should be turned clockwise until the wheel locks. Slacken off until the wheel spins freely then repeat on the next shoe.

Check that all brake pipe connections are tight.

Bleed the brakes. It may be necessary to do this two or three times, and providing

the expelled fluid is in a clean container it can be used again after allowing the air bubbles to disperse.

Fit the rear wheels and set the car on the ground.

Check that the suspension is working without fouling by bouncing the car up and down. If all is well the engine can now be fitted.

ENGINE AND GEARBOX

Components
Mounting bar.
Gearbox mounting rubber.
Top water pipe.
Bottom water pipe.
Radiator.
Exhaust pipe.
Silencer.
Propshaft.
SU carburetters and 4 branch manifold if required.

Check that oil filter bolt and all drain plugs are tight.

Remove the fan as this is not necessary.

Replace oil pressure switch with $\frac{1}{8}$" B.S.P. union body, sealing with a fibre washer.

Check that propshaft fits the gearbox tail shaft spline. Lay propshaft inside the tunnel but do not bolt to the pinion flange.

Fit speedo cable to gearbox. Slip rubber grommet on gearbox tailshaft casing with flat to the top. Lubricate the grommet with soft soap.

It is as well to protect the forward engine bay cross tube with a piece of slit rubber hose before fitting the engine.

Have two 2" x $\frac{5}{16}$" bolts ready to slip into the front mountings, and then lift the engine and gearbox into the car.

Fit the tunnel bracket clamp.
Two Nyloc nuts $\frac{5}{16}$".
Two flat washers.

Fit the flexible steel oil pipe to the $\frac{1}{8}$" B.S.P. union and run the pipe back horizontally to the bulkhead. Drill a $\frac{3}{8}$" diameter hole in the bulkhead next to the vertical tunnel tube and fit the pipe, using the thin lock nut. Screw on the conical end of the plastic oil pipe and run up to the oil pressure gauge, where a leather washer is fitted between the flat end of the pipe and the gauge.

Connect speedo cable.
Connect water temperature bulb to cylinder head.
Fit coil.

Bolts
Two bolts 1$\frac{1}{4}$" x $\frac{1}{4}$".
Two Nyloc nuts.
Four flat washers.

Connect leads to starter, dynamo, coil and distributor.

Fit exhaust pipe, using Ford clamp, to manifold.

Fit silencer to exhaust pipe with a Jubilee clip.

Bolts
Two bolts 2" x $\frac{5}{16}$".
Two spring washers.
Two flat washers

Connect hose to clutch slave cylinder and bleed, using brake fluid.

THROTTLE LINKAGE

Components
One cable.
One cable stop.
One clevis clip.
One pin.
One spring.
One clip.
One bolt 1" x $\frac{3}{16}$"
One Nyloc nut.
One flat washer.

Remove the cranked Solex throttle arm and straighten in a vice. Remove the ball from the arm by filing the burred over end. Refit the arm to the carburetter. Fit the return spring clip to the nearest manifold stud. Replace the existing bolt holding the choke cable clamp with the 1" x $\frac{3}{16}$" bolt.

Fit the cable stop bracket on the bolt and fasten with Nyloc nut and flat washer. Fit clevis clip to throttle arm with pin and fit return spring in pin hole and clip. Fit the cable between the cable stop and throttle pedal arm. The inner cable fits in a bracket on the lower frame member below the arm.

A plate is welded on the throttle arm to act as a return stop; this may need filing to position the pedal.

Fit throttle cable and clips.

Note the 4 degree crank of the anti-roll bar end. Both bars are the correct way up.

TWIN CARBURETTERS

Components
Two SU carburetters H2.
Two stub pipes.
Two gaskets.
Four bolts 1" x $\frac{3}{8}$".
Four Nyloc nuts.
Eight flat washers.
One mounting plate.
Four bolts 1" x $\frac{5}{16}$".
Four Nyloc nuts.
Eight flat washers.
One bonded rubber stud c/w nuts and washers.
One length petrol resisting hose.
Four Jubilee clips.
Two ball joints.
Four $\frac{3}{16}$" plain nuts.
One length $\frac{3}{16}$" studding.
Two spring washers.

Bolt carburetters to mounting plate and line them up with the inlet stubs. Drill a $\frac{1}{4}$" dia hole in line with hole in the chassis bracket.

Temporarily fit the bonded rubber stud, so that the stub pipes and rubber hose can be cut to length. Do not have a greater gap than $\frac{1}{2}$" between the two stub pipe ends. Fit together with Jubilee clips. Make up throttle link to your liking, using the $\frac{3}{16}$" studding and ball joints.

Cut throttle return spring to size and form end loops. Complete assembly by synchronising both carburetters and fitting the link and spring.

Fit choke cable. Fit side entry distributor cop. Place radiator in position, using the 'top hat' rubber grommets on the mounting pegs. Drill $\frac{1}{4}$" dia hole through the aluminium baffle plate in front of the radiator, using as a guide the lug soldered to the bottom tank.

Bolt together fitting a rubber grommet between the two.

Bolts
One bolt $\frac{1}{4}$" x $\frac{1}{4}$".
One Nyloc nut.
Two flat washers.

The fore and aft position of the radiator is located by the top water pipe.

Bolts
One bolt 2" x $\frac{1}{4}$" UNC.
One bolt $\frac{3}{4}$" x $\frac{1}{4}$" UNC
Two spring washers.
Two flat washers.

(Continued on page 59)

Close - up of the front wishbone assemblies and two - leading - shoe brakes.

LOTUSSEVEN

▶ Most people think of a Lotus as a sleek, aerodynamic missile like the Eleven, the Fifteen or the Elite. But for two years Lotus has been building — in ever-increasing numbers — a small, inexpensive, all-around sports car called the "Seven", which is just beginning to arrive in the States. Lotus has reverted to a one-number designation (at a time when the new rear-engined Formula car is called the Mark 18) to use the name that was saved for the successor to the square-cut Mark Six, the car that really put Lotus on the map as builders of competition machines. When written up by SCI in June, 1957, Lotus's Colin Chapman ascribed the omission of "Mark Seven" to the fact that this was already being used by Jaguar, a fairly transparent ruse.

The original Seven followed closely the basic layout of the Mark Six, having simple body panels wrapped around its sturdy space frame, cycle-type front fenders and negligible weather protection. Now a special variant has been produced for the U.S. market and dubbed the "Seven America". To adapt it to North American needs it has flared fiberglass front fenders that powerfully recall classic sports car lines. Less obvious are redesigned rear fenders, a thermostatically-controlled radiator fan, Elite-type windshield wipers, and the fitting of directional signals and big stop/tail lights. Several engines are fitted to the Seven in England, but the America comes standard with the full Healey Sprite engine, for which parts and service are readily available here. In our test car its power was transmitted by a Sprite clutch and gearbox to a BMC axle having a 4.875:1 ratio; other cogs are available to choice.

Like all other open Lotuses, the Seven has a Chapman-designed space frame. The front suspension is the now-standard Lotus parallel-wishbone layout, with the anti-roll bar forming one leg of the upper wishbone, while the live back axle is guided by parallel radius rods and a diagonal member. Springing is by coaxial spring/damper units at all four corners, and steering is by rack and pinion. The two-leading-shoe brakes work in eight-inch drums, bathed in a plentiful supply of cool air. Seen overall, this collection of time-proven machinery resembles a hybrid of an MG TC, a K-2 Allard and a California dragster. It's a basic vehicle, purely sporting, with an epidermis of red-painted aluminum encasing a businesslike mechanism. It makes no pretense to Detroit's — or, for that matter, Coventry's or Turin's — creature comforts. It's as spartan and unadorned as a rowboat.

Even before the engine is started it's obvious that this is an enthusiast's car. Since there are no doors, you step over the low cockpit side and shoehorn yourself into the non-adjustable seats. These have only an inch or two of padding atop a very firm surface and are a mere 16 inches wide, so they're a very snug fit. You're so low that you can press a palm flat against the pavement from the cockpit, and you're braced firmly in place by the prop shaft tunnel and the side of the body. In spite of the lack of adjustment, the seat position seems to accommodate varying heights efficiently, and the sparse cushioning is surprisingly comfortable. There's a carpet on the floor with rubber mats under the driver's heels, but this is the only concession to comfort. Everything else is intended for just one thing: driving.

Set at arm's length, the steering wheel is pleasant to use but its ivory plastic design seems out of keeping with the rest of the Seven. Its diameter is good; in fact it couldn't be larger or even a skinny driver couldn't get in the car, except through a trap door in the bottom. Neatly grouped on the dash are the speedometer, oil pressure gauge, water temperature gauge and ammeter, a tach being optional either in place of or in addition to the speedometer. The short shift lever is ideally placed within a few inches of the wheel — though its shift pattern was felt to be too lengthy — and

ROAD TEST

LOTUS Seven America

Price as tested:	$2795

Importers:
Lotus Cars of America, Inc.
4110 Lankershim Blvd.
North Hollywood, California

Suburban Foreign Car Service, Inc.
1907 Susquehanna Road
Abington, Pennslyvania

European Motors, Inc.
8811 East Jefferson Ave.
Detroit 14, Michigan

ENGINE: (BMC A-type)

Displacement	57.8 cu in, 948 cc
Dimensions	Four cyl, 2.48 x 3.00 in
Compression Ratio	8.3 to one
Power (SAE)	48 bhp @ 5200 rpm
Torque	52 lb-ft @ 3300 rpm
Usable rpm Range	800-6000 rpm
Piston Speed $\div \sqrt{s/b}$ @ rated power	2365 ft/min
Fuel Recommended	Premium
Mileage	26-35 mpg
Range	220-290 miles

CHASSIS:

Wheelbase	88 in
Tread, F, R	47 in
Length	132 in
Suspension: F, ind., coil, wishbones inc. anti-roll bar; R, rigid axle, coils, radius arms.	
Turns to Full Lock	1½
Tire Size	5.20 x 15
Swept Braking Area-drum	126 sq in
Curb Weight (full tank)	960 lbs
Test Weight	1300 lbs
Percentage on Driving Wheels-laden	62%

DRIVE TRAIN: (BMC A-type gearbox and rear axle)

Gear	Synchro?	Ratio	Step	Overall	Mph per 1000 rpm
Rev	No	4.66		22.74	3.1
1st	No	3.63		17.69	4.0
			53%		
2nd	Yes	2.37		11.57	6.2
			68%		
3rd	Yes	1.41		6.88	10.4
			41%		
4th	Yes	1.00		4.88	14.6

Final Drive Ratios available: 3.73, 3.89, 4.22, 4.55, 4.875, 5.125, 5.375 to one.

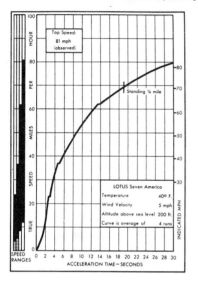

Performance graph:
Top Speed: 81 mph (observed)
Standing ¼ mile

LOTUS Seven America
Temperature 40° F.
Wind Velocity 5 mph
Altitude above sea level 200 ft.
Curve is average of 4 runs.

(Axes: HOUR PER MILES SPEED TRUE / INDICATED MPH; ACCELERATION TIME — SECONDS 0 2 4 6 8 10 12 14 16 18 20 22 24 26 28 30; SPEED RANGES)

Lotus Seven America

the handbrake is hard to get at, being away on the passenger side of the car. The view out over the long hood is inspiring, even taking in the brightly twirling knock-off nuts that stand out from the Lotus's narrow fenders.

The pedals are less inspiring. We'd suggest following the ancient Chinese custom of binding your feet for a few years before tackling this particular car. With skill it's possible to get a 9C shoe on the necessary controls, which feel about the size of a half-dollar. You find that your right foot just about covers both the brake and accelerator, so you control by rolling your foot to one side and the other instead of actually moving it sideways. This of course makes "heel-and-toe" work a cinch, but it can lead to application of the wrong pedal at the wrong time.

When the engine was fired up and the car put on the road, we found that the Seven cleverly combines a traditional sports car feel with the most modern techniques of frame design and suspension. It has amazing cornering power, thanks mainly to its extremely stiff space-framed chassis.

In this day and age the use of a live rear axle causes raised eyebrows in some quarters, but in the Seven this heavy assembly is so well located that you're seldom if ever aware that it's there. Whenever the tail can be broken loose — which is really only on wet roads — it does so very smoothly and controllably.

Light weight is as helpful for braking as it is for acceleration and handling, and on the Lotus Seven fantastic retardation is provided by very modest pedal pressures. The standard linings show no tendency to fade in normal road use, and even after a series of panic stops from speed they continued to halt the car squarely without any increase in pedal travel.

With its 4.875 axle ratio, the test car was obviously set up for acceleration rather than maximum speed, and it certainly did deliver far more sparkling performance than the Sprite engine provides in its original resting place. In top gear the most this engine will pull in the Lotus is 5500 rpm, which corresponds to only 81 mph — about what most Sprites will do, but the Lotus gets there a whole lot quicker.

For road use, however, extra speed is worth little unless you're keen to tangle with the police, and the Lotus provides all the exhilaration at 60 that some more lavishly equipped sports cars supply at 100. In fact, on a cold, dark winter's night 70 mph can feel like 140! There's nothing like it for blowing away the cobwebs of a city office.

The weather protection of the Seven can be summed up by saying that it would impress a motorcyclist but not a Jaguar owner. The simple canvas top is held in place by tubular supports and is clipped down all around by Dot fasteners. When not in use it's stowed behind the seats, and

it's fairly easy and quick to put up or down. When it's up, the Seven looks much better than do most roadsters with their canvas flying. But getting in and out under these conditions requires considerable agility, practice and a slender frame as well. If you weigh much more than 180 pounds you might as well forget it; you couldn't get your thighs past the steering wheel. It's like climbing into a frozen sleeping bag with a wooden leg. The best way to manage it is to leave the three right-hand windshield snaps unfastened, then reach up and hook them to the pegs after you get behind the wheel.

Despite all the shortcomings mentioned, the Lotus Seven has a remarkable attraction for enthusiastic drivers because it's far less of a compromise than are most sports cars today. Basically it's a racing car which can be used on the road without any of the snags normally associated with sports-racing machinery.

Yet roadholding, steering and braking are right up to racing car standards, and the instant steering and speedy gear shift all contribute to sheer driving pleasure. There are a lot of standard parts built into the Lotus Seven, but the chassis they're all attached to makes them seem a lot more desirable than they were in their parent vehicles. With the emphasis on competitive performance, it's hard to view this as a true all-purpose sports car unless you're a dedicated enthusiast — a *small* dedicated enthusiast. The Seven America is a genuine male automobile, tough, muscular and utilitarian.

—David Phipps and Mike Davis

LOTUS 7 AMERICA

What is it, daddy? It's a kit car, son

THE LEAST PRACTICAL and at the same time the most enjoyable sports car that we have driven in a very long time is the "new" Lotus Seven. As a design, the machine is rather dated; it is a development of the old Lotus Mark 6, which was the first of Colin Chapman's creations to reach series-production. Further, the Seven is drafty, brutally hard-riding and offers absolutely none of the comforts and niceties that are inseparable from the modern automobile. Yet, it has an enormous appeal; there is about it an air of spartan singleness of purpose and from any distance or angle the Seven looks exactly like what it is: a racing car with a passenger's seat and enough road equipment to be "legal." On an everyday, all-weather basis it is absurdly impractical—but therein lies its great charm.

Our test car was a Seven carrying the sub-designation "America," which means that it is made expressly for this market and differs from the English version. In English club racing, for which the Seven was primarily intended, regulations permit cycle-type fenders—and the corresponding American regulations do not. That is the reason for the swooping front "wings" on the America model; these satisfy the regulations and look quite dashing in the bargain.

The styling of the Lotus Seven provides us with an object lesson in how closely form can follow function. Actually, we suppose there isn't any styling involved, as the body panels are simply flat sheets riveted to the frame. The frame itself is typically Lotus, constructed entirely of 1 in. and 0.75 in. round and square section tubes—all having wall thicknesses of less than 0.050 in.—and the body panels contribute materially to the strength of the structure as a whole. The only compound curves to be found are in the fenders and the "GP-car" nosepiece,

which are of fiberglass. The resulting over-all appearance is rather slab-sided but it is quite functional and very, very light. We were all in favor of the lightness of the design, but wished that it were possible for the car to have doors. Unfortunately, structural considerations make that impossible.

The over-all fit and finish, both inside and out, was neatly done, but without the careful camouflaging of joints that is carried out in the average car. The exterior decor, paint over aluminum, was repeated in the interior, with a bit of leatherette along the area where the doors would be, if there were any, and on the instrument panel. Leatherette is also used on the seats, which have a common backrest and two shaped cushions (padded with foam rubber) on the floor. The flooring itself, also a sheet of light gauge aluminum, is covered by ribbed rubber mats and the transmission/driveshaft tunnel, between the seats, is padded with a bit of carpeting. The net effect is very "racing-car" and if it is not luxurious, then it is at least consistent with the rest of the automobile. The only clashing item was the steering wheel, which could be an inch smaller in diameter and look less as though it had been snitched from someone's sedan.

The lack of doors does not seriously complicate getting in or out—assuming a certain agility on the part of the persons involved. The passenger has the best of it; he can just step into the car and sit down. The driver, on the other hand, must slide his legs under the wheel while lowering himself into the seat and unless the right sequence of motions is followed, he will not get in at all. Once in, though, he will find that the car fits very well and that all of the controls fall nicely to the hand, or foot, as the case may be.

The instrumentation is very complete—none of these

warning lights—and the layout is particularly well suited to racing. Directly in front of the driver are the tachometer and the oil pressure and water temperature gauges; the speedometer and so forth are located over on the far side of the panel where they cannot cause confusion. Unmarked toggle switches control the lights, high and low beams, the horn and the windshield wipers—and there is a switch that turns on an electric fan placed in front of the radiator should one become bogged down in traffic. There is no engine-driven fan.

There is a top furnished with the Seven, and it is not too difficult to erect, but our experience with the car convinced us that it should be regarded as a desperation measure only. As we have said, the Seven has no doors, and with the top in place one has to enter the car through the window opening. This really isn't too difficult a feat, but it is one of those things that should never have to be performed in front of a crowd of hooting urchins.

Weather protection, such as it is, is completed by a pair of canvas flaps that snap along the sides of the cockpit. These also satisfy the racing regulations (for sports cars) that require a car to have doors. If any bad-weather touring were seriously contemplated, it would be absolutely essential to make up a set of full side curtains for the car.

Mechanically, the Seven is an oddly assorted mixture of parts "borrowed" from small British sedans. Engine and gearbox come from the Morris 1000—and they are used without any substantial alterations. A special intake and exhaust manifold (with two SU carburetors) is the only "racey" touch on an otherwise very everyday powerplant—the internals are absolutely stock. The rear axle, brakes, wheels and part of the front suspension come from the Triumph "10" sedan. Such a combination of parts isn't overly exciting, but any or all can be replaced easily and in a racing car, perhaps even more than any other

type, that is always a very welcome feature.

Whatever innovations may be lacking in the mechanical makeup of the Seven are more than compensated for by the advanced nature of the chassis. Colin Chapman knows a great deal about handling and how one gets it, and this knowledge has been put to good use in the Seven. The front suspension is of the unequal-length A-arm type, with a torsional anti-roll bar acting as part

of the upper A-arm—an arrangement proven on the late-series Lotus sports/racing cars. The "live" rear axle is located by trailing links above the axle and a wide-based A-frame that attaches under the differential housing at its center. In this way the rear roll center is placed quite low and the front wheels are forced to provide most of the roll resistance. Thus, even with the rearward weight bias, the car has a nice controllable understeer and there is never any tendency to lift the inside rear wheel in a corner.

The springing, at all four corners, is provided by coil springs mounted in concentric units with the shock dampers. The spring rates could be much lower if only street use were contemplated but they are just perfect in the use for which the car was designed.

We were fortunate enough to be able to drive the car for several hours and many, many laps around Riverside Raceway—in addition to our regular street testing. And, moreover, we were table to compare the Seven's behavior to that of the more exotically suspended Elite and the Lotus Junior. We are pleased to report that even in that

sort of company the Seven is quite impressive. Fast bends or slow, the Seven sticks marvelously well and will allow its driver almost any blunder.

During the performance testing phase, we found that the Seven makes the sort of standing start that we dream about. It goes away from the mark with the wheels spinning just enough to keep the revs up and no skill at all is needed to get the car's very best. Valve crash places the limit on top speed and on the maximum in each gear, and the car would perform better if stiffer valve springs were used.

All in all, we were tremendously impressed with the Lotus Seven America. It is not much of an all-purpose sports car, but it was not intended as such. However, one would have to go a long way to find a better car for inexpensive racing. Maintenance is much simplified by the lack of non-essentials and the machine can be purchased in kit form at a substantial saving. To us, the Seven appears to be an almost perfect answer for the man who wants a real racing car that can be taken on an occasional Sunday drive.

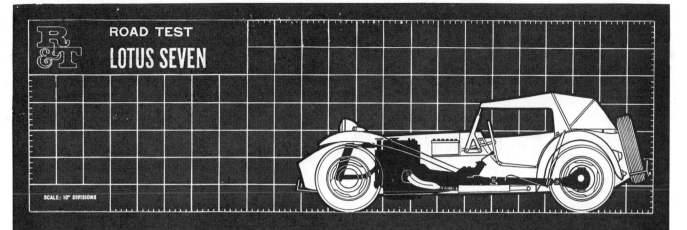

SCALE: 10" DIVISIONS

DIMENSIONS

Wheelbase, in	88
Tread, f and r	48.5/48.5
Over-all length, in	132
width	58.3
height	43.0
equivalent vol, cu ft	194
Frontal area, sq ft	13.9
Ground clearance, in	6.2
Steering ratio, o/a	n.a.
turns, lock to lock	2.7
turning circle, ft	28
Hip room, front	37
Hip room, rear	
Pedal to seat back	45
Floor to ground	6.2

CALCULATED DATA

Lb/hp (test wt)	32.7
Cu ft/ton mile	105
Mph/1000 rpm (4th)	14.6
Engine revs/mile	4120
Piston travel, ft/mile	2060
Rpm @ 2500 ft/min	5000
equivalent mph	72.8
R&T wear index	84.9

SPECIFICATIONS

List price	$2897
Curb weight, lb	960
Test weight	1310
distribution, %	48/52
Tire size	5.20-13
Brake swept area	110
Engine type	4 cyl, ohv
Bore & stroke	2.48 x 3.00
Displacement, cc	948
cu in	57.8
Compression ratio	8.3
Bhp @ rpm	40 @ 5000
equivalent mph	72.8
Torque, lb-ft	50 @ 2500
equivalent mph	36.4

GEAR RATIOS

4th (1.00)	4.55
3rd (1.41)	6.42
2nd (2.37)	10.8
1st (3.63)	16.5

SPEEDOMETER ERROR

30 mph	actual, 29.7
60 mph	60.0

PERFORMANCE

Top speed (4th), mph	85
best timed run	85.7
3rd (5800)	59.9
2nd (5800)	35.6
1st (5800)	23.3

FUEL CONSUMPTION

Normal range, mpg	25/35

ACCELERATION

0-30 mph, sec	3.6
0-40	5.1
0-50	9.2
0-60	14.3
0-70	22.0
0-80	35.0
0-100	
Standing ¼ mile	19.2
speed at end	67

TAPLEY DATA

4th, lb/ton @ mph	245 @ 48
3rd	360 @ 39
2nd	490 @ 30
Total drag at 60 mph, lb	89

ENGINE SPEED IN GEARS

4th
3rd
2nd
1st

2000 3000 4000 5000

ENGINE SPEED IN RPM

ACCELERATION & COASTING

90
80
70
60
50
40
30
20
10

MPH

SS¼
4th
3rd
2nd
1st

5 10 15 20 25 30 35 40 45

ELAPSED TIME IN SECONDS

LOTUS people are probably the most individualistic car manufacturers in the world. Guided by a near-genius with the energy of a reactor and the directiveness of a guided missile, they put out an astonishing range of sporting and racing machinery. Colin Chapman is as sage a businessman as he is an engineer. He aims his bread and butter machinery at the mass market, using proprietory parts (where available), to keep the cost down to reasonable levels. But he buys his publicity with remarkably ingenious racing cars, built at considerable expense.

In the case of the Lotus Seven, the car is available either off the assembly lines or in kit form, to be built at home. According to the factory, it takes between 80 and 100 man hours to assemble a kit, using nothing more elaborate than a power drill and a set of car tools. As a promotion stunt, a team of Lotus men managed to bolt a Seven together in a few hours in the New York Motor Show, but the average owner can expect to put in two or three week ends on the job.

In many ways Colin Chapman can be compared to Ettore Bugatti. His original approach to designing, his refusal to take anything for granted and his ability to enthuse owners with a respect amounting to fervor, are all reminiscent of the maestro. So, too, is the fact that Chapman always sacrifices comfort for lightness.

Small though it is, another similarity is that in common with Bugatti, Chapman does not keep his Type numbers in strict chronological order. The Lotus Seven, for example was produced some time after the Eight, which was the first of the aerodynamic Lotus models.

Why then does he continue to market what to some people is an old fashioned body design, when a more effective envelope body could be produced at a comparable cost?

The answer lies in the fact that the Lotus Seven is a dual purpose vehicle. It is a sports racing car in the true sense of the word. It does not pretend to compete with other British two-seaters, which are designed more as touring roadsters than strict sports cars. It is intended to form the basis of an effective racing car without a great deal more expense.

With fuel and spare wheel aboard, the Seven weighs only 8 cwt. It is available with a choice of three engines — BMC, Ford or Coventry Climax. All three units can be modified, if required, to turn the Seven into a true competition car. For example, in its standard form the BMC "A" series motor develops 37 bhp, but one Australian enthusiast has already boosted this power to a genuine 82 bhp, using almost every trick in the book.

Sixty bhp is by no means an over-ambitious target for this 945 cc motor and it goes without saying that an engine of this power in a two-seater weighing only 8 cwt will produce a quite exceptional sports-racing car at a modest cost.

Although the Lotus Seven stands knee high to almost anything you

The BMC A series motor in the du Cros Lotus.

SPLIT PERSONALITY

care to name, it is by no means difficult to get into. This much we learned during a recent visit to Beacon Hill near Sydney where we drove the first Lotus Seven to come to NSW.

It is owned by Mrs Wendy Du Cros and was imported in kit form. Her husband, Edward, aided by Keith Watts assembled the kit and the trio has now formed a racing stable, intending to enter the Seven in circuit and hill climb events. The other cars in the group include a Borgward and a very swift Peugeot.

The kit cost £1245 (in Sydney) including tax, which is at a lower rate than for a fully assembled motor vehicle. Thus, in price, the Lotus falls conveniently between the Sprite and an MG.

It is not a suitable vehicle for the man who merely wants fast transport because it is lacking in many of the home comforts found with most factory produced sports cars. The all-weather equipment keeps out the rain, but not the wind; the seats are comfortable but non-adjustable; the headlights

The cockpit, with handbrake resting against the passenger's knee.

The Seven equipped for the weather with Australian-designed side screens, like the Goggo Dart. But entry and exit is a real problem.

are adequate rather than impressive, and the exhaust has a fruity tone which could be heard by a policeman standing two blocks away.

But for the man who enjoys his motoring, who likes to live with his machine and who demands a high standard of safety with zestful performance, the Seven stands out way ahead of the field.

There is nothing complicated or exotic about the design. The multiple space frame is clad in a stressed aluminium body with a fibreglass nose cone and separate fibreglass mudguards. The engine is mounted at the front and drives a proprietory rear axle through a conventional transmission system. All four wheels are sprung on combined coil and damper units and rely on normal 8 in hydraulic brake drums, unless discs are specified as optional extras.

The current choice of engine lies between the A series BMC unit, a Ford Anglia (ohv), a Ford Ten (side valve) and the 1100 cc Coventry Climax unit. The latter is by no means easy to get because of production limitations and it is not likely that many will be seen here.

The Du Cros car is fitted with the BMC engine. It had only been assembled a few days before we drove it, consequently a full road test was out of the question. (We hope later to have this opportunity when the engine has been suitably modified). However, the Seven is not expected to give a startling performance in stock form.

Acceleration for the stock Ford version is quite creditable, with a standard quarter in 21.2 sec and 0-60 mph in 16.2 sec. Fuel consumption, once again influenced by the lack of streamlining, is not exciting for an 8 cwt car, working out at 38 mpg at a constant 40 mph.

This, of course, is an answer to anyone who argues that aerodynamics are over-rated. Lotus have built cars capable of 61 mpg at a constant 40 mph. The 1100 cc Mk IX is an example. Even at a constant 60 mph, its mileage worked out at 49.0 mpg. Maximum speed was 113 mph, from a 72 bhp Coventry Climax unit.

The compact dimensions of the Seven make it particularly useful in traffic. Overall length is a mere 11 ft, width 4 ft 5 in and wheelbase 7 ft 4 in. Although the height to the top of the scuttle is only 27½ in, the minimum ground clearance is 5 in. The turning circle is a fantastic 24 feet to the left and 30 feet to the right.

When assembled from the kit, the body is a dashing mixture of gleaming aluminium and red impregnated fibreglass. Like many owners, the Du Cros sprayed theirs a more suitable colour for road use.

Two features of the car are disappointing. One is the all-weather equipment. In standard form, it consists of a pair of hoops with a plastic top that normally sits behind the front seats. This top fastens into place with quick action studs. No side screens are

provided, so Edward Du Cros had a pair specially made up, based on Bill Buckle's Goggo screens. They were very necessary, too, because the Lotus front wheels throw up rain water with gay abandon.

The second disappointment concerns the headlights. In standard form, the Lotus is built to comply with safety regulations by fitting a permanently deflected Lucas fog lamp on the left and a Lucas long-range driving lamp on the right. In Britain this is legal provided the right-hand lamp is switched off when traffic approaches and the wing mounted parking lamp remains aglow.

But even if the arrangement would pass Australian traffic authorities, it has little to commend it. Therefore Edward Du Cros fitted a pair of dipping head lamps from an MG TC.

The instrument panel is neat and effective. An excellent view of the dials can be seen through the two spoked steering wheel. The speedometer is calibrated to 100 mph (?) and the three other dials are for the ammeter oil pressure gauge and water temperature gauge. Actually the Seven engine appears to run unnecessarily cool, despite the limited radiator opening. For this reason, Edward Du Cros fitted the number plate across the grille but even this did not bring the temperature up to normal working levels.

Of course after the engine has been suitably modified, it is likely that the cooling system will require no changes to cope with the extra heat.

The suspension system is a classic of simplicity.

CONTINUED ON PAGE 86

JOHN BOLSTER TESTS

THE LOTUS SUPER SEVEN

WITH COSWORTH-FORD CLASSIC ENGINE

THERE is a very real demand for a sports car which can be used on the road all the week and compete with success in club races at week-ends. The typical sports car of commerce is too heavy and too expensive and it generally has too much comfort and not enough roadholding. Now, I have discovered a really "hairy" sports car which meets all the requirements, and I have just spent

middle ranges, with 62 b.h.p. at 4,000 r.p.m. and 77 b.h.p. at 5,000 r.p.m.

This Cosworth-Ford unit costs only £182 complete. The tubular chassis and aluminium body assembly works out at £260 and the remaining components required total £157. Thus, the cost of assembling a Lotus Super Seven is £599. Provided that certain conditions are complied with, and that a genuine amateur

ing is employed. At the rear, cost considerations have dictated the use of a proprietary hypoid rear axle. It is located by tubular trailing arms at the top on either side, and a single "A" bracket beneath the differential, which also gives lateral location. The springs are helical, and the dampers are telescopic all round.

Drum-type brakes and bolt-on wheels have been chosen for reasons of cost,

a most exciting week of Le Mans motoring.

The Lotus Super Seven is descended from the Seven which all enthusiasts know so well, but it has been absolutely transformed by a new and much more powerful engine. Briefly, the unit is a Cosworth-tuned version of the 1,340 c.c. Ford Classic 109E. Fitted with two twin-choke Weber carburetters, this engine develops 83 b.h.p. at 6,000 r.p.m. and is still producing 82 b.h.p. at 6,500 r.p.m., which is the safe limit as at present developed. Much more important, however, is its immense "punch" in the

puts the car together himself, H.M. Customs and Excise, by a special concession, will levy no purchase tax.

A tubular space frame is the basis of the car, the floor panels and prop-shaft tunnel being also stressed members. The other body panels are secured by Dzus fasteners, rendering accessibility first class. The driver and passenger really sit "on the deck" with a minimum of seat padding.

The front suspension is by wishbones and helical springs, the anti-roll torsion bar also acting as the forward halves of the top members. Rack and pinion steer-

but are entirely adequate. A spare wheel and petrol tank behind the rear axle serve to balance the engine which is well forward, thus giving a high polar moment of inertia. The test car had close-ratio gears in its Ford box, which would cost £35 extra.

No attempt has been made to streamline the car. The screen is uncompromisingly flat and the lamps project. Some rather pleasant flared front mudguards do keep the mud off the screen, which the previous cycle-types did not, but they add a little more to the wind resistance. By stripping the screen, lamps and mudguards off the car, another 12 m.p.h. or so might be available, but on the short British circuits where club races are run, this is not of great importance.

The Super Seven is so low that one sometimes trips over it in the dark. It is easy to enter though slightly harder to leave, and the weather protection is adequate for driving without goggles. There were no sidescreens on the test car and I did not use the hood, though it seemed practical if a little "blind".

On moving off, it is at once obvious that the acceleration is phenomenally good. If you keep away from M1 you can beat any sports car short of the "E"-Type category. Acceleration from 0 to 60 m.p.h. in 7.6 secs. or a standing quarter-mile in 16.1 secs. are indications of the really immense performance of this red hot little machine.

With a weight of only 8½ cwt. and an 83 b.h.p. engine with tremendous torque, the car fairly shoots forward on any gear. Even on top gear, the Lotus will leap way up quite a steep hill and will soon be travelling at over 90 m.p.h.

I was able to achieve a timed 100 m.p.h., which is equivalent to 6,200 r.p.m. on the rev. counter. This speed can be obtained after quite a short run, but even on a long straight it seems about the limit. One imagines that the air is really piling up at this speed, so I did not bother to make numerous runs over the timed stretch as the ultimate maximum is not of prime importance.

Roadholding presents quite a problem with so light a car, for the back axle forms a large lump of unsprung weight. Let me say, straight away, that the cornering power is phenomenally high on a smooth surface, and much better than would be expected over bumps. The axle does hop on occasion, of course, but the effect on the line which the driver is following is remarkably little. After some practice, one can do almost anything with the car, and there is enough power for a lot of fun on the bends.

The natural characteristic is an understeering one but a full drift can be

INSTRUMENTS include (left to right) ammeter, speedometer, oil-pressure gauge, 8,000 r.p.m. rev. counter and water temperature gauge. There is no fuel gauge, but there is plenty of room to fit one if required for, say, touring purposes.

achieved by the application of maximum engine power. On wet roads, the tail does become more lively, and care must be taken not to lock the front wheels when braking. On dry roads, the brakes can cope well with the performance of the car.

As an ordinary road car, the Super Seven is the greatest possible fun. Of course, one takes a mackintosh along in case it rains, but the mud-in-your-eye of the old cycle guards has been avoided. The driver and passenger are in fact quite well protected and there is ample luggage space for a week-end for two. An

". . . enough power for a lot of fun on the bends"

electric fan may be turned on to keep the radiator cool in traffic and the sparking plugs do not soot or oil up in London. This machine is fairly stark, but it is quite practicable as an everyday business hack.

I covered a large mileage during my

SPECIFICATION AND PERFORMANCE DATA

Car Tested: Lotus Super Seven sports two-seater. Price in component form, £599; close-ratio gears £35 extra (see text).

Engine: Four-cylinders, 80.96 mm. x 65.07 mm. (1,340 c.c.). Pushrod-operated overhead valves. Compression ratio, 9.5 to 1; 83 b.h.p. at 6,000 r.p.m. Two twin-choke Weber carburetters. Coil and distributor ignition.

Transmission: Single dry-plate clutch. Four-speed gearbox with central remote control; ratios, 4.1, 5.248, 6.953 and 11.959 to 1. Open propeller shaft. Hypoid rear axle.

Chassis: Tubular space frame. Independent front suspension by wishbones and helical springs with anti-roll bar. Rack and pinion steering. Rear axle on helical springs with trailing arms and central "A" bracket. Hydraulic brakes in 8 ins. x 1¼ ins. drums (front) and 7 ins. x 1¼ ins. drums (rear). Bolt-on disc wheels fitted 5.20-13 ins. tyres.

Equipment: Twelve-volt lighting and starting. Speedometer, rev. counter, oil pressure and temperature gauges. Ammeter. Windscreen wipers.

Dimensions: Wheelbase, 7 ft. 4 ins. Track, 4 ft. ½ in. Overall length, 11 ft. Width, 4 ft. 10¼ ins. Turning circle, 28 ft. Weight, 8 cwt. 64 lbs.

Performance: Maximum speed, 100 m.p.h. Speeds in gears: 3rd, 80 m.p.h.; 2nd, 61 m.p.h.; 1st, 37 m.p.h. Standing quarter-mile, 16.1 secs. Acceleration, 0-30 m.p.h., 2.8 secs.; 0-50 m.p.h., 5.8 secs.; 0-60 m.p.h., 7.6 secs.; 0-80 m.p.h., 14.4 secs.

Fuel Consumption: 28 m.p.g.

test, driving the Lotus really hard and enjoying it to the full. One or two small parts needed securing from time to time, but absolutely nothing went wrong with any of the major components. I formed the opinion that this is a tough, sturdy little car, and that if it were conscientiously assembled by a careful amateur, using plenty of lock nuts, split pins and so forth, it would be exceptionally reliable. Modern short cuts in assembly are wonderful, but for a "hairy" sports car there is still a lot to be said for the old engineering methods of keeping things secure.

There is little that one can criticize in this car, for it achieves so much more than one would believe possible. For touring, the petrol tank is too small and one needs a gauge. For racing, I would be happier with a safety catch or a strap on the bonnet as the clips sometimes rattle loose. In general, though, this is a thoroughly practical car that has improved steadily, as a result of competition experience, with successive models.

The Lotus Seven is not all that comfortable and it definitely is not quiet. Furthermore, you need an extra pullover or two when the nights are cold. If you mind about this sort of thing, this car is too good for you, and you had better buy the dreary conveyance which you deserve. If you want shattering acceleration, the right sort of handling and a jolly good chance of passing the chequered flag while it is waving, the Lotus is your car. The Seven has always been fun, but with this new Cosworth-Ford engine it is a real ball of fire. I wish I could think of a good excuse to borrow it again! For further details, apply to Lotus Components, Ltd., Delamere Road, Cheshunt, Herts.

Lotus Super Seven

THE motoring writer is privileged to drive an amazing variety of cars, some of which afford him more enjoyment than others. Every so often there comes a test which he remembers as an extremely exciting experience, a highlight of his motoring life. The particular car may not be an expensive model nor even an uncommon one, but rather one which somehow contrives to have visual appeal, excellent mechanical features, extraordinary performance, impeccable handling or other virtues which appeal to the sporting motorist to make a car which is truly unforgettable. We found the Lotus Super Seven to have all these features and to be such a car.

Since its introduction in the early fifties the Lotus Seven has been steadily developed, one of the more obvious improvements being the provision of the attractive flared wings which first appeared on the Lotus Seven America in 1960, replacing the ineffective cycle type and thereby inhibiting further spreading of the malady commonly known as "Lotus elbow", the primary cause of which was the excess of water found on British roads. Up till now the Seven has been available with a variety of engines including Ford 100E, Ford 105E, BMC "A" series, and Coventry Climax FWA, but the latest addition to the range has been the Ford 109E engine which powers the Ford Consul Classic 315 and the new Capri.

Thus the Lotus Super Seven has a Cosworth modified 109E engine which develops 85 bhp at 5,800 rpm from its 1340 cc. The modifications are fairly simple and include a Cosworth Mark 2 camshaft, improved inlet porting, four-branch exhaust manifold, and two 40 DCOE 2 Weber carburettors on Cosworth inlet manifolds. The compression ratio is increased to 9·5:1. A rev limit of 6,500 rpm was imposed for the test, some 500 more than what might be considered desirable in normal use. The Seven has a multitubular space frame of one or three-quarter inch 18 gauge tubing while the floor and propellor shaft tunnel are stressed members. This form of construction gives the Super Seven a kerb weight of around 900 lb, so that the power-to-weight ratio is promisingly high.

One cannot but be impressed by the appearance of the Lotus Super Seven, for it is strictly functional and while it is obvious that it has been built to a price rather than to an artist's drawing the form is most pleasing. It is extremely compact, the overall length being only 11 ft, while the scuttle is a mere 27 in from the ground. The designer dispensed with doors and rather more agility than usual is needed to enter the little car, but if both feet are put in first and then the weight of the body supported on the hands as the feet are slid under the dash your can achieve the best sitting position immediately. The foam rubber seat squab is sufficiently long to give adequate support to the thighs, which is important for the drivers' legs are nigh horizontal. The seat back stretches the width of the car, its flat surface being well padded with foam rubber, and while it does not provide much lateral support it does not need to, for one is well located between the padded side of the car and the carpeted transmission tunnel, while the amount of roll experienced in the Seven is practically nil. The seat is not adjustable without the requisite tools, but the only complaint about the leg room was that there was too much, and this fault can be rectified without too much difficulty.

The lovely wood-rimmed steering wheel seemed at the ideal distance, while the pedals were nicely positioned, although not over-far apart. The gear lever was well forward on the transmission tunnel almost under the scuttle so that the left hand had to curl around rather than over the knob to avoid hitting the dashboard. Like the seats

and the sides of the cockpit the dash was covered in red vinyl material. Neat rubber matting lined the floor.

The Lotus Super Seven has almost a full complement of instruments, the one serious omission being a fuel gauge. Immediately behind the steering wheel and clearly viewed through it is the 8,000 rpm rev counter with tell-tale, as the maximum rpm register is called. To the left of the rev-counter is the oil pressure gauge and to the right the water temperature gauge. The 120 mph speedometer is placed immediately in front of the passenger, perhaps not too happy a choice because the readings are bound to instil a certain nervousness into the occupant. The passenger also has an ammeter to keep his (or, dare we suggest it?, her) eyes averted from the road, and might be called upon to operate the choke from time to time. There is a central group of three toggle switches which operate the lights and the electric radiator fan which is seldom required. The starter button is underneath the dash but quite easily reached while the ignition switch is in plain view. The handbrake is over to the left of the car and it is necessary to grope for it, although its operation in a horizontal plane is simple. It certainly is effective, however, and has the added virtue of being out of the way of the driver, if not the passenger.

The Weber carburettors on the well-tuned engine posed some problems in the starting procedure, but after a while we found that if the choke was pulled out the motor fired immediately whether hot or cold, and if the choke was returned straight away the engine would run smoothly. Once under way several of the car's virtues are immediately obvious. The steering, for instance, is so light and accurate that it must be experienced to be believed, which could also be said of the throttle response. The engine has remarkable flexibility for such a highly rated unit and even at revs below 2,000 small throttle openings will produce very brisk acceleration. The exhaust noise makes itself heard in no uncertain manner, and we were left with the impression that the silencer was little more than a token gesture towards the satisfaction of the Law. While it would be embarrassing to use full throttle openings in town, there is certainly sufficient acceleration at low rpm to ensure a good placing in most traffic light grands prix without attracting unwanted attention.

Impressed by the performance in the first couple of miles we took the earliest opportunity to try the little wonder at speed. A de-restricted stretch of the A10 not far from the Lotus factory at Cheshunt enabled us to learn a little more about the new baby. The acceleration through the gears was obviously fantastic, and the 105E Ford gearbox a joy to use. The short lever results in ultra-short movements which are very positive and make it possible to accomplish extremely rapid changes with the utmost confidence. We found the clutch pedal stiff but when the car was later returned to the factory it was discovered to be the result of maladjustment. It was also established that at high speeds (80 mph and over) the windscreen offered scant protection from the airflow and thereafter we invariably used goggles when high speed was anticipated, not because it was absolutely necessary to do so but because it was much more comfortable.

We were surprised how comfortable the ride was during the first few hours of our acquaintance with the Super Seven for while road shocks were certainly felt one was prepared for considerably less damping than that provided. Before setting off to do some high speed motoring later on the first day the tyre pressures were raised, for all tyres had less than 20 lb/in² and a couple considerably less. Accordingly they were raised to 26 lb/in² front and 28 lb/in² rear.

Upholstery is basic but the driving position comfortable (the seat squab is in place!)

Back on the road it was immediately noticed that pumping up the tyres had made the car much more sensitive to road shocks, but still not uncomfortably so. It might be said at this stage that even when the tyre pressures were low and irregular we had been most impressed by the handling although at that stage only fifty miles had been covered and mostly in built up areas. Considering the wet conditions so often encountered in this country there would be a good case for the Seven owner to run the tyres at low pressures except when prolonged high speed motoring was contemplated.

During the next few days the Lotus covered some 600 miles in all weathers and over a variety of roads, and these miles included some acceleration and maximum speed tests which were most enlightening.

First of all we will consider the handling. The steering is basically (and delightfully) neutral; the Seven goes exactly where it is pointed and the expression "it corners as though it were on rails" is more true of this car than any other road machine we have tested. Now liberal use of most of the 85 bhp will naturally cause some degree of oversteer at low speeds but one had the impression that the car cornered so fast on a trailing throttle that the best policy was to limit the oversteer. But on damp roads one could be forgiven for steering the car almost exclusively with the rear wheels. In these conditions the response to the throttle gave the impression of driving a much more powerful car; the sensation was sufficiently exhilarating to give some understanding of why the grand prix drivers complain of the low power/weight ratios of the modern formula one machines! Even at extremely high speeds the steering remains virtually neutral and only on one occasion when a very high cornering force was involved, was it necessary to wind on more lock than anticipated. Despite an anxious moment, the little car did all that was expected of it in the width of road available. The Lotus Seven is the type of car which invites fast motoring and this is just what she got during the test: it was impossible to avoid driving it in a much more enterprising manner than that devoted to most test cars. Despite this, never once was the Seven uncontrollable, nor did it ever once falter in responding to throttle, steering or brakes in exactly the manner that the driver intended. •

The hydraulically operated drum brakes were excellent and brought the car to a rapid standstill in a straight line from any speed, despite the low weight of the car. A single combined master cylinder in front of the scuttle serves both front and rear brakes. One feels that a car readily capable of over 100 mph deserves twin master cylinders but of course there are many more expensive cars that do not have this refinement. Much the same could be said of disc brakes when applied to the Lotus Seven. It is doubtful if the discs would improve the retardation factors, except perhaps from maximum speeds, but they might reduce the amount of pedal pressure required by the ability to use softer friction material. The synchromesh from fourth gear to third, and third to second, was so good that the braking supplied by the engine could be put to very good use, but the good arrangement of the throttle and brake pedals relative to each other invited the use of the heel-and-toe method of slowing, and therefore the tendency was to rely on double declutching, not because it was quicker—it just seemed more correct!

As is usual with road tests at this time of year we encountered a good deal of rain, so that the Seven's weather equipment was given some intensive testing. As mentioned earlier the new flared wings which stretch back to a point beside the cockpit afford much more protection than did the earlier cycle-type guards. The driver and passenger are safe from mud and water thrown up by the front wheels. A worthwhile suggestion that we have already made to the manufacturers is that the wings should be extended right back to the rear wing for the body behind the present wing soon gets well coated with mud and dirty water, spoiling the appearance and ready to brush off on clothing. Another sound argument for this improvement is that such a wing would cover the exhaust which now runs just outside the cockpit on the passenger's side—a trap which a lady would not appreciate falling into. Indeed the man who likes more variety in his feminine friends than in his cars could run up an unpleasantly large hosiery bill! And, it has to be faced, the Seven is not conducive to retaining the affections of most ladies.

The Super Seven is provided with a hood, and in the near future an ingenious form of sidescreen will be available. The hood is folded up and stowed away in the small compartment behind the seat. A light alloy frame is permanently pivoted just behind the seat and this is unfolded and fastened by the web belting which locates it and supports the hood. The hood is then thrown over this and the many push-fasteners secured. The belt which holds the spare wheel in place poses a problem initially, but it must be threaded through the slot in the hood before this is fastened. The erection of the hood cannot be accomplished particularly quickly, but as the owner of a Super Seven will no doubt have much the same spirit as the veterans of the classic long distance sports car races, he will no doubt enjoy developing a swift technique which will stand him in good stead on those occasions when time is a vital factor. An early Lotus Seven brochure says that "hand luggage may be stowed behind the seats . . ." we are disinclined to say more about the luggage accommodation.

But about the performance there is a lot more to say. The acceleration figures are tabulated elsewhere. If you have not already examined them, do so, and hark back to the test to be assured of their accuracy. We spent considerable time verifying these figures, and only one other journal having so far tested the Lotus Super Seven, (the test car being the prototype) we kept in close touch with the factory. They expressed disappointment when informed of the first figures, but when obtaining these we had not taken the engine revs much above 6,000 feeling that we

might be getting better torque immediately after upward changes. Early the next morning, therefore, more tests were conducted, with the air quite cool and absolutely calm. The 0-60 mph figure was improved from 7·2″ to a mean for four runs of 6·9″ while at the first attempt at 0-90 mph the little car achieved a fantastic 17·6″, an improvement of nearly four seconds on the mean of the first day's times. The driver thought the timer had made an error but at the next attempt exactly the same figure was achieved.

After 90 mph the acceleration tailed off suddenly and the four attempts at the magic ton took an average of over thirty seconds. Colin Chapman achieved the ton in 29 seconds during the initial tests but agrees that the figure is never twice the same. The maximum speed reached was 107 mph, some three mph down on what the manufacturer claimed but good enough in all conscience.

At very high speeds the Super Seven is sensitive to the slightest cross winds but if the natural tendency to grip the wheel firmly is overcome, the driver can feel the slightest changes through the fingers and only a minimum of movement of the delicately balanced steering is needed to keep the car running in a straight line.

As said before, the car was driven hard throughout the test yet the petrol consumption was very good, working out at 27·3 mpg overall, while the greatest mileage obtained from a five gallon tankful was 149 miles which is near as makes no matter to 30 mpg. If the car was driven in a normal fashion the very small throttle openings necessary to provide all the required speed would ensure consumption figures much better than 30 mpg and it will not be long before somebody is seriously claiming better than 40 mpg. It is certainly feasible with such an efficient engine in such a light car.

The faults which we encountered during the tests have deliberately been left until last for the reason that the buyer of a Lotus Super Seven will be putting it together himself and will naturally have to make all necessary adjustments himself. One of the more important faults concerned driving at night. The near-side headlight is a

Cosworth Classic engine looks decidedly businesslike behind its two twin-choke Webers

Driving compartment of stark simplicity is offset by the handsome wood-rim steering wheel

Frontal appearance, like everything else about the car, is uniquely purposeful

Lucas fog lamp of the "spread" type which remained lit when the lights were dipped. The off-side lamp was a "long beam" type which would have been excellent had it been mounted correctly, but it shone straight into the sky rather than on the road ahead, which made high speed work at night rather a tricky business. Until we took a

Three stages of hood erection. First, discover same.
Second, attach frame. Third, cover with fabric.
Surprisingly enough, it is very snug inside!

spanner to them both lamps tended to twist when the car was motored fast. Some type of locking device is required. The vibration experienced at high revs was sufficient to loosen all but one of the dashboard light-bulbs from its socket, so these would require stronger clips. The amount of exhaust noise might be listed as a fault: it is rather deafening from 4,000 rpm on, but it is certain that most drivers would find the amazing performance in this range more than sufficient compensation.

And of course there are faults which one anticipated and never found. It says great things of the rear suspension that it was difficult to induce wheelspin. In fact the whole rear-end is something of a marvel. It is surprising that a live rear axle, even located by twin parallel trailing arms and an A-bracket, in association with coil-spring damper units, could achieve such roadholding. The front suspension incidentally, is independent by transverse wishbones incorporating a roll bar, again employing coil-spring damper units.

In conclusion it might be said that the Lotus Super Seven provides motoring experience far removed from the ordinary. Extremely well suited to racing and a variety of club events it nevertheless remains a highly feasible road car. It combines so well the features that appeal to people of a sporting frame of mind, yet it is a fraction of the price of the average high-performance vehicle. At £599 the Super Seven represents value for money not easily found among sports cars. For those who appreciate the finer points of motoring fast and are of such an age or outlook that comfort is a secondary consideration, we recommend the Lotus Super Seven confident that it will give the same enjoyment over a long period of time as we experienced in our brief association.

SPECIFICATION

ENGINE:
Cosworth-Ford 109E. Four cylinders; bore 80.96 mm (3.187 in), stroke 65 mm (2.562 in). Cubic capacity, 1340 cc. Compression ratio, 9.5 to 1. Maximum bhp, 85 net at 6,000 rpm Maximum torque, 80 lb ft gross at 4,000 rpm. Two Weber 40 DCOE twin-choke carburettors on special inlet manifold. 12V battery.

TRANSMISSION:
Single dry plate clutch. Four-speed gearbox with synchromesh on top three ratios. Overall gear ratios: 1st, 11.99; 2nd, 6.97; 3rd, 5.26; 4th, 4.11. Hypoid bevel final drive. Central, remote control gear shift.

CHASSIS:
Suspension: front, independent by transverse wishbones and coil spring-damper units with anti-roll bar; rear, rigid axle and coil spring-damper units. Girling hydraulic brakes. Rack and pinion steering gear; three-spoke wood-rim steering wheel. Tyre size: 5.20-15.

DIMENSIONS:

	ft	in
Wheelbase	7	4
Track: front	3	11
Overall length	11	0
Track: rear	3	10½
Overall width	4	5
Overall height (to top of scuttle)	2	3½
Ground clearance		5
Turning circle	30	9
Kerb weight	8¾ cwt.	

PERFORMANCE:
Acceleration through gears:

m.p.h.	sec.
0- 40	3.6
0- 60	6.9
0- 90	17.6
0-100	35.2

THE Motor Road Test No. 45/61

Make: Lotus **Type: Super Seven**

Makers: Lotus Components, Ltd., Delamare Road, Cheshunt, Herts.

Test Data

CONDITIONS: *Weather: Wet, with rain at times. Gusty 10-30 m.p.h. wind. (Temperature 45°-55°F., Barometer 29.0 in. Hg.) Surface : Wet concrete and tarmacadam. Fuel : Super-premium pump petrol (100-101 Research Method Octane Rating)*

INSTRUMENTS
Speedometer at 30 m.p.h.	.. ..	3% fast
Speedometer at 60 m.p.h.	.. ..	4% fast
Speedometer at 90 m.p.h.	.. ..	1½% fast
Distance recorder ..	.. ..	accurate

WEIGHT
Kerb weight (unladen, but with oil coolant and fuel for approx. 50 miles) 8½ cwt.
Front/rear distribution of kerb weight 55/45
Weight laden as tested .. .. .. 12¼ cwt

MAXIMUM SPEEDS
Maximum at rev. limit of 6,000 r.p.m. (see text) ..	96.2 m.p.h.
Maximum at 6,400 r.p.m...	102.6 m.p.h.

"Maximile" Speed. (Timed quarter mile after one mile accelerating from rest.) As max. speed.

Speed in gears (at 6,000 r.p.m.)
Max. speed in 3rd ..	.. ..	75 m.p.h.
Max. speed in 2nd ..	.. ..	57 m.p.h.
Max. speed in 1st ..	.. ..	33 m.p.h.

FUEL CONSUMPTION
37.5 m.p.g. at constant 30 m.p.h. on level.
45.5 m.p.g. at constant 40 m.p.h. on level.
37.5 m.p.g. at constant 50 m.p.h. on level.
31.5 m.p.g. at constant 60 m.p.h. on level.
29.0 m.p.g. at constant 70 m.p.h. on level.
22.0 m.p.g. at constant 80 m.p.h. on level.
20.0 m.p.g. at constant 90 m.p.h. on level.

Overall Fuel Consumption for 1,212 miles, 47.7 gallons, equals 25.4 m.p.g. (11.12 litres/100 km.)

Touring Fuel Consumption (m.p.g. at steady speed midway between 30 m.p.h. and maximum, less 5% allowance for acceleration) .. 29.2 m.p.g.
Fuel tank capacity (maker's figure) .. 5 gallons.

STEERING
Turning circle between kerbs :
Left	25¾ feet
Right	26½ feet
Turns of steering wheel from lock to lock 2⅝	

BRAKES from 30 m.p.h.
1.00 g retardation (equivalent to 30 ft. stopping distance) with 110 lb. pedal pressure.
0.95 g retardation (equivalent to 31½ ft. stopping distance) with 100 lb. pedal pressure.
0.73 g retardation (equivalent to 41 ft. stopping distance) with 75 lb. pedal pressure.
0.65 g retardation (equivalent to 46 ft. stopping distance) with 50 lb. pedal pressure.
0.30 g retardation (equivalent to 100 ft. stopping distance) with 25 lb. pedal pressure.

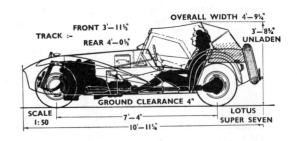

OVERALL WIDTH 4'–9¼"
TRACK :– FRONT 3'–11½" REAR 4'–0½"
3'–8¾" UNLADEN
GROUND CLEARANCE 4"
SCALE 1:50   7'–4"   10'–11¼"
LOTUS SUPER SEVEN

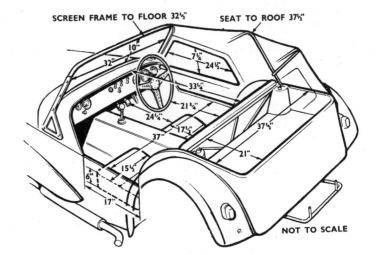

SCREEN FRAME TO FLOOR 32½"   SEAT TO ROOF 37½"
NOT TO SCALE

ACCELERATION TIMES from standstill
0-30 m.p.h.	3.3 sec.
0-40 m.p.h.	4.6 sec.
0-50 m.p.h.	6.4 sec.
0-60 m.p.h.	8.5 sec.
0-70 m.p.h.	11.1 sec.
0-80 m.p.h.	14.9 sec.
0-90 m.p.h.	19.2 sec.
Standing quarter mile	16.2 sec.

ACCELERATION TIMES on Upper Ratios
	Top gear	3rd gear
10-30 m.p.h.	—	5.6 sec.
20-40 m.p.h.	7.2 sec.	4.7 sec.
30-50 m.p.h.	6.0 sec.	4.2 sec.
40-60 m.p.h.	6.1 sec.	4.4 sec.
50-70 m.p.h.	7.9 sec.	5.3 sec.
60-80 m.p.h.	8.9 sec.	—
70-90 m.p.h.	8.9 sec.	—

HILL CLIMBING at sustained steady speeds
Max. gradient on top gear	..	1 in 5.8 (Tapley 380 lb./ton)
Max. gradient on 3rd gear	..	1 in 4.3 (Tapley 510 lb./ton)
Max. gradient on 2nd gear	..	1 in 3.0 (Tapley 705 lb./ton)

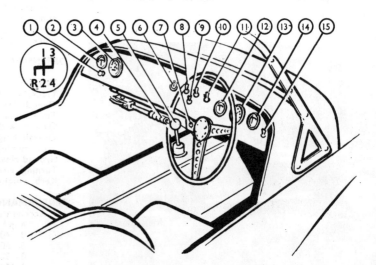

1, Choke. 2, Ammeter. 3, Speedometer (with non-decimal, non-trip distance recorder). 4, Handbrake. 5, Gear lever. 6, Ignition. 7, Starter button. 8, Windscreen wiper switch. 9, Electric radiator fan switch. 10, Dip switch. 11, Lights switch. 12, Oil pressure gauge. 13, Rev. counter. 14, Water temperature gauge. 15, Horn.

The Lotus Super Seven

The hood keeps out most of the rain but few of the draughts. Visibility to the side and rear is strictly limited with the top up.

In Brief

Price (including close ratio gears as tested), £681 plus purchase tax £350, equals £1,031.

Price in kit form (without c.r. gears), £599.

Capacity	1,340 c.c.
Unladen kerb weight ..	8½ cwt.

Acceleration:

20-40 m.p.h. in top gear	7.2 sec.
0-50 m.p.h. through gears	6.4 sec.

Maximum direct top gear gradient

	1 in 5.8
Maximum speed	96.2 m.p.h.

"Maximile" speed   As maximum speed

Touring fuel consumption   29.2 m.p.g.

Gearing: 16.03 m.p.h. in top gear at 1,000 r.p.m.; 37.5 m.p.h. at 1,000 ft./min. piston speed.

Phenomenal Performance for the Hardy Handyman

THE Lotus Seven is a sports car. The Lotus Super Seven, a version of the car fitted with a Cosworth-tuned Ford Consul Classic 315 engine, is even more so. With all the nebulous divisions that exist between touring, G.T. and true sports cars here is one that falls indisputably in the last category. *Pur sang* in being directly descended from the Mk. 6, which was the first production Lotus ever made, it offers performance with little regard for any other consideration save cost. Like most vehicles which pursue one goal to the exclusion of all others, it is exceptional in its own particular virtues.

The car is sold in kit form and although the price of a complete machine is quoted, few if any are sold in this country as most purchasers are prepared to spend some time (Lotus claim 20 hours) in assembly in order to avoid paying purchase tax. Having done this the owner has a car which offers very little in the way of creature comforts as regards ride and weather protection, but has a performance that allows him to say goodbye to virtually everything else on the road, both from a standstill and round corners. Furthermore it is an admirable type of machine for competition motoring on the club level.

The Mk. 6 was normally fitted with the side-valve 1,172 c.c. Ford engine, while the Seven has the latest o.h.v., 1.3-litre Ford Classic engine fitted with twin Weber carburetters, the engine being extensively modified internally though not up to Formula Junior standards. Thus a limit of 6,000 r.p.m. is suggested for long life, due allowance being

The Cosworth-tuned Ford Classic engine, with its massive twin-choke Weber carburetters, sits well forward in the chassis. Accessibility is good, save to the dipstick.

The Lotus Super Seven

made for the fact that it is extremely easy to exceed that limit. In fact in order to check its maximum speed we made a two-way run in top gear with 6,400 r.p.m. on the rev counter. This was reached after accelerating for about half a mile from rest. Acceleration times were taken using 6,000 r.p.m., carrying a full test load and under bad weather conditions. Even so it is difficult to single out any figure as of particular merit inasmuch as they are all in a class that is rarely met with when testing ordinary cars. A standing ¼-mile in 16.2 seconds and the ability to reach 90 m.p.h. from 70 in top gear in only 1.7 seconds more than are required from 20 to 40 indicates that the car's getaway is matched by its acceleration at high speed.

The engine gives its power very smoothly, the valve spring surge that was present at something over 5,000 r.p.m. in Cosworth-tuned 105E Anglia engines seeming to be absent although a very crisp exhaust note helps to hide other sounds. Flexibility is good, thanks to the larger engine capacity, and the car can be driven at below 20 m.p.h. in top gear remarkably smoothly provided that full throttle is avoided. A really smooth and long accelerator pedal action makes this easy and also adds to the pleasure of driving. Starting (the carburetters run very rich at low r.p.m.) is easy, particularly from cold, but care must be taken not to pump the pedal when the car is warm or the plugs may become wetted. Oil consumption was for some reason excessive and a smoky exhaust suggested that some of this was going down the valve guides. Previous experience of these engines in tuned form indicates that this unit was not typical in this respect.

On the open road the engine runs at above 80°C. and in traffic an electric fan, operated by a switch on the dash, is used to keep temperature down. This fan threw a blade during our test and the engine boiled, but even then there was no sign of running-on with 100 octane fuel.

The gearbox of the test car was fitted with close ratio gears which cost £35

Nothing that isn't essential—though the lighting arrangements are not completely ideal for fast night driving. Note the electrically driven radiator fan which is controlled by a facia switch.

extra unfitted, and are a worthwhile improvement. The change from first to second could easily be missed and the clutch pedal required a very heavy pressure.

The present engine, offering almost double the power of the units normally found in the old Mk. 6 and other 7s, has necessitated chassis and running gear development. Wishbone front suspension in place of swing axles and a more effectively located rigid rear axle are coupled with 13 in. wheels. Previously, a variety of larger sizes was used. Nevertheless the driver is still aware of the large quantity of unsprung weight as is only to be expected in a car which is so light; axle tramp can be provoked on rough surfaces and wheelspin in third gear was experienced in the wet. Equally, while those products of Cheshunt which have independent suspension all round offer very good riding qualities, the Super Seven is so firmly damped and sprung (in that order) that every road unevenness is felt, although this fault diminishes as the speed rises and the car floats over

the bumps. While this may not please comfort lovers, for whom the car is not intended anyway, the complete stability of the Lotus earns it high praise. On the worst surfaces it always lands square and we were able to sample its stability at maximum speed in heavy wind and rain without anxiety. A complete lack of pitching or roll adds to the general feeling of safety, but drivers not used to the exceptionally light and sensitive steering took some time to get used to its instantaneous response. Once it becomes familiar, however, it is a delight, and although the consequences of making hard contact with anything in the diminutive Seven do not bear thinking about, the situations from which it is possible to extricate oneself with a flick of the wrist or a touch on the accelerator pedal would often prove to be disastrous in less nimble and agile cars.

Cornering power is of a very high order and is really best appreciated on a racing circuit. The tail of the car tends to "hang-out" less when really motoring round a bend than was the case with

No one forgets the exhaust—least of all the passenger. The flared front wings keep most of the spray out of the cockpit. A useful amount of small luggage can be piled in the " boot ".

earlier models, although in the wet excessive use of the accelerator will induce rear-end breakaway.

The light weight of the car coupled with lack of streamlining and low gearing render brakes almost unnecessary, since the driver has only to lift his foot for an instant to lose speed almost as rapidly as he can gain it. Nevertheless the drum brakes, which are taken from the Triumph Herald, are there for emergency and work well, showing far less tendency to lock the wheels at low speed than previous systems used on similar Lotuses.

Only someone who had experienced an earlier version could, however, appreciate that advances have been made in providing comfort for the occupants. Pendant pedals mean that water is no longer able to enter the driving compartment from beneath. Nevertheless in wet weather the occupants suffer from what is known as "Lotus Elbow," a complaint which consists of a completely soaked elbow which has perforce been hanging out of the side of the car because of the limited room inside. This in turn means that damp can penetrate into the car, and although the seats are in other respects good the fact that some form of foam material is used in their construction means that they absorb this damp to the discomfort of the persons sitting on them. It should perhaps be recorded that during our test the weather was at its English worst, which undoubtedly heightened these shortcomings. Furthermore we did not have the optional extra sidescreens although a tonneau was fitted and this

did help. The windscreen is so placed as to produce considerable wind buffeting inside, and it becomes wet on both sides in the rain.

The Vynide-covered dashboard has few switches or instruments to distract the driver (even the rev counter is, surprisingly, an extra). They are reasonably well placed, but the cluster of three switches to the left of the steering wheel controlling wipers, electric radiator fan, and the extinguishing of one of the headlights as a means of dipping, were apt to be confused. Mounted below the dash the handbrake was not very accessible but the closely mounted pedals allow "heel

and toeing" at rest or when mobile. The lights consist of a wide-spread lamp and a long-range spotlamp and their tendency to move slightly so that they do not point in the right direction makes them less effective most of the time than in fact they can be.

As a study of the data will reveal there are no ashtrays, parcel shelves (there is a little "boot" space) or radio options, only the basic essentials for the sporting motorist. It is by no means everyone's car but for those of limited resources who want performance which is quite exceptional at the price, this is it.

The cockpit is sparse and strictly functional. Built-in seats (they are not adjustable) are more comfortable than they look. Ammeter and speedometer (left of facia) are difficult to read and invisible when the tonneau covers the passenger seat. Note the horizontal handbrake and stubby gear lever.

Specification

Engine
Cylinders		4
Bore		80.96 mm.
Stroke		65.07 mm.
Cubic capacity		1,340 c.c.
Piston area		31.92 sq. in.
Valves		o.h.v., pushrods
Compression ratio		9.5/1
Carburetters		Twin Weber 40DCOE2
Fuel pump		AC mechanical
Ignition timing control		Centrifugal
Oil filter		AC full flow
Max. power (gross/net)		90/85 b.h.p. at 6,000 r.p.m.
Piston speed at max. b.h.p.		2,562 ft./min.

Transmission
Clutch		s.d.p.
Top gear (s/m)		4.11
3rd gear (s/m)		5.26
2nd gear (s/m)		6.97
1st gear		11.99
Reverse		15.74
Overdrive		None
Propeller shaft		Single piece Hardy Spicer open
Final drive		Hypoid
Top gear m.p.h. at 1,000 r.p.m.		16.03
Top gear m.p.h. at 1,000 ft./min. piston speed		37.5

Chassis
Brakes		Girling hydraulic drum
Brake diameters		8 in. dia. front, 7 in. dia. rear
Friction areas		73 sq. in. of lining working on 118 sq. in. of rubbed area
Suspension:		
Front		Independent, by coil springs and wishbones
Rear		Live axle, located by "A" bracket and parallel trailing arms, with coil springs
Shock Absorbers		Armstrong telescopic, combined with coil springs
Steering gear		Rack and pinion
Tyres		5.20 × 13 tubed

Coachwork and Equipment

Starting handle		None
Battery mounting		Under bonnet in front of scuttle
Jack		None
Jacking points		Any convenient point on chassis
Standard tool kit		None
Exterior lights		2 side, 2 rear, 2 head, stop and number plate
Number of electrical fuses		Two
Direction indicators		Flashing indicators extra
Windscreen wipers		Twin-blade, electric, self-parking
Windscreen washers		None
Sun visors		None
Instruments		Speedometer with mileage recorder, oil pressure, water temperature, ammeter.

Warning lights		None
Locks		None
Glove lockers		None
Map pockets		None
Parcel shelves		None
Ashtrays		None
Cigar lighters		None
Interior lights		Instrument lights
Interior heater		Optional extra
Car radio		None
Extras available		Side screens, heater, close ratio gears, tonneau cover, flashing indicators, tachometer.
Upholstery material		Vynide
Floor covering		Rubber mats
Exterior colours standardized		Any colour at extra cost
Alternative body styles		None

Maintenance

Sump		4 pints, S.A.E. 40/50
Gearbox		1¾ pints, S.A.E. 80 EP
Rear axle		1¾ pints, S.A.E. 80 EP
Steering gear lubricant		Multi-purpose grease
Cooling system capacity		8 pints (2 drain taps)
Chassis lubrication		None required
Ignition timing		3° before t.d.c. static
Contact-breaker gap		0.014–0.016 in.
Sparking plug type		Champion N5
Sparking plug gap		0.025 in.
Valve timing		Inlet opens 40° b.t.d.c. and closes 76° a.b.d.c. Exhaust opens 76° b.b.d.c. and closes 40° a.t.d.c.

Tappet clearances (cold)		Inlet 0.017 in. Exhaust 0.020 in.
Front wheel toe-in		⅛-in.
Camber angle		1° positive
Castor angle		5°
Steering swivel pin inclination		9°
Tyre pressures		Front 22 lb.; rear 22 lb.
Brake fluid		Girling
Battery type and capacity		12 volt 38 amp. hr.
Miscellaneous		Trunnion to vertical link bearings requires filling with oil

AMAZING LOTUS Mk SEVEN

The movement of Lotus to the front rank of racing and sports car makers has undoubtedly been the foremost motoring success story of recent years.

Lotus designer, Colin Chapman, has already produced such successful cars as the Formula One, Formula Junior, Eleven and Elite, and one can expect that one or two more outstanding designs will place him in such company as Marc Birkigt, Ernest Henry, Ettore Bugatti and Ferdinand Porsche.

by J. L. Scheftstik

This is how you will receive the Lotus Seven kit. All the major assemblies are already in one piece and it is a simple matter to put the car together.

Unfortuntely, Chapman does not design engines. He is a chassis and suspension expert, one of the world's best. Lotus engines have been obtained from many sources, but principally from Coventry-Climax, Ford and B.M.C.

That Lotus cars go fast and corner as if glued to the road, becomes obvious to anyone lucky enough to get a drive in a Lotus Seven, a lightweight "Production Sports Car" now beginning to appear in Australia.

The Seven is a road and competition car with the frontal appearance of the 1960 Formula One Lotus, mudguards not unlike an M.G. T.F. (but of fibre glass), and a squarish back. Having an alloy and space-frame type body, weight is kept down to 8 cwt. and that includes the spare wheel and a full tank !

Owners receive the cars in kit-form and so benefit by the saving of much sales tax. Assembling could be expected to take two men two weekends, and not require special tools or much expert knowledge. Pending permanent agency arrangements for N.S.W., Lotus Sevens can be bought through Edward du Cross of Beacon Hill, and in the case of other States, from John Roxburgh in Melbourne and Derek E. Jolly Ltd. of Adelaide.

The Lotus Seven Ser. 2 comes with either a Ford 105E or a B.M.C. 'A' engine, and the price including tax is £1195. This places the Lotus at above the cost of a Sprite and below that of an M.G. 1600 (and it is evident that it is a most modern design and ideal for hillclimbs and the shorter road circuits.

For road use and the under 1½-litre Sports class, there is the Lotus Seven Classic, fitted with the new Ford 1340 c.c. engine and twin Webers. This is the same car, apart from the engine, and without special competition tuning it will provide 85 b.h.p. and 107 m.p.h. Sixty m.p.h. is attained in 6.2 secs. The Lotus Seven Classic has not been long on the market, and is expeced to sell in this country for £1,440.

The engine room of the Ford 109E (Consul Classic) engined Lotus Seven. This car, priced at £1,440 complete with 85 b.h.p. Cosworth tuned engine must be one of the best sports car buys on the market. It will accelerate from rest to 60 m.p.h. in 6.2 seconds and has a maximum speed of over 100 m.p.h. It is equally at home on the racing circuit or as a normal road car.

The performance of the smaller engined cars depends on whether the owner is content with the basic 40 b.h.p., or tunes for the ultimate figure of around 85 b.h.p. On the English circuits, speeds of 105 m.p.h. and more have been attained on the straights.

Recently I was able to try out a Lotus Seven on the road, the car belonging to Mrs. J. W. du Cross of Sydney. It is the same car that has been driven at Catalina Park and Warwick Farm by Edward du Cros and Keith Watts, and it is fitted with a 948 c.c. B.M.C. engine. I soon realised that this was a most lively and stimulating lightweight sports car. The suspension was firm but not uncomfortably so, and the cornering amazing. The better the driver, the more he or she would enjoy this car on a winding road. I agreed wholeheartedly with the remarks of an overseas expert, "plenty of power is needed all the way round the corners, after going in rather gently. Nothing dramatic is needed, sliding only slows this car down. The Seven does not understeer or oversteer — it just steers."

The du Cross Lotus that is entered for N.S.W. motor events by Team Ivory Tower, is also a very tractable car to drive on the road, with good torque and fuel consumption on long journeys of over 35 m.p.g. Compression has been raised, a new camshaft fitted, and the breathing has been improved. Locally obtained S.U. carburettors are used, alternative sets of twin 1¼ in. and 1½ in.

The brakes are most impressive, probably the best on any sports car of its size. With standard linings they cannot be made to fade or pull to one side. English motoring journalist, Michael Henderson liked the brakes so much that he said that he would welcome a trip over the notorious Stelvio Pass !

The fitting of disc brakes is not advised by Lotus, as they are not needed. For instance, to stop the very fleet Lotus Classic 1340 c.c. — competition linings are fitted as standard — not discs.

The Lotus I drove had been fitted with new flared-type front mudguards in place of cycle-types. The new ones look very handsome and the protection is also much improved.

The seating position is surprisingly comfortable, but those with under-endowed posteriors are wise to take a cushion on long journeys. The fashionable long-arm driving position is easily obtained, and heeling and toeing is also easy.

Space around the pedals is not really generous, and for the quickest pedal shunting during motor events it is best to wear gym boots. Visibility is excellent all round and still far from bad with the hood up.

Noise, which is considerable with the hood up, is no great problem when the car is open. Cruising can be carried out quietly, and whether the noise level is such as to bring police patrols up like bees to honey, depends on the style of the driver.

The exhaust note is unusual, and is unlike that of an M.G., T.R. or Healey. It is something between a busy hum and an angry buzz — peculiar but most pleasant.

The Morris 1000 gearbox has a short lever and it is a first-class unit, though not quite so easy to use as that of an M.G. or a V.W. Wendy du Cros' Lotus is equipped with an Aust.-made rev-counter, an electric type and quite efficient, and cylinder head conversion and other tuning has been carried out by Armstrong-Baker Ltd., of Brookvale, Sydney. Lack of suitable roads prevented any fast runs in top gear but I noticed that the engine went up to 6,500 revs very quickly and this represents 65 m.p.h. in 3rd. Features I noticed included an ultra-lightweight Exide battery, some luggage space, and 5.20 x 13 Firestone tyres, made specially for the Lotus Seven.

Front springing follows the same general plan as the Triumph Herald, though one should, no doubt, say that the Herald follows the plan of the Lotus. It is a double-wishbone system with an anti-roll bar and integral coil spring damper units. This is identical to the Formula 2 racing Lotus of about three years ago. As one would expect, steering is by rack and pinion, and the turning circle is very small — less than 25 ft.

The earlier Seven, the Series One, was basically an adapted Eleven space-frame, and there was room for a Climax 1100 c.c. engine. One or two such cars are in Australia. In England, it was more usual to find them with Ford 1172 c.c. motors. The Series Two was designed from the start for a ultra-light square tail body, and for the Ford 997 c.c. and B.M.C. 948 c.c. engines. It has a simple and strong space-frame. The nose-cowl and all mudguards are of fibre-glass, and the rest of the car is of light alloy. The rear-axle is located by single upper trailing links, and an "A" bracket, which extends from the bottom of the differential unit at the centre of the "A", to the mountings on the chassis below those for the trailing links. Integral coil spring damper units are used also at the rear, placed above a Standard-Triumph rear axle.

I noticed that the makers, realising that these cars will often be in sports events, arranged for the windscreen, held by four screws to be detachable in a matter of moments. Team Ivory Tower has fitted a small perspex screen behind the main screen. There is a wood racing-type steering wheel. Early Series Two's had a larger metal wheel which was heavy, and also inclined to be in the way when getting in and out. Head-lamps are the same as were fitted to the T.D. model M.G., and they are good enough for any speed of which the car is capable. Colin Chapman and his team have designed the car throughout with the utmost skill, and as it is also such an obviously up to date car, it should prove popular in Australia for the road and for sports events.

This is a handsome little car, most unusual and interesting, and stimulating both to driver and onlooker.

I believe the due Cros Lotus is the first non-Climax car of this make to be raced in this country. Looking around for features I disliked, I could find hardly any. I noted that the B.M.C. engine gives only 5 in. clearance under the sump. With a Ford 105E engine, there is more clearance, but this version has a much heavier gearbox than that of the B.M.C. It is also true that the handbrake takes up important space around the passenger's legs, but passengers soon become used to this, and, anyway, one wonders where else the designer could have put it.

Road Impressions:
LOTUS SUPER

Shattering performance from one of the simplest little sports cars ever made.

THERE is probably no other sports car in the world as stark and functional — yet still cunningly complying with road registration requirements — as the Lotus Super Seven. Then again, as far as Australian enthusiasts are concerned, there is certainly none currently available here with the same kind of exhilarating, **all-round** performance. With a dry weight of only 8½ cwt and more than 80 brake-horsepower to pull it along, this lively little package of *pure* sports car has an unladen power-to-weight ratio exceeding 200 bhp per ton, which approaches that of a modern-day Formula Junior. Add fuel, oil and occupants and the figure drops to about 150 bhp/ton, an outstanding net result.

Additionally, the Super Seven's exceptional roadholding qualities enable a reasonably competent operator to use *all* the power, which is more than can be said for many other fast cars which have impressive bhp but cannot hope to transmit it to the road except perhaps in a straight line. Only those fortunate few who have had previous experience with Lotus products will readily appreciate just how much the Super Seven defies centrifugal force when it is flung through corners at speeds which would seem absolutely impossible to the average motorist

At Warwick Farm, Leo Geoghegan shows a surprised editor just what the little car will do.

Super Seven owes its hairy legs to 85 bhp Cosworth-Ford engine equipped with two twin-choke Webers.

By MIKE KABLE

SEVEN - world's fastest "kit" car

In terms of sheer acceleration, the Super Seven is one of the fastest cars yet tested by SPORTS CAR WORLD, reaching 70 mph from a standing start in 10 seconds with two people up. While ours was not a full road test in the normal form known to readers, we really went one better and engaged the short circuit at Warwick Farm, which enabled us to get down to some serious motoring without interruption or — more important — breaking the traffic laws. Of course, the Super Seven really shines on a proper racing circuit where all the corners have been scientifically constructed and demand the utmost of a car and its driver.

The Super Seven is descended from the well-known Seven, which in turn was developed from Lotus' first production sports car, the Mk VI. Outwardly, the SS is identical to the Seven and for that matter there is really hardly any difference in appearance between the Seven and Mk VI. Whereas the Mk VI was equipped with an 1172 cc side-valve Ford 10 engine, the SS has a 1340 cc Ford Consul Classic (109E) engine tuned by Cosworth Engineering to give 85 bhp at 6000 rpm. The capacity is unchanged from the normal production unit, therefore the engine is considerably oversquare with its 80.96 mm bore and 65.07 mm stroke and gives off excellent torque at comparatively low rpm figures.

Power has been obtained by re-working the cylinder head fairly extensively, upping the compression to 9.5 to 1, fitting two twin-choke 40DCOE2 Weber carburettors and a special extractor exhaust system which pairs off cylinders 1 and 4 and 2 and 3 and runs them into a sports-

Outwardly, the Super Seven and normal Seven are identical, as this photograph shows.

type silencer mounted along the nearside of the car. The crankshaft, rods and bearings are standard Ford components as is the flywheel and clutch. The gearbox is also Ford, although our car was equipped with the optional close-ratio gears and a Standard 10 live rear axle equipped with a 4 to 1 final drive ratio is used.

Although light in weight the multi-tubular space frame is immensely strong and supports all the aluminium body panels. The fibreglass nose, swept-back front mudguards and wide, curved rear wings are easily detachable while the bonnet, a sheet of aluminium simply bent over at the sides, is held in place by four catches. Our car was equipped with a door on the passenger's side to comply with CAMS production sports car regulation, but there are no doors on the normal production model, which has low-cut sides around the cockpit to allow easy entry and exit.

Weather protection consists of a flat windscreen mounted against the bulkhead by V-shaped aluminium brackets and a hood, which despite its ugliness, is quite effective in case of a sudden shower of rain. Obviously, Colin Chapman never intended his cars to be driven with their hoods up anyway! Sidescreens are an optional extra and there are two windscreen wipers.

Other creature comforts, of course, are at the the barest minimums in the plain, no-frills cockpit which seats only two — no more — on two padded cushions on the aluminium undertray which also doubles as the floor. Legroom is adequate, allowing the legs to be stretched right out on both sides and the occupants are held from sliding by the square-shaped transmission tunnel. The pendant-type brake and clutch pedals seems oddly placed, being almost out of comfortable

LOTUS SUPER SEVEN Continued

reach for all but quite a tall driver and a chassis cross member directly underneath them often got in the way of the feet, which was fairly disconcerting.

Everything else was well tailored for fast driving, the wheel being a good distance away from the body and nicely raked, while the excep-

---

SPECIFICATIONS—PERFORMANCE
LOTUS SUPER SEVEN

Engine: Four cylinders, 80.96 mm x 65.07 mm — 1340 cc. Overhead valves operated by pushrods. Compression ratio 9.5 to 1, 83 bhp at 6000 rpm. Two twin-choke Weber carburettors. Coil and distributor ignition.

Transmission: Four-speed gearbox, central remote control. Ratios, 4.1; 5.248; 6.953 and 11.959 to 1. Single plate dry clutch. Open propeller shaft. Hypoid rear axle.

Chassis: Tubular space frame, with independent front suspension by wishbones and coil springs with anti-roll bar. Rack and pinion steering. Rear axle on coil springs with trailing arms and central A bracket. Hydraulic brakes, 8 in x 1¼ in drums front and 7 in x 1¼ in drums rear. Bolt-on disc wheels. 5.20 x 13 in tyres.

Dimensions: Wheelbase, 7 ft 4 in; track, front and rear, 4 ft ½ in. Overall length, 11 ft. Width, 4 ft 10¼ in. Turning circle, 28 ft. Weight, 8 cwt 64 lb.

Performance: Speeds in gears: first, 40 mph; second, 60 mph; third, 82 mph; top, 108 (estimated). 0-30 mph, 2.9 sec; 0-40, 4.2 sec; 0-50, 5.6 sec; 0-60, 7.2 sec; 0-70, 10 sec.

---

tionally small — six inch — gearstick falls easily to hand and is actuated by the wrist rather than the arm, so short are the movements between gears. The change from first to second is not all that could be desired, as reverse, which is left and down from the driver, can be accidentally touched. The other changes are easily accomplished, but the gearbox has a production saloon feel in that it is fairly stiff. Saving space, the lever-type handbrake sits transversely under the dash while the starter button is mounted out of sight against the wall of the bulkhead.

Necessary instruments and toggle switches are grouped along the vynide-covered dashboard and comprise (from right to left), horn button, water temp, tachometer (an extra), oil pressure, switches for lights, dipping, electric radiator fan and windscreen wipers, key ignition, speedometer, ammeter and choke. The headlights are of the spotlight variety and sit up cheekily between the guards and the bodywork in the traditional sports car manner while tail lights are set into the bottom of each rear guard. There is no glove box or map pockets but there is a small luggage space over the top of the fuel tank and this, at a pinch, could take weekend requirements. The stumpy tail is chopped off almost in line with the guards and carries the spare wheel which is strapped on an outrigger and acts as a convenient "bumper bar."

Our test car was the one currently being raced in production sports car events by Geoghegan Motors, the NSW-Queensland agents for Lotus and the leading Lotus exponents in this country. Ian Geoghegan simply romped away from the field in the Super Seven's first outing at Catalina Park and set a new lap record of 1 min 10 sec, faster than brother Leo's Elite ever managed. Then, competing against outright racing cars, it was second in the Oran Park 100 guineas event last April. Save for a tune-up, it was in standard trim, although the windscreen and spare wheel were removed.

Leo was anxious to show me just what the Super Seven could do — besides finding out what difference another occupant made to the road-holding — and took me for several rapid laps around the short circuit. Passengering at speed with one of the country's top drivers is certainly

not for the weak-hearted and the mental effects of being hurled up to a corner at 80 mph and upwards and thrown through at undiminished speeds are electrifying, to say the least. One knows exactly how those nerveless riding mechanics of the old days must have felt and how much confidence they must have had in their driver!

Despite our combined weight of some 23 stone, representing about 30 percent of the car's weight, the Super Seven was only three seconds slower around the circuit than with just the driver up. Leo's technique was to lock the car on understeer when it was well in the corner, wait for the tail to come out slightly, then accelerate and set it back on course again with a flick of the wheel. Just to show me how extremely controllable it was, he changed his line a couple of times and deliberately took an untidy path through a corner. The Lotus is a forgiving little machine, fortunately. Stability at high speed is exceptional and the car digs itself into a corner without a trace of roll or pitch, although the tremendous side stress forces on the chassis can be literally felt right through the seat of the pants.

During this period of rather exciting motoring, the engine boiled due to having a low-pressure instead of high pressure radiator cap and we made a "pit stop" before carrying on with the test. Our aim was to get straight line acceleration figures along Pit Straight and after the thermostat had been removed — an operation which took little more than five minutes — we lined up out of Leger Corner. By juggling three stopwatches, we obtained four separate readings in one run and then went back for the 0-70 figure. This was a phenomenal 10 sec, and those familiar with Warwick Farm will appreciate just how quick this is when I report that the speedometer was showing well over 70 mph before we reached the end of the pits, having made our standing start a very short distance back down the road. The 0 to 60 time was 7.2 seconds, which puts the Super Seven well and truly in the E-type Jaguar class as far as acceleration is concerned. The factory claims around 16 seconds for a standing quarter-mile.

The fun wasn't yet over and I took the car out for several solo runs, limiting the maximum rpm to 6000, although 6500 is safe. Cosworth is justifiably proud of the fact that its conversion brings up around 62 bhp at only 4000 rpm and 77 at 5000 rpm. Naturally, this endows the Super Seven with plentiful power right through the range and this, plus the close-ratio box, makes for extraordinary acceleration even though the car has a relatively high rear axle ratio of 4.1 to 1. Torque is such that third and top gears would be sufficient for most racing circuits — Ian Geoghegan never used second gear at Katoomba, except at the start—and the Super Seven will either potter along or accelerate sharply in top gear.

Speeds in the gears run out at about 40 in first, more than 60 in second and more than 80 mph in third, while the theoretical maximum speed approaches 110 mph. Considering the unstreamlined shape of the car, this is remarkable. Rising in intensity with the revs, the exhaust note from the muffler mounted along the nearside is rather raucous, but delightful to the ears of an enthusiast.

Whether or not it would offend the ears of a police patrolman is open to conjecture! At low speeds, however, it is not so audible.

While the drum brakes (8 in front, 7 in rear) were effective enough if heavy pedal pressures were applied, I felt disc brakes — at least on the front — would be a distinct advantage, as this car is very fast by any standards and definitely must have most efficient brakes. I believe discs can be fitted and they would be well worth the extra expense. The brakes were not subject to fade, which was understandable enough, as they are not enclosed in any way and therefore keep constantly cool in the stream of air.

The ride is rigid, being controlled at the front by the well-known Lotus layout of double wishbones locating on Triumph Herald support arms and dampers enclosed in coil springs. A live hypoid axle with coil springs, a central A bracket and trailing arms is used at the rear and it is doubtful whether this system could be bettered, as there is very little axle hop — none on smooth surfaces — and no suggestion of the car jumping off line on a bumpy corner. The light bodywork is commendably free from rattles, although the bonnet is inclined to whip about at speed and could do with a leather strap as an added safety measure.

Rack and pinion steering is employed and this is delightfully light and precise, being geared for 2¾ turns lock to lock and having a small turning circle both to left and right of under 30 ft. After a little practice, it becomes easy and effortless to hold the car in line through a corner without jerking the wheel.

Buying the Super Seven in kit form represents a saving of some £500 in Australia and it now sells for £1399. The car comes from the factory in two crates, one containing the engine and transmission, which is already assembled and the other carrying the body, which is virtually assembled, guards and other components. It is claimed that the whole vehicle can be put on the road, sprayed and all, in three days. Another version of the Seven with a 1340 cc 109E engine developing 65 bhp is available for £1235, while the normal Seven, equipped with a 997 cc 105E engine, sells for £1199. While this last-named Seven has only a stock engine, apart from twin SUs, it is not to be sneezed at, either, as we found out during a few laps with it before moving on to the Super Seven.

If you are a real enthusiast who is more concerned with the spirit than the comfort of a car, the Super Seven will have immense appeal. While it is not exactly the kind of car in which to make interstate trips, it is nevertheless great fun on the open road and once you've driven it you don't want to part from it.

There is hardly anything else on the road — certainly nothing costing under £2500 — to match its sheer poke and handling, and if a driver plans to participate in competition it represents really good value. An owner can carry out any number of improvements for his comfort if he so wishes and maintenance is certainly no problem as there are so many proprietary components on the car which can be bought over the counter at low cost.

Extreme simplicity has always marked Colin Chapman's products and the Super Seven is no exception to the rule. He has certainly come up with an answer to those old stagers who stubbornly claim there is no substitute for cc's. It is left to speculation just what would happen if one were to substitute the present engine with the 1500 cc, 126 brake horsepower Ford engine recently developed by Cosworth!   #

LOTUS SUPER SEVEN

Much less for the road than the track

HISTORICALLY, THE TREND in sports cars has been away from the stark, near-racing-car type of machine and toward the closed, comfortable and civilized Grand Touring car. On the whole, this is a Good Thing; it has transformed the sports car from a fussy toy into a practical piece of transportation and given it the kind of popular appeal that it otherwise could not have acquired. However, for a few this softening has removed some of the interest from the game; they would prefer the sports car to remain a racing car, with two seats (both small) and just enough lighting and muffling equipment to get the vehicle within the limits prescribed by law. For many years (too many, some say) there were no cars that met those specifications but now, in the Lotus Seven, the all-or-nothing, *pur sang,* I-*like*-rainwater-in-my-ear enthusiast can find happiness.

Our first acquaintance with the Lotus Seven came last year when we tested the Morris-engined Lotus 7-A, which had a considerable Spartan charm but only 40 bhp, and lacked the speed to match its excellent handling. Apparently this lack did not go unnoticed at home, for Lotus shortly produced a new version with a "tuned" Cosworth 109-E Ford engine and that car, the Super Seven, was, according to all reports, fast enough to satisfy almost anyone. Naturally we were eager to obtain one of these new cars for test, but expected some delay. It was a pleasant surprise, therefore, when Mr. Robert Anderson called out of the providential blue and asked if we would like to borrow his personal Super Seven. We would; and we did.

The Lotus Super Seven is in many respects exactly like the 7-A, but with some important differences—not all directly relating to the engine. It has the same frame, made up of many small round- and square-section steel tubes, and the same

suspension: unequal-length A-arms in front (with the anti-roll member acting as part of the upper suspension arm) and trailing links at the rear. Transverse location of the rear axle is provided by the lower suspension member, which is a wide-based A-bracket that trails back from the chassis structure and fastens to the axle at a single point on the bottom of the drive-gear casing. This layout gives a relatively low rear roll center and little rear-axle steering. Coil springs mounted concentrically on telescopic dampers are used at each wheel. The steering is of the rack-and-pinion variety, and at 2.75 turns, lock to lock, is not unduly sensitive—although it should be noted that there is a substantial amount of lock and the steering is far from slow.

A major change in the chassis is the engine location, which is much farther forward than was the case in the 7-A. The Lotus 7-A carried 52% of its weight at the rear and in the Super Seven the engine has been located to give the car an exact 50/50 balance (all figures being with the driver in place). We must conclude that Lotus felt the car would handle better with the 50/50 weight distribution, as the engine actually had to be moved into an inconvenient location to achieve this balance. In fact, the car's fiberglass nose-piece now partially enshrouds the front of the engine, and has been made quickly removable to give access for service. We might add that the Super Seven is slightly heavier (55 lb) overall than the 7-A.

The Super Seven engine is from Ford of England's Classic, and has the same displacement but, whereas in stock form the engine develops 57 bhp (@5000 rpm), it has 90 bhp after being given the Cosworth treatment. It is widely thought that this is the same engine that Lotus is using in its Formula Junior cars, but this is not quite the case. The F-Jr engines are very highly tuned and incorporate many internal modifications to allow them to operate above 8000 rpm. In Super Seven form, a special camshaft is used and there is some reworking of the cylinder head, but that is about all that is done inside and the engine is not too reliable above 7000 rpm. Externally, there are the very impressive and effective 40-DCOE Weber carburetors and a special extractor-type exhaust system. The compression ratio is up one full number (from 8.5:1) and premium fuel is a necessity. We mention this as a point of academic interest; people who buy this car will not be of the kind who fret over the cost of fuel. In the unlikely event that there is, somewhere, a person who wants a smooth and economical Lotus Seven, the car is offered with a near-stock Ford Classic engine—having SU carburetors—at a slight reduction in cost.

With the 7-A's Morris engine, one gets the BMC series-A transmission, which can be had with a close-ratio gearset, and—logically—the 109-E engine carries with it the Ford transmission (also available with close-ratio gearing). Frankly, we were happier with the BMC transmission; the Ford unit is fine when carrying the stock power loading and pulling the stock sedan, but it shows serious signs of weakness when subjected to the Cosworth-Ford's 90 bhp. The higher loading causes a galling of the splines on which 1st gear slides, and this makes fast shifts from 1st to 2nd virtually impossible. In our test car, this misfortune occurred in the original gears and also in the replacement parts that were installed to correct the trouble, so we assume that it is not a problem peculiar to our car. Anderson plans to try a set of the optional close-ratio gears and hopes that will solve the problem—and also improve the car's acceleration, which suffers greatly under the handicap imposed by the present setup.

In making our test runs, we were unable to use 1st gear; all starts were made in 2nd. This was not as great a handicap as one might assume. The Super Seven bogs down a bit in 2nd gear, but if you catch a few thousand revolutions and bang home the clutch, it will spin its wheels enough to make

A racing car—with lights and fenders.

a reasonably clean start. Had we used 1st gear, it would not have taken us far enough to make much difference. On the other hand, the wide spacing of the 3 speeds we used definitely slowed the acceleration. We note that in the British tests of a Super Seven equipped with close-ratio gears, standing-

Forward aspect with the hood removed. (The tach was out for repair.)

The test begins. Away, dull care!

LOTUS SUPER SEVEN

start ¼-mile times as low as 15.8 sec have been recorded and that seems to be a reasonable time for such a light car.

Except during the actual acceleration trials, we did not find the lack of a usable 1st gear much of a bother: even though tuned well beyond stock specifications the Super Seven's engine pulls strongly over a wide speed range and the car will perform satisfactorily when driven as though it had only 3 speeds.

Unlike the Lotus 7-A we tested last year, the Super Seven had left-hand drive, and this introduced a very interesting factor into our driving—a continuous hot-foot. The exhaust pipes are on the left, sweep next to the corner of the driver's foot-well and, as there is not the slightest trace of insulation, the heat comes right through. Also, several large gaps exist in the firewall where the steering column, etc., go through and the heat pours into the cockpit. Even though we expect a certain amount of discomfort with a machine like this, the Super Seven on several occasions gave us the distinct impression

We suppose this, too, is "advanced thrust."

that it was really on fire. Oddly enough, the car was equipped with a heater, too; we cannot imagine to what purpose.

Other discomforts are created by the narrow seats, which are a press-fit for even the slight of build, and the lack of doors, which made entrance and exit with the top erected an experience that neither we, nor any onlooker, will ever forget. The problem is compounded a trifle, too, by the location of the exhaust pipe along the side of the car. This pipe curls outward at its end, and it is altogether too easy to get one's leg against the tip—another thing that left an indelible impression on at least one member of our test crew.

With all its discomforts, the Lotus Super Seven was one of the most inviting cars ever to fall into our collective hands. It is the very embodiment of that "thinly-disguised racing car" people are always talking about and, while it has serious shortcomings for day-in, day-out transportation, few cars offer as much excitement and fun. Actually, the Super Seven should be classified as a racing car, pure and simple, and the fact that it can also be driven on the street is just an incidental advantage, not its primary function. Only on a race track can the car be driven as it should be.

As a racing car, the Super Seven has considerable merit. It handles and corners like a real racing car with no modifications needed after purchase. Its fiberglass and flat-panel-aluminum body is easily repaired, and most of the pieces can be quickly stripped off for servicing. All of the mechanical elements are from low-cost, mass-produced sedans and routine maintenance should present no difficulties in either price or ease of procurement.

The one big drawback is purchase price—and even that is not as bad as it might seem. The U.S. agents for Lotus are asking $3395 POE New York for the Super Seven, and that is shockingly expensive. On the other hand, the same car may be purchased in England for slightly over $1900, and that includes the close-ratio gears. Getting the car shipped here, the duty paid, and licensed in your home state would raise the tab, naturally, but we cannot imagine how one could spend more than $2500. Still expensive, we grant you; but this is a limited-production racing car. All things considered, it is a most appealing package.

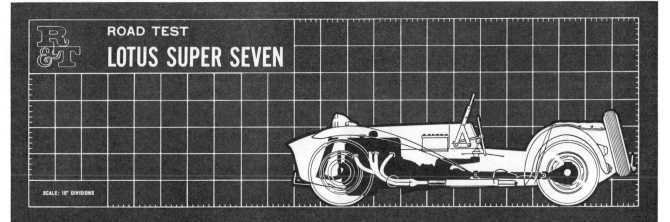

ROAD TEST
LOTUS SUPER SEVEN

SCALE: 10" DIVISIONS

DIMENSIONS

Wheelbase, in	88.0
Tread, f and r	47.5/48.5
Over-all length, in	131.2
width	57.2
height	44.7
equivalent vol, cu ft	194
Frontal area, sq ft	14.2
Ground clearance, in	5.0
Steering ratio, o/a	n.a.
turns, lock to lock	2.7
turning circle, ft	26
Hip room, front	2 x 15.5
Hip room, rear	n.a.
Pedal to seat back, max	42.0
Floor to ground	5.0

CALCULATED DATA

Lb/hp (test wt)	14.9
Cu ft/ton mile	131.5
Mph/1000 rpm (4th)	16.1
Engine revs/mile	3720
Piston travel, ft/mile	1590
Rpm @ 2500 ft/min	5850
equivalent mph	94
R&T wear index	59.2

SPECIFICATIONS

List price, poe N.Y.	$3395
Curb weight, lb	1015
Test weight	1340
distribution, %	50/50
Tire size	5.20-13
Brake swept area	118
Engine type	4 cyl, ohv
Bore & stroke	3.19 x 2.56
Displacement, cc	1340
cu in	81.8
Compression ratio	9.5
Bhp @ rpm	90 @ 6000
equivalent mph	97
Torque, lb-ft	n.a.
equivalent mph	n.a.

GEAR RATIOS

4th (1.00)		4.11
3rd (1.41)		5.79
2nd (2.37)		9.74
1st (4.12)		16.5

SPEEDOMETER ERROR

30 mph	actual, 28.8
60 mph	58.8

PERFORMANCE

Top speed (4th), mph	102
best timed run	103
3rd (6500)	75
2nd (6500)	44
1st (6500)	26

FUEL CONSUMPTION

Normal range, mpg	19/25

ACCELERATION

0-30 mph, sec	4.0
0-40	5.2
0-50	7.4
0-60	9.9
0-70	13.1
0-80	18.1
0-100	31.0
Standing ¼ mile	16.9
speed at end	78

TAPLEY DATA

4th, lb/ton @ mph	340 @ 65
3rd	495 @ 50
2nd	off scale
Total drag at 60 mph, lb	95

ENGINE SPEED IN GEARS

4th
3rd
2nd
1st

2000 3000 4000 5000
ENGINE SPEED IN RPM

ACCELERATION & COASTING

90
80
70
60
50
40
30
20
10

SS¼
4th
3rd
2nd

MPH

5 10 15 20 25 30 35 40 45
ELAPSED TIME IN SECONDS

BUILDING AND RUNNING A LOTUS SUPER SEVEN

The story of how three staff members built a Lotus Super Seven, together with road impressions after the car had covered 5,000 miles

MOTOR SPORT'S Proprietor is reasonably indulgent when members of his editorial staff try to convince him that their present car is worn out and that a new mount is of the utmost urgency, but even he was a little shaken when a new recruit to the staff demanded a Lotus Super Seven. The young man was Ted Wilkinson (Yes, the same E. L. W. who doesn't know that a Ford 8 cylinder head won't fit a 100E engine!) and as he had joined the staff primarily to report trials and hill-climbs he felt he ought to have a suitably spartan machine, to which idea the other members of the staff agreed, having had to lend him their cars for trips to all corners of the country. The Proprietor finally capitulated when told that the building of a kit car would provide good copy for the magazine as well as giving one or two staffmen some competition experience in hill-climbs and the like. So an order was placed with Lotus for a Super Seven and within a month the Lotus van arrived at the Assistant Editor's house with all the bits and pieces on board. The Assistant Editor's house was chosen for the task as his was the only one with enough spare garage space to accommodate the car as well as his own Sprite. Staff photographer Laurie Morton was press ganged into helping mainly because he had the best set of tools and also because he was required to take photographs throughout the construction stage.

Lotus claim that the car can be assembled with normal hand tools in 22 hours but we spent about 20 of the 22 sorting out all the various parts. (*See Photo 1.*) Actually, unless you happen to get the car on Saturday and want to race it on Sunday it is wiser to take plenty of time and in fact due to our heavy commitments at week ends it was over two months before the car was running on the road. The Lotus arrives in a pretty fully assembled state with the bodywork riveted to the space frame chassis and all instruments, wiring and the petrol tank in position and construction merely a matter of adding the front and rear suspension, brakes, steering, engine and gearbox, radiator, lights, front wings and a number of smaller components. The Purchase Tax regulations do not allow instructions to be given with a kit car as this constitutes professional help and there are one or two items on the Lotus which can be fitted incorrectly as the Lotus Service Department will testify having seen many a Seven arrive with nose pointing up in the air, the owner having put the front suspension wishbones on the wrong side of the car. However, having placed the chassis/body unit on a couple of trestles and laid the various components in their approximate positions we were fairly confident of not having too many pieces left over when the car was completed.

The first job was the front suspension which consists of a lower wishbone with a single top arm and an anti-roll bar. (*See Photo 2*). Our ideas that this would go together like a piece of Meccano were soon dispelled and a fair amount of work removing paint and swarf was required before the rubber bushes of the wishbone would slip over the chassis lugs. It is necessary to fit the wishbone on the correct side of the chassis and this can be determined by fitting it with the mounting point of the coil spring/damper unit projecting below the centre line of the wishbone. The upper link was then fitted along with the coil spring/damper unit as they have a common upper mounting point. The modified Triumph Herald king post and Girling front brake assemblies were fitted next, care being taken not to tighten nuts more than finger tight until the car was on its wheels.

We fitted the anti-roll bar next but this is incorrect and should

(**Photo 1.**) *TWO INTREPID Lotus builders surrounded by all the bits and pieces of the Super Seven prior to beginning the assembly.*

(**Photo 2.**) *FIRST job to be tackled was the front suspension which soon dispelled the idea that building a Lotus was merely a matter of doing up some nuts and bolts.*

not be done until the car is on its wheels, or at least should not be tightened up until then. It is located at each end by two Metalastic half bushes working in the upper link arms and on the chassis by alloy blocks bolted to the uprights of the front box section. The anti-roll bar was finished in black paint and it was necessary to clean off this paint and lap the bar in with grinding paste. When the roll bar was working smoothly the paste was wiped away, the blocks tightened up and the grease nipples fitted. Another prevalent fault is to fit the anti-roll bar on upside down; the correct way is to have the cranked ends of the bar parallel with the ground when the car is at normal ride level. This is the main reason why the bar should not be finally fitted until the car is on its wheels.

The steering came next, this being a modified Triumph Herald rack and pinion unit which is located on the chassis by two light alloy mounting blocks. Here we met our first snag as Lotus had drilled the holes in the fabricated steel platform on the chassis too near one side so that a nut could not be fitted to the bolt. However, this was resolved by filing a larger flat on one side of the bolt head and passing the bolt upwards through the casting rather than downwards. (*See Photo 3.*) The coupling of the tie rods was then done, a note being made of the fact that the ⅛ in. toe-in had to be set when the car was on its wheels.

The rather fragile looking steering column was then slipped through the facia mounted bush and down to the rack assembly to which it is connected by a splined universal joint. Great care was taken to push the column well onto the splines and also to push the u.j. well down onto the spline of the rack as there is very little clearance between the u.j. and a chassis tube. The u.j. pinch bolts were then tightened.

Attention then moved to the rear end and the axle (taken from the Standard Companion and fitted with Herald 1200 gears) was placed in position after having slipped the Hardy Spicer propeller shaft into the tunnel. Two "U" bolts secure a platform to each end of the axle casing into which the lower end of the coil spring/damper unit is bolted. (*See Photo 4.*) Having secured the damper units to the axle they were then secured at their upper ends just behind the seats making sure that the rubber bushes were fitted in the correct sequence with one rubber and two steel caps below the chassis bracket and one rubber and one steel cap above the bracket. The "A" bracket was then fitted, a great deal of reamering being required before the bolts would go home. Lastly the radius arms were fitted, the upper mounting point being on a lug on the chassis within the rear mudguard and the lower mounting is on the same bolt which locates the coil spring/damper unit. Care should be taken to fit the radius arms the right way up. The arm should curve down from the spring/damper unit. The brakes are already fitted to the axle when delivered so we were now able to fit the wheels and lower the car off its trestles.

The next step was to fit the 1,340 c.c. Ford Classic engine which had been breathed on by Cosworth to the tune of 85 b.h.p. It was supplied with the modified cylinder head already fitted but the twin Weber carburetters and manifolds had to be fitted later. A hoist is a necessity as some manoeuvring is required to persuade the engine and gearbox into the chassis. (*See Photo 5, page* **46**.) Before lowering the engine we removed the remote control gear lever, distributor cap and petrol pump sediment bowl and covered vulnerable parts like hydraulic pipes, with rags or split rubber hose. After fitting the tubular steel engine bearers to their rubber mountings on the chassis (*See Photo 6, page* **46**) the engine was lowered, making sure the tail shaft entered the tunnel first and that the single point gearbox mounting went home. The splined propeller shaft was slipped into place and the four-point mountings on each side of the engine were then tightened up and the hoist removed. The remote control, which is a modified Triumph Herald component was then replaced together with a new paper gasket at which point it was discovered that the gear lever was too long, almost fouling the lower edge of the facia. However, Lotus cut and re-threaded the lever at the 500-mile service.

When connecting up the various accessories connected with the engine such as oil pressure pipe, clutch piping, temperature gauge we discovered that we had made a ghastly error in not fitting the right angle speedometer drive take-off to the offside of the gearbox and there was insufficient clearance between the gearbox and the tunnel to fit it while in position. Bilking at the thought of removing the engine we cut a hole in the tunnel, fitted the speedometer drive and riveted a piece of aluminium over the hole.

The radiator, which is held by two top-hat rubbers, one bolt and the water hoses, was fitted next, the hoses being rather difficult to fit. In fact it is best to fit the radiator before the steering rack as some complicated juggling is required to get it into position when the rack is in place. Fitting of the Weber carburetters and exhaust manifolds came next and a considerable amount of time was taken in sawing and filing the various flanges to obtain a good fit. The manifolds are secured to the head by Allen screws and due to the angled inlet pipes are very difficult to tighten, requiring a specially made Allen key. (*See Photo 7, page* **47**.) When the Webers are bolted to the inlet manifolds they have rubber "O" rings inserted in between and adjusting the tension on the double spring washers so that the carburetter intake pipes have a total vertical movement of about ⅜ in. will ensure correct carburation, as loose carburetters will allow air leaks and too tight ones will cause frothing. The throttle linkages came next and caused a fair amount of trouble as there are a large number of threaded rods, ball joints and so on, but careful study of a Formula Junior Lotus in the paddock at Silverstone showed us how it all went together. The fuel lines and throttle cable were then connected up but we did not fit the choke cable as we had an idea that there would be no starting problems with those two big Webers and later events proved us right.

By now there was only a very small pile of pieces left over on the bench and the car was very near completion. The front wing stays were fitted and the flared glass fibre wings attached, care being taken to incorporate the piping between wing and body. The sidelamps were then attached to the wings and the wiring connected. The windscreen fitted easily and the wiper motor was bolted into position under the bulkhead, care being taken to fit the spacer tubes over the wipers rack. If this is not done the cables will flex themselves and not move the wiper blades at all. The pedals

(**Photo 3.**) THE modified Triumph Herald rack and pinion steering is attached to the Lotus chassis by light alloy mounting blocks. Due to incorrect drilling the steering was difficult to fit in our car.

(**Photo 4.**) FITTING the steel platform to the Standard Companion estate car axle to which the coil spring/damper unit and radius arm is attached.

were then fitted, this operation requiring some ingenuity and a reclining posture under the bulkhead. (*See Photo 8, page 47*) This was followed by the handbrake and its linkage after which the hydraulic piping was connected, the master cylinders filled and the brake and clutch systems bled. The coil was then fitted to the driver's footbox using the steel backing plate provided, the silencer bolted to the outside of the passengers side of the car and the flexible piping attached to the exhaust manifold down pipe by a Jubilee clip and the two-blade fan bolted to the water pump pulley with the two aluminium spacer blocks in between so that the blades did not touch a chassis cross tube. By now all that remained was the hood, this being supplied complete except for the Lift-the-Dot fasteners which were fitted with the fabric laid over the hood sticks so that a good fit was obtained.

Finally the engine, gearbox, rear axle, radiator and petrol tank were filled with the appropriate fluids, the wooden steering wheel slipped on its splines and bolted down and with some trepidation the ignition was switched on and the bulkhead-mounted starter button pressed. After a few seconds delay while the carburetters filled with fuel the engine burst into noisy life and idled happily while the proud builders looked on affectionately.

HISTORY

Since the Editorial Lotus Super Seven passed its 500-mile factory check the car has done nearly 6,000 miles at the time of going to press. Whilst still in the final stages of running in it was apparent that such a light vehicle would cause problems in wet conditions. The lesson was not fully learnt until an argument with a London Transport 'bus occurred on a narrow railway bridge on a soaking wet August Bank Holiday. A mangled off-side front suspension and torn sump brought home the lesson that locked brakes on a wet road changes the Lotus from a car to a toboggan. With the damage made good the teething troubles commenced and it took several visits to the Lotus Service Department at Panshanger, and finally the fitting of a new rack and pinion before the car began to steer and brake efficiently again.

The electric horn, which is mounted on the nearside engine bearer, suffered from acute vibration which culminated in a replacement being fitted and, at our suggestion, the re-mounting of the unit on a firmer chassis point. At 2,342 miles the water-pump casting split as a result of the pump bearings seizing and a new water-pump was supplied free of charge. Just before 3,000 miles were up the mechanical cooling fan broke at speed and came

(**Photo 6.**) *ENGINE MOUNTINGS for the Classic engine consist of tubular steel struts which are bolted to the normal four-stud fixing points on the block and to single rubber-cushioned mountings on the chassis.*

through the fibreglass nose cowling, severing the upper radiator hose in the process. As this occurred on the Motorway section of the A1 at about 10.00 a.m. on a Sunday, few of the Ford agents in the area would help out, being content to sell petrol and oils, yet still calling themselves Ford agents and having the sign "Garage" or "Service Station" over their portals. However The Bawtry Motor Co., some twenty miles from where the breakdown occurred showed enterprise in opening their stores on a Sunday morning and willingly sold a Ford 109E fan blade for 2s. 9d. The damaged fibreglass was repaired by the Lotus Service Department effectively but far from invisibly. Three other water-pumps were fitted at intervals of less than 200 miles and it was not until the mechanical fan, which required a heavy spacer to clear a chassis cross-tube, was replaced by an electric fan thus relieving the undue weight on the water-pump bearings that the trouble was finally remedied.

The electric fan, mounted in front of the radiator appeared to suffer from the airflow to such an extent that within six days of being fitted by Lotus the blade had fallen off. This was re-fitted by Lotus but came off again within two days and is now in the process of being returned to the factory for examination.

As soon as full performance was usable it was noticed that the bolts locating the differential housing were working loose, allowing the oil to escape on one occasion when the car was driven for nearly 50 miles with no oil in the axle save for a slight plating of Molyslip which could well have contributed to the fact that no damage had been done. An attempt by the Lotus Service Department to rectify this fault did not prove successful and the remedy has been to drill the bolt heads and wire them. It is understood that Lotus have now developed a special taper bolt which is supplied on all new models which will keep the differential housing in place.

Apart from the above the car has been trouble free with the exception that one baffle plate is now loose in the exhaust system but does not appear to have altered the silencing qualities in any way except for a slight rattle audible when throttling back. The Lucas spotlamps have been removed, having proved inadequate for fast night driving and we are at present experimenting with a pair of matching Butler spot and foglamps; the foglamp proving a distinct advantage while the spotlamp is not quite up to the standard of the Lucas spotlamp. The original rubber mats wore out within 2,000 miles and were replaced with a pair of fitted rubber-link mats made by Typrod of Brighton. These are competitively priced, unaffected by oil and are guaranteed for ten years.

A 5s. can of bitumastic paint sufficed to completely underseal the body, in particular the pop-rivet seams where water came in very rapidly, and to protect the engine bulkhead which had been attacked by battery acid. On such a low-slung, high performance car a windscreen washer is essential and a Tudor Accessories washer, using a flat water container has been fitted. A further modification which will be carried out in the near future is the

(**Photo 5.**) *A HOIST is essential for lowering the engine as the tailshaft has to be manoeuvred into the tunnel before the rest of the engine is lowered.*

(**Photo 7.**) *FINGERS AND THUMBS: Considerable dexterity is required when fitting the Weber carburetters as the Allen screws are rather inaccessible due to the angled inlet manifolds.*

making of a gull-winged detachable hard-top incorporating a wrap-round rear window and lockable doors. The throttle cable is being altered to use a copper tube packed with grease as an outer cable to overcome a tendency of the existing cable to slip out of its retaining bucket. The awkward fuel filler cap is being modified by means of a curved piece of radiator hose, jubilee clips and another filler neck to take the cap outside the body.

The pleasure of driving such a potent piece of machinery on the open roads, the envy of one's friends with their buzzing Minis and Sprites completely outweighs the earlier trials and tribulations of Lotus owning although they, in turn, laugh at the 17-20 m.p.g. fuel consumption of the Lotus! The only regret is that the 1,340 c.c. Super Seven was superseded by the later model incorporating the 1,500 c.c. 5-bearing crank engine with all synchromesh close-ratio gearbox and such extras as sidescreens, better view p.v.c. hood, revolution counter, disc brakes, sealed beam headlamps all for the same price just after the Editorial Super Seven was put on the road!

DRIVING IMPRESSIONS

Some people liken driving a Lotus to a visit to the dentist—it's awful while it's happening but wonderful when it stops—but these people are seldom Lotus owners and if one is a Lotus owner then one is prepared to make many sacrifices such as pre-war Bugatti owners must have done. To refresh his memory as to what Lotus driving was like the Assistant Editor set out one morning when the cold spell was at its height for a long run in the car which he had helped to build.

Getting into the car provides some exercise especially with the hood and sidescreens in position and until the drill is learned the driver usually manages to tramp his muddy boots all over the seat cushions or get his leg stuck through the steering wheel. Once in position he is held securely between the body side and tunnel and his legs disappear into an ever-narrowing tunnel where one size-10 shoe seems to cover all the pedals at once. We found it best to drive in plimsolls or shoes with no welts. Even in the bitter cold weather we have been experiencing recently the engine started first time from cold without a choke and ran with a delightful burble, the temperature rising to around 80°C, at which point it remained whatever the road speed. Tuned by Cosworth to give 85 b.h.p. at 6,000 r.p.m. the engine is by no means silent, especially as the exposed exhaust system runs within a few inches of the passenger's ear. The gearbox is the standard Ford Classic version which at the time we built the car had no synchromesh on first gear but even so is delightful to use, except for a slight tendency to snick reverse when changing from first to second. This is presumably a fault of the particular remote control fitted.

With only 8½ cwt. the acceleration of the Lotus is pretty sensational although as there is no rev. counter on our car (it being a £17 10s. extra) we treated the engine with respect. With standard

gear ratios (close ratio gearbox £40 extra) there is a fairly wide gap between second and third but such is the acceleration in second that this would only become an embarrassment on a race track as the speedometer needle can be taken to 60 m.p.h. in second with no sign of stress. Third is good for an indicated 85 m.p.h. and on more than one occasion the needle went past the 100 m.p.h. mark in top. Practically nothing can live with the Lotus on the road especially if there are any bends in sight but even in a straight line it will stay with an E-type Jaguar up to 80 m.p.h. Almost as exhilarating is the punch the engine gives when vivid acceleration is required for overtaking long strings of traffic, while the car will run along at 30 m.p.h. in top gear with no fuss at all.

The ride is uncompromisingly hard and roads which we had previously thought to be particularly smooth suddenly became full of bumps and potholes although the car was only deflected from its intended course by serious bumps. A number of rattles were with us almost permanently and there seems little hope of curing these with the present stiff suspension. Despite the generous use of bitumastic paint all over the underside there are numerous draughts which manage to creep in around the driver's feet, while a stiff blast of cold air freezes his right elbow. Some heat comes back from the engine and the optionally extra heater (£12 16s. 7d.) is not really necessary.

Cornering of the Lotus on smooth roads is quite exceptional and with 2¾ turns from lock to lock the merest flick of the wrist gets the car round quite acute bends. Bumps do tend to displace the rear end but the car can be driven hard round acute bumpy bends without fear of completely losing adhesion, the limiting factor being the amount of jolting the occupants can endure.

The windscreen surround and sidescreen leading edge cause a considerable blind spot which renders the negotiation of roundabouts and hairpin bends hazardous and the car is so low that signposts are difficult to read with the sidescreens in place.

The brakes work very well and haul the car down from its habitual 90 m.p.h. cruising speed with no fuss at all, although a little grab was experienced when the drums were cold.

The normal driver of the car has made several modifications to make the car more habitable (which are detailed elsewhere) and is contemplating more. Certainly anyone intending to use a Lotus Seven as everyday transport would need to make several modifications and be able to put up with petty annoyances such as the lack of a fuel gauge, little luggage space, the need to lift the hood to fill the fuel tank, and to remove the bonnet panel to check oil and water. Judging by our experiences he should also be able to cope with a number of teething troubles as they occur as the car is guaranteed for only 90 days. All in all the Lotus owner will need to be a hardy soul as the majority of creature comforts present in much cheaper saloons are absent while the casual attitude of Lotus to such serious troubles as the inability of the rear axle to withstand the power of the engine will not endear the car to impecunious owners. Fortunately for Colin Chapman there appear to be plenty of people about who are willing to endure these hardships.
M. L. T./E. L. W.

(**Photo 8.**) *THIS UNDIGNIFIED position has to be adopted to fit the pedals correctly. Note the close proximity of the gear lever to the facia. Lotus eventually shortened the lever.*

THE LOTUS SUPER SEVEN 1500 COSWORTH

THE Lotus Seven, in its various forms and with different engines, has been tested from time to time by AUTOSPORT. Now, the Super Seven 1500 Cosworth has come along and has been duly put through its paces. This particular Lotus is of course intended for the type of enthusiast to whom performance and handling are everything and comfort is a dirty word. It can at once be said that, for such people, the latest Super Seven provides more sheer performance for less money than any other car.

Bought in do-it-yourself form, the Super Seven 1500 costs £585, which is increased to £645 when the Cosworth version of the five-bearing engine is fitted. Among the extras on the test car were a close-ratio gearbox at £40 and an oil-cooler at £15. For this moderate expenditure one gets a vehicle which is ideal for racing on short circuits and which can out-accelerate almost anything on the road below 100 m.p.h.

The well-known Lotus multi-tubular chassis with aluminium panels needs no description. The front suspension is by wishbones, an anti-roll bar forming part of the top linkage and the steering being by rack and pinion. The rear axle is on radius arms and an "A" bracket, the suspension medium being helical springs and telescopic dampers all round. Disc brakes

BOLSTER enjoying himself at Brands Hatch in the Lotus . . .

in front and drums at the rear have the by no means arduous task of stopping the little projectile. A parking brake lever lies horizontally above the passenger's knees.

The engine is the 1,500 c.c. five-bearing Ford unit, with two twin-choke Weber carburetters and Cosworth modifications. The clutch is fitted with very strong springs and the gearbox has synchromesh on all ratios, the selection being by a very short central lever. The propeller shaft tunnel and the body sides form the driver's and passenger's armchairs, a minimum of padding increasing the luxury of the ensemble. A greatly improved hood and really practical sidescreens have been added since our last Super Seven test.

I never used the choke, even after all-night parking in the open, a few prods of the accelerator always ensuring an instant start. The power unit is quiet mechanically but has a throaty exhaust note, particularly on the over-run, which could be muted with advantage for road use. The idling is a little uneven but once the engine is pulling it is astonishingly flexible, even on top gear.

The clutch is excellent, though the pedal pressure is fairly high. At first I disliked the gearchange, but some fast laps at Brands Hatch served to loosen things up, after which it became easier to select the ratios. There was some friction in the remote control linkage, but absolutely no vibration was transmitted to the lever. Probably the change would continue to improve during a considerable mileage.

With 95 b.h.p. in a car weighing 9¼ cwt., fuel and oil aboard, it is obviously extremely easy to spin the wheels on a dry road and discretion must be used in the wet. To accelerate from a standstill to 60 m.p.h. in 6.8 secs., or to 80 m.p.h. in 12.6 secs. is quite an experience in so small a car. These excellent times could actually be improved with a really well run-in gearbox, which would permit faster changes. The maximum speed was restricted by the gearing. When I timed the car at 102.2 m.p.h. the rev. counter was steady at 6,400 r.p.m., which is past the peak. However, the axle ratio chosen is ideal for British circuits and a higher gear would bring no great benefit as the exposed lamps, flat screen, and open mudguards render extremely high speeds out of the question.

During the speed testing, a side wind was blowing which caused the car to wander a little, but one could ignore this with experience. The brakes are excellent and the old trouble of locking the front wheels has been eliminated. The right front wheel occasionally flaps a little during high-speed

retardation, but this has no adverse effect on stability.

The ride is hard, bumps being felt through the very thin cushions. I tended to roll about in the car on corners, which affected my confidence at Brands Hatch. I notice that those who race these models invariably modify the seating to give better location and this could be done very cheaply. The propeller shaft tunnel does prevent the driver and passenger from colliding and there is plenty of room in the car for two people.

The roadholding is rather remarkable, and though some practice is desirable before one drives on the limit, it is eventually possible to corner with great abandon. The back axle can be felt over bumps, but the effect on the directional stability is much less than would be expected. The Lotus has quite a high polar moment of inertia, and being of an under-steering disposition it is fundamentally stable. The characteristic can be swung towards over-steering, either by a suitable application of power or by going onto the over-run, according to circumstances. There is an astonishing similarity to the steering response of the Ferrari Testa Rossa, and I would say that both cars respond well to rather "hairy" driving methods. The steering is quick enough for the enterprising negotiation of a crowded circuit, while remaining light at parking speeds.

The test car was fitted with a very neat all-over tonneau cover at £6 10s., which incorporated detachable side pieces to keep rain and mud off the driver and passenger. The hood is excellent, being quite devoid of any flapping at 100 m.p.h. The sidescreens also earn full marks, and they are instantly detachable when extra ventilation is required. Entry with the hood up is much easier than would be expected when the drill has been learnt. It is also possible to leave the car quite expeditiously, though never with dignity. With the hood and sidescreens buttoned up, the interior is very cosy indeed, a good deal of heat arriving from the engine compartment, not to mention plenty of noise from the "fruity" exhaust.

One does not expect to find a vast luggage boot in such a car, but in other respects it is a practical vehicle for touring. It would be better if the petrol filler cap were outside the boot and the absence of a fuel gauge is a nuisance. Apart from this the instrument panel is well stocked with gauges and the lamps are remarkably powerful, permitting 100 m.p.h. driving at night. With the car open, the sound of the exhaust does not bother the occupants,

ACCELERATION GRAPH

though it may attract the attention of you-know-whom. The sheer ease of travelling, as steep hills drop astern at 90 m.p.h. and corners are taken with a slight movement of the wrists, is something that endears the Lotus to the true enthusiast.

The Super Seven is not the wear for the pompous and the portly but an uncompromising sports car for the young in heart of all ages. The essential requirements of a genuine sports car are that it shall go, steer, and stop, all of which this Lotus does in a very big way. If you're interested in getting £2,000 worth of performance for £645, this is your car.

SPECIFICATION AND PERFORMANCE DATA

Car Tested: Lotus Super Seven 1500 Cosworth sports two-seater. Price, in kit form, £645. Extras on test car: Close ratio gears £40. Oil cooler £15. Full tonneau cover £6 10s.. Flashing direction indicators £7 15s. Heater £17 10s.

Engine: Four-cylinders 80.96 mm. × 72.75 mm. (1,498 c.c.). Compression ratio 9.5 to 1. 95 b.h.p. at 5,000 r.p.m. Pushrod-operated overhead valves. Two Weber twin-choke carburetters. Lucas coil and distributor.

Transmission: Single dry plate clutch. Four-speed gearbox with synchromesh on all speeds and central remote control, ratios 4.11, 5.26, 6.97, and 11.99 to 1. Open propeller shaft. Hypoid rear axle.

Chassis: Multi-tubular space frame with aluminium panels. Independent front suspension by wishbones with anti-roll torsion bar. Rack and pinion steering. Rear axle on radius arms and "A" bracket. Helical springs and telescopic dampers all round. Hydraulic brakes with front discs and rear drums. Bolt-on disc wheels fitted 5.20-13 ins. tyres.

Equipment: 12-volt lighting and starting. Speedometer. Rev. counter. Oil pressure and water temperature gauges. Ammeter. Windscreen wiper. Extras: Flashing direction indicators. Heater.

Dimensions: Wheelbase 7 ft. 4 ins. Track (front) 3 ft. 11½ ins. (rear) 4 ft. 0½ in. Overall length 13 ft. 6 ins. Width 4 ft. 9 ins. Weight 9 cwt. 1 qr.

Performance: Maximum speed 102.2 m.p.h. Speeds in gears: 3rd 82 m.p.h., 2nd 60 m.p.h., 1st 41 m.p.h. Standing quarter-mile 15.4 secs. Acceleration: 0-30 m.p.h. 2.4 secs. 0-50 m.p.h. 5.2 secs. 0-60 m.p.h. 6.8 secs. 0-80 m.p.h. 12.6 secs

Fuel Consumption: 18-20 m.p.g.

MAKE: Lotus *TYPE: Super Seven* 1500

MAKERS: Lotus Components Ltd., Delamare Road, Cheshunt, Herts.

THE Motor

ROAD TEST ● No. 17/63

TEST DATA:

CONDITIONS: *Weather: (Temperature 46°-54°F., Barometer 29·2-29·3 in. Hg.) Surface: Damp during most tests except acceleration and braking. Fuel: Premium grade pump petrol (98 Octane by Research Method).*

MAXIMUM SPEEDS

Flying Quarter Mile

Mean of four opposite runs ..	102·8 m.p.h.
Best one-way time equals ..	103·4 m.p.h.

"Maximile" Speed: (Timed quarter mile after one mile accelerating from rest).

Mean of four opposite runs ..	102·2 m.p.h.
Best one-way time equals ..	102·9 m.p.h.

Speed in Gears

Max. speed in 3rd gear	81·0 m.p.h.
Max. speed in 2nd gear	60·0 m.p.h.
Max. speed in 1st gear	40·0 m.p.h.

ACCELERATION TIMES From standstill

0-30 m.p.h.	2·6 sec.
0-40 m.p.h.	3·7 sec.
0-50 m.p.h.	5·7 sec.
0-60 m.p.h.	7·7 sec.
0-70 m.p.h.	10·2 sec.
0-80 m.p.h.	13·9 sec.
0-90 m.p.h.	17·7 sec.
0-100 m.p.h.	27·7 sec.
Standing quarter mile..	15·9 sec.

ACCELERATION TIMES on upper ratios

	top gear	third gear
20-40 m.p.h.	6·2 sec.	3·7 sec.
30-50 m.p.h.	6·0 sec.	3·4 sec.
40-60 m.p.h.	5·5 sec.	4·1 sec.
50-70 m.p.h.	5·8 sec.	4·2 sec.
60-80 m.p.h.	6·6 sec.	5·4 sec.

HILL CLIMBING

Max. gradient climbable at steady speed

Top gear	1 in 4·7 (Tapley 460 lb./ton)
Third gear	1 in 4·3 (Tapley 510 lb./ton)
Second gear ..	1 in 3·0 (Tapley 705 lb./ton)

FUEL CONSUMPTION

Overall Fuel Consumption for 1,082 miles, 44¾ gallons, equals 24·8 m.p.g. (11·4 litres/100 km.)

Touring Fuel Consumption (m.p.g. at steady speed midway between 30 m.p.h. and maximum, less 5% allowance for acceleration) 22·4 m.p.g.

Fuel tank capacity (maker's figure) .. 8 gallons

Direct top gear

28¼ m.p.g. ..	at constant 30 m.p.h. on level
28¾ m.p.g. ..	at constant 40 m.p.h. on level
25½ m.p.g. ..	at constant 50 m.p.h. on level
23¾ m.p.g. ..	at constant 60 m.p.h. on level
23¾ m.p.g. ..	at constant 70 m.p.h. on level
22 m.p.g. ..	at constant 80 m.p.h. on level
18½ m.p.g. ..	at constant 90 m.p.h. on level

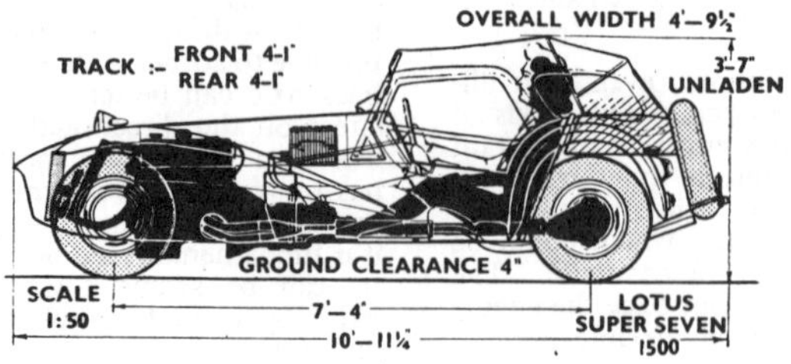
OVERALL WIDTH 4'–9½"
TRACK :– FRONT 4'-1" REAR 4'-1"
3'-7" UNLADEN
GROUND CLEARANCE 4"
SCALE 1:50
7'–4"
10'–11¼"
LOTUS SUPER SEVEN 1500

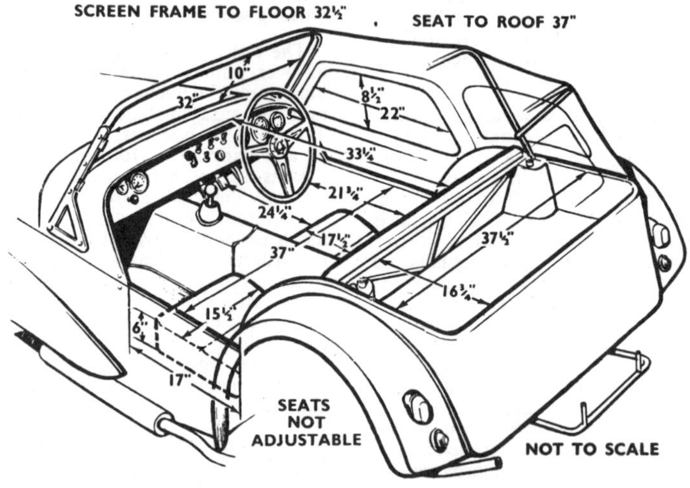
SCREEN FRAME TO FLOOR 32½"
SEAT TO ROOF 37"
10"
32"
8½"
22"
33¼"
21¾"
24¼"
17½"
37"
37½"
16¾"
15¼"
6"
17"
SEATS NOT ADJUSTABLE
NOT TO SCALE

BRAKES

Deceleration and equivalent stopping distance from 30 m.p.h.

1·00 g with 115 lb. pedal pressure ..	(30 ft.)
0·94 g with 105 lb. pedal pressure ..	(23 ft.)
0·70 g with 75 lb. pedal pressure ..	(42¾ ft.)
0.61 g with 50 lb. pedal pressure ..	(49¼ ft.)
0·28 g with 25 lb. pedal pressure ..	(107 ft.)

STEERING

Turning circle between kerbs:

Left ..	25¾ ft.
Right ..	26½ ft.
Turns of steering wheel from lock to lock	2¾

INSTRUMENTS

Speedometer at 30 m.p.h.	9% fast
Speedometer at 60 m.p.h.	accurate
Speedometer at 90 m.p.h.	1% fast
Distance recorder	accurate

WEIGHT

Kerb weight (unladen, but with oil, coolant and fuel for approximately 50 miles) ..	9½ cwt.
Front/rear distribution of kerb weight	55/45
Weight laden as tested	12½ cwt.

Specification

Engine

Cylinders ..	4
Bore ..	80·63 mm.
Stroke ..	72·75 mm.
Cubic capacity ..	1,498 c.c.
Piston area ..	31·92 sq. in.
Valves ..	Overhead (pushrod)
Compression ratio ..	9·5/1
Carburetters ..	Two 40 DCOE Webers
Fuel pump ..	AC Mechanical
Ignition timing control	Centrifugal
Oil filter ..	Full flow
Maximum power (gross) ..	95 b.h.p.
at ..	6,000 r.p.m.
Maximum torque (gross) ..	95 lb. ft.
at ..	4,500 r.p.m.
Piston speed at maximum b.h.p.	2,870 ft./min.

Transmission

Clutch	8 in. Borg & Beck s.d.p.
Top gear (s/m) ..	4·1
3rd gear (s/m) ..	5·79
2nd gear (s/m) ..	6·98
1st gear (s/m) ..	10·31
Propeller shaft ..	B.R.D. open
Final drive ..	Hypoid bevel
Top gear m.p.h. at 1,000 r.p.m. ..	15·3
Top gear m.p.h. at 1,000 ft./min. piston speed ..	31·9

Chassis

Brakes:	Girling disc and drum
Brake dimensions:	Front discs: 9½ in. dia. Rear drums: 7 in. × 1¼ in. wide
Friction areas:	44¼ sq. in. of friction lining area
Suspension:	
Front:	Unequal length wishbones with coil spring damper units
Rear:	A-bracket with parallel radius arms and coil spring damper units
Shock absorbers: Front, Rear	Armstrong telescopic
Steering gear:	Alford and Alder rack and pinion
Tyres:	4·50—13 Dunlop C41 or India C.46 Autoway

Lotus Super Seven (1500)

AS a tool for satisfying the "racer" in most of us, the Lotus Super Seven is an unqualified success. It does it at such a low price as to be remarkable and it would be unreasonable to expect very much comfort or refinement. There is plenty of performance and good road-holding but except for the arch-enthusiast, it would not be acceptable for everyday transport. As in most Lotuses up to the monocoque 25 Grand Prix racing car, the basis of the Super Seven is an extremely light tubular structure, and with the five-bearing 1½-litre Ford Classic engine tuned to produce 95 b.h.p., it has a power to weight ratio close to 200 b.h.p. per ton. Consequently, acceleration is very fierce indeed; the equal of almost any other vehicle on the road. Disc brakes match the performance and good handling complements it so far as smooth roads go. The ride is stiff and uncomfortable at low speeds and weather equipment, although an improvement over previous Sevens, remains rather sketchy. Cockpit space and luggage room are restricted, emphasizing that the Lotus is intended for the enthusiast to whom low-cost performance is worth extreme sacrifices. More specifically, it is aimed at the enthusiast with the ability and time to assemble his own car and save the purchase tax on works-completed vehicles.

Acceleration

THE bite of the Lotus is even worse (or better according to how one looks at it) than its bark which is considerable. The exhaust is full-throated and loud; definitely not for the town, where it could give serious offence, but a delight to the enthusiast

Spare-looking (*top*) the Lotus bonnet is only a little over knee high. The oil cooler and electric cooling fan can be seen through the front grille. (*Below*) The small wood-rimmed steering wheel and the low build of the car encourage a reclining, long-arm driving position. The speedometer, of secondary importance to the tachometer, is placed in front of the passenger.

In Brief

Price (without the extras mentioned in text) £695 plus purchase tax £173 15s. equals £868 15s. Price in kit form (without extras) £645.

Capacity	1,498 c.c.
Unladen kerb weight	9½ cwt.
Acceleration:	
20-40 m.p.h. in top gear	6.2 sec.
0-50 m.p.h. through gears	5.7 sec.
Maximum top gear gradient	1 in 4.7
Maximum speed	102.8 m.p.h.
Overall fuel consumption	24.8 m.p.g.
Touring fuel consumption	22.4 m.p.g.
Gearing: 15.3 m.p.h. in top gear at 1,000 r.p.m.	

Lotus Super Seven

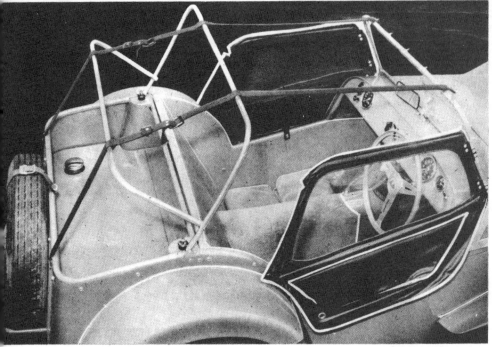

Without the sidescreens shown here (*top*) the Lotus has an almost fragile appearance. The stoneguards at the front of the rear wings are a practical innovation. (*Left*) The hood frame folds up and the fabric buttons on with press studs all round. The hood will stow in the space behind the seats which is also the only possible luggage accommodation. A neat tonneau cover may be supplied. (*Below*) The Cosworth-modified five-bearing Ford Classic engine. The dipstick is hard to get at under the plastic nose cowl ahead of the front carburetter. Rubber hoses alongside the engine lead to the test car's heater at the top of the picture.

in the right place. The sharp crackle is more than mere noise however. It is the voice of a Cosworth Ford with two double-choke Weber 40 DCOE carburetters, modified manifolds, cylinder head, and non-standard camshaft. At 6,000 r.p.m. it is producing 95 b.h.p. and over-enthusiasm from a standing start can leave long black lines of tyre tread on dry concrete. 50 m.p.h. can be reached in under 6 seconds and the quarter-mile mark passed in less than 16. The Lotus is one of the few cars which will accelerate to 100 m.p.h. and brake to a stop again in a time approaching the half minute, and it is almost certainly the cheapest production car ever to approach this. The maximum speed of nearly 103 m.p.h. was achieved at around 6,400 r.p.m. and the engine was taken to 6,500 in the indirect gears during the performance tests and on the road quite frequently without any apparent ill effects.

The smoothness of the five-bearing crankshaft makes the new engine a suitable choice and although there is no red line on the tachometer it appeared capable of revving higher if there had been any need. There is a good deal of mechanical clatter as well as hoarse sucking noises from the Webers to a listener standing at the front of the car, but inside this is all drowned by the exhaust. Idling is uneven and seemed to vary between 900 r.p.m. and about 1,800 r.p.m. with very richly set carburetters which were responsible for the heavy low-speed fuel consumption. The choke was never found necessary even after the car had been left standing out all night but care had to be taken with the throttle when starting the engine hot in case sudden floods of neat petrol drowned the plugs. This was really the only trace of temperament the engine had, although, not surprisingly, the power only starts asserting itself above 2,000 r.p.m.

Cooling is by the draught through the radiator when the car is moving, assisted by an electric fan which is switched on in traffic. This was seldom found necessary; in fact the temperature remained under 80°C. during all normal running (away from slowly shuffling traffic) one day when the outside temperature hovered round 50°F. (10°C.). During the test, this fan became inoperative and it was occasionally necessary to bring the interior heater blower into service in its place. This, together with the warm air which blows in from the engine compartment at speeds over 50 m.p.h. could make the interior uncomfortably hot. The oil cooler with which the test car was equipped is an optional extra at £15.

Close ratio gears

THE competition clutch was so heavy as to be difficult to operate at all, and the pedal uncomfortably angled which made traffic driving most unpleasant. For fast gearchanges however, it is much more suitable and has a short travel. The gear lever is stumpy and needs a quick, firm movement with care for going from first to second owing to the weakness of the reverse stop; otherwise, the changes are clean. The test car was supplied with the close-ratio box which costs an extra £40, gave splendid fast changes and seemed worthwhile to allow the engine to give its best. The standing-starts proved too much for first gear however, which failed during the test.

Like the clutch, the brakes need a firm pressure. They are Girling discs on the front with drum rears and while extremely resistant to fade, they were sometimes a little uneven when stopping from high speeds. The handbrake above the passenger's knees worked on a 1 in 3 test hill but it is extremely difficult to operate. The light steering has very little self-centring action and feels rather dead, although there is some kick-back on bumps. High speed stability is impaired by this and by engine torque reaction which can deflect the car off course when the throttle is opened or closed.

Cornering on smooth roads, the Lotus behaves in an exemplary fashion. There is a pleasant understeer and at speed the car behaves precisely as directed with a mild breakaway at the rear. In the wet, discretion is called for with the throttle, especially in the lower gears and the steering is very high geared making over-correction of slides rather easy for the unpractised. Smooth roads in the dry however, are sheer joy and fast, open, main road bends can be negotiated on "lines" in the prescribed manner with scarcely any body roll.

On rough surfaces, the firmness of the damping gives a bumpy ride and the rigid back axle shows itself to be rather unruly. The tubular chassis frame whips, giving a good deal of scuttle shake, making the front wings and headlamps vibrate rather alarmingly. The springs have a good deal of movement, demonstrated when the back tyres scuffed the inside of the rear wings with the increased g force on the M.I.R.A. bankings but they hardly budged over small bumps. Main road undulations are coped with well at speed but potholes cause some discomfort and can upset the car's stability on a corner.

Sacrifices

HAVING dwelt at some length on the fine performance, and the exhilaration of driving this splendid and truly sporting car, stock must be taken of the drawbacks of owning one. The driving position gives a clue to what conditions must be like in the cockpit of a current Formula Junior or Grand Prix racing car. It is small and cramped, with a diminutive 15-inch steering wheel at arms' length and the elbows overhang the driving seat, the left resting on the transmission tunnel and the right overhanging the frame tube at the side of the car. Non-adjustable seats demand a semi-reclining position fitting different heights of driver remarkably well; heavy coats, however, are difficult to accommodate, and so are large-sized shoes on the narrow toe-board.

The wood-rimmed steering wheel is quite comfortable although most drivers would prefer a thicker rim. Instruments are limited to a tachometer, oil pressure gauge, and water thermometer in front of the driver and a speedometer and ammeter on the passenger's side. A fuel gauge seems a curious omission.

Weather protection is a great improvement on earlier Super Sevens and sidescreens are now available. New transparent panels in the hood make the car much easier to see out of, and with the hood and sidescreens in position the interior is really quite cosy, if not very draught or waterproof. A good way of motoring the Lotus is solo with a tonneau cover over the passenger's seat and a segment filling the cutaway by the driver's right elbow. The flared glass-fibre wings deflect most of the spray from a wet road but the hot exhaust pipe is very close to the legs of passengers getting in or out. Space behind the seats will hold the hood when the tonneau is in place, or the tonneau when the hood is up, but proves a little small for the sidescreen frames. The inside fuel filler is reached by unbuttoning a corner of the hood so that luggage in the rear well may get splashed with petrol.

Climatic

OUR affection for the Lotus Super Seven quite literally would change with the weather. On a good day, driving it over open main roads without the hood was thrilling, but in hot damp traffic the heavy clutch and the drips and the draughts made it miserable. Depending on one's acceptance or rejection of its discomforts and starkness, the Lotus will be accepted or rejected. Its suitability for club racing, sprints, or driving tests is obvious although it might prove a fragile rally car. It is quite outstanding for low-cost, high-performance sporting motoring.

The much improved hood gives the Lotus a slightly dragster look. There was little ground clearance for the exhaust system which now comes out at the back instead of the side.

Coachwork and Equipment

Starting handle	..	..	.. None	Sun visors	..	.. None	Cigar lighters	.. .. None
Battery mounting	..	.. Under bonnet	Instruments: Speedometer with total mileage			Interior lights	.. .. None
Jack	..	..	.. .. None	recorder, oil pressure, water temperature,			Interior heater	.. .. Optional extra
Jacking points	Any convenient point on chassis			ammeter.			Car radio	.. .. None
Standard tool kit	..	..	.. None	Warning lights	.. .. None		Extras available: Sidescreens, heater, tonneau	
Exterior lights: 2 side, 2 rear, 2 head, stop and				Locks:			cover, flashing indicators, tachometer.	
number plate.				With ignition key	.. .. Ignition		Upholstery material	.. .. .. Vynide
Number of electrical fuses	..	.. 2	With other keys	.. .. None		Floor covering	.. .. Rubber mats
Direction indicators	Self cancelling flashers extra			Glove lockers	.. .. None		Exterior colours standardized: Any colour at	
Windscreen wipers	.. Two-blade, electric,			Map pockets	.. .. None		extra cost.	
		self-cancelling		Parcel shelves	.. .. None		Alternative body styles	.. .. None
Windscreen washers	.. .. None			Ashtrays	.. .. None			

Maintenance

Sump	..	.. 4 pints, S.A.E. 40/50	Sparking plug gap	.. .. 0.025 in.	Steering swivel pin inclination .. .. 9°
Gearbox	..	.. 1½ pints, S.A.E. 80 EP	Valve timing: Inlet opens 40° b.t.d.c. and closes 76°		Tyre pressures:
Rear axle	..	.. 1¾ pints, S.A.E. 80 EP	a.b.d.c. Exhaust opens 76° b.b.d.c. and closes		Front .. .. 22 lb.
Steering gear lubricant	Multi-purpose grease		40° a.t.d.c.		Rear .. .. 22 lb.
Cooling system capacity	.. 8 pints (2 drain taps)		Tappet clearances: (cold) .. inlet 0.017 in.		Brake fluid .. .. Girling
Chassis lubrication	..	.. None		exhaust 0.020 in.	Battery type and capacity 12 volt, 38 amp.-hr.
Ignition timing	..	3° before t.d.c. static	Front wheel toe-in	.. .. ⅛ in.	Miscellaneous: Trunnion to vertical link bearings
Contact breaker gap	.. 0.014-0.016 in.		Camber angle	.. .. 1° positive	requires filling with oil.
Sparking plug type	..	.. Champion N5	Castor angle	.. .. 5°	

CHRIS BECK DRIVES

THE SENSATIONAL SUPER SEVEN

WHAT sports car has the look of a praying mantis, the comforts of a gaol cell, a price tag of £1395 and yet accelerates to 80 mph quicker than an E-type Jaguar? Those who said "a Lotus Super Seven" take a bow and go to the head of the class.

Anything bearing the magic name Lotus must be good; we at SPORTS CAR WORLD formed this opinion after testing the ordinary Seven. Now the Super Seven has confirmed this. It is a car that did nothing but amaze us; and every time we accelerated from traffic lights or entered a corner our wonderment increased.

The Lotus Super Seven is a complete paradox. It is not in the least stylish; in fact the body line is classically stark. It is one of those "racing improves the breed" cars — by this I mean that it was originally a road derivation from Chapman's mark six racing machine. It was, our staff members felt, the ideal second, sporting, member of a two car family. But for those who cannot afford the luxury of a stable of automobiles the Super Seven, if the owner were prepared to put up with its austerity-plus-character, would suffice.

The expressions on many of the puzzled,

LIKES	DISLIKES
● Acceleration	● Seats and seating position
● Roadholding and handling	● Handbrake position
● Braking	● Ride harshness
● Gearbox ratios	● Absence of turn indicators
● Engine flexibility	● Difficulty of entry and exit
● Steering	● Lack of luggage space

Functional, with the classic "square rigger" line, the Lotus Super Seven wears old-fashioned clothing.

questioning faces that eyed the test car conveyed one of two thoughts. Several men complimented us on the excellent finish and asked where we had bought such a nice brand-new 1949 sports car. Others shrugged their shoulders and said, "Backyard jobs are always funny-looking, aren't they?"

The main difference between the Super and the standard Seven we tested last year is in the mechanicals. Instead of the 997 cc 105E Ford Anglia motor tweaked to produce 43 bhp the Super uses the 1498 cc, five bearing, 116E Cortina inspiration with modifications from the house of Cosworth, developing a meaty 95 bhp at 6500 rpm. This is almost 36 bhp more than the production Cortina 1500 motor.

Cosworth gets the extra power by radically reworking the cylinder head, almost to full race specifications, fitting larger valves and double valve springs and raising the compression ratio. Carburetion is dealt with by twin double choke 40DCOE Webers connected to stub inlet manifolds. A full extractor system pulls the spent gases from the head into a large bore exhaust pipe and then into a thin tube-type silencer which runs along the passenger's side of the car. As is natural with a "warm" motor the rev limit inevitably rises and to combat wear and the possibility of damage by the factory parts not holding together Cosworth adds special conrods and has the flywheel, clutch, crankshaft and conrod assembly dynamically balanced.

The most noticeable thing in this modified Cortina engine is the camshaft; it offers a gruff note when idling and the full effect of the semi-race grind is felt around 4000 rpm. When the motor is warm it is easy to accelerate steadily and quickly in top gear from 1000 rpm — 16.8 mph — without it snatching or being temperamental in any way. Cosworth must be praised for producing such an extremely flexible unit, which, while not being as velvety as some

Interior finish is not in Aston Martin class, but simplicity and accessibility make the driver's job easy.

sports car motors, is hard to fault.

Around town it was best to hold the car in second and third gears, but when a bit of open space permitted fourth gear was used. For quick overtaking second or third gear proved ideal although in top the car would gallop away with a deep roar from the Webers. In fact it accelerates from 30 mph in top harder than a Malcolm-modified editorial Mini in second.

Starting from rest presented a real problem.

Anything above 2750 rpm sent the car snaking wildly up the road and on the change to second the wheels would spin violently and rev counter soar. In third the needle would again spin round the face of the Smiths electric tachometer at an alarming rate. There seemed to be a never-ending supply of power. Only during acceleration runs did we extend the car to its fullest, for we found no other time where the situation warranted it. It was the complete proof of a theory we have expounded at SCW that a car with an abundance of power has a greater margin of safety — if driven properly — in a ticklish situation than something less powerful.

Straight from the Cortina, the gearbox is hard to fault. First is an ideal ratio, and so are third and top, but the staff had some misgivings about second gear. It was not quite high enough and the close ratio option — which gives a maximum of 65 mph — would be better suited. Maximum in first was 35 mph while the change to second lifted the road speed to 57 mph. Third is exhausted at the 90 mark and top takes the car up to almost 110 mph. Although we saw this figure on the speedometer during our runs the actual was closer to 105 mph. It is interesting to note that the Super Seven, formerly raced by the brothers Geoghegan, now owned by that small, intrepid Lotus driver, Bill March, recorded a top speed of 122 mph through the flying eighth on Conrod straight at Mount Panorama. The car's lap times were comparable to the best of D-type Jaguars that once raced there. Gear graunching is almost impossible due to excellent synchromesh.

A disc/drum braking combination is used and is most effective, hauling the car down from maximum speed without any trace of brake fade. Nine-inch Girling discs are fitted at the front — the same units as used on the Triumph Spitfire — and eight-inch drums take care of the rear. After several crash stops from 60 mph the brakes seemed to get better, not worse. One thing we found more of an ornament than an effective piece of equipment was the horizontally-mounted pull-up, ratchet-type handbrake on the passenger's side. As well as being difficult to operate it was not particularly effective.

An Alder and Alford rack and pinion steering unit is used, giving two and a quarter turns lock to lock. This allows quick manoeuvrability and immediate and precise changes in direction. On rough — even tar aggregate roads — the steering reflected intense vibrations, making the driver's job quite difficult. It is hard to see why Cheshunt has not incorporated a shock damper in the system.

A car with such stunning performance would not be a great car unless it had roadholding and handling to match. The Lotus Super Seven has handling and roadholding that would, 10 years ago, have been considered advanced for a GP car. Suspension at the front is independent, using double wishbones connected to a Triumph Herald spindle support and the springing is by a combined coil/shock absorber unit. The location of the live rear axle by parallel trailing arms and a triangulated A-bracket again damped by coil spring/shocker units seems to be the car's secret. Unlike earlier imported Sevens the ride, while very choppy and harsh, is not offensively hard or uncompromising. Off bitumen roads the Seven is a nightmare; it jumps, tosses and bucks. So the word is that you don't take them on anything but tar roads, and then these would preferably be hot-mix.

Roadholding is nothing short of phenomenal. During the test we kept cornering harder and harder and *harder* and still could not find the ultimate limit. Sliding is the basic essence in driving the Super and with the available power it is not very hard; but it is very hard to do it properly, on line and quickly. This is where it sorts the men from the boys on the race track. It was hard to define the test car's handling. Sliding through a 50 mph corner on a closed throttle resulted in a heavy, pronounced, but not uncomfortable understeer. On a trailing throttle the car was almost neutral, but when

A brace of twin-choke 40 DCOE Weber carburettors feed the Cosworth-modified motor, but consumption is not excessive.

SPECIFICATIONS

CHASSIS AND BODY DIMENSIONS:

Wheelbase	7 ft 6 in
Track, front	4 ft 3½ in
Track, rear	4 ft 2⅛ in
Ground clearance	3 in
Turns, lock to lock	2.25
Overall length	12 ft 2 in
Overall height	2 ft 10½ in

CHASSIS:

Steering type	Rack and pinion
Brake type	disc front, drum rear
Suspension, front	independent, wishbones and coil springs
Suspension, rear	live rear axle, parallel trailing arms and A bracket, coil springs
Shock absorbers	telescopic hydraulic
Tyre size	5.20 x 13
Weight	9 cwt
Fuel tank capacity	7 gals
Approx. cruising range	250 miles

taken with the power full on the tail snapped out quickly. We found the quickest way through any corner was to close the throttle for the entry, gradually opening up until full power was being used at the exit. If one changes lines in a corner suddenly the car goes where the front wheels are pointed — nothing frightening or nerve shattering happens. I think I can say, with some certainty, that it is the safest and best-handling car we have ever road tested.

Body styling, while not the most handsome of all small sports cars, is functional and light. At the front the mudguards and nosepiece are of fibreglass. The rest of the bodywork is aluminium, except the rear mudguards, which are also of fibreglass. In the tradition of the classic sports car the headlights, completely detachable units, nestle in the valleys between the mudguards and the nose. At the rear there is a small parcel tray atop the seven gallon fuel tank and the rear is completely squared-off, with only the spare tyre for decoration. The Lucas brake/taillight units are attached to the rear 'guards.

Immediately in front of the driver, at less than arms' length is the wood-rimmed steering wheel with the grey, yellow and green Lotus boss in the centre. On the passenger's side of the dash panel there is an ammeter and a mechanical Smiths 130 mph speedometer, incorporating an odometer.

Across to the right of these is the key-ignition switch and then almost immediately above the gearlever is a triangle of toggle switches which operate the wipers, headlights and parkers and the electric cooling fan. In front of the driver is an 8000 rpm Smiths electric tachometer, flanked by an oil pressure and water temperature gauges. On the far righ is a spring loaded toggle switch actuating the horn. The starter button is under the dash on the aluminium scuttle. It, like the handbrake, is difficult to operate.

The gearshift is a remote unit from a Triumph Herald and has short, stiff throws. It needs little more than a flick of the wrist to go from one gear to the next. Once inside the driver finds the cockpit quite comfortable, although if he is a small man the non-adjustment of the seat and pedals makes things a little difficult. At speed the Super Seven attracts more draught than a medieval castle. At anything over 60 mph the hair blows and tangles.

As an everyday sports car for Australian roads the Super Seven is a little impractical, but if one were prepared to put up with the inconvenience and almost impossible situation of never driving over rough roads then it would be ideal. But its austerity, simplicity and ungainly appearance and tremendous performance make it an excellent car in which to go Jaguar hunting.   #

ENGINE:

Cylinders	four, in line
Bore and stroke	80.9 mm by 74.6 mm
Cubic Capacity	1498 cc
Compression ratio	9.5 to 1
Fuel requirement	100 octane
Valves	pushrod, overhead
Maximum power	95 bhp at 6000 rpm

TRANSMISSION:

Overall ratios

First (Synchro)	15.81
Second (synchro)	9.34
Third (synchro)	5.50
Fourth (synchro)	3.90
Final drive	3.90 to 1

PERFORMANCE

Rpm limit on test	6000 rpm
Top speed average	106 mph
Fastest run	106.5 mph
Maximum, first	35 mph
Maximum, second	57 mph
Maximum, third	90 mph
Maximum, fourth	106 mph
Standing quarter mile average	16.0 seconds
Fastest run	15.8 seconds
0 to 30 mph	2.3 seconds
0 to 40 mph	3.8 seconds
0 to 50 mph	5.7 seconds
0 to 60 mph	7.6 seconds
0 to 70 mph	10.1 seconds
0 to 80 mph	13.0 seconds
0 to 90 mph	18.8 seconds
0 to 100 mph	NA
40 to 60 mph	5.8 seconds
50 to 70 mph	6.2 seconds
60 to 80 mph	6.7 seconds
Brake fade resistance on test hill	98 percent
Fuel Consumption, overall	25 mpg
Fuel Consumption, cruising	30 mpg

After the Numbers Wear Off:
LOTUS SUPER SEVEN

BY ALAN GIRDLER

EVERY SPORTS CAR enthusiast should own a Lotus Super Seven—and probably would if the cars could be sold with a guarantee that never again would rain fall, temperatures drop, roads be rough or other drivers park by ear.

I have it on good authority that rain, cold, bad roads and worse drivers will always be with us. This cost analysis of the care and feeding of a Super Seven should be considered, then, as more of a love letter than practical information.

To say that I didn't buy the car for its looks is probably superfluous. I doubt that the Lotus Seven could be described as styled; it just sort of happened. The Seven has the simplest possible space frame, with the body panels wrapped around it and a fender tacked on each corner. Top down, it looks like an old MG reworked by a dry lakes dropout. Top up, it has all the esthetic charm of a 1935 Chaparral.

My excuse for purchase was rationalized economics. I'm a club racer, just good enough to know how good I'm not. Even this unsolicited testimonial won't cause Colin Chapman to offer me a place on the team. I race only on the local track, three or four times a year, and I can't justify buying a car to drive for a few hours annually. A racing car that I can drive to work whenever my MG-TC is laid up for repairs (that is, one or two days a week), is an excusable investment. It also promotes good feeling at home because I can promise my wife that I won't appropriate her station wagon.

New list price on my 1963 Super Seven, equipped with all Cosworth mods and options, was $4500. I got more than a generous discount; bought the car used in late 1965 for $1800. For every bargain, there's a reason. Before I could start the engine, I paid $13.75 for engine parts, $9.95 for a generator rebuild, $15 for a battery and $15 to have cracks in the differential welded shut and broken frame tubes replaced. Before I could drive the car on the street, I bought a set of used road equipment—muffler, top, top bows, side curtains and windshield wiper motor—for $65.

Three of the tires that came with the car were badly worn and the fourth had a broken sidewall. New racing-grade

tires, $140. The safety regulations had been strengthened since the car's last race. Wide seat belt and shoulder harness, $29. My first practice lap revealed a very independent suspension. New shock absorbers, $138.

On paper then, the car cost $1800. Realistically, by the time I had worked my used car into a usable car my investment in car, parts and services that a semi-skilled mechanic like myself couldn't perform, was $2225.70.

Gas mileage will have to be an estimate. I'm not really sure what the tank capacity is and the odometer isn't connected. I drive about 25 miles daily and one dollar's worth runs the car for two days. With premium gas selling here for 37¢ per gallon, I work that out to be around 20 mpg. With my heavy foot and the car's 4.11:1 final drive, that's reasonable. On a daily basis, the car is more expensive to park than to drive. A Lotus Seven has no bumpers. The body is alumi-

---

1963 LOTUS SUPER SEVEN

Costs for 5000 miles and seven races

Purchase price	$1800.00
Immediate replacements and repairs	425.70
Actual cost	$2225.70
Street operation:	
Gasoline	$100.00
Parking	200.00
Licensing	114.28
Insurance	108.00
Total	$522.28
Race entry fees:	
Four regional races	$100.00
Three national races	90.00
Total	$190.00
Maintenance, all purposes	$175.55
Total operating costs	$887.83
Total costs	$3113.53
Less present value of car	1800.00
Cost of 2 years' ownership	$1313.53
Cost per mile (see text)	either 10.4¢ or 22.4¢
Cost per race (see text)	either $113.14 or $27.14

LOTUS SUPER SEVEN
Owners Report

num and thin fiberglass. Parallel parking is out. The car exerts a hypnotic attraction on passersby. They succumb to urges to lean on it and some even climb inside and whip the steering wheel back and forth to assure themselves, I guess, that it steers. Public parking is out.

I have a deal with the attendants at a downtown parking garage. They are no more anxious to drive the car than I am to let them, so I park it myself in the safe, secluded basement. Costs me $1 daily and better insurance I never bought.

More mundane insurance is also reasonable. The Lotus is the third car in a 2-driver family. I'm 30 years old, with one wife and four children, which puts me in a good insurance bracket. Liability insurance costs me $54 a year.

Oklahoma collects its property tax on cars through the tag agency so the license price is based on the car's retail price when new. They don't care what I paid, they look up the retail price and they charge me $54.14. I don't argue. I learned my lesson when I tried to explain that my TC actually sold for $1895 rather than $2395 because of the devaluation of the English pound years ago.

The highest cost listed in my maintenance account could also be listed as operating cost, or even insurance. A competitor broke a rear axle and shed a wheel one day, so I decided to have my axles Magnafluxed. The test cost $2 but machine work was required to take the things apart and I discovered that the teeth were flaking off the pinion. The entire project, including new wheel bearings and a new ring-and-pinion, set me back $91.

Mind, I'm not complaining. Magnafluxing stressed parts on racing cars is a good thing and I'd rather replace parts too soon than too late.

The car is serviced regularly, indeed, continually, by me. During the past two years I've bought 32 quarts of oil, $24; one set of ignition points with condenser, $3.60; two sets of hot (street) plugs and two sets of cold (racing) plugs, $10.40; and an oil-pressure booster kit, $1.75. That's not a complete list, but I've forgotten the prices of the various hoses, belts, brake parts and so forth. I'll add $50 to the maintenance total to make up for my lack of records.

Depreciation of most cars is routine. The car loses a set percentage of its value when it leaves the showroom floor and so much more every model change. Depreciation of a production-class racing car depends largely on the vagaries of the Sports Car Club of America, which are considerable.

Lotus Super Sevens compete in class C Production. When I bought my car the Lotus Elans had just been moved up from C to B production, leaving the Super Sevens to compete against rare and expensive Porsche Carreras and Supersport Morgans. A Super Seven had a good chance of winning the class and a sound one sold for $2500.

Since then, the Elans have been moved back to class C, bringing the Sunbeam Tigers with them. The Carreras are still around, aided by their rich relatives, the 911s. The new 2-liter Datsuns are doing very well in CP. Even gentlemen drivers take these things into consideration and judging from the classified ads, my race-ready Super Seven is now worth $1800, or what I paid for the rough material two years ago.

Having added it all up, I don't know how to divide it. If I claim the Lotus is a racing car, driven occasionally on the street, then only the actual road expense —gas, parking, tag and insurance—applies against 5000 street miles. Cost per mile, 10.4¢. All other items went into the racing fund, and each race cost $113.14.

It's probably more accurate to say the car is a street car, used for racing a few times a year. I do need a third car and I did rationalize my purchase as a third car that could also race. On that basis, only the race entry fees can be deducted from the total expenditures. The cost per mile more than doubles, to 22.4¢, but each race cost only $27.14. I'd almost have to pay that much for trophies at the trophy store.

To say I'm pleased with the car is an understatement. I'm delighted. Highly tuned and lightly built, my Super Seven has displayed all the temperament of an electric clock. Never a break-down on the street and the only mechanical derangement at the races came when the exhaust pipe fell off. It was recovered by a brave corner worker without damage to it or him.

True, there have been cloudy days with snow expected when I had a choice of a car with heater and no windshield wipers or a car with wiper and no heater.

True, not being able to leave the Lotus unattended is inconvenient, the ride is fierce, the rain comes in and driving with the top up is comparable to riding inside a bass drum.

But there is no cheaper way to go racing and I don't know of any other car that is so much fun to drive, anywhere, any weather. Plus, to my wife's surprise and pleasure, I haven't snuck off with her wagon since I bought the Lotus.

How to Build a Lotus Seven
CONTINUED FROM PAGE 13

Fit bottom water pipe with angle hose to radiator.
Fit the propshaft.

Bolts

Four bolts 1" x $\frac{5}{16}$"
Four Nyloc nuts.
The remote gear control can then be fitted into the tunnel and fastened with
Six bolts $\frac{1}{2}$" x $\frac{3}{16}$".
Six Nyloc nuts.
Six flat washers.
for which you must drill $\frac{3}{16}$" holes in the tunnel sides.
Cut a hole in the tunnel cover for the gear lever. Cut a 3" dia hole in the centre section with a slit to the edge and fit the rubber boot to control rod.
Fit horn.

Bolts

Two bolts $\frac{1}{4}$" x $\frac{3}{16}$".
Two Nyloc nuts.
Four flat washers.
Fit battery.
The suspension bolts can now be tightened.
Set front wheel track to $\frac{1}{8}$" toe in at hub height.
Fit steering wheel.
Fit the front wings and stays with the headlamp mountings to the rear, allowing for full bump clearance inside the wings.

Bolts

Eight bolts $1\frac{1}{4}$" x $\frac{3}{16}$".
Eight Nyloc nuts.
Sixteen flat washers.
Eight bolts, special coach.
Eight plain nuts.
Eight flat washers.
Drill wings for side lamps.
Run wires through wing stays and connect to side lamps.
Fit headlamps, noting that in the dipped position the offside lamp is switched off.
The number plate lamp is mounted on the "D" shaped plate which is in turn bolted to the rear number plate.

Bolts

Two bolts 1" x $\frac{3}{16}$".
Two $\frac{3}{16}$" Nyloc nuts.
Four $\frac{3}{16}$" flat washers.
Two bolts $\frac{1}{2}$" x 5/32"
Two plain nuts.
Two spring washers.

READY FOR THE ROAD

Lubricate all grease nipple points.
Fill engine, gearbox and rear axle with their respective oils.
Fill water system.
Set the tyre pressures to 20 lb sq in front and rear.
On starting the engine check that there is oil pressure, that the dynamo is charging and look for oil and water leaks.
Adjust the carburetter. If you have 2 SUs requiring synchronisation, the Lotus Works will be pleased to provide tuning instructions.
After a short road test check again for leaks.
The running-in speed can be as high as 45 mph in top gear.
When you have completed 500 miles replace all oils and check over nuts and bolts.
The weather proofing can be improved by filling all pop rivets and joints which are subject to wetness with Sealastic or a similar preparation. Obviously it is preferable to do this before assembling the car.
If you plan to paint the car yourself, it is as well to remember to use an etching primer before filler coats and colour.

AUTOTEST

LOTUS 7 TWIN CAM SS (1,558 c.c.)

AT-A-GLANCE: Super-sporting two-seater, offering shattering performance and excellent handling, in kit form only. Accommodation spartan and rather cramped. Poor streamlining affects economy and top speed. Without equal on performance-for-money basis and tremendous fun to drive.

MANUFACTURER
Lotus Components Ltd, Norwich (NOR 92W), Norfolk, England

DISTRIBUTOR
Caterham Car Sales, 36-40 Town End, Caterham Hill, Surrey.

PRICES
Complete kit	£1,250 0 0	(£1,250.00)
Purchase Tax	Not applicable (available only as a kit)	
Seat belts (approx.)	£6 5 0	(£6.25)
Total (in G.B.)	£1,256 5 0	(£1,256.25)

EXTRAS (inc. P.T.)
Metallic paint finish	£25 0 0	(£25.00)
Roll-over bar	£14 0 0	(£14.00)
*Tonneau cover	£9 10 0	(£9.50)
Tinted windscreen	£6 0 0	(£6.00)
*Oil cooler	£15 0 0	(£15.00)
* Goodyear Rally Special tyres	£17 4 7	(£17.23)

*Fitted to test car

PRICE AS TESTED £1,297 19 7 (£1,297.98)

PERFORMANCE SUMMARY
Mean maximum speed	103 mph
Standing start ¼-mile	15.5 sec
0-60 mph	7.1 sec
30-70 mph through gears	7.2 sec
Typical fuel consumption	19 mpg
Miles per tankful	150

THERE is a lot of stuff written these days about what some people call "fun cars". Sadly, "fun" usually means odd, also ostentatious, but rarely enjoyable to drive. Therefore it is particularly good for one to drive the Lotus Seven Twin Cam SS, which is real fun. Putting 125bhp in a little over half a ton of very controllable space-frame chassis—and not much else—which sits on four fat and quite well-connected little tyres, cannot help being very entertaining for anyone who likes to drive fast. To drive this vehicle on a lonely, open road (there are still some if you look hard) is to be reminded most firmly that the genuine and the best "fun car" is still a pure sports car. And that, without any possiblity of argument, is exactly what this Lotus is.

The original Lotus Seven first appeared at the London Motor Show 13 years ago, and was a descendant of the popular and successful club-racing Lotus Mark VI. Although there are obvious differences—including an increase of 2.6cwt since our last Super Seven test—this latest Lotus is something of a nostalgic throwback to the early days of a most remarkable marque. Suspension is independent in front, using some Standard-Triumph parts in a double-wishbone and anti-roll bar layout, with a Ford live-axle behind located by a shallow A-bracket and trailing arms; combined coil-spring and damper units are used at each end. Steering is rack-and-pinion, and delightfully high-geared and tight-locked, 2.7 turns for 29½ft mean turning circle between kerbs. Because of the small overhang, it needs only 2in. more between walls.

To make it go, there is a Holbay-tuned Lotus-Ford twin-ohc 1,558c.c. engine which delivers a claimed 125bhp at 6,200rpm via a four-speed all-synchromesh gearbox and 3.9-to-1 final drive (with Hewland limited-slip differential) to Goodyear Rally Special low-profile radial tyres on 5½in. Dunlop cast-alloy wheels. To make it stop there are Girling 9in. discs in front, with drums at the rear. In spite of burying the engine partially under the nose section (which therefore has to be removed every time you check the oil level), weight distribution is only just front-heavy with no occupants and half a tank of petrol. With the tank filled—8 gallons only—it is virtually 50-50.

Before going any further it should be stated that, with its now slightly thicker seat-padding on seats that are non-adjustable anyway, the Lotus is best suited to drivers between 5ft 8in. and 5ft 10in. tall. With the hood down—the

Below: Open is the only way to drive the little Lotus. Removing the very flexible bonnet uncovers the rear two-thirds of the engine and the carburettors. Four Dzus fasteners, accessible by sixpence rather than a penny, release the glass-fibre nose section for, amongst other things, inspection of oil-level. A flush aircraft-type trap-door in the top of the nose over the dipstick would help greatly without seriously spoiling the aerodynamics

Left: Erecting the hood isn't as quick as the car. Anyone used to modern sports-cars or saloons must at first remember that those big back wheels stick out quite a way sideways from where one is sitting. The temporary towing bracket on the spare wheel is not for caravans

Below left: You must crouch to see horizontally through the sidescreens

LOTUS 7 TWIN CAM SS (1,558 c.c.)

ACCELERATION

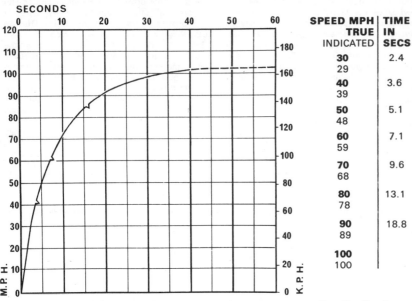

SPEED MPH TRUE INDICATED	TIME IN SECS
30 29	2.4
40 39	3.6
50 48	5.1
60 59	7.1
70 68	9.6
80 78	13.1
90 89	18.8
100 100	

SPEED RANGE, GEAR RATIOS AND TIME IN SECONDS

mph	Top (3.90)	3rd (5.45)	2nd (7.84)	1st (11.59)
10–30		5.2	3.3	2.4
20–40	7.0	4.5	2.8	—
30–50	7.0	4.6	3.0	—
40–60	7.2	4.4	—	—
50–70	8.1	4.5	—	—
60–80	9.4	—	—	—
70–90	11.2	—	—	—

Standing ¼-mile
15.5 sec 82 mph
Standing kilometre
29.8 sec 98 mph
Test distance
800 miles
Mileage recorder
6 per cent
under-reading

PERFORMANCE
MAXIMUM SPEEDS

Gear	mph	kph	rpm
Top (mean)	103	166	5,700
(best)	106	171	5,860
3rd	90	145	7,000
2nd	63	101	7,000
1st	43	69	7,000

BRAKES
(from 70 mph in neutral)
Pedal load for 0.5g stops in lb

1	55	6	52–62
2	53–55	7	55–62
3	48–50	8	60–67
4	45–62	9	60–63
5	45–58	10	58–62

RESPONSE (from 30 mph in neutral)

Load	g	Distance
20lb	0.17	177ft
40lb	0.29	104ft
60lb	0.44	68ft
80lb	0.60	50ft
100lb	0.70	43ft
120lb	0.89	34ft
140lb	1.00	30.1f
150lb	1.02	29.5f

CLUTCH
Pedal 50lb and 4.7in.
MOTORWAY CRUISING
Indicated speed at 70 mph	68 mph
Engine (rpm at 70 mph)	3,870 rpm
(mean piston speed)	1,850 ft/min.
Fuel (mpg at 70 mph)	22.1 mpg
Passing (50-70 mph)	4.5 sec

COMPARISONS

MAXIMUM SPEED MPH
Jaguar 4.2 E-type Roadster	(£2,294)	140
Morgan Plus 8	(£1,647)	124
Lotus Elan S4 Drophead S/E	(£1,942)	124
Lotus 7 Twin Cam SS	**(£1,250)**	**103**
	(in kit form)	
Lotus Super Seven (1961)		—

0–60 MPH, SEC
Morgan Plus 8	6.7
Lotus 7 Twin Cam SS	**7.1**
Jaguar 4.2 E-type Roadster	7.4
Lotus Super Seven (1961)	7.6
Lotus Elan S4 Drophead S/E	7.8

STANDING ¼-MILE, SEC
Jaguar 4.2 E-type Roadster	15.0
Morgan Plus 8	15.1
Lotus 7 Twin Cam SS	**15.5**
Lotus Super Seven (1961)	15.8
Lotus Elan S4 Drophead S/E	15.9

OVERALL MPG
Lotus Elan S4 Drophead S/E	30.0
Lotus Super Seven (1961)	22.9
Jaguar 4.2 E-type Roadster	21.8
Lotus 7 Twin Cam SS	**19.2**
Morgan Plus 8	18.3

GEARING (with 195-13in. 70 series low-profile tyres)
Top	18.1 mph per 1,000 rpm
3rd	12.9 mph per 1,000 rpm
2nd	9.0 mph per 1,000 rpm
1st	6.1 mph per 1,000 rpm

TEST CONDITIONS
Weather: Overcast, occasional rain. Wind: 8—16 mph. Temperature: 6 deg. C (43 deg. F). Barometer 29.6 in. hg. Humidity: 81 per cent. Surfaces: Damp concrete and asphalt.

WEIGHT:
Kerb weight 11.2 cwt (1,258lb–571kg) (with oil, water and half-full fuel tank). Distribution. per cent F, 51.7; R, 48.3. Laden as tested: 14.8 cwt (1,654lb–741kg).

TURNING CIRCLES:
Between kerbs: L, 29ft 9in.; R, 29ft 3in. Between walls: L, 29ft 11in.; R, 29ft 5in. Steering wheel turns, lock to lock, 2.7.

Figures taken at 2,500 miles by our own staff at the Motor Industry Research Association proving ground at Nuneaton.

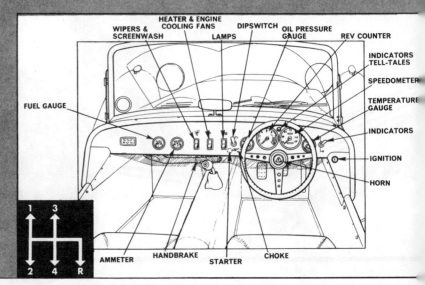

CONSUMPTION

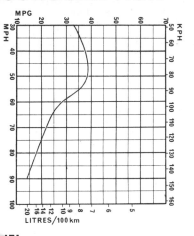

MPG / KPH graph

LITRES/100 km

FUEL

At constant speeds—mpg)

mph	. . . . .	32.8
mph	. . . . .	37.5
mph	. . . . .	38.5
mph	. . . . .	28.4
mph	. . . . .	22.1
mph	. . . . .	18.1
mph	. . . . .	14.1

Typical mpg 19 (14.9 litres/100km)
Calculated (DIN) mpg 20.1 (14.1 litres/100km)
Overall mpg 19.2 (14.7 litres/100km)
Grade of fuel
    Super Premium, 5-star (min. 100 RM)

OIL

Consumption (SAE 20W/50) . . . . negligible

SPECIFICATION

FRONT ENGINE, REAR-WHEEL DRIVE

ENGINE
Cylinders . . . . 4, in-line
Main bearings . . 5
Cooling system . Water; pump, electric fan, thermostat
Bore . . . . 82.6mm (3.25 in.)
Stroke . . . 72.8mm (2.86 in.)
Displacement . 1,558 c.c. (95.19 cu.in.)
Valve gear . . Twin overhead camshafts
Compression ratio 9.5-to-1 Min. octane rating: 100 RM; 5-star fuel
Carburettor . . Two double-choke Weber 40 DCOE
Fuel pump . . AC mechanical
Oil filter . . . Full flow
Max. power . . 125 bhp (net) at 6,200 rpm
Max. torque . . 116 lb.ft (net) at 4,500 rpm

TRANSMISSION
Clutch . . . Borg and Beck, diaphragm spring, 8.0 in. dia.
Gearbox . . . Four-speed, all synchromesh
Gear ratios . . . Top 1.0
    Third 1.40
    Second 2.01
    First 2.97
    Reverse 3.32
Final drive . . . Hypoid bevel, 3.9-to-1, Hewland limited-slip differential

CHASSIS and BODY
Construction . . Tubular steel space frame, aluminium alloy body panels, glass-fibre mudguards and nose section.

SUSPENSION
Front . . . . Independent, double wishbones, anti-roll bar, coil springs, telescopic dampers
Rear . . . . Live axle, trailing arms, A-bracket, coil springs, telescopic dampers

STEERING
Type . . . . Rack and pinion
Wheel dia. . . . 13 in.

BRAKES
Make and type . Girling, disc front, drum rear
Servo . . . . None
Dimensions . F 9.0 in. dia.
    R 8.0 in. dia. 15 in. wide shoes.
Swept area . . F 150 sq. in. R 75.4 sq. in.
Total . . . . 225.4 sq. in. (304 sq. in./ton laden)

WHEELS
Type . . . . Dunlop cast alloy, 4-stud fixing 5.5 in. wide rim.
Tyres—make . . Dunlop SP Sport (Goodyear Rally Special optional extra)
    —type . . Radial-ply tubeless (Low profile, 70 series Goodyear)
    —size . . 165-13 in. (195-13 in., Goodyear)

EQUIPMENT
Battery . . . . 12 volt 39 Ah
Generator . . . Lucas 42 amp d.c.
Headlamps . . . Lucas F700 120/90 watt (total)
Reversing lamp . None
Electric fuses . . 2
Screen wipers . Single speed, self parking
Screen washer . Standard, electric
Interior heater . Standard; re-circulating, single-speed boost fan, on/off cock on engine
Heated backlight . Not applicable
Safety belts . . Extra
Interior trim . . Pvc seats, pvc headlining
Floor covering . . Carpet, with rubber heel pad for driver.
Jack . . . . None supplied
Jacking points . No specific points—under lower wishbones at front, under axle at rear
Windscreen . . Laminated
Underbody protection . . No special treatment

MAINTENANCE
Fuel tank . . . . 8 Imp. gallons 36.4 litres
Cooling system . 12.5 pints (including heater)
Engine sump . . 7.5 pints (4 litres) SAE 20W/50 Change oil every 6,000 miles. Change filter element every 6,000 miles
Gearbox . . . . 1.75 pints SAE 80 EP Change oil every 6,000 miles
Final drive . . . 2 pints SAE 90 EP Change oil every 9,000 miles
Grease . . . . 6 points every 1,500 miles
Tyre pressures . F18:R22 psi (normal driving) F20:R24 psi (fast driving)

PERFORMANCE DATA
Top gear mph per 1,000 rpm . . . . 16.8 (18.1 with Goodyear Rally Special tyres)
Mean piston speed at max. power . . . 2,964 ft/min.
Bhp per ton laden 169

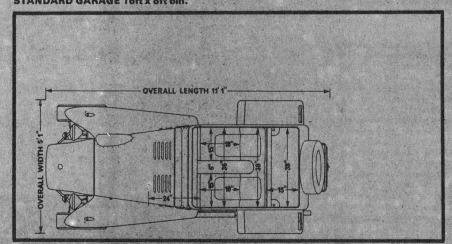

STANDARD GARAGE 16ft x 8ft 6in.

OVERALL LENGTH 11' 1"
OVERALL WIDTH 5' 1"

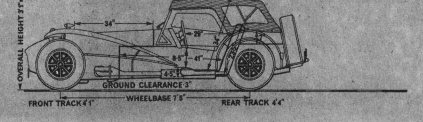

OVERALL HEIGHT 3' 6"
GROUND CLEARANCE 3"
FRONT TRACK 4' 1"
WHEELBASE 7' 5"
REAR TRACK 4' 4"

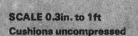

SCALE 0.3in. to 1ft
Cushions uncompressed

best way to drive it in any circumstances—our 6ft and 6ft 2in. testers could get behind the wheel fairly easily, though knees were uncomfortably close to the wheel rim. With the hood up, either of these same testers had to poke his trunk across until his head was above his passenger's lap, then bring his feet in from outside to the small space behind the wheel, afterwards twisting himself past the wheel and into place. Keen but tall drivers all regret that they are not made more welcome, but once in place agree that the struggle is worthwhile.

Both the rich mixture control for the two twin-choke 40DCOE Weber carburettors and the big button of the starter switch are hidden under the facia on the engine bulkhead. Starting is good, and during the cold wet weather, which reigned throughout the test period, rich mixture wasn't needed for more than the first minute of running. Requiring a 50lb shove, the Borg and Beck clutch is heavy, but fully up to its job. The very short gearlever is extremely close to the wheel and has a positive, precise and sometimes slightly notchy action; in the main it is a delight.

The car warms up quite quickly to around an indicated 90deg.C. which it holds no matter what is happening. There is a non-automatic electric fan for the radiator, but we never had to switch it on, even in the heaviest traffic. Once it is warm, and if the road is clear, you feel free to start using the engine to the full.

Performance

As our acceleration figures show, the performance is fierce. In order to reduce one of the car's built-in headwinds slightly, performance measurements were taken with the hood up; that makes little difference to the noise you hear, which is dominated by the hard beat of the unsilenced induction trumpets which becomes a snarl at high revs. Exhaust noise—a most unexpectedly lusty hiss not unlike that made by a contemporary Rolls-Royce accelerating flat-out—is only audible to bystanders. Standing starts were best made by feeding in the clutch at 4,500rpm, which produces least wheelspin, sometimes a little axle-tramp and some snaking nearly all the way to 30mph, 2.4sec from rest; such take-offs, achieved two-up (with test gear, a total of 358lb payload), are extremely impressive and exciting. Brief wheelspin and a wriggle marked each hustled gearchange thereafter; 50mph comes up in 5.1sec, 60 in 7.1, and 80 in 13.1; corresponding times for the last E-type Jaguar we tested (open 4.2 model, *Autocar* 12 October 1967) are 5.6, 7.4, and 12.4sec. Aerodynamic influences are felt overcoming the uncompromising body shape after 90mph, reached in 18.8sec; top speed is 103mph mean, 21mph slower than the much "cleaner" Special Equipment Lotus Elan (which, however, gets to 60mph in 0.3sec after its forebear). One must of course pay for the performance in fuel consumption, which at a typical 19mpg is heavy. During performance testing, this dropped to around 15mpg, which might be fairly typical if one raced the car.

The engine is pretty flexible, pulling reasonably and without snatch from as little as 800rpm. It begins to get into its stride at around 3,500rpm and really gets going at 4,500 to all the way beyond the beginning of the red mark on the rev-counter at 6,500rpm. No ignition cut-out was fitted to the test car and we were told that it was permissible to rev

to 7,000rpm for brief periods during our acceleration runs. The "official" 6,500rpm limit gives speeds in the closely spaced gears of 40, 58 and 84mph, more than enough for most purposes. This is one of those cars where overtaking is made so much easier and safer by its tremendous get-away. One can overdo violent standing starts, however; possibly because "our" car had already been the subject of a number of tests by other periodicals, our first attempts at taking figures were halted when the A-bracket locating the back-axle buckled during acceleration runs. The greater care exercised by an owner should avoid this trouble.

Handling and roadholding are the Lotus Seven Twin Cam's other great virtues. Anyone used to cars with less accurate steering will at first drive the Lotus in a series of darts; there is virtually no free play and the effort needed at the wheel rim is low. After a while, directing the car becomes a mainly fingertip exercise, seemingly more mental than manual—until, in the appropriate place, one starts cornering at more than ordinary speeds. What little roll there is is amplified visually by the wing tips. The car of course, is, basically an understeerer, though not too much so. If the road is smooth it takes a good deal of power to break the tail away, though it isn't that difficult even on a good dry surface. On a track, one soon discovers the true worth of the steering mechanism, which being high-geared and capable of large angles of lock enables one to hold almost any slide one might get into. Adhesion is excellent, dry or wet, though one must watch it on wet surfaces. The essence of the car in these respects is that it is not in the least treacherous.

Its security includes the brakes which hardly fade at all and, on those remarkable tyres, surprised us by giving a 1.02g maximum retardation on quite damp MIRA surfaces. Pedal effort is akin to a racing car, abnormally high. The handbrake is a thing to avoid using because of its awkward position under the facia. Two-up, it would just hold on 1-in-4, and had a very sticky pawl release. We couldn't help thinking that no one would mind greatly if it were re-positioned trials-fashion outside the cockpit on the driver's side.

The ride is simply very firm. You watch out for the larger potholes for fear of the crashing noise everything makes if you hit one. One accepts this as part of the car's character.

Seating is basic but not uncomfortable for the right size of driver specified earlier. You are located sideways simply by the cockpit wall and the side of the high transmission tunnel, and forwards, not quite well enough, by the shape of the seat cushion. If it were not for the fact that getting knees past the steering wheel would become more difficult as things are at present, one would like more "lip" at the front

of the cushion to stop one moving forward more effectively. One is at little more than elbow-length from the 13in. dia. wheel; slide correction for long-legged drivers is made a little awkward because hands on the wheel's rim hit one's thighs.

Instrumentation is good, lacking only an oil temperature gauge, though this probably doesn't matter much with such a well-cooled engine. The ammeter deputizes for an absent ignition warning light. The speedometer surprised us by consistently under-reading by 2mph over much of its range. Switches are neatly identified by symbols; the washer and wiper controls are combined and so are the radiator and recirculating heater fan switches; first position is for the former only, second for both. Heater temperature is either hot or cold, depending in the first place on whether the heater water cock under the bonnet is turned on and, as far as your feet are concerned, on whether or not you have the blower fan on.

One badly needs a clutch foot-rest. Persuading one's left foot past the clutch pedal is awkward and withdrawal slow, so that you daren't rest it while on any sort of twisty going if you are having to use the gearbox a lot. Accelerator and brake pedals are well-placed for easy flat-of-the-foot heel-and-toe changes for the shorter driver and side-of-the-foot ones for the tall.

Erecting the hood, if you must use it, is somewhat laborious but not impossible. At speed it does keep the rain off your head but not off your knees and some areas of the back of the windscreen; spray blows in past the very vision-blinkering side-screens. The tonneau cover was not a good fit on the test car. Another item which interferes with vision is the position of the spare wheel relative to the mirror; the latter is too low—wing mirrors would help greatly when two are in the car; travelling two-up in the Lotus is the personification of togetherness. The headlamps are no longer fog or spotlamps and when aimed correctly work average well. Maserati air-horns are fitted, which give the easily overlooked little Seven a legal voice in the affairs of those around it, apart from its raucous intake roar.

Summing up, one can say that in terms of vulnerability, comfort, control, performance and sheer enjoyment, the Lotus Seven Twin Cam SS is a four-wheeled motor-bike. Despite testing it at one of the worst possible times of the year, those of us who drove it found it most satisfying. We would like to see a little development in accommodation and some other details—there are several things we have mentioned which could easily be much better without spoiling the car's purpose. But, overall, it is most effective in what it sets out to do; as one of us put it "I'd be quite happy to race it as it is." □

In the Lotus it is as easy to get into this sort of situation as out of it, thanks to the superb steering. Here the slide was "put on" for the photographer's benefit; the fast way through any track corner is to enter quickly which produces a fair amount of understeer, and to balance this with throttle. On ordinary roads the roadholding is so good that one need never approach this state, yet still be cornering much faster than anything else.

RUMBLINGS

"Having been flown up on the Sunday (to Hethel), we thought it only decent to depart in a Lotus." The Editor about to drive from Norfolk to Radnorshire in the latest Lotus 7.

■ **LIVING WITH THE LOTUS 7.**—In May, to attract people to Wymondham to see the Group Lotus Car Companies' factories and to raise funds for the Norwich Lads' Club, Graham Hill opened the Lotus Open Weekend of 1970, at which a display of historic Lotus cars, modern Lotus cars, a fairground, midget car racing, a flying display which included a visit by a Hurricane, a dance, and other jollies were laid on. Having been flown up on the Sunday in a Piper Twin Commanche, appropriately one wearing a competition number, a legacy from the London-Sydney race, we thought it only decent to depart in a Lotus. Which we did, in a Series 4 Seven, scorning to erect the hood, so that the journey to Wales tied in with what we wrote last month about sports cars and the joys of open-air motoring . . .

It was our intention to write about what it is like to live with a Lotus 7 but there wasn't one to spare, the car we borrowed being the personal property of Mike Warner, Managing Director of Lotus Components Ltd., which had to be returned within the week. However, it is possible from this necessarily brief encounter to convey something of what this cheeky little modern sports car is like.

We realised almost as soon as the security police had permitted us to get out on to the road that the Lotus 7 puts the fun back into motoring in no uncertain manner. But the smooth, quiet running of the car and its civilised suspension came as a surprise. The accelerator is in close proximity to the foot-brake and maybe because Warner's car was very new (it showed only 527 miles on its odometer) the gear-change was extraordinarily stiff, third impossibly baulky, and the clutch very "sudden". That apart, the Lotus 7 is simplicity to drive, the short central gear lever well placed, the steering very light and responsive to scarcely more than wrist movements, 2⅝ turns of the little leather-rimmed wheel taking it from one full lock to the other. This example had the Cortina GT engine, which ran quietly, with a subdued exhaust note, yet when the throttle was opened things happened—fast, the little red two-seater accelerating to the eager note of efficient machinery. The car's light weight (10 cwt. 3 qr. empty, but with about four gallons of fuel) is reflected in the ready response to the accelerator even in top gear. At 70 m.p.h. the tachometer reads just below 4,000 r.p.m. and an indicated 100 m.p.h. comes up quite quickly.

There is nothing dramatic about driving this Seven, apart from steering shake as the wheel plays through one's fingers and some frenzy from the bonnet and the "power-bulge" in front of the driver, which can reflect the sun into one's eyes. It is not to be compared to vintage motoring and, indeed, offers fewer amenities. It is, however, enormous fun, and light though it is to handle, it provides plenty of exercise, because, being doorless, getting in and out becomes a bit athletic—and may well have been planned with mini-skirts in mind ! The detachable sidescreens serve as doors but to release them an awkwardly-placed single external turn-stud has to be manipulated through the sliding window and there is nothing to hold up the "door" as you climb out. Getting out when the hood is up must be almost impossible, and quite claustrophobic . . .

The seats, like those on early Morgan Plus Fours, are fixed (but the pedals can be adjusted). On the Lotus they are a snug but not very comfortable fit, because you lie rather than sit in them, but not to the extent that a racing driver lies in a GP car, so driving the Seven can put a bit of a strain on the lumbar muscles. But snug fit they are, to the extent of leaving the seat harness to be sat on unless it is worn (the Lotus belts were easy to use, says W.B.'s wife) and with the side pieces up there is not much elbow room. Provision for a tonneau cover would have been appreciated.

Otherwise, this Seven is very civilised. Hood and sidescreens stow in the boot, which has a cover easy to fit thanks to Tenax fasteners, which are an improvement of "lift-the-dots" as well as being neater, although one pulled out of the fabric. There is full, easy to read, Smith's instrumentation (heat 70 to 80°C.), a Smith's Series 3 heater, and winkers with side repeaters on the front mudguards—and they are *real* mudguards. Four press-buttons on the centre panel work lights, heater-fan, wipers and washers. The bonnet releases absurdly easily to hinge forward and reveal most of the mechanism, including the Weber carburetter topped by a Nordic air-cleaner. The finish of the fibreglass body is excellent and the frog's-eyes Lucas headlamps, black on this car in contrast to the red paintwork, give an effective beam. The spare wheel lives on the tail (Dunlop SP Sport radials were fitted), there is a quick-action fuel filler in the broad n/s rear wing, and the Lotus 7 comes with roll-over bar, ready to race.

Leaving Norfolk on our solo drive to Wales we were soon making good progress along the A11, picking off the dodderers with impressive bursts of effortless acceleration. It was very much open-air motoring, however, in the bitter gale that was sweeping off Thetford heath and Newmarket plain and in the Snetterton area (where a race meeting was presumably in progress for a Chain-Gang Frazer Nash was seen abandoned on the adjacent straight). We endured the buffeting from the wind until St. Neots, before pausing to erect the side bits, which plug in easily and make open-car motoring much less tough. (Sports cars of the 1920s didn't habitually go at the pace we were extracting from the Lotus and their aero screens probably created less backdraught than the Lotus' upright one.) In the softer country beyond Bedford the run became extremely pleasant, for there is nothing quite like this Seven, which rattles and shakes a bit but clings to the road like a limpet and steers with the accuracy of a micrometer. The 258-mile journey was accomplished well within the six-hour target in spite of several more pauses, to map-read and refuel, and much crawling Sunday traffic with which to contend. The fuel gauge went to zero just before Tewkesbury, suggesting a usable range of some 200 miles, at very roughly 30 m.p.g. The gear-change got progressively more horrid, however, until it was almost impossible to shift, due to clutch drag, which adjusting the pedal wouldn't cure (to do which a country garage charged at the rate of 45s. an hour!), but the adequate ground clearance up the rough house-drive that marked journey's end was another pleasant surprise, although eventually the exhaust tail-pipe bracket fractured.

This short acquaintance with Mr. Chapman's boy's-racer confirmed what enormous fun the latest Seven is (until the transmission went solid) and now we want to try the hotter twin-cam version.

Series 4 Seven for the Seventies

By SIMON TAYLOR

THIS week Lotus introduce the Series 4 version of the famous Seven, which continues the line begun with the first Lotus 7 more than 12 years ago, and is still very much in the tradition of the first serious Lotus production car, the Six, which made its bow in 1953. The new 7 Series 4 still uses a simple multi-tubular chassis frame, stressed with steel sheet and using wishbone front suspension and a rigid rear axle, but a much more elaborate fibreglass body makes the car a better proposition for everyday transport without detracting from its essential "fun-car" character.

Had the Formula F100 rules been a little different, the 1970 Lotus 7 might have been rear-engined. When the new category was first announced an idea was put forward at Hethel for a car based on the Formula Ford Type 61, using the same suspension parts but with a wider two-seater chassis and cycle-type front wings. The machine would have been available in raceable FF100 form and also as a road car. However, the FF100 rules called for an all-enveloping body, which would

have made the car more expensive and elaborate and far removed from the Lotus 7 image, so the idea was dropped. However, the connection with racing is maintained by the 7X currently being campaigned by Tim Goss, which was recently built by Lotus Components; the centre section of the chassis is similar to the production car's, although they have nothing else in common.

Front suspension on the 7 S4 uses Europa components, with rubber-bushed wishbones and coil-damper units, while the location of the rear axle (an Escort TC component) is unusual in that it uses an upper leading arm and lower trailing arm each side. Thus when the car rolls the axle itself is in torsion, and acting as its own anti-roll bar, although the rubber bushes on the pickup points of the arms allow some movement. Coil-damper units provide the suspension medium.

Although the standard engine is the unmodified 84 bhp Cortina 1600 GT unit, the 1300 Escort GT motor can be specified. Other options are the pushrod 1600 Holbay Clubman engine as used in the Lotus 7S,

which develops 120 bhp, and the Lotus twin-cam unit in standard (115 bhp) and Holbay (125 bhp) forms. Steering is Burman rack and pinion, and standard wheels are 5J steel affairs shod with 165-13 Dunlop SP Sport radials, although Brand Lotus cast alloy wheels are an option. Braking is by 8½ins front discs and 9ins rear drums.

It is the body of the 7 S4 which shows the greatest change. The car is 14½ins longer, mainly due to the all-enveloping tail which houses a much more generous luggage space than before. The nose cone and bonnet make up a one-piece fibreglass moulding which hinges forward to give excellent engine accessibility, and the rest of the body structure is a one-piece bolted-on fibreglass shell replacing the alloy panels of earlier cars.

This has allowed a larger and much more habitable cockpit with heavily padded seats, increased leg and elbow room and moulded-in fibreglass dashboard. The bigger overall cockpit size means that with the hood and sidescreens erected visibility is enormously improved; the rigid sidescreens have sliding

Engine accessibility is improved by the new bonnet/nose unit (left). The all-enveloping tail makes the S4 over a foot longer (right).

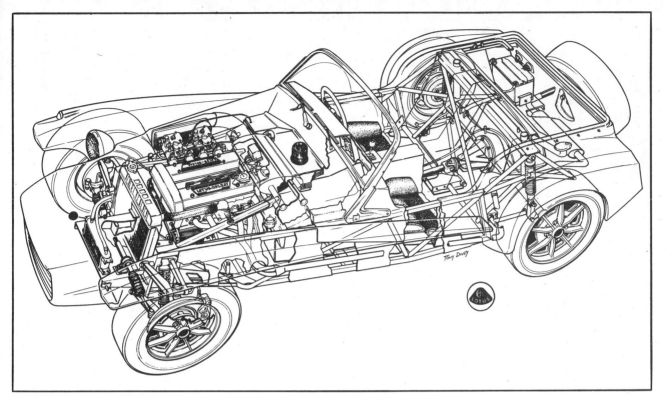

Perspex panels. These, plus the long front mudguards which now continue to the fronts of the rear wings, should stamp out Lotus Elbow, the familiar malady suffered by hardy Lotus 7 drivers and their passengers in inclement conditions.

Interior trim varies according to specification—the dash is naked fibreglass as standard, but can be finished in an attractive simulated leather finish which is sprayed on—but there is full instrumentation and a leather-rimmed steering wheel. The rubber floor covering can be replaced with carpeting at extra cost, and another option is a roll-over bar. In basic trim the 7 S4 weighs almost exactly half a ton.

Track impressions

Last week I visited Hethel and, although the new wild-shaped Formula 1 Type 72 and monocoque Formula 2 Type 69 cars were under frenzied construction behind closed doors, I was able to see the first 7 S4s under construction in the Lotus Components area, and also to try a couple round the dogleg-

shaped Lotus test track, which has three fast corners and two tight ones, plus a long straight which has to be negotiated with a bit of care as Colin Chapman may be landing his twin-engined Navajo on it at the time (or Big Graham Arnold his Little Auster, for that matter).

Both the cars I tried were very new prototypes and had only just been finished, and apart from their engines both had equally basic specification with nothing in the way of extra trim. First I tried one with an unmodified 1600 GT engine, which proved to have fairly brisk performance despite a very tight new engine. Very lively indeed was the twin-cam version. The controversial rear suspension probably helped to give the car its roll-free cornering; the rear end seems to break away easily, but it all happens progressively and the little machine can be driven like a go-kart with fistfuls of opposite lock and plenty of entertainment. The suspension is softer that before, and on bumpy surfaces under really heavy cornering I found that the propshaft or diff casing could clout the fibreglass undertray.

There is certainly more room inside than in previous 7s, and one seems to sit rather higher in the glass-fibre tub than one did in earlier cars, when one was wrapped in the alloy panels that stressed the frame. In the basic trim cars and with the hood up the noise is pretty deafening, although the de luxe trim kit would obviously help.

The car's appearance is rather an acquired taste, but I found that I liked all but the rather high, square nose, which is not an aesthetic improvement on the rounded nose-cone of the S2 and S3 versions. The car isn't as cheap as it was—the basic 1600 cc version costs £895 in kit form —but its performance-per-£ factor is still very high, and as a fun car it seems bound to carry on the Lotus 7's reputation and sell well at home and abroad. It's very much a road machine and in its present form would hardly be a competitive clubmen's formula racer, but perhaps the BARC and BRSCC will accept it as a mod sports car before too long, and then it should give the lightweight Spridgefires (and the Elans) something to think about.

The three most recent Lotus 7s : left to right, the 7S, the Twin-Cam SS, and the new Series 4 with its different nose treatment.

Ton-up lightweight

MOTOR TESTED

Reborn 7 with stylish glassfibre body and better
cockpit; tractable Cortina GT engine; exhilarating to drive;
precise agile handling, skittish in wet; excellent gearbox
but heavy clutch; quite expensive as a stark kit car

It used to be easy to spot the owner of a Lotus 7; he was agile, perhaps even a contortionist, walked with a stoop, had a damp right sleeve and a watery eye. He was a die-hard wind-in-the-face enthusiast prepared to sacrifice all, or nearly all, creature comforts and convenience in pursuit of performance and the pleasure of driving an open sports car in its simplest and perhaps purest form.

Lotus mark numbers are now up to 72, so the 7 was clearly an early one. In fact it is 13 years since it first saw the light of day. Since then it has remained the epitome of a fun car and until this year had changed very little apart from the fitting of a succession of different engines into the light, simple tubular space-frame in accordance with the latest thinking at Dagenham.

It is an open secret that Lotus have been trying to kill the 7 for some time. It was not really an economic proposition under the new set-up at Hethel and hardly in keeping with the image of performance with refinement set by the Elan and Europa. That it

survives today is largely due to the efforts of Graham Nearn of Caterham Car Sales who obtained the sole concession for the 7 some years ago. It was he who put up the idea of civilizing and glamorizing the little tin box for its series 4 form. He plans to sell 250 kits this year.

Inevitably some people will say that the car has gone soft and lost much of its character in the revisions which include a stylish one-piece glassfibre body in place of the previous conglomorate of mouldings and alloy panels; a completely new console and facia with instruments designed to be read on the move; and more comprehensive easy-to-work protection against the elements. There is now hardly a bare frame tube in sight since the whole of the interior is lined with a neat black moulding to give a monocoque effect. The seats are still not adjustable, and you either fit or you don't, but they are now comfortably shaped and no longer cushions laid on the floor.

We didn't think it had lost any of its appeal as a fun car; in fact the more aggressive shape of the new body would, we think, do far more to win friends and influence people than the old one. It is slightly heavier than the last we tested and the standard crossflow 1600 unit develops a little less power than the tweaked 1500 Classic engine used then. But it will still reach a genuine maximum of 100 mph, scorch up to 60 mph in under 9s and pull strongly from as low as 15 mph in top gear. This should be

Price: £950 (component form only, no purchase tax); magnesium alloy wheels £42; heater £17; roll-over bar £15; screen washers £3 5s; air horns £4 15s; tonneau cover £10; **Price as tested £1042**
Make: Lotus. **Model** 7 SE. **Makers:** Lotus Components Ltd, Norwich, NOR 92W.

good enough for most fun seekers; if not the latest engine options include the Holbay Clubman and the Special Equipment twin-cam.

The ride is surprisingly good for this kind of car though there is still a trace of scuttle shake. Too much power through a bumpy corner will lurch it off line and it tends to slide around like a bar of soap in the bath on wet roads. Otherwise, it goes where it's pointed and its inherent swervability and light, direct steering are ideal for jinking in and out of traffic. Although the car is a lot more civilised than before most of our criticism still relates to the total lack of amenities. There is space for no more luggage than the proverbial week-end suitcase, rather less with the hood down; and once the neat rear tonneau is in place there is nowhere to stow even a packet of Polo. With the hood up clambering in and out through the small opening afforded by the hinged side screens is tiresome. The screens themselves are fiddly to release from inside and we lost count of the number of techniques adopted by young ladies attempting to enter the car with a degree of decorum; none were successful. The new hood no longer has three-quarter panels so visibility has suffered. But

perhaps this doesn't matter to the damp-sleeve fraternity.

The 7 was built to give pleasure from the moment the lorry dumps the formidable pile of seemingly unrelated parts in your front garden. Considering that all of the £950 it costs goes to Lotus and none to the government, it may seem rather expensive fun but even after 13 years there are still no serious imitations.

Performance and economy

First impressions can be misleading. With its rakish lines, prominent outside exhaust curling away from the fabricated bunch-of-bananas system, and obvious performance potential we expected the 7 to be fierce and raucous, our bright red test car to be an immediate target for every copper in Z division. It is fierce certainly, as we would expect with a power/weight ratio of 150 bhp per ton, but after the harsh bellow of the Cosworth 1500 with its twin 40 DCOE Webers, the standard 1600 cross-flow unit is almost an anticlimax. Some enthusiasts might even say it was too quiet; we thought the level about right and it was a pleasant change to drive a sports car which was as tractable and

PERFORMANCE

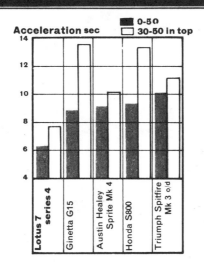

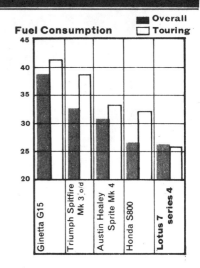

Performance tests carried out by *Motor's* staff at the Motor Industry Research Association proving ground, Lindley.

Test Data: World copyright reserved; no unauthorised reproduction in whole or in part.

Conditions

Weather: Warm and dry, wind 10-12 mph
Temperature: 56-60°F
Barometer: 29.6 in. hg.
Surface: Dry tarmacadam
Fuel: 98 octane (RM) 4-Star rating

Maximum Speeds

	mph	kph
Mean lap banked circuit	100	161
Best one-way ¼-mile	108.5	175
Direct top gear		
3rd gear ⎫	82	132
2nd gear ⎬ at 6500 rpm	58	93
1st gear ⎭	39	63
"Maximile" speed: (Timed quarter mile after 1 mile accelerating from rest)		
Mean		99.1
Best		101.2

Acceleration Times

mph		sec
0-30	. . . .	3.0
0-40	. . . .	4.5
0-50	. . . .	6.3
0-60	. . . .	8.8
0-70	. . . .	11.8
0-80	. . . .	16.0
0-90	. . . .	24.2
Standing quarter mile		16.0
Standing Kilometer		31.4

mph	Top sec.	3rd sec.
10-30	. . . .	5.2
20-40	7.1	4.8
30-50	7.2	4.5
40-60	7.5	4.5
50-70	7.9	5.3

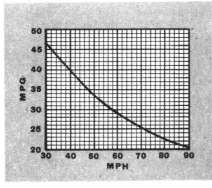

60-80	. . . . 9.3	7.6
70-90	. . . . 13.0	—

Fuel Consumption

Touring (consumption midway between 30 mph and maximum less 5 per cent allowance for acceleration) 25.9 mpg
Overall 26.3 mpg
(= 10.8 litres/100km)
Total test distance 1460 miles

Brakes

Pedal pressure, deceleration and equivalent stopping distance from 30 mph

lb.	g.	ft.
25	0.38	79
50	1+	30
Handbrake	0.30	100

Fade Test

20 stops at ½g deceleration at 1 min. intervals from a speed midway between 40 mph and maximum speed (=70 mph)

	lb.
Pedal force at beginning	30
Pedal force at 10th stop	30
Pedal force at 20th stop	30

Steering

Turning circle between kerbs:	ft.
Left	30½
Right	29½
Turns of steering wheel from lock to lock	2¾
Steering wheel deflection for 50 ft. diameter circle 0.8 turns	

Clutch

Free pedal movement	. . . .	½in.
Additional movement to disengage clutch completely		2in.
Maximum pedal load	. . . .	50lb.

Speedometer

Indicated	30	40	50	60	70	80	90
True	29	39	49	58	67½	76	85

Distance recorder 2 per cent fast

Weight

Kerb weight (unladen with fuel for approximately 50 miles)
11.4 cwt
Front/rear distribution 48½/51½
Weight laden as tested 15.2cwt

Parkability

Gap needed to clear 6 ft. wide obstruction in front
4ft. 11 in.

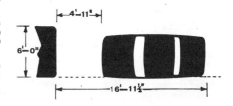

69

unobtrusive in city traffic as it was exhilarating when given its head on the open road.

The GT engine with the normal compound Weber downdraught carburetter produces 84 bhp at 5400 rpm compared with 95 bhp at 6000 rpm of the old Cosworth 1500. Torque is about the same, 92 lb.ft., but it reaches a maximum much lower down, at only 3600 rpm which makes it a much more docile and tractable unit. The cross-flow engine is not noted for smoothness; in fact with the light weight and firm engine mounts of the 7 it tends to be rather harsh throughout its range, though there are no serious vibration periods or flat spots and it will pull cleanly and strongly in top gear from speeds at which many sports car engines would be trying to jump out of the bonnet: witness the 30-50 mph top gear time of 7.7 seconds. Breathing seems rather restricted at the top end and the engine seemed reluctant to rev in the orange sector of the rev counter which ends at 6500 rpm. This has little effect on acceleration, though, especially as hard standing starts are easy.

Our best mean lap of MIRA in rather blustery conditions was exactly 100 mph but we managed a best quarter of over 108 mph

with an engine that was still a little on the tight side. The car did not like being held at high speeds for long though; either the air intake is inadequate or it chokes itself at speed since even after a fairly short spell at 85-90 mph the temperature climbs well above normal and the oil pressure settled to 25 psi or less, enough to make the more mechanically sympathetic lift off. Fortunately readings returned to normal very quickly.

We were a little surprised that the 7 did not return a better touring consumption figure than 25.9 mpg for cruising at 65 mph although an overall figure of 26.3 mpg is pretty good for a sports car driven hard. Even so the range with the eight gallon tank is only a little over 200 miles. Refuelling is not the nuisance it used to be now that the filler cap has been moved from the floor of the luggage compartment to an external position in the nearside wing. Being a standard engine, it is virtually free of temperament and runs quite happily on four-star petrol.

Transmission

The excellent 2000E semi-close ratio gearbox is a standard fitting on the SE model we tested. There is no frictional resistance or

Thanks to easy entry into an open cockpit, above, our man made a clean getaway on this occasion. Inside, below, it's a snug fit

The fixed seats are comfortably bolstered and provide a good driving position if you're not tall. The handbrake fouls your knee

Still starkly functional, above, but striking and not inelegant

Hood and sidescreens can be stowed in the "boot", above, leaving little room for other luggage. Erecting the hood, below, is a fairly quick but fiddly process with all those pop fasteners

free-play in the sturdy gearlever and the synchromesh is unbeatable yet hardly notchy, let alone obstructive. Our only complaint is that the very narrow gate sometimes leads to snicking reverse on the way down into second. We liked the ratios of this box, too, particularly the uprated second gear which can hurl the car up to nearly 60 mph. After flirtations with various final drives (Graham Nearn once used to scour the dealers for spare Standard 10 axles) Lotus have now settled on the 3.77 to 1 Escort axle which gives 17.8 mph per 1000 rpm in top gear, a reasonably long-legged cruising ratio.

Compared with the change the clutch is intolerably heavy; it needs a push of 50 lb. to release completely. Fortunately only the slightest dip of the pedal is required to effect a smooth change, but it is a good cure for drivers who ride the clutch at traffic lights. The car started easily on the 1 in 3 test hill.

Handling and brakes

Since the 7 was first made, Colin Chapman has gone on to show in cars like the Elan that superlative handling can be combined with an acceptably soft ride. The 7 remains comparatively wooden, though it doesn't jar even on very bad surfaces. But it is firm enough for the road surface to have a fairly significant influence on cornering behaviour.

The front suspension now consists mainly of Europa components but that at the rear is completely new and best described as a double Watts linkage, with trailing links to the bottom of the axle and leading links from a rearward extension to the chassis. It relies heavily on rubber bushes for compliance, an A-bracket for lateral location, and the geometry is such that roll is resisted by twist on the axle case which thus serves as a giant anti-roll bar.

On smooth surfaces, the handling is very neutral, the fat Dunlop SP sport tyres have tremendous adhesion and the car can simply be steered round on a steady throttle at seemingly impossible speeds. Put the power on too early and the car is undecided whether to plough straight on with understeer or push the tail out. The result, a rather untidy lurching motion and a lot of tyre squeal. If the road is bumpy, the back end always goes first as the tyres patter and lose adhesion and very high rear roll stiffness unloads the inside wheel. Roll is very well controlled, virtually non-existent, but there still seems to be some lateral movement in the rear suspension as there was evidence of the near side rear tyre having fouled the wheel arch after our performance tests.

Though our only chance to try the 7 in the wet came after a prolonged dry spell when the roads can be treacherously slippery, we were not impressed with wet road adhesion; considerable care was needed with the throttle to keep the rear end in check. The steering is very light and direct—2¾ turns lock to lock and 0.8 turns for the 50ft. circle—but it lacks self-centring which makes it feel rather dead at times. Rough surfaces cause some dither and kick-back which it is sometimes necessary to minimize by holding the wheel between finger and thumb on the spokes. Although the new body is now much stronger, and the wings and headlights no longer vibrate, there is still enough whip in the chassis to produce scuttle shake. Undoubtedly the 7 is at its best on fairly smooth twisty roads on which it is as manoeuvrable and exhilarating to drive as perhaps any car in the world. Being so light it builds up very little momentum through a series of bends and it can be swerved under complete control almost as fast as the driver can turn the wheel. The same attributes coupled with the exceptional tractability of the engine also make it extremely easy to get around town in heavy traffic.

The brakes are not servoed but still extremely effective, 50 lb. pedal pressure being sufficient to produce a 1g stop. They were unaffected by our fade test and recovered almost immediately after a soaking in the water splash. Admittedly in need of adjustment the pistol-grip handbrake is still an unsolved problem; we doubt that it could ever be made to hold the car on the 1 in 3 slope.

Comfort and controls

Lotus 7 customers presumably don't list comfort very high on their priorities. It is designed purely as an instrument of pleasure, an objective it achieves superbly. It is still cramped for any driver over 5ft. 10in. tall; getting in and out with the hood

Rear threequarter visibility is hampered by absence of side panels

The sidescreens hinge forward but the roof is low and the sill high

up calls for considerable agility; and the toe-board is so narrow that it is unwise to attempt to drive fast without proper driving shoes. Otherwise the car has been refined about as thoroughly and effectively as it could be without sacrificing any of its sporting character. In addition to the one-piece glassfibre body the redesigned chassis now has sheet steel sections along the cockpit sides and farther forward to provide mounts for the front suspension. The cockpit seems to be completely waterproof. It is also slightly bigger with more elbow room and an extra 2¼in. in the wheelbase, most of which has gone into the cockpit. As a result most people will now be able to hold the neat and comfortable leather rimmed steering wheel at arms' length without hanging their right elbow over the side.

The new seats are still fixed but extremely comfortable and support the occupants rather than simply wedge them in place. With the left arm resting comfortably on the padded transmission tunnel the gearlever is perfectly placed though most people will want more leg room or somewhere to rest the left foot off the clutch without having to bend the knee. Otherwise the pedals are well placed for heel-and-toe changes.

The car is most pleasant to drive with the hood off and the sidescreens in place; there is too much draught round the sides of the windscreen when these are removed. In this form entry is quite easy; a single fastener allows the screen to pivot like a front-hinged door and you climb in over the side without too much difficulty. The new wings now extend right down to meet the rear wheel arches so there is no longer any risk of passengers burning their legs on the outside exhaust which used to be rather exposed on that side. The new screens have sliding Perspex windows but it is still a rather fiddly job to reach the fastener from inside the car.

The hood is well made and fits snugly, making a watertight seal with the screens. But with more than a dozen poppet fasteners to do up it is necessary to anticipate a shower well in advance.

1 dipstick. 2 electric air horns (optional). 3 voltage regulator. 4 clutch reservoir. 5 brake fluid reservoir. 6 fuel pump. 7 carburetter. 8 distributor. 9 coil.

With the hood up the car is now quite cosy; provided the screens are tensioned to press firmly against the body sides very few draughts intrude and nobody complained of getting wet. Visibility to the sides and rear is good—until the Perspex gets scratched, which it will in time. The elimination of the clear panels from the rear corners seriously cuts visibility in that direction and you have to cut across road junctions at right angles, Europa fashion, to be able to see what's coming. Getting out of a closed 7 is laborious and inelegant especially as the angle of the screen hinges stops them staying open.

Luggage room is restricted to the well behind the seats into which the hood and its folding frame must be fitted when the car is open. With careful planning it should be possible to stow a fair sized suitcase and some soft baggage on top of the hood and then secure it neatly with the tonneau which is permanently attached behind the seats. With this in place there is nowhere to put a map or the odd bar of chocolate out of sight—annoying as there is room behind the new facia panel to incorporate a locker or cubby on the passenger's side.

Fittings and furniture

The new facia is neat and attractive with speedometer, rev counter, oil pressure and water temperature gauges immediately in front of the driver. A centre console contains the ammeter and a fuel gauge (a new addition to the equipment) and piano key switches for the wipers, electric washers, side lights and heater. As usual with the Herald steering column there are two stalks, for indicators on the right and main beam dip and flash on the left. Climate control is strictly limited; there is no means of ventilation and the heater is a simple recirculating unit with a tap under the bonnet, a single speed fan, and no provision to demist the windscreen. Still, it does seem possible to provide enough heat to warm the tiny cockpit very quickly when necessary. Among the external modifications are separate direction indicators beside the radiator intake with repeaters on the wings, moulded-in parking lights and much more elegant rear light clusters incorporated in the rakish squared-off tail. Safety has not been neglected either; lap and diagonal seat belts are very well mounted and comfortable to wear and a substantial rollover bar is an optional extra and a reminder of the 7's racing ancestry. The headlights have very good range and spread.

Accessibility and maintenance

The whole of the front section of the new body now hinges forward on releasing a catch at the base of the windscreen. It checks open with a strut and fully exposes the engine and front suspension. No chassis maintenance is required except for occasional oiling of clevis pins and cables, but the engine requires the usual Ford service schedule and oil change every 6000 miles. No tools are included as standard but a roll containing jack and wheel changing equipment is offered as an optional extra for £3 10s.

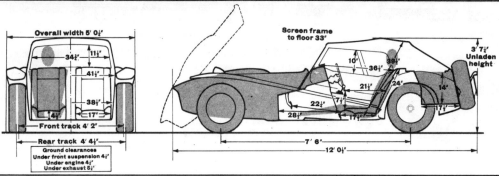

1600 cc front engine driving rear wheels through live axle; tubular and sheet steel frame; separate glassfibre body

Engine

Block material	Cast iron
Head material	Cast iron
Cylinders	4
Cooling system	Water
Bore and stroke	8.98 mm (3.188in.) 77.62 mm (3.056in.)
Cubic capacity	1599 cc (97.6 cu. in.)
Main bearings	5
Valves	Pushrod ohv
Compression ratio	9:1
Carburetter	Weber compound downdraught
Fuel pump	AC mechanical
Oil filter	Full flow
Max. power (net)	84 bhp at 5500 rpm
Max. torque (net)	96 lb. ft. at 3600 rpm

Transmission

Clutch	8-in. sdp diaphragm
Internal gear box ratios	
Top gear	1.00
3rd gear	1.40
2nd gear	2.01
1st gear	2.97
Reverse	3.32
Synchromesh	All forward gears
Final drive	3.77:1
Mph at 1000 rpm in:	
Top gear	17.8
3rd gear	12.7
2nd gear	8.9
1st gear	6.0

Chassis and body

Construction	Tubular chassis with stressed steel side panels, sheet steel front assembly, glassfibre body bolted on with separate front wings and bonnet

Brakes

Type	Disc/drum
Dimensions	9in. diameter discs front 9in. diameter drums rear
Friction areas:	
Front	14.7 sq. in. of lining operating on 34.6 sq. in. of disc
Rear	47.2 sq. in. of lining operating on 99 sq. in. of drum

Suspension and steering

Front	Double wishbones and coil springs
Rear	Live axle located by double Watts linkage and coil springs
Shock absorbers	Telescopic front and rear
Steering type	Rack and pinion
Tyres	165 x 13 HR Dunlop Sport Radial
Wheels	Pressed steel disc (alloy wheels optional)
Rim size	5½J

Coachwork and equipment

Starting handle	No
Tool kit contents	Spare wheel kit (optional extra)
Jack	Screw scissors
Jacking points	Under chassis side rails
Battery	12 volt negative earth 35 amp hrs capacity
Number of electrical fuses	2
Headlamps	60/45 watt sealed beam
Indicators	Self cancelling flashers
Reversing lamp	No
Screen wipers	Two speed electric
Screen washers	Electric (optional extra)
Sun visors	No
Locks:	
With ignition key	Ignition only
Interior heater	Recirculating (optional)
Upholstery	Ambla
Floor covering	Rubber mats
Alternative body styles	None
Maximum load	1650 lbs all up weight
Maximum roof rack load	None

Maintenance

Fuel tank capacity	7½ galls
Sump	5.8 pints SAE 10/30
Gearbox	2.4 pints SAE 80 EP
Rear axle	2 pints SAE 90 EP
Steering gear	0.25 pint SAE 90 hypoid
Coolant	12 pints (1 drain plug)
Chassis lubrication	None
Minimum service interval	6000 miles
Ignition timing	
Contact breaker gap	0.025in.
Sparking plug gap	0.023in.
Sparking plug type	Autolite AG22A 14 mm
Tappet clearance (hot)	Inlet 0.0012in. Exhaust 0.022in.
Valve timing:	
inlet opens	27° btdc
inlet closes	65° abdc
exhaust opens	65° bbdc
exhaust closes	27° atdc
Front wheel toe-in	0–$\frac{1}{16}$in.
Camber angle	0°
Castor angle	5°
King pin inclination	8½°
Tyre pressures:	
Front	16 psi
Rear	22 psi

Safety check list

Steering Assembly

Steering box position	in front of engine
Steering column collapsible	yes
Steering wheel boss padded	no
Steering wheel dished	yes

Instrument Panel

Projecting switches	no
Sharp cowls	no
Padding	none

Windscreen and Visibility

Screen type	laminated
Pillars padded	no
Standard driving mirrors	interior
Interior mirror framed	yes
Interior mirror collapsible	no
Sun visors	none

Seats and Harness

Attachment to floor	permanently fixed
Do they tip forward?	no
Head rest attachment points	no
Safety harness	lap and diagonal

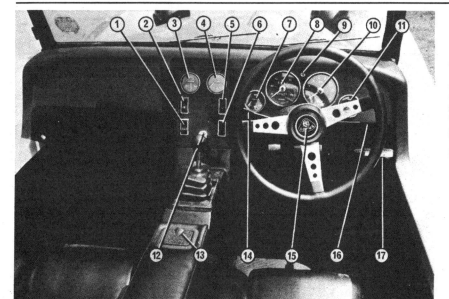

1 heater boost fan. 2 side lights. 3 ammeter. 4 fuel gauge. 5 wipers. 6 electric washers (optional). 7 temperature gauge. 8 speedometer with trip and total mileage recorders. 9 indicator tell-tale. 10 rev counter. 11 oil pressure gauge. 12 ignition/starter switch. 13 ash tray. 14 main/dip/flasher stalk. 15 horn. 16 indicator stalk. 17 handbrake.

THE KIT CAR THAT MADE GOOD

Lotus Super Seven A
by Jim Gilbert

As proponents of the taxation system, the British are not what you'd call visionary. Two hundred years ago they blew it royally with the colonies, and in recent years they've been working over car owners—particularly performance car owners.

But where there's a will, there's a way. Our forefathers cried "Taxation without representation" and "Up the British," and gave birth to the one revolution Americans respect. The British aren't quite as radical about things as their American "cousins," but they do their thing to avoid unnecessary taxation whenever they get the chance. Instead of a revolution,

they rallied around the "kit car."

The kit car was an aphorism for tax dodge. See, the parts of a kit car were not subject to British purchase tax. This meant you could *build* the same car for a lot less than you could *buy* it. It was a boon to the home mechanic with a bent for things automotive and a yen for saving a pound. And it brought forth such automotive classics as the Tornado, Eb Debonair (Eb?), Falcon, Turner, Rochdale, Fairthorpe, TVR, Elva, Marcos and Gilbern. You've heard of all those fabulous cars, haven't you? Well, one you have heard of is Lotus. The Colin Chapman brainchildren have excelled in racing beyond credibility. Yet they, too, were once kit cars.

Chapman's exquisite Lotus Elite was a build-it-yourselfer in its prime, but most models found in America today were pre-assembled at the Cheshunt, Hertfordshire, factory. At the time, however, crafty Englishmen

could save close to $1900 on the Elite by buying it in kit form.

The car came absolutely complete, but in pieces, and only required step-by-step assembling. With a little help from his friends, and a case or two of British brew, the thrifty Briton could build an Elite in a weekend.

The kit car found its way into the American heart, as well. Long a nation of do-it-yourselfers who usually botch the job and resort to paying twice as much to get it put right, America's expedition into this field started with a sports car kit (along with some hot rod bodies, too). Back in the "old days" there were Fiberglas bodies for the tiny Crosley car, and for old Ford V-8s and others. You tried to bolt this body on and when you got done you had a new car. This was all refined when Bill Devin came along with his approach to total concept kits where an entire car could be put together

CAR KIT

by the buyer. This, of course, has since manifested itself in the current dune buggy industry, pioneered by Bruce Myers and the Meyers-Manx.

But we digress. What we're here to talk about is another of Colin Chapman's off-springs, a kit car called the Lotus Super Seven A.

The Super Seven A is a refinement of the Seven, and sort of a Formula Car with fenders, or an overgrown kart, or maybe it is just Basic Automobile. It looks like a Praying Mantis, but it goes like locust through a farmyard. By American standards it's a silly car, but by the car nut's criteria it's what this whole crazy phenomena is all about.

It is so much fun to drive that you quickly forget about the lack of doors, the race driver's slide under the steering wheel, the lack of seat adjustment, the ridiculous protection against the elements (what protection?), the right-hand drive, and the screams of anguish from your passengers who inevitably burn themselves on the inconveniently-placed muffler right where they step out of the car. Mere trifles.

How about when you run out of gas because there isn't a fuel gauge—only a dip stick to measure the level in the tank. You quickly learn what "sporting motorist" means.

But what you marvel at is the sheer simplicity of it; everything straightforward and basic. You can hardly fault a car for that in this day of complex contraptions. And some get starry-eyed and burble things about the Lotus' Honesty, Purity and Commitment.

If ever there was a car to instill enthusiasm in the mundane driver, this is it. The Super Seven A is so much enjoyment that it prompts exuberance, yet it is forgiving if your verve exceeds your ability. There are limits, of course, and you could easily get yourself incarcerated for your automotive antics. Law 'n order, you know. It brings out the child in the "stuffy, mature" silent majority.

However, we've yet to find one single owner of the Lotus Seven or Super Seven A that wasn't an enthusiast and a competent driver whose abilities exceed those of your average Rambler, VW or boulevard Camaro driver. Besides, anyone who doesn't see the Lotus for what it is has to be ready for the coo-coo place anyway. No *normal* person would spend the money for one!

So, at any rate, let's suppose you get your hands on one of these. What can you expect?

You can expect a car with bodywork so basic you can unbolt it in minutes and have a stripped car standing there (a boon for thieves!). It's composed primarily of BMC parts which makes for easy accessibility throughout the country. The frame is a light-tube space frame with aluminum panels and Fiberglas parts forming the body.

The front suspension is fully independent with a common lower A-member bolted to a vertical support from a Triumph. The upper A-arm is joined with a stabilizer bar and the unit has a coil-shock springing set-up.

The rear end is a live axle braced by trailing links and a lower support member in the center; springing is quite stiff.

Brakes are 8½-inch BMC drums and quite adequate for the car due to its low weight of 1200 lbs.

In this particular version, the Super Seven A, the engine is about as hot as you can get without going to full racing tune. The "A" indicates dual Weber 40 carburetors, sidedraft variety. They're mounted on a Cosworth-Ford 109E, one of *the* engines for small displacement racing, and the base for many Formula cars. It displaces 1340 cc of rasping, gut-grabbing power through an English Ford four-speed with close-ratio gears. The super stiff clutch is hydraulic.

The engine itself has been given a thorough going-over to clean it out and make it work at peak efficiency. Among the performance changes are matched valves with dual springs to get the mixture in and exhaust out quicker and more efficiently.

With this modification, the Super Seven revs right up to the maximum on the tach, 8000 RPM, before the valves float. This is nothing but power and few could use anymore than that on the street. It's a torquey little car and great for blowing off more expensive, powerful, and sexy street racers (horrors!).

Though it goes on and on through the gears, second cog can be used all day long for town driving. There is ample torque and revs to keep the engine cleaned out and the power on.

The Seven variety is a popular car for club racers and slalom events. It is ideal for a budding race driver who, with a bit of guidance, can develop his talent to utilize all of the Lotus' potential on the track. And for an occasional blast on the streets, the car is ideal for curing the blues, the yellows, and whatever else ails you.

This is not your garden variety car. It's special. And the driver should be a little special, too. That lets out about 95 of the yo-yo's on the streets who masquerade under that title.

How about you? ●

LOTUS SUPER 7
TWINCAM

Not importable, but more fun than you can have in just about any other way

DEPLORABLE TASTE, this report on the Lotus Super 7 Series 3 Twincam. You are going to learn that:

The Twincam Super 7 is the finest sort of thinly-disguised racing car;

The Series 3 is no longer in production, and

We can't tell you how to get one.

Chances are this news will not cause you to eat out your heart. Either you are not interested in Lotus 7s (and if Colin Chapman doesn't care—and he doesn't—why should you?), or you care very much, and already know that the Series 3 has been replaced by the Series 4.

Cries of anguish. Consumption of broken hearts. The Series 4 is, as they say in Detroit, longer, lower and wider. It is for those so effete as to wish to check the oil supply without removing both hood and radiator cowling. It has been styled. Not re-styled, mind, but styled. Somebody drew lines and made the body conform to them. Not like in our day, b'jove, when Colin welded tiny tubes into a space frame, riveted aluminum sheets over that and bolted a fiberglass fender to each corner.

The Series 3 then is (was?) the last of the originals. As such, it arrived at the best and worst of times. The Seven is an assembled car. Lotus makes the body/frame and suspension links. The engine, transmission, rear axle, brakes, etc., come from other, larger, factories.

Lotus and Ford of England are allies, so the Super version of the Seven S3

LOTUS SUPER 7 TWINCAM

received the twincam 1600 as used in the Elan, with the close-ratio transmission and shift tower developed for the better-known car. Ford had just introduced the Escort and Lotus selected that car's live rear axle, which is well matched to both engine and transmission and is incomparably stronger than the Standard-Triumph unit used in the earlier Sevens.

The S7S3, to abbreviate, is stronger and more powerful than its predecessors, without being larger or less starkly appealing. But its introduction coincided with the U.S. safety standards. The S3 was federalized; rocker switches for the instrument panel, an outside gas filler, larger signal and tail lights, side reflectors and so forth, but official importation never got beyond the talking stage.

The same is true for the Series 4, but none of them are here yet. There is a Twincam Series 3 in the U.S. It is here, in this country and this magazine, because Jeff Johnson, the owner of this car and the Europa tested in the May issue, is a determined man. As you'll learn presently.

But on to the test. The first thing the car did was wreak havoc on the test form. The procedure for determining driver comfort is to measure the door size and opening angle,

BILL MOTTA PHOTOS

LOTUS SUPER 7 TWINCAM

the distance from steering wheel and pedals with the seat at its extremes of travel, etc. The Seven has no doors, and the seats don't adjust.

For a person of average size and agility, this is not the problem you might suppose. One clambers over the side and inserts feet, rather like putting on a bag of golf clubs. Once inside, the small, leather-covered steering wheel is an arm's length away, the pedals fall readily to foot. The shift knob just barely clears the lower edge of the instrument panel, but it's the proper sort of short, quick gear change. There are two eccentricities: The starter solenoid is a push button bolted to the firewall, and the hand brake is horizontal, pivoting from the left side of the cowl across the transmission tunnel. The starter can be coped with, the handbrake is best forgotten.

For median sizes, the Seven is surprisingly comfortable. The padding is thin, but correctly placed, the position is perfect. Drivers of less than 5 ft 8 in. can add padding, or even replace the stock back and cushion with a narrowed bucket seat. Those taller than 5 ft 10 in. can remove padding to suit.

The Seven has no trunk as such, but there is a shelf over the fuel tank behind the seatback. Not roomy to begin with, and this car had a permanent, stout roll bar over the cargo area. The usual measurements do not apply, but a carry-on suitcase will fit. The luggage capacity of a Seven, then, is the volumetric equivalent of the space beneath an airliner seat.

Performance is ferocious, up to a point. Curb weight is astonishingly low and the car must be the lightest real car there is. Through the gears the Twincam S3 is the quickest 1600-cc car we've tested. Which is as it should be; that's why it's so light and carries such a powerful engine.

The engine has no temperament and pulls with just a trace of grumbling from idle. It's quick off the mark, with a leap forward and spinning tires. Up to 60, it's a match for almost any car, with no need to apologize for the engine size or justify the price. It covers short distances faster than the Elan, the Europa, the 914/6 or the Morgan Plus 8. Satisfying.

But aerodynamically, the S7S3 is a 1200-lb barn door. A large percentage of the car's frontal area is flat windshield, and the blunt nose and clamshell fenders don't help either. Once over 70, wind resistance matters, and the Elan, Europa or 914/6 will whistle past. Luckily, top speed is not a valid worry in most tests. The Elan with the same engine and incomparably cleaner shape is much faster, and any sporting sedan worthy of the title will top the S7S3's best.

Oddly, the least sporting note, when power is being used, is the exhaust note. The larger muffler and longer tailpipe combine to reduce engine noise to a hiss, like an enraged Rover 2000.

The controls are hard and sharp. Both clutch and gearshift are heavy to operate but the distances involved are so short that the effort required is soon forgotten.

The brakes are almost the only sign of the car's assembled nature. They are not balanced and the front tires tend to lock under pressure. The stopping distance is short and straight. Considering that the front discs came from a Triumph Spitfire and the rear drums from a Ford Escort, and that neither pair knew it would be working with the other, the brakes are very good.

Driving the Twincam 7 is a delight. There is no other word. The lowness to the ground, the cramped, spartan cockpit, the tautness of the steering and the vibrating body panels all leave no doubt: this is a racing car with license plates. Given some luck and fragile competition in class, you can fit racing tires and roll bar, and qualify a SCCA-approved showroom-stock Super 7 for the national championships. People have done it.

Given the right conditions—low to medium-speed corners and smooth pavement—the Seven will out-corner anything you'll ever meet. Not for nothing did the west coast slalom clubs set aside a class limited to Super 7 and Corvair-powered Meyers Manxes.

Cornering power isn't everything. The Twincam's weight distribution is 50/50, right down to the pound. There is no play in the steering. It is very quick, and the car will go directly to where the driver points it. Corrections are instantaneously heeded. There's mild understeer, just enough to need more lock. The fast way through is to simply drive, adding enough power to keep the front of the car in line with where the wheels are pointed.

You are going to have to learn this first hand. The handling is so good that it can't be demonstrated on public roads. Long before the ragged edge is reached, the passenger will have his eyes closed and the driver will be under arrest.

Transients are mild. You can get away with all manner of foolish tricks; braking in the middle of the turn, hanging the tail out with power, anything. The quick steering comes with a tiny turning radius. It's Chapman's theory that if you can make 45-degree corrections, you can get out of 45-degree powerslides, and he's right.

There are drawbacks. Driving on rough pavement is like being strapped to a jackhammer. Worse, on standard or racing tires, the bumps will walk the car sideways. Radials help; the skips become ripples. Avoid bad roads.

But to those who want a car like this, the appeal is irresistible. Before telling you how Jeff Johnson got his car, you should be reminded that magazines are not allowed to practice law. In passing this information along, we are serving merely as historians. We are not interpreting the statutes, nor are we saying that you could do what Jeff Johnson did.

What he did was, he wrote to an agent in England. This man bought the Series 3 Twincam, from Caterham Car Sales (36 to 40 Town End, Caterham Hill, Surrey, England), the sole outlet for Sevens. The agent then arranged to have the car shipped by air to Denver. Johnson picked up the car at the Denver airport, after it cleared the customs office there. He paid the import and excise taxes, took the papers to the state motor vehicle offices, registered the car and drove it home.

Shortly afterwards, he received a form, from the federal customs people. The form contained the various blanks to be checked, as in "car imported solely for racing, testing and/or exhibition." Johnson crossed this out, wrote in "not imported for resale," and sent the form back.

The cost was high. Base price for the S7S3 in England was $3501.60. When you include the excise tax, $325.71; the air freight bill, $948.90; the import duty, $158; and the broker's fee of $32.50, the car cost $4966.71. And there was the Colorado sales tax, and the license fee. When he drove the car home, the bills totaled $5450.

Worth every penny, Johnson feels. He was serious when he wrote in that not for resale notice. He plans to keep the car forever.

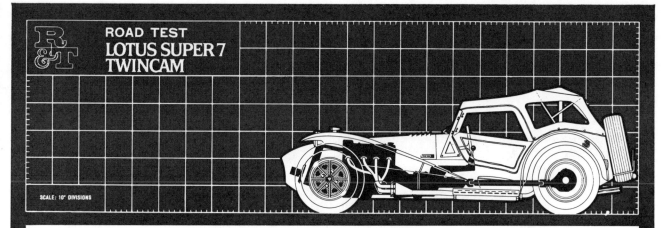

ROAD TEST
LOTUS SUPER 7 TWINCAM

SCALE: 10" DIVISIONS

PRICE

List price (England)........$3502
Price as tested, Denver, Colo.$5450

IMPORTER

Not imported for resale (see text)

ENGINE

Type.....Lotus-Ford dohc inline 4
Bore x stroke, mm.....82.6 x 72.8
Equivalent in........3.25 x 2.86
Displacement, cc/cu in..1558/95.2
Compression ratio...........9.5:1
Bhp @ rpm.........125 @ 6200
Equivalent mph...........107
Torque @ rpm......116 @ 4500
Equivalent mph.............78
Carburetion...two Weber 40 DCOE
Type fuel required......premium
Emission control........PCV valve

DRIVE TRAIN

Transmission.......4-spd. manual
Gear ratios: 4th (1.00).....3.90:1
3rd (1.40).............5.46:1
2nd (2.01).............7.84:1
1st (2.97)............11.58:1
Final drive ratio..........3.90:1

CHASSIS & BODY

Layout.....front engine/rear drive
Body/frame: space-type frame of
steel tubing and stressed alumi-
num panels: fiberglass fenders
and nose cowling
Brake type: front, 9-in. disc; rear,
8 x 1.5-in. drum
Swept area, sq in........225.4
Wheels...........alloy 5.5J x 13
Tires.........Dunlop 165 HR 13
Steering type......rack & pinion
Turns, lock-to-lock.........2.7
Turning circle, ft.........29.6
Front suspension: lower A-arm and
single link, coil springs, tube
shocks, anti-roll bar
Rear suspension: live axle with
trailing arms and A-brackets, coil
springs, tube shocks

ACCOMMODATION

Seating capacity, persons.......2
Seat width...............2 x 18.0
Head room.................34.0
Seat back adjustment, degrees...0
Driver comfort rating (scale of 100):
See text

INSTRUMENTATION

Instruments:speedometer,tachom-
eter, water temperature, oil
pressure, ammeter
Warning lights: directionals, high
beam

MAINTENANCE

Service intervals, mi
Oil change................6000
Filter change.............6000
Chassis lube.............1500
Minor tuneup........as needed
Major tuneup........as needed
Warranty, mo/mi...........none

GENERAL

Curb weight, lb.............1210
Test weight.............1520
Weight distribution (with
driver), front/rear, %....50/50
Wheelbase, in..............89.0
Track, front/rear......49.0/52.0
Overall length............133.0
Width..................61.0
Height.................37.0
Ground clearance...........3.0
Overhang, front/rear......18/26
Usable trunk space, cu ft..see text
Fuel tank capacity, U.S. gal....9.6

CALCULATED DATA

Lb/bhp (test weight)........12.2
Mph/1000 rpm (4th gear)....17.3
Engine revs/mi (60 mph)....3470
Engine speed @ 70 mph....4050
Piston travel, ft/mi.........1655
Cu ft/ton mi...............166
R&T wear index............58
R&T steering index........0.80
Brake swept area sq in/ton....332

ROAD TEST RESULTS

ACCELERATION

Time to distance, sec:
0–100 ft.................2.8
0–250 ft.................5.2
0–500 ft.................8.3
0–750 ft................10.9
0–1000 ft..............13.2
0–1320 ft (¼ mi).........15.7
Speed at end of ¼ mi, mph....80
Time to speed, sec:
0–30 mph.................2.7
0–40 mph.................3.9
0–50 mph.................5.6
0–60 mph.................7.7
0–70 mph................10.5
0–80 mph................15.6
Passing exposure time, sec:
To pass car going 50 mph....5.7

FUEL CONSUMPTION

Normal driving, mpg..........20
Cruising range, mi.........192

SPEEDS IN GEARS

4th gear (5500 rpm)..........96
3rd (6200)................79
2nd (6200)................54
1st (6200)................36

BRAKES

Panic stop from 80 mph:
Max. deceleration rate, % g..75
Control.................good
Pedal effort for 50%-g stop, lb..55
Fade test: percent increase in pedal
effort to maintain 50%-g deceler-
ation rate in 6 stops from 60
mph...................10
Parking: Hold 30% grade?......no
Overall brake rating.....very good

SPEEDOMETER ERROR

30 mph indicated is actually...32.5
40 mph....................43.0
60 mph....................63.7
70 mph....................74.1
80 mph....................85.5
Odometer, 10.0 mi.....not taken

ACCELERATION & COASTING

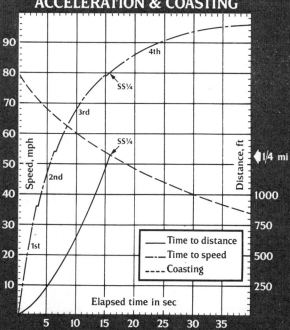

79

Ideal for the 23-year-old bachelor, and a boost to those not so fortunate in years, the 7 remains much the same since its announcement in 1957.

Learning to love the 7

Most Lotus cars are mechanically up to the minute. But there is one model in the range which, despite some fairly extensive modifications last year, remains essentially the same as when it was announced in 1957. Even then the designer of the Lotus 7 must have forgotten to change his calendar for many years. Along with Peter Morgan's well-loved cars, the Seven is the last of a dying breed of windswept, bumpy, fast, exhilarating, awkward, lovable sports cars.

It is an impractical car which an owner would come to accept, love and cherish. I have a friend who has owned one for several years. Although he is not a typical Seven owner — that's a 23-year-old single man according to David Wakefield, a director of Caterham Cars — his attitude is characteristic. His car is old enough to have been the first off the assembly line. It has an old 1-litre BMC engine, has been involved in at least one major accident, regularly shakes many of the nuts loose, has farcical weather protection and is the veritable apple of its owner's eye.

He tells fisherman-like fibs about its performance and reliability, spends hours fiddling, adjusting, modifying, drives the breadth of Britain in all weathers with the hood down, fishing rods tucked heaven knows where. I used to regard his attitude as eccentric. Frankly, after a spell with the latest Series 4 I have more understanding and sympathy.

While driving the car I adopted John Bolster's maxim of imagining myself as the typical owner. The Seven did not suit my family needs but it would ideally suit those of that 23-year-old bachelor. First, it is a Lotus, born and bred by a tremendously successful racing car constructor. Cars that have this sort of heritage tend to have good seating positions, steering, road-holding, performance. The Seven certainly has those, and if there isn't a plastic wood-style fascia, what matter!

The current Seven, whose ancestry goes back to the Lotus Mk 6, has a pigmented glassfibre body around the familiar strong tubular/sheet steel chassis. It has a more square look than the older alloy-bodied versions. Access to the engine is complete as the whole bonnet lifts forward.

Front suspension is by twin pressed steel wishbones with coil spring/damper units and an anti-roll bar. At the rear is a live axle located by trailing and leading links and equipped with coil spring/damper units. Front brakes are 8½ in discs and at the rear there are 9 in drums. The attractive 5½J alloy wheels are fitted with 165 x 13 Dunlop Sport radial tyres.

The canvas and perspex doors open completely, and there is a definite knack to getting in. (It's a real test of girl's elegance.) The low slung PVC seats are extremely comfortable, and with the padding, transmission tunnel and body sides, there is no question of being thrown about in cornering. You get in and are simply wedged there, in the nicest possible way.

The fascia is matt black plastic. Why put in anything more fancy if it's only going to be rained on? The Smiths instruments reveal all one needs to know—speed of the engine, speed of the car, oil pressure, water temperature, how much petrol is left in the rear-mounted 7½ gallon tank and the state of the battery. There are rocker switches to control the two-speed windscreen wipers, the washers, heater (what are Sevens coming to!) and side and main lights. Further lighting control is on the steering column, along with the direction indicators.

The 13 in PVC-bound steering wheel contains a Lotus badge on the boss, just to remind you of the type of car you are driving. With that fabulous Burman rack and pinion steering, who could forget? Lap and diagonal seat belts are fitted, and there are mounting points for full shoulder harness. Just behind the driver's head a stout roll-over bar sprouts out of the chassis. A sheet of canvas at the back neatly covers the hood when not in use—which it rarely is—and the small luggage space.

The seating position suited me perfectly. The steering wheel was the right distance

The cockpit is a snug fit and data that one needs to know is well presented by ample instrumentation.

" The rear wheels began to bite immediately the critical point was reached."

44-17-3

away and the short, notchy gear lever a few inches away. The good handbrake is of the umbrella variety located under the right of the fascia. But although the seating position suited me, a lanky colleague who tried the car said he simply could not fit in. There is only just enough room for the three pedals, and when not in use, the left foot was a bit of a problem to park. I developed a naughty habit of lightly resting it on the clutch—there was nowhere else—but the left leg of a tall person might clash with the pedal and steering wheel.

The essence of the Seven is its performance. The standard Series 4 comes in kit form for £995 with a Ford 1600 GT engine developing 84 bhp. With less than 12 cwt to cart around, that performance is pretty exciting. But for a bit more money you could have a lot more performance. The car which I borrowed at short notice from Caterham Cars' Finchley Road branch had a Holbay Clubman engine pushing out a " guaranteed 120 bhp " at 6200 rpm. It felt like it too! Price in component form is £1,265, slightly more than the twin-cam version (£1,245) and rather less than the Big Valve twin-cam (£1,295). That Big Valver must be the hairiest road-going Seven of all time because the Holbay version had more power than it could sometimes put on the road. The t/c versions apparently have a smoother torque profile.

The Seven is a *sports* car, and considering how much performance you get it is not that much money. It's true that in order to avoid paying tax you have to build it yourself. If the reports that the Government are to introduce new laws in order to obtain that tax are true, then I would recommend any would-be purchaser to buy now. With the dreaded PT it obviously wouldn't be such an attractive buy.

The Holbay is fed through two twin-choke Weber 40 DCOE carburetters, has a hairier R120 camshaft and is fitted with all the best parts that can be mustered. Power reaches the back wheel via a 2000E gearbox with standard ratios, and a 3.7 Escort differential. The clutch on the car I tried was exceptionally stiff, and was very much an in-or-out job; the rear wheels began to bite immediately the critical point was reached.

Operating the clutch in London traffic gave me Charles Atlas-style left leg muscles, but I was very impressed with the car's behaviour in the kind of conditions which obviously do not suit it. The engine ran smoothly throughout the worst traffic jams, never coughing or spitting and remaining at a constant, low

temperature. It was extremely tractable, and through all conditions returned a creditable 22 mpg.

But town is not the real habitat of the Seven. It's a country car which will rush up to the legal limit in about 9 sec. At 70 mph in top gear the engine was ticking along at just under 4000 rpm with another 2½ to go. It hadn't even reached its maximum torque, which is produced at 4200 rpm.

Neither is it a motorway car. Although it will tank along at very high speeds, reliably too, the wind and the roar are a little unnerving. I found myself travelling along the motorway more slowly than I do in my Fiat saloon, unwilling to live with the noise but happy in the knowledge that if I wanted to I could bound into the distance.

On minor roads, however, it was a pleasure to drive. It was shatteringly quick, which made for safe over-taking. The road holding was good, certainly in excess of my own capabilities. It was possible to slide the back—perhaps practised Seven owners abuse

their cars more than I did—but in normal use it never broke away. The brakes were well up to the job but the pedal needed a good deal of pressure for effect.

The other feature which struck me was the steering. It was several months since I had previously driven a Lotus, and I had forgotten just how precise the steering was. It came as a revelation, simply to flick the car around a corner with the smallest of movements of the steering wheel. With 2¾ turns lock to lock, hands in the easy quarter to three position on the wheel, lying in a well padded seat so close to the ground, it had a real racing feel about it.

Driving the Seven, hood down and wind-blown, the thought crossed my mind that I had discovered something for which man has been searching for centuries. Is the Lotus 7 the answer to ever-lasting youth ?

RICHARD FEAST

The Holbay clubman engine produces 120 bhp at 6200 rpm.

LOTUS SEVEN SERIES IV

If you think of it as a car, you will be disappointed.

Dear Mr. Claus:

I just wanted to write and thank you for dropping off those three boxes with, "If lost, return to Racing Engines Ltd., Norwich, Nor 92 W" stenciled on the side. I guess that you could tell from that one open wooden crate that there were the parts to a kit car inside. Not the kind of kit car I asked for last year . . . that 1:4-scale MRC Honda. (Incidentally, I actually built that thing . . . just like it said in the instructions it took 40 hours. Two days after it was finished the cat stepped on the front suspension and broke both uprights and I had to throw it out.)

Anyway, this year's kit was the real thing, a Lotus Super Seven Series IV and, honest to god, 25 hours after I dumped out the parts (hasn't anyone ever told those people in England that after you throw the parts in the proper carton that there's stuff like excelsior and chopped-up paper to keep them from banging into one another?), anyway, 25 hours after I got the parts all spread out on the garage floor, and picked all the tree tinsel out of the chassis, 25 hours after first taking "spanner twixt thumb and forefinger," the Lotus Seven, *my* Lotus Seven that I had built *myself*, was out on Littleworth Lane running circles around Porsche 914s.

And, quite frankly, Mr. Claus, that's about the best handling car I've *ever* driven.

Actually, even if I made it myself, I can't really claim that it's much of a car, but *damn*, whatever it is, it sure is fun. But, hey, Mr. Claus, I don't want to seem ungrateful or anything but I think you may be able to save a couple of bucks if someone else asks for one of these things next year. I checked and found that you paid $3136 for the body, chassis, wheels, tires—everything except the engine—which is fine. But then you sprung an extra $1200 to get the Lotus Twincam engine. Next time, I suggest that you just drop off the kit without the engine and let the guy who gets it scrounge around junkyards for an old Cortina 1600 motor . . . maybe, if he's lucky, he'll even find a *Lotus* Cortina. I bet that he could save almost a grand that way even if the junker engine has to be rebuilt.

I'm sure glad you didn't go all the way and pick-up the Lotus "Big Valve" engine. Even if it does make 130 horsepower, $1500 extra is a pretty heavy tariff to pay unless you're go-

PHOTOGRAPHY: RUSS PFEIFFER

ing SCCA racing.

Speaking of racing, my next door neighbor is complaining that my Seven sounds like a whole E-production race just pulling out of the driveway by itself every morning.

And I guess cops must have the same impressions after they hear all that rrrrraa-rrrrrrppp-prrraarrrrruuuhhhh going by them, and see the semi-outside exhaust system, and no bumpers and start ticking off all the violations they can find out of their copies of the *GSA Nonconforming Vehicles in Silhouette* handbook. But that's the great thing about this car, it's strictly legal. Lotus has only built 500 of the Series IV kits and only 300 of those ever got to the U.S. and all the required kit car stuff—like approved hydraulic brake

hoses, and laminated glass, approved tires and wheels, seat belts and even approved brake fluid—comes right in the kit so you don't have to worry, you're legal.

Of course, if you really *like* to worry there's a whole bunch of stuff that the Lotus Super Seven doesn't have that should keep you happy. I mean some pretty basic stuff like . . . well, doors. When you're building the thing, not having to worry about a precise task like hanging a pair of doors is great, but after a few times of aiming your butt in the general direction of the seat and doing a backwards half-gainer into the car, the thrill kind of wears off. (And if the top is in place you can add about four points to the degree of difficulty rating.) And if you find

you've forgotten a pack of cigarettes once you're in there, it's better to abstain than to try and get out again. The unadjustable molded fiberglass seats with fairly thick upholstery padding don't just "gently caress your body to hold you in place"—they bite down on your pelvis like an enraged giant clam. The only parts of your body that you can move are your arms, and, to a very limited extent, your feet. (The driver's footwell is completely filled by the three paddle-type pedals and if you can figure out someplace besides the clutch to rest your left foot, please let me know.)

It's really tight in there, just what you'd expect from something that's an old race car. And even if the car does have a new fiberglass body replacing the old Super Seven's rattly metal, and a new rear suspension, it is an old car—remember that it is a Lotus *Seven* and the current Lotus race car is the 72. (And that means that something like 65 other Lotus projects—and 14 years—have gone by since it was introduced.)

And even though it's now supposed to be a road car, you can't avoid the feeling that underneath it all, the Lotus Seven Series IV is nothing but a late-Fifties club racer—it even looks like the fiberglass cowl is laid up from an old Lotus 18 plug. The feeling is, of course, abetted by the fact that you are sitting so low and so far back in the car. You can reach out and drag your knuckles on the ground if you'd like and you can blame the car's fat-looking rear end on the fact that both the driver and passenger seats are actually between the rear wheels, positioned in a genteel semi-slingshot style.

It's strictly and solely appealing to real hard-core wind-in-the-face drivers. I really do mean wind in the face, the windshield is so far away from the driver and mounted so vertically, that it hardly shields any wind—you finally become resigned to the fact that its sole function is to act as a front support for the single-layer fabric top.

If you persist in thinking of the Seven as a car, I suppose you're going to hate it. All those passenger amenities that we've come to take for granted are either missing—like the doors, or any trace of cockpit upholstery or sound insulating materials—or only gratuitously included. In the latter category, you can include the items like the sidecurtains, a handbrake that must have come from a fire sale on

(Text continued on page 86)

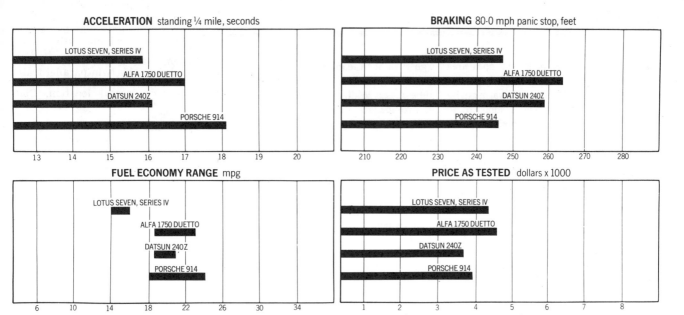

ACCELERATION standing ¼ mile, seconds

LOTUS SEVEN, SERIES IV
ALFA 1750 DUETTO
DATSUN 240Z
PORSCHE 914

13 14 15 16 17 18 19 20

BRAKING 80-0 mph panic stop, feet

LOTUS SEVEN, SERIES IV
ALFA 1750 DUETTO
DATSUN 240Z
PORSCHE 914

210 220 230 240 250 260 270 280

FUEL ECONOMY RANGE mpg

LOTUS SEVEN, SERIES IV
ALFA 1750 DUETTO
DATSUN 240Z
PORSCHE 914

6 10 14 18 22 26 30 34

PRICE AS TESTED dollars x 1000

LOTUS SEVEN, SERIES IV
ALFA 1750 DUETTO
DATSUN 240Z
PORSCHE 914

1 2 3 4 5 6 7 8

LOTUS SEVEN, SERIES IV

Importer: Lotus Central
35093 Schoolcraft Road
Livonia, Michigan

Vehicle type: Front engine, rear-wheel-drive, 2-passenger convertible

Price as tested: $4336.00
(Manufacturer's suggested retail price, including all options listed below, Federal excise tax, dealer preparation and delivery charges, does not include state and local taxes, license or freight charges)

Options on test car: Base car with Cosmic wheels, $3136.00; Lotus twin cam engine, $1200.00

ENGINE
Type: 4-in-line, water-cooled, cast iron block and aluminum head, 5 main bearings
Bore x stroke . . . . .3.25 x 2.86 in, 82.5 x 72.6 mm
Displacement. . . . . .97.6 cu in, 1600 cc
Compression ratio . . . . .9.5 to one
Carburetion . . . . .2 x 2-bbl Weber
Valve gear . . . . .Chain driven twin overhead cams, mechanical lifters
Power (SAE) . . . . .115 bhp @ 6000 rpm
Torque (SAE) . . . . .108 lb-ft @ 4000 rpm
Specific power output . . . . . . .1.18 bhp/cu in, 71.9 bhp/liter
Max recommended engine speed . . . . .6500 rpm

DRIVE TRAIN
Transmission . . . . .4-speed, all synchro
Final drive ratio . . . . .3.77 to one

Gear	Ratio	Mph/1000 rpm	Max. test speed
I	2.97	6.0	39 mph (6500 rpm)
II	2.01	8.9	58 mph (6500 rpm)
III	1.40	12.8	83 mph (6500 rpm)
IV	1.00	17.9	100 mph (5600 rpm)

DIMENSIONS AND CAPACITIES
Wheelbase . . . . .91.0 in
Track, F/R . . . . .48.8/51.5 in
Length . . . . .146.3 in
Width. . . . . .60.5 in
Height . . . . .44.0 in
Ground clearance . . . . .6.5 in
Curb weight. . . . . .1300 lbs
Weight distribution, F/R 56.1/43.9%
Battery capacity . . . . .12 volts, 35 amp/hr
Generator capacity . . . . .286 watts
Fuel capacity . . . . .7.5 gal
Oil capacity . . . . .4.5 qts
Water capacity . . . . .8.0 qts

SUSPENSION
F: Ind., Unequal length control arms, coil springs, anti-sway bar
R: Rigid axle, lower trailing arms (A-frame one side), upper trailing arms, coil springs

STEERING
Type . . . . .Rack and pinion
Turns lock-to-lock 2.8
Turning circle curb-to-curb .33.5 ft

BRAKES
F: . . . . .9.0-in solid disc
R: . . . . .8.0 x 1.5-in drum

WHEELS AND TIRES
Wheel size . . . . .13 x 5.5-in
Wheel type . . . . .Cast aluminum alloy
Tire make and size . . . . .Goodyear, 165 SR 13
Tire type . . . . .Radial
Test inflation pressure, F/R . . . . .24/24 psi
Tire load rating . . . . .1010 lbs per tire @ 32 psi

PERFORMANCE

Zero to	Seconds
30 mph	2.6
40 mph	4.2
50 mph	6.0
60 mph	8.7
70 mph	11.4
80 mph	14.8
90 mph	19.0
100 mph	24.5

Standing ¼-mile . . . . .15.8 sec @ 82.4 mph
Top speed (at redline) . . . . .116 mph
80-0 mph . . . . .247 ft (0.86G)
Fuel mileage . . . . .14-16 mpg on premium fuel
Cruising range . . . . .105-120 mi

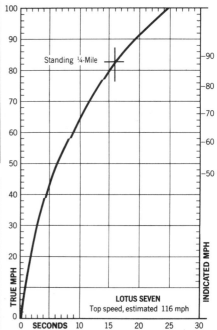

LOTUS SEVEN
Top speed, estimated 116 mph

LOTUS SEVEN, SERIES IV

Plymouth Wayfarer parts, the open area behind the seats which is the only storage compartment in the car, and a valve tap on the cooling system which is supposed to supply a heater. There's a small core high up under the dashboard that is supposed to heat air ducted into the passenger compartment, but the one or two BTU's that squeeze through are immediately sucked out through gaps in the sidecurtains. (Not unexpectedly, there isn't even a half-hearted attempt to provide any windshield defrosting.)

Passenger comfort, in other words, has never been a priority design requirement for the Seven. And things haven't changed with the Series IV, which, incidentally, earned its new designation after being revised by the men of Lotus Racing Components . . . a make-work project for off-duty Formula One mechanics in a manner of speaking. And you certainly can see their influence. The steering wheel, with its quick 2.8 turns lock-to-lock, is nicely positioned for an arms-out driving style, the small shift handle with narrow gate 4-speed pattern is also well located high on the central backbone/console (although it is possible to beat the Ford 2000E transmission's synchro—particularly from first to second), the high-effort but easily modulated foot controls and instrumentation that includes a large tach and oil pressure gauge along with all the standard engine monitoring gauges—all these items betray the car's long heritage as a racer. Even things like the gas tank seem to have been designed for sprint racing rather than afternoon motoring down country lanes. It's mounted right behind the driver and is about the size of an "FIA suitcase," so although you can get around 14 miles-per-gallon even if you drive with your foot on the floor all the time, you're going to have to stop at a gas station about every 100 miles.

I mentioned earlier that I thought the Twincam engine came close to being monetary overkill, but it sure is an absolute bear in this 1300-lb. car. That's right; 1300 lbs. fully loaded with gas, oil, water and ready to go. With the 3.77-to-one rear axle and 115 horsepower (at 6000 rpm) available, the car not only is a responsive sports car but in the stoplight to stoplight Summernationals it has put a few surprised Super Car drivers on the trailer—as long as the stoplights aren't too far apart. But hell, that's just a bonus. The Seven was really meant as a road racer, and for that it's just about unbeatable. The rear suspension with its coil springs and lower trailing arms (actually a sort of double Watts link-

age with both leading and trailing arms plus a single A-arm on the right side of the tube chassis leading to the differential case to provide lateral location—which essentially turns the light Ford Escort axle into a giant anti-roll bar) keep the rear tires on the road no matter how quickly you enter a turn. And the quick steering and throttle response allow corrections no matter whether the car understeers (as it will most of the time) or adopts an oversteering attitude (which it will on occasion, depending more on the road surface than speed). You can really "drive" around almost any turn and the car will remain flat and predictable, even if you can feel signs of definite chassis twisting and flexing. Still if you want to experiment there seems to be no limit to the evil, even dumb, attitudes with which you can go into a corner and still be able to exit it neatly. It has to be the most forgiving and fun-to-drive car in this aspect that you can buy for the street. And because of the car's light weight, rather than super-efficient brakes, the Seven stops in less than 250 feet from 80 mph—and will do so time after time without showing signs of brake fade or loss of controllability.

Surprisingly, the ride quality isn't that Heim-jointed harshness that you would expect from a racer. The front suspension components (most of which are the same as used on the Europa models) are permanently and inalterably mounted in heavy rubber bushings which absorb, or at least soften, a good bit of road shock. Still, a lot of vibration does get through and it seems like the car's bodywork as well as chassis must absorb most of it. At cruising speeds you can see the scoop fenders and headlights frantically vibrating and the dashboard is trembling so badly that you can hardly read the smaller instruments. (At night the headlight vibrations spread the beams all over the road—well, not just the road but anywhere vaguely in front of the car. It's like driving into a road show version of the Electric Circus.)

All in all, I suppose it's really a pretty stupid thing to have built, because it really doesn't do many of the things that a "car" is supposed to do. But, Mr. Claus, if you happen to have three more of those crates lying around someplace that you want to get rid of, you can drop them off with me any time. I've had more fun with this car than anything I've driven on the street in the past four years and, at least to me, *that's* what a car is supposed to be all about. By the way, what am I supposed to do with all of that coal I discovered in the trunk?   ●

CONTINUED FROM PAGE 22

The IFS uses transverse wishbones with an anti-sway bar and a pair of combined coil springs and telescopic dampers. The rear suspension has a BMC "A" series axle, located by twin parallel trailing arms and a diagonal member to provide lateral location. Coil springs with in-built dampers are also used.

Nine inch brake drums provide very powerful stopping, because of the low all-up weight. Disc brakes are available as optional extras, so are wire wheels.

In the first series Lotus Sevens, the battery was located at the back for weight distribution reasons. Now a lightweight battery (24 lbs) is placed behind the engine. The fuel tank has also been reduced in size to five gallons, so as to augment the luggage space.

Roadholding gives extraordinarily good cornering power and though the springing is understandably firm, the ride is not uncomfortable. Body roll just does not exist and the car handles with the sureness and confidence of a thoroughbred. It is eminently safe, and provides remarkably enjoyable motoring.

The Lotus Seven is classed as a production sports car and can enter races in this category. But because of its lack of streamlining, it is obviously best suited to short circuits and hill climbs. In Britain, it is a most popular car for mud trials, known as scrambles, where a unique type of motoring has been brought to a thrilling perfection.

For those owners who wish to convert the Seven into competition trim, Lotus market a wide range of optional extras, including a banana exhaust system, close ratio gearbox and non-standard rear axle ratios.

Australian enthusiasts will have noted that their £1245 buys basic sports car specifications. But actually, it buys more. The Seven is a dual purpose vehicle. Apart from its sporting nature, it is a genuine racing car, particularly suitable for the novice and then equally suited (with a much modified engine) for the experienced man. It can be driven to and from a race track without using a trailer and offers alternative transport for weekend or even for day-to-day motoring.

You have only to sit in the cockpit to realise that it is a true sports car, with no concessions to comfort. The driving controls are placed for rapid action, apart from the handbrake. This is located above the passenger's knee, a starting point for many conversations without doubt. Because of the high power to weight ratio, top gear is most flexible and it is only necessary to use the gearbox if a really brisk performance or maximum cornering power is needed.

SUMMING UP:. The lotus Mk Seven is a quite delightful unusual type of sports car, appealing to the section of the market that demands a traditional sports car with the temperament of a true racer.   #

Lotus Seven
There's nothing like it!!!

By Christopher Hilton

It was love at first sight. In the very beginning, I loved her for her beautiful body; and, later, for her heart, too . . .

Of course, as my friends keep reminding me, I am a creature of impulse, I bought a house without ever going inside it and now there I was with a Volkswagen 1300 parked outside the showroom and all kinds of exotic machinery around me.

Then I saw her. Curves and soft lines. Smooth and radiant. Well bred. A suggestion of Aix-en-Provence rather than Chorlton-cum-Hardy. She might have been a model.

A salesman was hovering some distance away. I beckoned him over. It was, he said in a discreet whisper, a Lotus. A what? A Lotus Seven. "I suppose we might be able to arrange a test drive," he added.

I told him I didn't want a test drive. I wanted the car.

"But you don't even know if you'll fit in it!" He seemed mildly amazed by my ignorance. "My dear chap, you have to have been created the right size. The seats are not adjustable." He pointed. Oh, I thought, so those black clamps are the seats . . .

I did get in and thanked God and parents that I was, indeed, the right size, and when he had explained that you had to build the thing yourself and it came through the post, as it were, I knew I wanted a Lotus Seven. Odd, I suppose. I never actually drove one until the pieces had been delivered and it was built. I won't ever forget that day.

The first moment with the car in motion, I thought it had gone mad. First the engine gurgled, then gave forth a gutteral roar which reached such a pitch that it seemed to be snarling and spitting at me. My foot was thrown back by the heavy clutch pedal and the thing took off along the road. Every small mark on the road surface sent a shock-wave rippling through the car—and me. Every time I twitched my trembling fingers on the tiny steering wheel, the car twitched too . . . here, there, everywhere.

Only when I had reached a lay-by, switched off (better to do that, because the car might have a mind of its own) and calmed down did I begin to have doubts. A month later they had all been resolved. I knew I had entered a new world of motoring, so far removed from the ordinary saloon-sports car scene that comparisons aren't valid.

I was now living with a sleek yellow glassfibre beast. Odd, too, that the drawbacks which any road test would highlight—draughts (truthfully, a free passage of wind through the car), doors which did not lock, an open well in the back for luggage, a cramped cockpit to sit in—didn't really matter after a while.

I used to give people runs in it. As we went, I could see them noting these drawbacks. It's nice, they'd say politely, but what did you buy it for?

Well, I did resent the draughts at first—but I got used to that. (In Germany once, it snowed inside the car, lovely, thick flakes). At first I worried about the lack of luggage space, but I learned to plan accordingly, and I used to feel too enclosed in the cockpit until I realised that the position in which the seat held you was precisely the position you should have been in anyway to drive the thing.

But I came to treasure the road-holding. Circling a roundabout in Essex to demonstrate this to a friend, he cried out and covered his face with his hands. We were still comfortably circling the roundabout when he removed his hands to verify, correctly, that we were still very much alive.

Once, too, I came upon an Alpine-Renault—the rally car—in the Vosges Mountains in France. Seeing the Seven on his tail, he began to accelerate round the hair-pin bends. What he resented, I'm sure, was not so much that the Seven was capable of staying with him, but that I was just waiting for the first stretch of straight road to overtake. He definitely didn't like seeing me go past.

The performance, which seemed to press your back against the seat, very much as a big aeroplane does when its engines are suddenly given full throttle to take off, was outstanding.

From traffic lights, no car ever pulled away from the Seven. If you fancy your car a bit and find that statement irksome, there's a very simple test. Find a set of traffic lights with a Seven waiting at them, and see what happens to you.

Then one fine day I parked it and went to work. When I came back in the evening it was gone—"borrowed", taken to Bristol and broken up to remove and sell the 1600 GT Ford engine.

My insurance company provided me temporarily with a Morris Marina. I collected it from Victoria Station, and almost crashed it three or four times. The car just did not do what I wanted it to. The steering was hopeless—like trying to control a trawler in a storm somewhere off Iceland. I tried other cars, and tried honestly to adjust to them. They were all the same: big oblong containers meandering vaguely forward.

Six months later, my twin-cam Seven was on the road. Having learned from the first one, this one was refined by stages (no wind, rain, fog or even snow inside) to the point where I even managed to make all the side lamps work at the same time (a noteworthy feat, judging by other Sevens I have seen). And with the engine properly balanced, there was no need to spend each Sunday morning combing under the bonnet for bolts which had shaken loose during the week.

A whole era is coming to an end if, as Lotus say, the Seven goes out of production.* This brutal, forgiving, funny, frightening little vehicle is the only one around which makes no effort whatsoever at compromise and does exactly what any driver with some beef in him will tell you a vehicle should do.

When you get the hood down—a force nine gale plucking at your face and the level road rising like a tide under your chin—you and the car blend into one unit to make beautiful curves round impossible corners. There just isn't anything like it.

I'm sorry, Mr Chapman. They did say that the road-holding of your Lotus Elans was positively outstanding so I went out of my way to drive one. It's not in the same street.

And another thing. "What do you propose I tell my children and grandchildren when they find a set of old photos in the attic of a yellow, sleek rocket and ask what in the name of goodness it was?" I know what I'll tell them, "Son, you don't know what you missed." □

*New Sevens are at present available in kit form from Caterham Car Sales Ltd., Seven House, Town End, Caterham Hill, Surrey and they will continue to sell Sevens in fully-built form after the introduction of VAT in April.

Super Seven

Now built by Caterham Car Sales, the Super Seven continues in production
with the Lotus Twin Cam Big Valve engine.
Shattering performance better than ever. Still as stark and purposeful
as the original Lotus Six of two decades ago.

*Above: Chris Goffey models the
garments which are almost
mandatory when driving the Super
Seven in wet weather*

*Below: Happiness is an open
road, the wind in your hair and a
Super Seven*

*Above: The Series 3
body is much starker
and more functional
than the more
streamlined and
now defunct Series
4; there are
indicators beneath
the headlamps and
repeaters on the
front wings*

*Right: The
Technical Editor
proves that you can
squeeze a driver 6ft
2in. tall, weighing
16½ stone into the
tiny cockpit*

NOBODY WANTED the Lotus Seven to die, least of all Caterham Car Sales who had for some years been the main distributors of the kit versions. So when Lotus announced the cessation of the Series 4 version, Caterham decided to keep the car alive. They bought from Lotus everything that remained – jigs, body-moulds, chassis and spares, in fact, all that was left of the car that started Colin Chapman on the road to success.

It was not difficult for Caterham to decide to revert to building the Series 3 model, since this was the one most loved by enthusiasts. Mike Warner's Series 4 Seven had not been the commercial success that £30,000 of development money tried to make it; and while nobody would deny that it was more practical than earlier versions, it was not what the market wanted. Caterham Cars decided that since the Super Seven should represent ultimate performance, they might as well use the most powerful suitable engine – the Big Valve version of the Twin Cam engine. With its power output of over 120 bhp, this engine could not fail to give the 10·3cwt car blistering performance, which was exactly what we found on re-acquainting ourselves with it.

Performance

Only a handful, and a tiny handful at that, of cars can match the performance of the Super Seven in accelerating from rest to 100 mph in 22sec, and none that we have ever tested reach 30 mph in only 2·3sec. It is simplicity itself to attain such figures since dropping the clutch sharply at 3,000 rpm produces enough wheel spin to enable a delicately-played throttle to keep the engine exactly at maximum torque; when the tyres have stopped spinning, the accelerator can be floored. The change to second gear can be made as quickly as the hand can move just at the moment when the engine revs reach 6,550 rpm, the point at which the rev limiter cuts in. As second is taken and the clutch thumped home another shriek of wheelspin is heard. By now you are doing 40 mph and second gear takes you to just below 60 mph when again the diminutive gear lever can be slashed across the gearbox and

Above: The spare wheel is strapped onto a "space frame" carrier, which also holds the number plate; the body is aluminium, the wings black glass fibre

Below: The spartan cockpit, with fixed seats, tiny steering wheel and neatly Dymo-taped signs for the switches

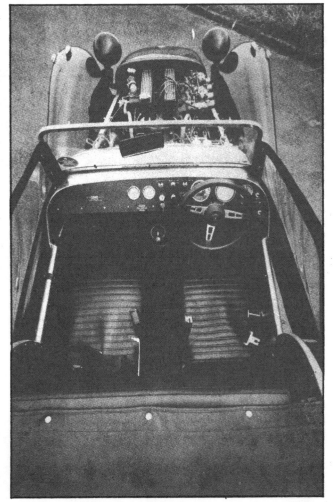

Above: A pair of big Webers lurk behind the right hand headlamp, their gobbling intakes totally unprotected

Left: Seven times Seven: Less agile drivers have to reflect on how to get into the car when the hood is up

Below: The Super Seven is leaned into a right-hander, perfectly under control, although the ride leaves a good deal to be desired

yet *another* cheep of wheelspin is heard as the little car leaps forward in third gear. This is held until 80 mph comes up before the change to top gear is made. You have not yet passed the ¼-mile mark and there is another ¾ of a mile of straight to cover. The ¼-mile and 90 mph come up together and then the affect of the poor aerodynamic shape begins to tell. Another 7sec are needed to reach 100 mph, which is passed only 22sec after leaving the start line. On a slightly windy day for testing 110 mph was reached in only one direction, yet with only a light tailwind this was achieved in 23·5sec.

No less impressive is the acceleration in each gear, especially in third in which only the 20 mph increment from 50 to 70 mph occupies more than 4sec. In top gear, you get a chance to listen to the changes in engine note as the combination of load and rpm change. Snapping open the throttle at 20 mph produces that hollow gulping sound so typical of unsilenced single side draught chokes for each cylinder. As the revs rise to 3,000 rpm, the exhaust note becomes suddenly hard and gruff. As the revs continue to rise, it goes quieter at 3,500 rpm, and then suddenly hard and very purposeful at 4,000 rpm. After this it just gets more and more shrill as it climbs to its limited maximum of 6,500 rpm, an engine speed reached from 20 mph in just a fraction over half a minute.

Since we used the full performance as often as possible, it was still a pleasant surprise to find that the overall fuel consumption worked out at 23·8 mpg; this can be regarded as a typical figure that an enthusiastic owner might attain. For interest, we took steady-speed fuel consumption figures which showed that at a steady 80 mph, the consumption was still 24 mpg. The DIN consumption figure is 23·4 mpg, which means the 8gal fuel tank gives a range of barely 200 miles.

Roadholding, ride and handling

The roadholding is marvellous, the ride is diabolical and the handling is on the nervous side of reassuring. With so little weight, good grip from the Goodyear G800 tyres and race-proved suspension, one should expect the roadholding to be good. Light steering with plenty of feel tells you exactly what is happening and allows instant correction of the result of any careless or excessive use of the right foot. Basically the Super Seven understeers unless you use power to balance the car, which it is possible to do with only a little practice. The ride is very hard and harsh, even though Caterham have wisely avoided the temptation to use tyres of wider section than is necessary. There is little tendency for either the front or the back of the car to hop over a mid-cornering bump and one would only criticize the tyres for the amount of bump-thump which they transmit.

Despite an overall height of only 3ft, the Super Seven is affected by sidewinds and a sensitive hand must be kept on the steering wheel when passing fast-moving lorries. In still air there is a tendency for camber changes or undulations to cause some self-steering, but it is self-correcting provided that the steering wheel is not held too tightly.

Comfort and controls

The producer of an out-and-out sports car is fortunately relieved of the responsibility for providing too many creature comforts in his cars. Caterham take their lack of responsibility rather seriously, avoiding comfortable seating and any spare room inside the cockpit. They do, however, provide full instrumentation, a tiny thick leather-rimmed steering wheel and the gear lever with about the shortest, sharpest movements on record. The pedals too are designed to be used quickly and often, and on the basis that your foot is rarely off the clutch pedal, they provide nowhere to rest it. However, the combination of brake and accelerator is ideally placed to allow heel-and-toe movements provided that you leave your Cuban-heeled shoes at home.

Bearing in mind the likely use of the car on High Days and Holidays, a heater is a listed option which, in the recent weather we have enjoyed, was unnecessary. Since the heater matrix retains any hot water that is in it, whether or not the water valve is switched off, it is wise to put the water valve in the off position whenever the car is left for any period to avoid the likelihood of unquenchable heat adding to that which comes from the engine and gearbox anyway.

Unlike earlier Lotus Sevens, the Super Seven uses proper headlamps which give good spread and beam, both dipped and main, but side and headlamps must be switched on for daytime flashing. The tiny windscreen boasts washing as well as single speed wiping but the tiny windscreen wipers lift off the screen badly over 80 mph.

Space and stowage

Only the diminutive space behind the fixed and thinly padded seats can be used to stow anything, including the hood when it is in the down position. Thus luggage needs to be of the

Confrontation: scant attention is paid to aerodynamics, and the negative camber of the front wheels makes the car look almost aggressive

squashable variety and there cannot be much of it.

Although the position of the seats, pedals and steering wheel are all fixed there is, in fact, adequate room for drivers or passengers of average build up to six feet in height but you need to be very athletic to climb in and out when the hood is erected; our largest staff member (6ft 2in. and currently 16½ stone) was unable to do so at all. With the side screens in place, visibility to the side is severely limited by the inadequate depth of the Perspex panels and with the hood up as well, visibility is limited to the rear, especially when the rear panel gets wet in rainy weather. The rear quarter panels are useful for three-quarter rear vision.

In conclusion

Since September 1974, Caterham Car Sales have managed to maintain a very full book of domestic and world-wide orders for this intriguing little car, to the satisfaction of lovers of fast driving whose budget is limited. You will not see many Super Sevens on the roads of Britain because nearly 95 per cent are exported (mainly to Japan, Germany and Northern Europe). Luckily for us, sales abroad enable Caterham to offer the Super Seven here for less than a Ford Capri 1600GT which, when you consider the performance available, can surely be considered good value for money.

When they took over the manufacture of the car from Lotus, Caterham Cars gave the construction of the chassis to Arch Motors, well-known for their racing car work. Fuller triangulation of the side members was specified to reinforce the radius arm pick-up points, and in addition the engine bay is tri-angulated at the bottom and the front bulkhead is strengthened by two additional tubes. The steering rack mounting points have now been connected and a steel-tube integral gearbox mounting reinforces the tunnel and floor area. The result of all this work is that the current car feels sturdier and by stiffening the chassis the handling has definitely been improved.

For those who might wish to use an alternative power unit the car can be supplied as a rolling chassis less engine and gearbox for the extremely attractive price of £1,300 (inc VAT) thus avoiding car tax at the same rate as a completed car. The level of this tax is then determined by the purchaser's local Customs and Excise official dependent on the value of the engine and gearbox fitted.

Anyone looking for the creature comforts of today's family car would, of course, be terribly disappointed by the Super Seven, but then a Seven owner would be more than disappointed by the family car's lack of performance. This is a car for the enthusiast, for the man whose car has to feel like an extension of his own will and personality, the extrovert, the competitor. Caterham Cars admit that few owners do long journeys and most use the cars for those occasions when only real performance will send the blood coursing through the veins and bring a sparkle back into their eyes – we loved it. □

Maximum speeds

Gear	mph	kph	rpm
Top (mean)	114	184	6,550
(best)	114	184	6,550
3rd	81	130	6,550
2nd	57	92	6,550
1st	38	61	6,550

Acceleration

True mph	Time secs	Speedo mph	Steady mpg
30	2.3	30	
40	3.2	42	
50	4.5	53	
60	6.2	64	
70	8.3	75	
80	10.9	87	
90	15.0	98	
100	22.0	110	—
110	—	122	—

Standing ¼-mile: 14.9sec 88 mph
Standing kilometre: 28.2sec 108 mph

mph	Top (1.0)	3rd (1.4)	2nd (2.01)
10–30	—	4.0	3.0
20–40	6.0	3.7	2.6
30–50	5.9	3.6	2.3
40–60	6.4	3.8	—
50–70	6.5	4.3	—
60–80	6.7	—	—
70–90	7.9	—	—
80–100	11.0	—	—

Consumption

Overall mpg: 28.3 (11.9 litres/100km)

Specification

Engine: 4-cyl 82.6×72.8mm (3.25×2.86in.), 1588 c.c. (95.2 cu. in.); CR 10.3 to 1; Dellorto 40 DCOE carbs, 126 bhp (DIN) at 6,500 rpm; max torque 113 lb ft. at 5,500 rpm.

Transmission: Front engine, rear drive. Manual gearbox, ratios, top 1.0, third 1.40, second 2.01, first 2.97, rev 3.32. Top gear mph/1,000 rpm 17.4. Final drive, 3.89 to 1.

Suspension: Ifs, unequal length wishbones, coil springs, telescopic dampers, anti-roll bar. Rear, Live axle, A-bracket, trailing arms, coil springs, telescopic dampers. Steering, rack and pinion, 2.7 turns lock-to-lock.

Brakes: 9in. front discs, 8.0×1.5in. rear drums.

Dimensions: Wheelbase, 7ft 5in. (206cm); front track 4ft 1in. (124cm), rear track 4ft 4in. (132cm). Overall length, 11ft 1in. (336cm), width 5ft 1in. (155cm), height 3ft 1in. (94cm). Turning circle 29ft 6in. (9m). Unladen weight 1,162lb (527kg).

Others: Tyres Goodyear 165HR×13in.; 5½in. rims; Fuel 8 gallons (36 litres).

MANUFACTURER:
Caterham Car Sales, 36–40 Town End, Caterham Hill, Surrey

PRICES		Extras	
Basic	£1,690.00	*Goodyear alloy wheels	£68.58
Special Car Tax	£142.83	*Seat belts	£16.74
VAT	£146.63	*Stainless steel exhaust	£24.30
Total (in GB)	**£1,979.46**	Full tonneau cover	£20.20
		*Oil cooler	£24.84
		*Heater	£27.00
		Aeroscreen	£10.26
		*Adjustable dampers	£21.60

Fitted to Test Car

IF THE Lotus Seven was any car other than the Lotus Seven we would have to condemn it out of hand as setting a new low for creature comforts. If it was a product of the Seventies it would be drummed out of the nation's showrooms, laughed into oblivion by its total disregard for what is practical car design.

And we would not have it any other way because we cannot remember when the staff of this magazine had so much fun testing a car. We enjoyed it for its startling performance, its incredibly deft fingertip control through traffic, its rails-run handling, but above all for the inexplicably exciting feeling of freedom you get by exposing the top portion of your person to the elements.

The Lotus Seven is instant nostalgia for those old enough to remember and instant envy for those young enough only to have experienced the sterile survivors of a hot-blooded motoring era. It is simply a remnant of the heady rag-top Fifties, a remnant that someone thankfully forgot to turn off in the onwards rush to make tomorrow today.

What has to be remembered about the Lotus Seven is that it is a development of a track-oriented sports car introduced by Lotus chief Colin Chapman in 1957. In effect it was (and to some degree still is) a racing car with mudguards and lights to make it legal on the Queen's highway.

In almost 20 years of development and through four model changes the accent has been on mechanical and performance improvements. The Seven started life with a 1.2 litre side valve engine, that breathed just enough fire to get 60 mph in 16.2 seconds.

Some life was injected into the performance four years later with the introduction of the 1340 cc Ford Classic engine and by 1963 the Seven was running 1.5 litre engine which had pulled top speed over the ton and halved the original car's time to 60 miles an hour.

These days it runs a 1.6 litre Lotus twin cam, big valve engine which puts out 126 hp (94 kW) at 6500 rpm. Since it weighs only 500 kg, the current Seven has a power weight ratio of 250 hp per ton which is something like a Datsun 180B powered by the General's 5 litre V8!!

The engine sucks its air-fuel mixture through two twin choke Dellorto carbies (one throat per pot), the gases flow quickly past the big valves and get a free and easy passage out through individual extractors that eventually become a single pipe somewhere under the passenger's feet. Power is transmitted through a Lotus Ford close ratio gearbox and Ford Escort diff. And does it ever go. There's not a car that we can think of within $20,000 that can match it on our test strip.

Place it on the start line of the quarter (400 metres), tickle the twin cams to the tune of around 4000 rpm, drop the clutch and suddenly you are a very busy boy. First of all there's the quick correction needed as the back axle hops sideways across the tarmac until the tyres take a mouthful of bitumen and the little Seven rasps off towards the 400 metre marker.

It's barely straight before your realise the rev counter is flashing through the orange warning sector. Three fingers leave the left side of the steering wheel and draw the gear lever through two short notches like it's a toggle switch. The Dellortos bark and smoke rises from the tyres as the Seven gets another hefty correction. It comes straight and there's that push in the back once more

LOTUS
TWIN SCRAM

as the rev counter gets into the energy belt between four and a half and six and a half thousand rpm.

About now you remember you should have hit the split on the stopwatch for 60 km/h but she's already gone 90 and rising and anyway it's time for third. Zap, and the tyres let up a little yelp as they nip the road surface on the change. The marker's coming up fast and it's a toss-up whether to drop it into top or hang on to third all the way to the line and to red line of 6900 rpm. We hold it and complete the distance at 141 km/h in 15.7 seconds. The split needle showed that she was pulling 100 km/h in just 6.8 seconds.

On the following run we dropped into top before the end of the quarter and managed a 15.5 but most of the runs were 15.7 seconds. In fact our figures are not all that fast compared with what other motoring writers have squeezed out of Sevens and having the hood up would not have helped; however the morning was very frosty indeed and there is a limit to how dedicated you can be to any job. Also there is a school of thought that suggests that slipping the clutch rather than dropping it gives a far quicker departure from the line and improved times.

This extremely rapid acceleration can be put to good use because you can draw well clear of other cars away from traffic lights without overdoing speed limits and this means you can travel in the clear road ahead of the bunch you left behind and behind the bunch ahead. It's a nice feeling because the Lotus is quite low and inspecting Holden bumpers from head height is not the most comforting experience.

The Seven S4 comes into its own in traffic. Steering response is so quick, the gear stick so handy and changes so fast and engine so responsible to commands that the little Lotus can be zapped from gap to gap without interfering with a progress of those around. If your timing's right you should be able to get through the whole bunch without raising an eyebrow, let alone hackles.

Its handling largely depends on how well the car is set up for the corner. It will throw up anything from understeer washout at the front to spectacular oversteer but get it right and it's a positive joy. In short it's right twitchy when pressed. But that's really only because it hangs on so well that drivers tend to give it more stock and press on harder than normal.

In an age when power-boosted brakes are the rule rather than the exception, the un-boosted system on the Lotus comes as something of a surprise on first application. It has very good stoppers in fact, however, it is necessary to work hard to get results.

The suspension is tuned for handling rather than comfort and ride is not one of the

When it comes to a new sports car the Lotus Seven is your starting point on price. John Mellor tests it and finds that if you have the necessary eight and a half thousand it is worth every cent.

Lotus Seven's strong points. In short it is a bone-shaker in the best traditions of the sports car. It feels every bump and on heavily patched road surfaces the body moved around and flexed in so many directions we wondered if it was going to turn inside out.

For all its ferocious behavior the Seven packs a pleasant surprise at the bowser and we got an average figure of 29 mpg throughout the test. That just shows how efficient the twin cam engine is and shows just how light a car it is. And it is a light car because when it's all boiled down there is not very much to it — a space frame chassis,

engine and running gear enclosed in a tight-fitting fibreglass body. There's room for two people, a tonneau and a toothbrush and that's about your lot.

There are no doors although the side curtains, with sliding perspex windows, hinge out in a door-like manner and can be removed by withdrawing the hinge pin.

The hood is a separate unit which does not fold back into the boot but is rather draped over the supporting frame and then clipped into place. With practice you could erect it quickly enough we suppose but you'd get pretty wet if you were caught in a sudden downpour.

TEST DATA

MANUFACTURER .... Steel Bros. (NZ)

MODEL .... Lotus Seven S4

FROM: Bradshaw Auto Service, Maling Rd, Canterbury, Vic.

PRICE (Including Sales Tax) $8440

PRICE AS TESTED $8634

ENGINE:
Location .... Front
Construction .... Iron/alloy head
No. of cylinders .... Four
Configuration .... In-Line
Valve gear .... Twin overhead camshafts
Carburation Two, twin choke Dellorto 40 DHLA
Capacity (litres) 1.558
Compression ratio 9.5:1
Bore x stroke (mm) .... 72.7 x 82.5
Power, SAE at 6500 rpm
  /bhp) 126
Torque,
  lb. ft.) .... /113

TRANSMISSION:
Type .... Four speed manual
Control location .... Floor
Drive .... Back Wheels

Ratios:
1st 2.97:1
2nd 2.00:1
3rd 1.39:1
4th 1.00:1
Final drive 3.77:1

PERFORMANCE:
Test conditions:
  Track surface .... Dry
  Wind .... Still
  Temperature .... 2°
  Odometer (km) 3625
Speedometer error (km/h):
  Indicated: 60 80 100 120
  Actual: 60 78 97 116

Acceleration (seconds):
Zero to:
  60 km/h 3.5
  80 km/h 5.7
  100 km/h 6.8
  120 km/h 10.0
  140 km/h 14.2
  30-70 km/h 3.0
  50-80 km/h 2.5
  60-100 km/h 3.5
  80-110 km/h 4.8

Standing 400 metres:
  Elapsed time (seconds) 15.7
  Speed (km/h) 141

Maximum speed in gears (km/h)
at 6900 rpm
  1st 67
  2nd 99
  3rd 141
  4th 175
Braking 110-0 km/h
(metres/ft.):

Best 53.9/177
Worst 54.2/178
Average 54.0/177

BODY/CHASSIS:
Construction .. Tubular space frame chassis
Panel material .... Fibreglass
Weight (kg) 500

Dimensions (mm):
  Length 3716
  Width 1537
  Height 1080
  Wheelbase 2285
  Track F 1275
  R 1336
  Clearance 165

SUSPENSION:
Front ...... Independent, double wishbones,
  Coil springs, anti-roll bar.
Rear .... Live axle, double watts
  links, coil springs
Brakes:
  Type of system .. Non-boosted disc/drum
  Front .... 8.5 in. discs
  Rear .... 9 in. drums

STEERING:
Type .... Rack & pinion
Steering wheel diam. .... 13 in.
Turns lock to lock 2.75
Turning circle .... 9 metres

WHEELS/TYRES:
Wheel type .... Globe Volante alloy
Diameter/rim width (in.) 13/6
Make of tyre .... Firestone Cavalino
Type: .... Radial ply
Dimensions .... 175 SR 13

a touch of Nostalgia

AH, THE lost idealism of youth.

The days of wind in the hair, raunchy exhaust note, bonnet strap, dual spare wheels, cycle guards and a desirable blond (or brunette — or anything) sitting alongside as you carried out your long arm driving style impressions of Fangio at his best.

From age 18 until age 29 when I was first married I owned (or rather the hire purchase company owned) a range of sports machinery which continually thrilled and/or exasperated me.

TCs, half a dozen of them, occupied most of my time and they ranged in class from the ex-Barney Dentry all-alloy panelled competition TC to a very scruffy Norm Beechey trade-in which I drove for six months without a hood. Not that I was addicted to fresh air — simply I couldn't afford a hood.

Still it was all good sport.

Wandering the road from side to side with that incredibly poor

TC steering and being totally shattered when I was completely dusted off by my first encounter with a chopped and channeled V8 hot rod — later I realised I should have suggested we go around some corners instead of in a straight line. Even then, I'm doubtful if I would have seen which way it went.

But the idealism remained and we scoffed at the uninitiated who drive tin tops with heaters, 'screen wipers that worked, and windows which didn't let the rain in — not to mention the wooden floor of the TC which also let in the rain and finally succumbed to dry (or damp) rot.

Then I graduated to a couple of XK 120s which handled in truck-like fashion but were sufficiently potent to blast off most TCs in a straight line.

Time passed and requirements changed but I still clung valiantly to those early ideals. Now married and committed to a VW which I refused to admit was any more comfortable than the TCs, I managed to indulge my idealism by racing odd things such as a Nota Sportsman, Formula Vee, Austin 7 (!) and other open air type machinery.

Growing older all the time I failed to notice my transition to a tin-top owner, Falcon, Holden, Fairlane, Twincam Escort, Torana XU1 and currently a GTS Monaro

.... and then I took the Motor Manual test Lotus Seven with twin cam engine for a 250 km drive — and it was instant nostalgia.

The hood support, which folds back into the boot area, is spring-loaded so the hood can be tensioned to allow for stretch.

One of the most reassuring aspects of the modern Seven is the substantial roll bar mounted behind the seats with diagonal struts to further support it. These struts actually severely limit what would otherwise be quite a useable boot but we'd opt for the struts any day.

Visibility all round is obviously good with the top down and pretty good with it erect. The inside mirror is like a refugee from a powder puff and we wouldn't give two bob for the outside mirror, either.

When it comes to getting behind the wheel it is worth pointing out that you don't actually get into a Lotus Seven, you sort of put it on. If you suffer from painful ailments of the joints you can stop reading here. Suffice to say that success in this department is entirely dependent of the driver getting his left foot on the left hand side of the steering wheel. Fail at that and you walk.

The next step is to get the right foot aboard and then shoehorn the body down into the seat. If the hood is up the exercise is essentially the same except it is done from a squatting position. Maybe it's Lotus' way of saying that if you can't get in you're beyond it anyway.

The seats are not adjustable although the steering wheel can be adjusted if there's a spanner handy so if you happened to be very tall or very short a car would have to be tailored to your build.

The cockpit is neatly trimmed in carpet and vinyl and the seats are exceptionally comfortable and well-fitting. There is however a home-made air to the interior (originally the Seven was sold in kit form) no doubt reinforced by the instrument panel which is finished in that imitation wood grain stick-on stuff that comes by the yard at the local hardware store. It is used on the inside of the side curtains, too. The switches are something of a collection from different eras as well and the umbrella handled handbrake appears to be a survivor from the last Austin Lancer into the crusher.

The instruments and switches do their job alright (except a handbrake turn we'd like to see). The driver's foot well is fairly confined and there is literally nowhere to put the left foot except on the clutch. Heeling and toeing requires a foot of clown-like proportions.

The heater is a strange unit with an inordinate bias for the passenger side, controls down near the firewall and a strange rheostat fan control tacked on under the passenger fascia. Also there's no ash tray.

The Lotus Sevens coming to Australia are built in New Zealand and flown complete across the Tasman. Steel Bros, the New Zealand manufacturer, is apparently content with the interior and concentrates on handling and performance. However by the time the car gets on to our market it gets a price tag worthy of more devotion to detail. Maybe Bradshaw's should look at fitting their own heater, switchgear, fascia trim and handbrake. Also a few extra herbs out the headlights would help and a stronger horn, too.

The Lotus Seven costs about $8500 and is the cheapest sports car in the country if you don't count the Moke. No-one would ever buy it for practical reasons and it has its blemishes but these pale before the sheer flexibility of its performance, its incredibly quick and accurate response to commands and the gut pleasure of being such an intimate part of such a machine.

Changed very little in appearance from those Lotii of 15 years ago I was rapt at recapturing those long gone youthful years.

However, it was right about then that I found my one time idealism had been largely replaced with middle-aged practicality. It took me about 10 minutes to actually work my way into the driver's seat (hood was up) and once there I recalled that vision was never really all that good in sports cars anyway.

Unfortunately the seat is fixed in position so I couldn't adjust it, but at least it was extremely comfortable.

Locating the ignition (somewhere under the dash panel) I fired it up and sat for a recommended 3 minutes while the engine warmed up and then, having located reverse in a funny backward position on the left of the H gearshift, I dropped the clutch — and stalled.

From here on in I worked my way homeward through peak traffic.

Panic stricken most of the way as I peered at the hub caps of trucks which were now at eye level — I even had a nasty moment when a large dog looked suspiciously as though it was going to cock it's leg against the window.

That night I headed out for a drive up through the hills where the sportscar is at its best; wind in the hair, running eyes, and leaping along the bitumen like a mad thing at any sign of a bump.
BUT IT WENT . . .
Boy did it went; fantastic acceleration through the close ratio box and a rapid 6000 in each gear, through corners like a train on rails, and that long-remembered raunchy exhaust note thundering away through the night.

My wife informed I looked like a 10 year old with his first Dinky toy and I think she was probably right.

The Lotus on reflection is impractical, attractive in a circa 1950 fashion, rough to ride in, noisy, cold and without virtually anything to update it to the late 70's.

It's also bloody lovely to drive, ego boosting, incredible fun and, in my mind at least, what real motoring is all about.

Would I buy one?

As quick as a flash if I had the money and didn't have a largish type family.

Thank you Lotus for my trip back into nostalgia and the times of motoring idealism — and to hell with people who could ever consider hanging emission crap on to such a superb little machine.

LEN SHAW

THE SUPER SEVEN LIVES!

If eating a lotus makes a person dreamy and forgetful of home and friends, what will driving one do?

BY DOUG NYE

PHOTOS BY GEOFFREY GODDARD

TWO TRADITIONAL BRITISH sports cars have always had an attraction bordering on the addictive. One, the Morgan, has thrived for years and looks like soldiering on forever. The other, the Lotus Seven, was almost killed off by its parents but luckily found a good foster home. It is still alive and well in the town of Caterham, south of London.

Caterham Cars Ltd (Seven House Town End, Caterham, Surrey, England) has lived with the spartan little Lotus for 17 years, ever since they became Lotus' first agents in 1959 when Colin Chapman stopped selling Sevens direct from the Cheshunt works. In 1968 Graham Nearn, Caterham Cars' Managing Director, arranged a sole concession to take all the Seven kit cars that Lotus could build. Then Lotus Components decided to take the model up market and meet growing export legislation. In April 1970 they replaced the classic old S3 aluminum box and its race-bred performance with a kind of trod-upon Tupperware beach buggy known as the Seven Series 4. The new model was more roomy, more civilized and more legislation-complying than the deposed S3 but lacked much of the old hair-shirt character. It was a kind of "squeezed out of a tube" car and Lotus sank some £30,000 into development to break into the MGB/TR6 market: It failed dismally.

When Lotus moved even further up market the basic Seven theme became just too *infra dig* to survive. Nearn and Caterham Co-Director David Wakefield knew there was still a demand to be supplied and they acquired total manufacturing rights for the Seven, including all the jigs, body molds, components and spares.

They set up Seven Cars Ltd in a corner of their modest Caterham works and began production with the S4 only to confirm their suspicions that it wasn't quite what the Seven customer wanted. The decision to ax the unloved and unlovely

S4 and resurrect the aluminum-paneled S3 virtually made itself. Ultimate performance was to be the idea and with the Big Valve version of the 1558-cc Lotus-Ford twin-cam engine, the tiny 1162-lb Super Seven really fills the bill. Its 126 bhp gives it a power-to-weight ratio reminiscent of the downfield runners in the 1961 Grand Prix season! It is virtually identical to a strong Formula Junior or cooking Formula 2 for 1963–1964 and as a road car that makes it exciting enough to be real fun.

Seven Cars produced their first S3 Twin Cam in September 1974, and that car has spent some happy months in Hong Kong and is about to accompany its owner on a move to Hawaii. After an initial rush of home orders as the good news spread, 90 to 95 percent of the Sevens were supplied to export customers. Today home demand is growing, but export orders still take up most of Caterham's productions.

Component supply has always been a problem in maintaining a steady flow of Sevens and while Nearn and Wakefield would like to build four or five a week they are currently averaging less. A current dearth of engines from Lotus clouds the immediate future, but still the demand appears insatiable and Seven Cars is in the happy position of not wanting too much publicity in case they can't keep pace.

The Seven is available in knocked down and completed form, the kit including a virtually assembled rolling chassis. Its body/chassis unit is complete with wiring, instruments, wiper motor, weather equipment and holes drilled for wing fittings. The engine and gearbox are complete and placed in the chassis with the driveshaft, while the suspension is loosely fitted to ease loading onto a trailer. David Wakefield reckons almost anyone could have the car running on a Sunday evening after taking delivery on Friday and just to assure the worried customer his company offers a complete post-build inspection. Delivery currently takes five or six months but the basic kit could be simplified to save some time.

Although the Lotus Seven spirit has been retained, Caterham has not been afraid to make some improvements. Space frames have extra diagonals to limit flex and there is a new mounting for the Triumph Herald steering rack. The battery has been relocated to prevent the bonnet shorting it out and such legislative devices as a collapsible steering column and steering locks are now available. Optional extras include a heater, air horns, full tonneau cover and adjustable dampers all around.

Basically the Super Seven, as the Caterham car is known, is pure Lotus, with independent coil and wishbone front suspension and a Ford Escort live rear axle sprung on coils and controlled by an A-frame and trailing arms. Wheels and tires are by Goodyear, 13 x 5½Js shod with 165-13 G800 radials.

The Super Seven is a very narrow car, made to just barely accommodate two slim people. I'm far from slim and 6 ft tall, so when Wakefield eased me into the driver's seat we looked around for a tire lever to get me out again. I felt like the man who fell into Rob Walker's cider press. My knees hadn't been so friendly for years. I could feel nothing but anonymous pedals beneath my shoe leather and there was only one thing to do—remove my shoes. I stored them on the comfy passenger seat and my piggies could then differentiate 'twixt clutch, brake and throttle, and find a resting place beneath them. The thick-rimmed steering wheel sat perfectly at arm's length and the tiny gear lever snuggled into my palm. Good instrumentation includes a fuel gauge, ammeter, tachometer redlining at 6500 rpm, an optimistic 130-mph speedometer and combined oil pressure/water temperature dial. A bank of olde English toggle switches surround the ignition lock in the dash center.

So David hinged in the sidescreen and fastened it with turnbuckle and pop-stud while explaining about "our burst-proof door locks." Out on the road my initial impression of the Seven is of an abiding flatness and lowness, just the colored wings flaring into view on either side of its polished aluminum bonnet and those vintage headlamps up front to sight along. And it flies.

From a standstill it's simple to drag away with spinning wheels and the engine pulling hard from around 3000 rpm. The Elan Sprint gearbox has the shortest lever I've ever seen and you just blink to snatch 2nd, blink again for 3rd then top with the tires chirping with wheelspin in each intermediate cog! Sitting with the back axle fighting away just behind one's lumbar region, there's a lot of car up front, which was embarrassing in tightly twisting lanes and at junctions where visibility was poor. Ninety-degree corners find the wavy sidescreens an embarrassment too, for you want to see through them, cannot and attempt the Super Seven neck-stretch as you try to peer over them.

Roadholding is incredible. There's a deal of self-steering over ripples but the Seven runs true if you hold the wheel loosely and slinging through curves and corners is just a matter of lifting one fist or the other an inch or two. With very little practice the Seven can be slammed around at will, flicking into smooth fishtails out of tighter turns but always willing to come back and scurrying cross country at astonishing average speeds.

The disc/drum brakes are smooth and powerful but the car is so light that an over-enthusiastic downshift can lock the rear wheels momentarily, which makes things sound more exciting than is seemly. Ride? Well, yes, you can ride in it . . . one can hardly say more, but ride quality isn't the point. This little car is fun—so much fun you just can't believe it's still allowed.

During our day with the Seven we had only two nasty moments. One was when some horsemen appeared ahead, right arms extended, wanting to turn across the road. I slowed and waved them over, then snicked into 2nd and the tractable little Seven burbled round behind them. Just then I glimpsed the last horse's towering rump, fully 4 ft above my head—and its tail was lifting! Thank the Lord for quick cars. The tires smoked and we escaped, but it did demonstrate a potentially pungent problem with such a low roadster.

Then while Geoff was taking some stationary pictures I turned to say something and found the rear mudguard exactly at kneecap reflex height. Can't say I recommend that either.

But for the enthusiastic motorist the Super Seven with its super car potential is a back-to-nature experience not to be missed. It's crude, it's uncompromising, but it's also sheer, unadulterated, unbelievable fun.

The Lotus Seven frame of mind

By Eoin S. Young

Top: The Lotus Seven in its element — hillclimbing. Above: Patrick Depailler started racing in 1964 in this Lotus Seven

PATRICK DEPAILLER was exhausted but supremely contented, tired more by the barrage of interviews he had been giving non-stop since he won the Monaco Grand Prix in his Elf-Tyrrell. "Now," he said with a smile, "Now, I can afford to buy my car!" Patrick could, of course, buy just about any car he cares to fancy, but the boyish little French driver tends to share his fascination of money with the Scots — he loves making it quite a lot more than he loves spending it . . . .

The car Patrick wants to buy is a twin-cam Lotus Seven as a reminder of those weekends in 1964 when he raced a car for the first time. It was a stripped Seven, and looking back on it, he loved it. Lotus Sevens are not really cars in the ordinary sense of the word, they are more a frame of mind, a

habit you find yourself falling into.

The latest Series 3 Super Seven from Caterham Cars in Surrey would comfortably beat the performance of Depailler's racing Seven. In road-going form with the Lotus 1600cc twin-cam engine, the Super Seven is close to being the fastest accelerating production car to sixty miles an hour, a speed that arrives in a hectic fraction over six seconds. It doesn't accelerate, so much as explode off the line. Top speed is fairly academic in a car like this because you tend to use the rivetting performance through the gears, arriving at your cruising speed just short of the total discomfort barrier — 70 mph is a woffling 4,000 rpm. For the record, *Autocar* tested maximum velocity on the Super Seven at 114 mph. The Lotus Seven grew from Colin Chapman's earliest sporting

interest in Austin Seven specials and the Seven today embodies all the elements of those early cars — electrifying performance from a lightweight car, swift steering, wind in the hair, minimal weather equipment, that essential element of discomfort so that you *know* you must be enjoying it, a Vintage theme with modern mechanicals.

When Colin Chapman took his Lotus group of companies upmarket with the Elites, Elans and finally the Esprits and Eclats, he had to make the decision to leave the spartan Seven behind. Lotus had tried to civilize the Seven with the Mark IV version but it rather fell between two stools — it was *not* a car with the same Vintage spirit as the Series 3, it was more modern and glass fibre. When Lotus decided to bury the Seven, small specialist companies stepped in to

take over. Graham Nearn, managing director of Caterham Cars at Caterham in Surrey, had built up a strong business selling and servicing Sevens, so he arranged to take over the rights and equipment to manufacture the Series 3 Seven. David Dixon, marketing manager for Steel Brothers half a world away in New Zealand, saw the Lotus Seven as a relatively simple addition to the assembly of lorries and heavy earth-moving equipment, so he picked up the later-model Series IV Seven to serve the Colonies. Yet another Seven arrangement was made with a Spanish company to build the Series IV using Fiat running gear.

The fact that Colin Chapman and his Lotus company had decided to move away from the Seven concept didn't mean the concept was dying — simply that Lotus had outgrown it. The market was very definitely still there as Caterham Cars and Steel Brothers were able to show.

The evolution of the Seven has been barely perceptible since leaving Lotus, apart from those modifications required by modern regulations governing safety in the construction of motor vehicles. The other major balk in the path of Seven progress was that the customer didn't want it any other way than the way it was. Doors and wind-up windows would have been the beginning of the end for the man who wanted a Seven because it was still the way Colin Chapman had designed it 20 years ago. It isn't that those original Lotus Seven customers out-grew the car over two decades because Seven enthusiasts grow like carrots — every year there is a new crop of young enthusiasts with bobble hats and scarves. Graham Nearn doesn't categorise his customers into age groups, saying simply that his customers are ''car enthusiasts, mainly.'' If there is any determining factor to age it is insurance, and for this reason Nearn says the money-up buyers tend to be 22 and older. There is no doubt that Nearn could increase his production to more than 150 cars a year and cut the six-month wait for delivery, but it makes more sense to preserve the almost cottage-industry aspect of Seven-building along with the

six-month security of a full order-book.

As the supply of Lotus 1,600 c.c. twin-cam engines began to dry up, Nearn negotiated a supply of engines based on the 1,600 c.c. Ford engine with an actual capacity of 1,598 c.c., instead of the previous engine based on the old 1,500 c.c. Ford unit bored out to 1,558 c.c. Power output on the earlier engine was 126 bhp (DIN) at 6,500 rpm with a compression ratio of 9.5 to 1, whereas the new engine with an extra 40 c.c. maintains the horsepower figure while running with a compression ratio of 8.5 to 1 on 4-star petrol instead of 5-star premium petrol which is becoming more difficult to find in Britain.

The hood of the Lotus Seven is one of the less lovely things in the world of motorcars and getting in or getting out with the top up requires a very special knack. It is a car meant for top-down motoring, a high days and holidays car for use preferably when the sun is shining. At the wheel of the Seven, your eyes are a mere 3ft from the road and you sight down a louvered bonnet between the

Right: Twin cam Lotus engine as installed in the Mk 3 Caterham-built Lotus Seven

Below: The Mk 3 Seven combines vintage qualities with modern mechanicals. You get the same ''wind in the hair'' fun from £3,000 worth of Lotus Seven as you do from £13,000 worth of vintage Bentley

headlights. It doesn't take a very determined flight of fancy to imagine the lights are P100s and the long louvered bonnet is that of an SS 100 Jaguar . . . . Except, of course, that the Seven is a great deal faster than the SS100 was. It really is a four-wheeled version of a Superbike with many of the attendant stimulations for the arteries.

The Steel Brothers Series IV Seven in New Zealand is on the verge of a major revision within the parameters of the traditional styling. The changes have been demanded by the need to maintain a reasonable volume of production by investigating markets beyond the rather restrictive confines of New Zealand. ''In 1977 we put together the idea of fitting the 2-litre Elite motor and five-speed gearbox into an extended and developed Series IV, so that we could offer a car suiting the pollution and safety requirements of the more developed markets in either right- or left-hand drive,'' says David Dixon. ''Our initial prototypes have proved that the new 16-valve engine and five-speed gearbox marriage to the Seven is practical and successful and results in a smoother, faster car with adequate appeal for the international sports car market. Our next step is to improve the cockpit by fitting a new modular dashboard layout to suit left- or right-hand drive, increasing the cockpit room and improving the weatherproofing. We hope this will extend the car beyond the market of the enthusiast only.''

The new 2-litre car will be officially known as a Lotus 907. The engine bay has been increased by three inches in length and four inches in width and the engine itself is canted over at an angle of 45 degrees. The new Lotus engine/transmission package is 50lb heavier than the old. Overall length has been increased by eight inches. The cockpit comes in for

may be easier to attain on paper with a gear ratio chart than it is on the open road.

Use of the Elite engine means Steel Brothers can offer their car with ''domestic'' or ''Federal'' versions where export markets require them. Thus the 907 for the New Zealand market will be fitted with the 160 bhp version of the engine, and the Americans will have the anti-pollution 130 bhp version.

Following completion of Dixon's development programme on the 907, overtures have already been made to the obvious overseas export markets. It is not beyond the bounds of possibility that the New Zealand-built car will be imported to Britain for sale in the Panther Lima segment of the sports car market.

I drove an early prototype — one was already in the States, another in Australia for local evaluation — and as a Lotus Seven it was transformed. The engine develops 160 bhp at 6,200 rpm and the extra urge, compared with the Caterham Seven, comes through in a much more refined manner. The Caterham car is unashamedly a front-engined Formula Atlantic car in a moderate state of tune for public consumption. Motoring hard in the Caterham car brings with it the all-round sound of hard motoring. The blast of air through the carburettor intakes almost drowns the rorty exhaust note and over everything you have the roar of the wind in the rigging. This sonic dimension is one of the extras that customers are delighted to pay for with a Caterham Seven, but out in New Zealand the Seven is being de-noised. The car has become smoother and more civilised to extend it, as Dixon says, beyond the market of the pure enthusiast. Both Dixon and Nearn may be right in their separate ways of pursuing customers since their markets now seem unlikely to clash.

The market which caters for wind-in-the-hair enthusiasts may be an invigorating one but it has to be inevitably low volume and this was the main reason why Lotus cut the Seven adrift. Colin Chapman, the man behind the automotive perfection of the latest Lotus 79 Grand Prix car and a string of

trend-setters and winners before it, was also the designer of the Seven and he has never really abandoned his thoughts for a ''fun car.'' He still talks wistfully about building a ''Son of Seven'' one day when the pressure is off, but you get the distinct impression that pressure, with A. C. B. Chapman, is never off or even turned down a little. He is a man with a total commitment to success; second place, to Chapman, is losing. He thinks a successor to the Seven might be a three-wheeler, a modern Moggie trike. It would have no refinements like doors, just step-over cutaways for elbows because it would be a ''elbows-out'' sort of motorcar. As with the original Morgans, Chapman thought the best form of power unit would be a motorcycle engine — perhaps one of the latest four-cylinder Superbike motors with close to 100 bhp, or a more traditional large-capacity vee-twin slogger like a Harley Davidson. Two wheels at the front, one at the rear.

The way Colin Chapman discussed the little car that exists only in the back of a busy mind, you have the distinct impression that it might not mirror the success of the Esprit and the Eclat on the showroom floors of dealers around the world, but wouldn't it be fun?

Chances are that Chapman will never get around to the spare moments he needs to commit his ''fun car'' to paper, so the present Lotus Seven in its traditional Series 3 form in Britain or in its revitalized 907 form in New Zealand will remain as the ultimate for the enthusiast who wants to get the feel of what sports cars were all about. □

Caterham Cars,
Seven House, Town End, Caterham Hill, Surrey CR3 5UG, England.
Steel Brothers (NZ) Ltd,
PO Box 11-077 Sockburn, Christchurch 4, New Zealand.

Top: The hood is not one of the car's more attractive features

Above: 2-litre engine cants at 45 degrees in New Zealand Lotus 907. Engine bay is 4 in. wider, 3 in. longer

Prototype Lotus 907 at Ruapuna race circuit near Chistchurch beside a 500c.c. Cooper-Norton. Bikes in background: 500 Manx Norton, 750TZ Yamaha

major attention and will be four inches wider and three inches longer to allow more elbow room as well as adjustable seats. Dixon plans to have New Zealand wool carpets and leather upholstery. New sidescreens have been designed which incorporate proper handles and locks. The fuel tank has been increased from 7.5 gallons to 8 gallons. Early test figures show the 2-litre 907 capable of a standing quarter mile in 14.5sec with a top speed quoted at around 130 mph although this

With superb roadholding, quick steering and immense acceleration, the Super Seven is the ultimate fun

CATERHAM SUPER SEVEN

A ball of fire

As all motoring enthusiasts know, the famous Lotus Super Seven was taken over by Caterham Car Sales, who produce a much improved version. Now fitted with the big-valve twin-cam engine, this little ball of fire packs 126bhp into a machine weighing 11cwt, and that ain't hay.

First of all, let's get one thing straight. I'm tired of reading that the Super Seven is not a practical, everyday car. When I was a lad, I used sporting vehicles, such as the chain-driven Frazer-Nash and the 30/98 Vauxhall, as my sole means of transport. These splendid vehicles had none of the luxury of the Super Seven, which has sidescreens and even a heater, while their gearlevers and hand-brakes were outside in the cold. Yet, I thought it perfectly normal to attend social functions in white tie and tails and would certainly do the same in the car from Caterham, though dinner jackets are more usual in this less formal age.

The design follows that of the earlier Seven and the later, more plasticky variation has been forgotten. The improvements are unseen, but they make an enormous difference. The chassis is still a space-frame with a stressed aluminium skin, but it is far more rigid, thanks to additional triangulation. The location of the rear axle has received a great deal of attention and the beam itself has been stiffened by a full-length, welded-on web. This has also overcome the old problem of the bolts moving and letting out the oil. The front suspension is still that of the original Formula 2 Lotus single-seater.

The improvement in ride and roadholding is almost beyond belief. This is particularly noticeable in the form of vastly better traction, the hopping of the rear axle having been eliminated, which is also advantageous on bumpy corners. The ride is not nearly as hard as I expected and on most road surfaces one travels in quite reasonable comfort.

After all these years, the twin-cam engine has become outstandingly reliable and, although it produces a lot of power from 1558cc, it develops massive torque in the middle ranges and has good low-speed flexibility. Praise must be given to the two twin-choke Dellorto carburettors, which give instant starting and immediate throttle response.

While the exhaust note at high revs is inspiring, it makes rather a flat sound at low speeds and might attract unwelcome attention — I would prefer to have a more absorbent silencer. The open carburettor chokes are not too noisy for this sort of car, but pancake filters would keep road dirt out of the engine — they are available.

Vintage shape

With so much power and so little weight, the Super Seven can see off any of the £25,000 exotica in initial acceleration and the easy gearchange, with a very narrow gate, assists this sparkling performance. The car reaches 90mph extremely quickly, but thereafter the vintage shape takes its toll. The headlamps, wings, and screen create an enormous aerodynamic drag, and although acceleration continues past 100mph, this is reflected in the far greater power needed to propel the machine. Very economical of fuel below 90mph, the Super Seven becomes thirsty at higher speeds.

I remember testing a TT Replica Frazer-Nash which would not lap at more than 80mph round the Brooklands outer circuit. Upon removing the lamps, front wings, and screen, it immediately achieved more than 100mph, with a best lap at 103mph. It is understandable, therefore, that the Super Seven is not at its best at very high speeds, but does this matter? Speed limits are tending to restrict continuous fast driving and perhaps many people will be content to call it a day at 112mph or so. To drape the car with aerodynamic bodywork would destroy much of its unique appeal, and the additional weight would make it less of a Lamborghini-eater from a standing start.

The driving position is excellent and all the controls are well placed, though there is no free space for the left foot. A well-built driver might find himself wedged in the Super Seven, but a spot of amateur panel-beating would soon produce some extra bum-room. I feel that the sidescreens are a bit too vintage, for their wide edges and rippled panels make driving in London an awkward business; perhaps something a little more rigid could be devised. The hood causes entering and leaving the vehicle to become a gymnastic feat, but it should not be beyond the wit of man to devise something better. This is an open car and one would not use the hood for real driving, but it's useful to be able to erect it for town work.

Marvellous fun

The whole point of the Super Seven is that it's marvellous fun to drive. There's nothing difficult about it and almost anyone would enjoy it, but only a competent *conducteur* can make it display its full magic. In the hands of a real coachman, there is practically nothing on wheels that can look at it on a winding road. This combination of roadholding, quick steering, and immense acceleration adds up to about the safest car that's made anywhere. When you flick past a mimser who is wandering all over the road, you are past him and gone before he has time to hoot his pathetic little horn in his fury.

There is no need for fine weather in order to enjoy the Super Seven. With the hood down, I roared through rain, hail, and even a little snow without getting wet, and the powerful heater kept my feet and legs warm. The petrol tank is on the small side and the luggage space is far from generous, but the Super Seven is so enjoyable to drive that one forgives it for a few imperfections.

When I road tested its predecessor, the Lotus Mark 6, the price of the kit was £425. However, that was with a side-valve 1172cc Ford engine and a three-speed gearbox. The price of the Super Seven may seem steep for so compact a vehicle, but to find another car that will accelerate from a standstill to 60mph in 6secs you will have to pay many times its price.

Unfortunately, you must be prepared to wait nine months for delivery and, for idiotic legal reasons, you must do the last bit of the assembly yourself, even though the total price now includes tax and VAT. Such things may frighten away the dilettante, but the real enthusiast will be willing to spend some time and trouble to get his hands on this little gem of a car. Although I suppose I am old enough to have reached years of discretion, I reckon that the Super Seven is the ultimate for fun on wheels. ∎

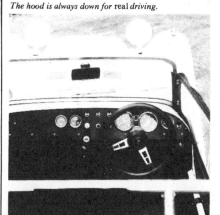

The hood is always down for real driving.

Specification and performance data

Car Tested: Caterham Super Seven open sports 2-seater, price £4464. Extra: seat belts £19.87, heater kit £41.58, light alloy 6in wheels and Goodyear Grand Prix tyres £102.60, rollover bar £26.46, air horns kit £12.91.

Engine: Four cylinders 82.55x72.75mm (1558cc). Compression ratio 10.3 to 1. 126bhp DIN at 6500rpm. Twin chain-driven overhead camshafts. Two twin-choke Dellorto carburettors.

Transmission: Single dry plate clutch. 4-speed synchromesh gearbox, ratios 1.0, 1.40, 2.01, and 2.97 to 1. Hypoid rear axle, ratio 3.54 to 1.

Chassis: Tubular space frame with stressed aluminium panels, glassfibre wings and nosecone. Independent front suspension by wishbones, coil spring damper units and anti-roll bar. Rack and pinion steering. Live rear axle on trailing arms, central A member, and coil spring damper units. Disc/drum dual-circuit brakes. Bolt on light-alloy wheels, fitted 185/70 HR 13 tyres (extra).

Equipment: 12-volt lighting and starting. Speedometer. Rev counter. Oil pressure, water temperature, and fuel gauges. Heater. Windscreen wipers and washers. Flashing direction indicators.

Dimensions: Wheelbase 7ft 5in. Track 4ft 1in/4ft 4in. Overall length 11ft 1in. Width 5ft 1in. Weight 11cwt.

Performance: Maximum speed 112mph. Speeds in gears, third 88mph, second 62mph, first 42mph. Standing quarter-mile 14.5s. Acceleration: 0-30mph 2.2s, 0-50mph 4.5s, 0-60mph 6.0s, 0-80mph 10.8s.

Fuel Consumption: 22 to 28mpg.

The lusty, 126bhp, big-valve, twin-cam engine.

MILES
Behind the Wheel

FIRST THEY tried to tax it out of existence, then there were attempts at killing it off with something called Type Approval, but like a hardy mountain flower the Caterham Cars neé Lotus Super Seven lives on. It is one of the very few true sports cars left in the world.

When the kit car attracted purchase tax and such basic machinery failed to fit into Lotus' ever more up-market future, Colin Chapman handed over the licence to build the Super 7 to Caterham Cars. Since then, CC boss Graham Nearn reckons they have supplied around 400 kits with that delightful 126bhp 1,558 c.c. Lotus, but now Caterham Cars-built, big valve Twin Cam and perhaps 100 with the increasingly popular 84 bhp 1,598 c.c. Ford Kent pushrod engine. Could Mr Chapman be having second thoughts about the deal?

At the moment they cost £5,416 and £4,684 respectively, so are no longer

cheap, especially by the time you have added "extras" like a heater, tonneau cover, seat belts, perhaps a set of 6in. wide alloy wheels, shod with 185/70 tyres. These and a roll over cage graced our smart pushrod Super 7. Only the roll cage was missing from the Twin Cam.

Looked at coldly, the Super 7 is a stark, noisy, hellishly uncomfortable, leaky, bucket of a car. But then what other machine can offer such initial acceleration, running economy, handling, dry weather grip and sheer motoring fun? More than ever the Super 7 catches a lady's attention. On a summer's day, the difficulty seems to be keeping the opposite gender out. It seems that a car's attractiveness is at least sometimes inversely proportional to its size.

For the Super Seven is tiny. Apart from detail improvements the simple alloy panelled spaceframe remains unchanged, as does double wishbone front suspension that is an amalgam of fabricated wishbones and Triumph uprights. The sturdy Escort RS 2000 rear axle is located by two trailing arms at the top, and an A bracket at the bottom. Similar

running gear serves both cars as does a gearbox from the now defunct Corsair 2000E.

I had never sat in a 7 until Nearn offered *Autocar* one of each. They are narrow — snug fitting. Body width has apparently been decided by doubling the average backside measurement and adding the width of a transmission tunnel. A six foot driver has just tolerable leg room but a five foot sixer would probably need a cushion to push him forward. Random switchgear confronts the driver. The pedal box is typical of early Lotus, i.e. narrow enough to make it all too easy to press the brake and accelerator simultaneously if you wear bigger than size nine shoes. If you are tall, you find yourself hunching shoulders rather, to look through the screen. With the hood up all round visibility is at best limited; more so at night, or in the wet — worse still on a wet night — when you peer through a clearish patch swept by tiny wipers grinding back and forth. Hood up or down, I learnt never to trust the single mirror but to look round motorcycle style. Surprisingly hood-up headroom is adequate and anybody reasonably athletic can swing the sidescreens back, climb in, then button up to get cosy. A briefcase, a couple of anoraks and a decent sized handbag will fill the luggage space behind the driver.

As ever, the essentials are mostly right. A stubby gearlever pokes out of the transmission tunnel within a few inches of a left hand placed on the steering wheel. The change is notchy, narrow gated, but accurate. On both cars clutch action is heavy yet precise but accelerator movement disappointingly jerky. The unservoed brake

pedal is like pressing on a board, but anybody who has raced a car will appreciate its reassuringly solid feel.

You are sitting near the ground, seemingly *wearing* a generously tyred road racer with 120 bhp per ton laden on tap in pushrod form and more like 180 bhp per ton laden with a Twin Cam under the bonnet. The steering is superb, which is to say ideally geared with 2¾ turns from lock to lock, about perfectly weighted and wonderfully direct — the Super 7 cries out to be flicked around.

I had forgotten what open air motoring was about. The ever building wind roar, having one's face blasted by the occasional road chipping, and when stuck fast being forced to breath diesel odours belched out at low level. Both cars suffer quite dramatic induction noise as soon as the throttle is opened wide — the warble of those twin Dellortos drowns most else on full chat. Wind, tyre, inlet and exhaust noises blend into an almost unbearable cacophony at 70 mph which I can only liken to that experienced during my one and only flight in the front cockpit of a Tiger Moth.

Motorway cruising is a bore for the incessant noise and tremendous buffeting (always take a bobble hat) also because what seem at first to be tolerably comfortable seat cushions soon take on the compliance of a board. I found myself sliding down and around in the seat to maintain circulation and get as far out of the blast as possible.

Who cares? These are things the avid sports car fan will gladly put up with for the compensations. Handling and roadholding are as stunning as eve Admittedly, on really slipp ry surfaces those lightly

Seven sensations

XPE 116S

For motoring fun there is still little to touch the Super Seven but Caterham's is no longer cheap

Getting in and out with the hood up (above) is just about possible if you don't mind bending double. The Super 7 Twin Cam corners (right) very securely, very fast, and with a trace of understeer

VPH 753S

laden tyres are prone to slither early.

But this is a sunny day car, a true sports car. Roll is there but sitting so close to the ground you don't seem to notice it. Smooth road cornering power is simply phenomenal. It seems ludicrously easy to keep up with the inevitable "trier", or drop him for dead through a series of bends. Ultimately there is understeer, and oddly more of it with two people on board. Surprisingly this is in a slightly rearward weight biased car. Lifting off in mid corner produces the usual mild tightening of line. In the dry, the standard Super 7 does not quite have the power to kick out the rear, whereas in second gear the Twin Cam one just does, which says something for the way both rear wheels stay driving in mid corner without the aid of a limited slip differential. The Twin Cam is so balancable and chuckable you feel it could be taken straight to the race track and acquit itself well.

Tolerable ride quality comes as a surprise. It's certainly better than a Morgan. Quite soft rear springs and dampers absorb smooth road undulations well. Sharp bumps do cause the occasional crash as the rear suspension runs out of travel or the rear to step out momentarily if in mid corner and there is some kickback through the wheel over poor surfaces but no more than you would expect in a light wide tyred car. The wider tyres may also contribute to the way the 7s wander mildly over any road camber changes yet they do this without feeling inherently unstable. Braking power only needs mentioning because of the contemptuous ease with which both cars walked through the standard *Autocar* fade test.

But perhaps best of all is the way these little cars go. In most respects I found the Kent engined Super Seven most fun. Where it lacks the Twin Cam car's ultimate performance it has much better low down acceleration bite in the gears. The test Twin Cam just may have been slightly off colour, nevertheless, a glance at the figures is enough to illustrate its far peakier power curve. It has to be turning over at around 1,500 rpm before it will accept full throttle without hesitating and does not even begin to pull hard until turning over at 3,500 rpm, i.e. precisely where the Kent motor is giving peak torque. In cars that have the same overall gearing this makes the more prosaic model far nicer to drive round town, neither does it have to be "rowed" along like the Twin Cam on the open road. In fact acceleration in third and top below 60 mph actually proved somewhat better in the standard Super 7.

Nor is the difference in outright performance as large as one might expect. Taking either off the line is most entertaining. Dumping the clutch with 5,000 rpm showing, the Kent engined car screeched off the line to 30, 60 and 70 mph in an amazing 2.4, 7.7 and 10.7 sec compared with 2.3, 6.5 and 9.1 sec for the Twin Cam; initial acceleration that threatens such exotic machinery as non-Vantage Aston Martin V8s, the Maserati Khamsin, Porsche 911SC, and Mercedes Benz 450SEL 6.9. Suffice it to say the basic Super Seven must be the only car with less than 90 bhp that can cover a standing ¼ mile in 15.7 sec.

Of course it can't last. At the top end the acceleration curve suddenly flattens. You can plainly feel the Super 7s struggle harder as their impossibly inefficient aerodynamics take charge over 80 mph — dramatically so towards the magic ton. No matter how hard I tried, I simply could not persuade the pushrod car to better a mean maximum of 99 mph. The hood was billowing and shuddering, the side screens had popped outside the hood at the top, but even with two occupants willing it on it would not do it. The Twin Cam did a mean 103 mph. Even the very best ones are unlikely to break 110 mph. Both had that rare thing: a pessimistic speedometer. Such speeds in a Super Seven are uncomfortable enough to be academic. What matters is the incomparable way they handle, grip, and accelerate; a sentiment still echoed by every member of the *Autocar* test team.

They are simply built and economically run. Driven hard the Super 7 averaged 27.1 mpg, while the Twin Cam returned a still quite good 26 mpg overall. The sheer pleasure of driving an extension of oneself through the country lanes overrode all. We didn't mind driving in the wet, or even at night, but please Caterham could we have some labelled switches, a thermostatically switched radiator fan (it is manually operated at the moment), a handbrake lever that is not placed horizontally on the passenger's side firewall, and a method of attaching the hood round the rear body that does not require the spare wheel to be time consumingly loosened, oh, and a stone guard, or filter for the down-draught carburettor on the Kent engine. In the meantime my memories are of watching reflections of roadside trees dance over a speeding bonnet, and of never having to drive unaccompanied . . . ☐

Caterham Car Sales Ltd.
Town End,
Caterham,
Surrey.
Tel. Caterham 46666 / 7.

The driving position is a shade cramped for a 6 footer

Far left: Pipe runs on the Super 7 "Kent" are a bit untidy, but service items are easy to check apart from the water which means removing the nose cone. Note the lack of air cleaner or stone guard on the carburettor The Twin Cam looks far more imposing. Water can be checked without removing the nose cone. The clutches are hydraulic. The flat box nestling atop the footwell on both cars is the heater

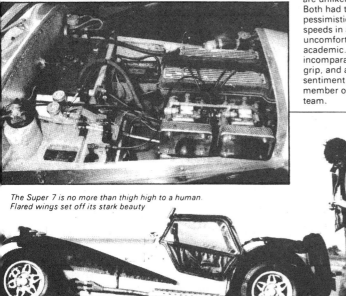

The Super 7 is no more than thigh high to a human. Flared wings set off its stark beauty

Above: From the rear the Seven's lines are most pleasing. Both cars were fitted with the optional alloy wheels and wide tyres. The roll over bar is also an extra

CATERHAM SUPER 7 Acceleration		CATERHAM SUPER 7 T.C.
true mph		
30	2.4	2.3
40	3.7	3.6
50	5.3	4.8
60	7.7	6.5
70	10.7	9.1
80	14.6	11.9
90	22.9	18.3
100	—	29.9

Standing ¼ mile:	Standing ¼ mile:
15.7 sec 88 mph	**15.0 sec 87 mph**
Standing kilometre	Standing kilometre
31.0 sec 93 mph	**29.0 sec 99 mph**

mph	Top	3rd	2nd	Top	3rd	2nd
10-30	—	5.0	3.2	—	—	3.5
20-40	7.1	4.5	3.0	—	5.3	2.1
30-50	6.8	4.5	3.0	7.7	4.8	2.8
40-60	7.0	4.4	—	8.1	4.5	3.1
50-70	7.8	5.1	—	8.8	4.5	—
60-80	9.3	7.1	—	9.2	5.1	—
70-90	13.6	—	—	11.1	—	—
80-100	—	—	—	18.6	—	—

DSK 7 Turbo

The four-wheeled motorcycle.

• Wind-in-the-face motoring is almost totally extinct. Entire generations of drivers, my own included, have matured without knowing the trials and rewards of driving as a one-with-nature activity. Those who crave this direct communication with their natural surroundings have been forced to keep their ancient British roadsters going, switch to motorcycling, or take up some slower-moving outdoor sport.

The last and the best of the true roadsters was the Lotus 7. It was the purest embodiment of the maximum-performance, minimum-comfort, no-barriers-to-the-environment school of sports-car design. Remarkably, the concept lived until the early Seventies, when it finally succumbed to Lotus's move upmarket. Afterward the burden of carrying the purist's torch fell to specialty firms like Caterham Cars, Ltd., in England and DSK Cars in America.

DSK started as merely a supplier of Lotus 7 parts, but soon it began to de-

velop improved versions of the more frangible 7 pieces. Both competition and the increased loads imposed by modern tires and engines had brought out the inherent weakness of many of the original parts (the original 7 weighed well under 1000 pounds, had three-inch-wide wheels, and but 27 hp). Eventually there were more DSK than original pieces in many of the cars, so DSK decided to market complete, upgraded car kits, somewhat as Colin Chapman did 25 years ago.

This may seem like quite an undertaking for a small company located in Marblehead, Massachusetts, a sleepy New England seacoast village. But in addition to having a spiritual resemblance to old England, Marblehead is in the center of a small cottage industry of automobile-racing parts fabricators that blossomed during the early Seventies to support Autodynamics, then a major force in racing. Moreover, nearby Boston is a source of multifarious technical

assistance.

DSK tapped all these resources to build the DSK 7, a radically updated and strengthened car that is true in character to Colin Chapman's original. In appearance, the DSK 7 is closest to the S3 versions of the Lotus 7. It takes a highly discriminating Lotusphile to distinguish a DSK car from the real article.

The foundation of this modern 7 is an all-new DSK chassis. Other than the basic dimensions not much is left. Larger or heavier-gauge tubing is used in most areas, along with additional bracing and triangulation where DSK's experience—and engineering-department studies by MIT—have shown it to be necessary. The individual tubes are hand-fitted and assembled by low-temperature brazing. The floor is a riveted-in-place aluminum sheet, and the outer skin is a hand-formed 0.050-inch aluminum sheet. The complete assembly weighs about 225 pounds, 60 pounds more than the original, but torsional rigidity

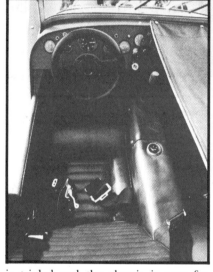

An integral roll bar, however, comes with every DSK 7.

Any standard Lotus 7 powertrain will fit into the DSK car. Ours was fitted with a turbocharged Ford pushrod 1.6-liter and a Ford four-speed transmission. This custom turbo installation was designed by DSK and fitted to satisfy the eventual owner's request, and to demonstrate the power-handling capabilities of the new chassis. It consists of an IHI turbocharger (located above the bell housing) drawing through a Lichtman-modified SU carburetor. Maximum boost pressure is 12 psi, and detonation is controlled by liberal water injection under boost. Despite its primitive design, the system worked well, with good throttle response and no flat spots. Its performance in the standing quarter-mile—14.1 seconds at 98 mph—attests to its power output. However, the engine is definitely in the non-emissions-certifiable category.

Driving the DSK 7 is an experience completely removed from the realm of modern automobiles. It's really much more like a four-wheeled motorcycle. There is, in fact, very little wind in the face—the flat windshield sees to that—but there is intense buffeting from all other sides. What little air the windshield leaves alone is broken up by the flowing fenders, and conveniently pours in over the low-cut sides. The seating position is extremely low, but the cushions are quite comfortable. There's copious lateral support from the transmission tunnel on the right and the body on the left. The steering wheel and the pedals are well positioned, and the gearbox has the toggle-switch feel for which Loti are famous.

The 7's cockpit is also motorcycle-like, with fantastic all-around visibility that makes precise car positioning almost subconscious. The steering helps, being quick and precise but still very light (the front tires carry but 650 pounds). It feels as though there's a direct communications link from the brain to the tires, acting via subtle pressure on the steering wheel.

Not only does the DSK feel great, but it also really hugs the pavement. Our 0.86-g skidpad result is the highest we've ever seen on a street-driven car. Furthermore, the DSK is quite controllable at that neck-straining level. There's mild understeer under power, which changes to slight oversteer when the throttle is lifted. The resulting tail-out attitude can then be maintained

is tripled and the chassis is now far more likely to stay in one piece. A tray for a battery and a fuel cell is located behind the passenger compartment. The classic flowing fenders are executed in fiberglass.

DSK adds its own front and rear suspension components to this chassis. A new front upper control arm locates the top of the Triumph upright without needing help from the anti-sway bar the way the original design did. The lower control arm is also new, having a reinforcement in a fracture-prone area. Specially valved coil-over Koni shocks complete the suspension. Not only is this suspension stronger than the original one, but it also eliminates the Lotus's binding friction for an improved ride.

In the rear, the suspension surgery is even more extensive. The Ford Escort axle is located by four trailing links and a Panhard rod instead of by two trailing links and a trailing lower control arm. In one swoop, this design improves durability, axle location, and ride.

The brakes are the original Triumph non-vented discs in front and Ford drums in the rear, but DSK fits a racing-style, dual-master-cylinder, adjustable-balance-bar arrangement for precise braking adjustment. Fat Pirelli 205/60R-13 P6 tires on six-inch-wide aluminum wheels put the various tractive forces to the ground.

The interior is mostly original and very basic, though our test car was upholstered in sumptuous leather. The flat dashboard holds a full complement of VDO instruments, and toggle switches control everything electrical. Our test car was fitted with neither a heater nor a folding top, although both are available.

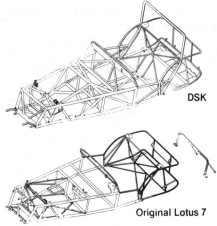

DSK

Original Lotus 7

with more throttle.

Out on the road these capabilities translate into going very fast well within the 7's limits—especially with the strong turbomotor slingshotting the car from corner to corner. Throughout all of this the ride is quite good. It is certainly firm and well controlled, but without much harshness. Even expansion joints and lane-divider dots are handled comfortably.

The only legitimate chassis complaint is with the brakes. While they managed a single stop from 70 mph in 175 feet—almost a record for a street-driven car—they fade under heavy use. The acceleration is too high and the grip too firm for the small, non-ventilated front rotors to cope with. This should be the next area for DSK's attention.

Our particular car, with its special features, cost $40,000. But the basic chassis kit will be available for about $10,000, and it seems well worth the price. At no point did our DSK show a hint of weakness, despite lots of wheelspinning, brake-smoking, skidpad-loading abuse. And with a lighter powertrain, perhaps an even better 7 can be made. Best of all, the DSK 7 is pure fun. It's a fantastic toy, one without equal on four wheels.   —Csaba Csere

Vehicle type: front-engine, rear-wheel-drive, 2-passenger roadster

Price as tested: $40,000

ENGINE
Type	turbocharged 4-in-line, iron block and head
Bore x stroke	3.19 x 3.06 in, 81.0 x 77.7mm
Displacement	98 cu in, 1600cc
Compression ratio	8.4:1
Carburetion	1x1-bbl SU
Emissions controls	none
Turbocharger	IHI RHO 5
Waste gate	integral
Maximum boost pressure	12 psi
Valve gear	overhead valves, pushrods, solid lifters
Power (mfr. estimate)	175 bhp @ 6000 rpm
Torque (mfr. estimate)	178 lbs-ft @ 4000 rpm
Redline	6000 rpm

DRIVETRAIN
Transmission 4-speed
Final-drive ratio 3.55:1

Gear	Ratio	Mph/1000 rpm	Max. test speed
I	2.92	6.4	39 mph (6000 rpm)
II	1.69	11.1	67 mph (6000 rpm)
III	1.28	14.7	88 mph (6000 rpm)
IV	1.00	18.8	113 mph (6000 rpm)

DIMENSIONS AND CAPACITIES
Wheelbase	88.0 in
Track, F/R	58.0/54.0 in
Length	132.0 in
Width	64.0 in
Height	40.0 in
Ground clearance	5.0 in
Curb weight	1350 lbs
Weight distribution, F/R	48.1/51.9%
Fuel capacity	10.0 gal
Oil capacity	9.0 qt

CHASSIS/BODY
Type . . . . full-length steel-tube frame
Body material . . . sheet aluminum and fiberglass-reinforced plastic

INTERIOR
Front seats	bucket
Recliner type	none
General comfort	poor fair **good** excellent
Fore-and-aft support	poor fair **good** excellent
Lateral support	poor fair good **excellent**

SUSPENSION
F: . . . . ind, unequal-length control arms, coil springs, anti-sway bar
R: . . . . . rigid axle, 4 trailing links, Panhard rod, coil springs, anti-sway bar

STEERING
Type	rack-and-pinion
Turns lock-to-lock	2.7
Turning circle curb-to-curb	29.6 ft

BRAKES
F:	9.0 x 0.4-in disc
R:	9.0 x 2.0-in cast-iron drum
Power assist	none

WHEELS AND TIRES
Wheel size	6.0 x 13 in
Wheel type	cast aluminum
Tire make and size	Pirelli P6, 205/60R-13
Test inflation pressures, F/R	24/22 psi

C/D Test Results

ACCELERATION
	Seconds
Zero to 30 mph	2.4
40 mph	3.4
50 mph	4.2
60 mph	5.6
70 mph	7.1
80 mph	8.8
90 mph	11.7
100 mph	15.1
Standing ¼-mile	14.1 sec @ 98 mph
Top speed	113 mph

BRAKING
70–0 mph @ impending lockup	175 ft
Modulation	poor fair good **excellent**
Fade	none **moderate** heavy
Front-rear balance	poor fair **good**

HANDLING
Roadholding, 200-ft-dia skidpad	0.86 g
Understeer	**minimal** moderate excessive

Building a legend

No longer a Lotus, but still in kit form —
Jeremy Coulter solved the Caterham jigsaw
and John Heseltine photographed it

Above left, having organised all the pieces and identified most of them, my first step, was to tighten the suspension fixings at front and rear. I should have done it last! Above right, the engine bay fixings next: this is the nearside engine mount which is easily accessible before the exhaust manifolding is fitted.

Above left, the outer section of the exhaust manifold must be fitted before the inner. Above right, the remainder of the exhaust system assembles easily although I had to resort to the hacksaw to get the centre bobbin mounting to fit. As this shot shows, it's quite possible to work in a small garage.

Above left, each headlight is mounted on a bracket which doubles as the front wing support. Above right, the wing mounting bolt holes lined up exactly and fitting was straightforward apart from holding the rubber sealing strip in place. It's advisable to drill the wing surface bolt holes from above, using masking tape to stop the drill slipping and scratching the smooth glass fibre.

Until recently, I disported myself in a stately Rover 100, but that has now been sold and replaced by a vehicle that is its antithesis in almost every respect, except perhaps in terms of individuality. It's a Caterham (née Lotus) Super Seven Sprint, the most popular of Caterham's current line-up.

A penalty — or attraction — of Caterham/Lotus Seven ownership, depending on your viewpoint, is that it turns heads. Fellow motorists fire questions from two feet above your head when you pull up alongside. Most frequent traffic light question is: "Did you build it?". During the first week of using the car I explained that I did, but that it's not really too difficult, as it comes from the factory with all the really tricky bits complete, so you don't need any special tools or expertise. However I soon tired of this and now just say "yes" and leave people to marvel at my technical skills!

In fact it took me just one weekend, plus a couple of evenings to build the car, although the job could quite probably be done in less time than that. The temptation, of course, is to rush the assembly simply to get the car on the road. But

having waited several months for delivery, will a day or two saved at this stage make all that much difference?

When Colin Chapman announced the very first Seven back in 1957, assembly wasn't reckoned to take much longer than a weekend even though the 'kit' was then quite literally a box of bits. Early sales literature proclaimed, "complete assembly with normal hand tools has been achieved in under 12 hours", which strains credibility slightly. The latterday Caterham arrives not as a 'box of bits' but as a rolling chassis with all the unattached parts loaded inside.

The Seven was introduced as a kit mainly to side-step swingeing purchase tax, but such tax advantages no longer pertain and kits now attract standard rate VAT as well as a hefty car tax. The reason the Seven remains a 'kit', however advanced (and in the UK is available only as such), is that home-assembled cars are exempt from National Type Approval. Boss of Caterham Cars, Graham Nearn, reckons that putting his cars through Type Approval would cost an unaffordable £60,000, which includes submitting several cars for crash testing.

Lack of Type Approval doesn't mean that the Seven is a dangerous car. Far from it. Its blend of performance and agility makes it very safe. It's just that the Seven is an idiosyncrasy that doesn't quite fit into today's bureaucratic scheme of things.

£5533 inc car tax and VAT will buy you the basic Cortina-engined 1600GT Seven and £5916 inc car tax and VAT, the faster Sprint version. The Twin Cam is now no longer available as supplies of the Lotus engine are exhausted. A Seven less engine and gearbox costs £3555 plus VAT. As a 25th anniversary celebration, Caterham are offering the Silver Jubilee Seven, resplendent in Silver paint, stainless exhaust and luxury trim. This desirable vehicle retails at £1400 more than the basic car. There's a waiting list of around three months for a new Seven. Of course, if you really can't wait, Caterham have a small selection of warranted used cars at their Caterham Hill HQ, but used Sevens hold their value remarkably well so you'll get only a ragged SIII example for less than £3000, although that sum should buy a decent example of the less popular SIV.

If you buy a new Seven, you'd be well advised to specify a number of optional extras. In a list of essentials, I'd include seat belts, heater kit, electronic ignition, rollover bar, tonneau, rear wing protectors, air horns — not an affectation, but vital to make your presence known in such a low-slung car — and also the alloy wheels and Goodyear G800 tyres. This collection will add around £400 to the total price of a new Seven.

My 'boxed' car arrived exactly on schedule with all these extras and was duly wheeled up the drive and positioned in front of the garage one Saturday morning. Lotus Sevens, and indeed Elites, Elans and Europas too, were never supplied with assembly instructions, which were deemed to constitute 'professional help' and invalidated the kit appelation. This tradition prevails with the present-day Caterham so the first task I set myself was to unload the car, then organise and identify all the parts.

At first sight it looked remarkably complete and I immediately had a vision of zooming off down the road that afternoon! However, as the colour photograph underlines, when all the pieces were spread out, it became clear that there really was plenty of work to do and the vision faded. The engine and gearbox were already installed, and the suspension, braking and steering systems fitted, as was the wiring loom, facia instrumentation and various ancillaries, not least the twin DCOE 40 Weber carburettors.

As far as tools for the job are concerned, I found that my modest DIY mechanics' toolbox sufficed. With the engine and gearbox in place, there's no need for any heavy lifting gear, and no special tools are called for. A good selection of spanners, a socket set, screwdrivers, pliers, grips and a pop rivet gun will account for most jobs. Useful aids, apart from an assistant — desirable, but by no means essential — are an hydraulic trolley jack and a pair of chassis stands.

Having identified just about everything, I took a deep breath and with the car on the ground taking its own weight started at the front by tightening all the suspension fixings. A useful aide-memoire is to mark each tightened nut or bolt with a small blob of paint so you can be sure that every fixing has received attention.

Moving to the rear of the car I tightened the rear axle linkage, including the A-bracket mounting on the differential casing. I learned afterwards that I should in fact have tightened the suspension fixings as one of the last operations!

It's now permissible to jack up the car and attend to the differential casing, propshaft and gearbox rear flange bolts, as well as checking the tightness of all brake pipe unions. While in position underneath I found it convenient to check both the differential and gearbox oil levels. These jobs complete, I lowered the car to the ground. Having said that, I'm still suffering from an aching

Building a Legend

back from bending over, so it might have been better to leave the car raised to give a more orthopaedic working height.

Job number one in the engine compartment was to tighten the engine mountings as well as any other nuts and bolts in the vicinity. The Weber carbs are mounted on rubber O-rings which are compressed the correct amount in the works, so the carb nuts shouldn't be touched. The exhaust manifolding is in two parts, an inner and an outer, and as I found out, the outer section must be fitted first. I experienced some difficulty fitting the remaining pipework for no matter how I pushed and pulled, the central rubber bobbin mounting wouldn't line up. In the end, I resorted to cutting half an inch from the second section and, hey presto, everything lined up and I was able to drill and secure the tailpipe bracket.

Various connections to the engine were next in line — the oil pressure pipe, heater and radiator hoses, speedometer drive and throttle cable. The latter, contrary to first impressions, leads in from above the carbs and sticks up. I now find that care has to be taken when fitting the bonnet, otherwise the cable can be trapped, giving a jerky throttle action. Achieving a satisfactory throttle setting necessitated some judicious bending of the throttle pedal before it could finally be set with the threaded adjuster. One unidentified item in the assortment of bits turned out to be a crankcase breather extension pipe which fixes to a bellhousing bolt.

After connecting the engine earth straps and setting the fan belt tension, I removed the plugs and rocker cover and checked the valve settings. Other jobs in the engine bay included fitting the electric fan, attaching the coolant overflow tube to the radiator filler neck and linking up the alternator wiring. I was relieved to find the contact-breaker-less ignition pack ready mounted and wired, which saved time musing over a circuit diagram.

Fitting the clutch cable was straightforward, the only tricky operation being refitting the actuating arm rubber boot into the bellhousing. Clutch adjustment is carried out at the gearbox end of the cable and I set it to give 2mm free play at the pedal.

By now it was late afternoon, and I was keen to get the engine running, so I set the ignition timing to the specified 12° BTDC using one of the repeater indicators as a test bulb. The bulb wouldn't light, which was hardly surprising as the battery wasn't connected! It's a negative-earth car and the arrangement of the several auxiliary leads to the terminals was self-evident. With the battery connected, timing the engine was simple as the timing marks are particularly easy to see on the crankshaft pulley. However, the distributor clamp bolt is most awkwardly placed. In fact the distributor itself is so badly located beneath the inlet manifold that simply removing the distributor cap becomes a major operation. Caterham are aware of this problem and have an improved manifold under development.

Having poured a gallon of petrol directly into the tank (the filler neck wasn't in place), filled up the radiator — a job I almost forgot — checked the engine oil level, and finally made an inspection for anything I could possibly have overlooked, I turned the key and the engine turned over sweetly. It whirred . . . and whirred . . . and oil pressure built up nicely but nothing happened except a couple of 'pops'. I rechecked everything and finding all the ingredients of successful ignition to be present, tried again but to no avail. In the end the battery flattened, so proceedings for the day came to an end.

Day two dawned wet, cold and dismal, but shrugging off the conditions I carried on! I abandoned the attempt to start the engine and turned my attention to the bodywork, fittings and trim. The headlamps and front indicators are mounted on an ingenious bracket which doubles as the front wing stay. It was a simple matter to position the brackets then wire and mount the light units.

Predictably I forgot to feed the wires through the grommetted hole in each side of the body and had to disconnect the wires and repeat the operation.

Wings next: I was reluctant to drill out the bolt hole indentations in the glassfibre mouldings in case they weren't correctly placed, but I needn't have worried, as each lined up exactly with its captive nut on the bodywork. Fitting the sealing strip between the wing and body was awkward, but once in place and with all the mounting nuts tightened, I cut off the dangling ends and then drilled and attached the intermediate wing support. The final job on the wings was to fit the repeater flashers. These slipped tightly into the pre-marked holes and the wires linked easily into the main loom.

Next on the list came the rollover cage which has a simple four-bolt mounting arrangement, although some attention with a rubber mallet was needed to line up the rearward mounting holes and allow the bolts to drop home. The interior trim, such as it is, fits in like a jigsaw and the carpets drop nicely into place, although the section for the 'luggage well' must be cut to fit round the rollover bar members. I measured wrongly and cut too generously, so this carpet doesn't look very good.

The petite windscreen wipers, rear view mirror and seat belts went on without problems but the fuel filler neck and locking cap needed some strong-arm persuasion. This left only a handful of further tasks, including fitting the grille to the nose cone and attaching the three badges, one fore and two aft, before I once again tried to start the engine.

Having installed the revitalised battery, with great dexterity I removed the distributor cap and checked the orientation of the rotor arm with the engine set to the 12° BTDC static timing position. To my eye, it seemed to be pointing to the correct cylinder, so I once again tested for fuel, and sparks and double-checked the valve clearances. Still nothing — so I retired for the night!

A phone call the following morning to Caterham's helpful Works Manager, Peter Cooper, put me on the right track. At his prompting, I drained the carbs and fuel line before refilling the tank with fresh petrol. Apparently the pipes are occasionally contaminated with tank-test fluid, though seldom enough to prevent starting. Also at this stage I did something I should have done earlier and balanced the carbs roughly by equalising the throttle butterfly angles while looking through the progression holes which are exposed when the cover screws are removed.

Next I rechecked the rotor arm orientation but in attempting to do this I became so frustrated with working under the carburettors that I decided to remove the inlet manifold, complete with the carbs. Common sense deserted me at this stage and I loosened the four manifold nuts without first draining the radiator. It's a water-filled manifold, and the result was that cylinders two and three filled with water!

Cringing at my incompetence I pressed on, and with the carbs out of the way and the distributor clearly exposed, found that the shaft *was* in fact 180° out. I repositioned it, refitted the distributor cap and carburettors before removing the spark plugs and giving the engine a quick whirl on the starter to expel the errant water which fountained out quite dramatically! As a matter of course, I changed the contaminated engine oil, then refilled the radiator.

It was downhill all the way from then on as the engine started first time accompanied by healthy oil pressure. After a stroboscopic timing check and carburettor adjustment plus sundry other ministration it ran perfectly. I was a little alarmed to find that the electric fan didn't cut in at 90°, but a quick piece of detective work revealed that I'd forgotten to connect up the thermostat wires which are hidden at the base of the radiator.

These jobs complete, I fitted the nose cone

Above left, the rollover cage going into place; the location of the fuel filler neck can be seen in this shot which also illustrates the extent of the 'luggage space' in a Caterham Seven! Above right, the seat back slots into place, needing no fixings. Below, the completed car raring to go. Summer's coming too!

EGP 73X

Building a Legend

and bonnet and set out to register the car for the open road. Predictably, this took longer than anticipated, not least because on my first visit to the local vehicle licensing office in Wimbledon I found it shut!

I went back next morning and spent a tedious 30 minutes waiting in a slow-moving queue only to be told that before I could register the car I had to get a receipt for car tax from the local Customs and Excise office. This levy is calculated at 10 per cent of the car's wholesale value — just over £400 in this case. A visit to the local HM Customs and Excise office yielded the appropriate piece of paper in exchange for the cash, and so equipped returned to the licensing office where I duly filled in form V55/5.

The licensing assistant looked puzzled as he studied the form then told me that the car would have to be inspected for roadworthiness and that this would be done "within a fortnight if you're lucky". Naturally I argued volubly and brandished the *Certificate of Newness* from Caterham. Faced with my firm queue-holding-up resolve, the assistant eventually disappeared to seek advice from a higher authority. The result was entirely satisfactory as it was decided that inspection wasn't necessary and the car was duly given the registration number EGP 73X, along with a road fund tax disc. I was told that the details would be passed on to Swansea and that a registration document would be sent to me in the near future.

A set of while-U-wait acrylic number plates was purchased on the way home and bolted on to the pristine Seven. After one last check, I strapped myself in, fired up the engine, snicked the stubby lever into first and gingerly pulled out of the drive, heading off down the road with a broad grin on my face, almost exactly five days after the 'kit' had been delivered. There are a couple of remaining jobs that I must get round to, including fitting the pop-rivet-attached rear wing protectors and the carpet locating studs.

Unfortunately I've already fallen victim to the Super Seven syndrome — I don't ever want to get out of the driving seat! ⏃

Below, a few final checks, the bonnet slips back into place and then its all systems go! I'll be reporting on the Seven in *Our Cars* each month.

The Caterham Connection

A glance at the history of the Super Seven, in this its 25th anniversary year

The present-day Caterham Super Seven is still easily identifiable as a near relative of the Lotus Seven that Colin Chapman introduced back in 1957. Although it looks similar, the car has in fact been changed and improved in many respects over the years. The current Seven is faster, stronger and not quite as spartan as its predecessors but it hasn't lost any of its essential character.

There have been five distinct stages of Seven development. The Series 1 began the line and was based around an aluminium panelled light tubular spaceframe similar to that of both the Lotus Six and Eleven, but with fewer tubes to keep the cost down. UK price for the basic car fully assembled with the 1172cc Ford Prefect engine and three-speed gearbox was £1036 7s which included £346 7s purchase tax.

Above, Colin Chapman officially hands over the Seven to Caterham's Graham Nearn in June '73. Right, cutaway of the radically different S4 Seven with moulded glass fibre body and in colour, the unmistakable Caterham profile.

If you elected to build it from a kit it was yours for £526. For comparison, an MGA stood at £995 17s and a TR3 was listed at £1021 7s. Lotus offered four engines for the new car — a standard or tuned version of the Ford 100E, the BMC 848cc unit and, lastly, the potent 1097 Coventry Climax FWA, which made it a real flyer although even in standard form its acceleration, tractability and handling, if belied by the 80mph top speed, were highly praised.

The Series 2 Seven came in 1960 and benefitted from various changes to the steering, suspension and weather protection, while more engines and states of tune were added to the list. One retrograde step was to cut down further still on the number of tubes in the chassis to prune costs. Later Series 2s sprouted flowing wings to replace the rudimentary cycle type.

By 1968 the days of the Seven seemed numbered as Colin Chapman steered his company's image up market. Despite relegation to a backwater at the new Hethel factory where the burgeoning company had moved in 1966, the car managed to survive, due in part to the unfailing enthusiasm of Seven owners, its steady sales and the efforts of one Graham Nearn, Managing Director of Caterham cars, by then sole distributors of the Seven. Caterham was one of

the first "Lotus Centres", dating back to 1959.

The Series 2 Seven was further refined to become the Series 3, in 1968. In terms of performance, handling and braking it became the definitive model. Lotus by now had their sights set on a larger more 'middle-of-the-road' market and the Series 4 Seven which replaced the 3 in 1970 was a very different machine. Although more comfortable and better equipped, it looked uninspiring and the glass fibre body carried on a steel ladder chassis never found favour with Lotus aficionados. It still performed very well, though, especially when fitted with the 125bhp Holbay-modified twin cam engine.

From its production peak in 1970/71 Series 4 sales dwindled and Lotus stood ready to wield the axe in 1973. Graham Nearn and his Caterham co-Director David Wakefield, by this time realised that there was no chance of persuading Colin Chapman to change his mind and saved the Seven in the best possible way. He took over the jigs and mouldings, plus all the spares and was granted licence to manufacture the car.

So Caterham kept the Series 4 going, having renamed it the Caterham Seven. However after only one year of production, insurmountable problems with the supply of subcontracted parts led to Caterham ending production. Foreseeing these problems, they'd been formulating alternative plans and in 1974 came the coup de grâce — Caterham replaced the Series 4 with a

revised Series 3, which had always been the enthusiasts' favourite. What's more, it was easier to make!

Caterham didn't simply reproduce the Series 3, for they improved it in several respects, including adding spaceframe triangulation to give greater strength, and revising the rear axle — latterly a BL unit has superseded the Ford. The enthusiastic ten-strong team at Caterham produce three or four cars per week and their waiting list shows no signs of shortening. There are several interesting new developments in the pipeline at Caterham and *T&CC* will be reporting on them in the near future. ⏃

Seven production 1957 — 1982
Series 1 (1957-1960) approx 242
Series 2 (1960-1968) approx 1350
Series 3 (1968-1970) approx 350
Series 4 (1970-1973) approx 1000
Caterham Series 4 (1973-1974) approx 47
Caterham Super Seven (1974 to date) 1003 and rising
Figures courtesy of *Legend of the Lotus Seven* by Dennis Ortenburger. Osprey, £11.95.

Hatton

AUTOSPORT's Marcus Pye tries out the current state of the Black Brick art at Goodwood.

The Black Brick

MARCUS PYE siezed upon the opportunity to talk to Rob Cox-Allison about his Caterham Super 7 Modsports machine and put it through its paces at Goodwood.

Motor racing at a National level has all too few true individualists among its competitors although the intrepid Rob Cox-Allison certainly falls into this category. Back in 1980, after a 10-year lay-off from the circuits, the Surrey businessman returned to the modified sports car class with a development of the Caterham 7 project, pioneered the previous season by David Bettinson. Despite the length of his 'retirement' Cox-Allison was competitive immediately — at the height of the class's popularity — and the intervening seasons have proved later versions of his 'Black Brick' theme to be the quickest of the contemporary modsports contenders. Three of these outrageous-looking ultra-lightweight machines have emerged from Geoff Rumble's stable in

East Horsley and, in Cox-Allison's hands, all have been successful both in terms of results and their crowd-pleasing capabilities.

Throughout the 1970s Rob continued to follow modsports and he keenly recalls watching David Bettinson hurtle a Caterham 7 around in his efforts to beat the then-dominant Porsches. Bettinson struggled to have the car accepted for modsports — many people felt it would be more at home in the clubmans formula where Lotus 7s originally competed — and Cox-Allison was one of several people to write to the motoring press in support of Dave who, after all, was beating some highly exotic machinery with a budget racer. Eventually the Caterham car was offically recognised and, by the end of 1979 Rob had decided

to rejoin the fray and to build another car.

"I bought a Panther Lima initially — I was well in with them at the time — and was going to develop a modsports version. Due to the class structure of the category it was agreed however that the Vauxhall-powered car would not be competitive so the works went into production sports racing with Chris Meek when I shelved the idea. I then saw the Bettinson car 'for sale after the last Thruxton race' but the advert was placed before he raced that weekend and he wrote it off.

"We went down and bought the remains but little did we know what we had bought . . . Virtually nothing was usable. Basically the engine, gearbox, rear axle and wheels were salvaged and

grafted onto a new spaceframe. Everything else was new. What we did get was David's knowledge on the project, which proved most invaluable, so we effectively continued its development. He suggested that F2-type front suspension should be fitted so that the 7 could stay with the Elans round the corners, so Chevron uprights were fitted to the car.

"At the first STP round of 1980, at Brands Hatch, I was second fastest to Pat Thomas in practice and I led the race. By the time I arrived at Paddock on the first lap I was about 20 yards up on everybody — I had a flier — but Pat hauled me in along top straight and passed me as if I wasn't there. I realised then that my little Caterham 7 was fantastic round the corners but it was like driving a brick in a straight line. The car was painted black so Ted suggested that we called it 'Black Brick'.

"It was very competitive that year with Nicky Ellis, Paul Berman and Thomas in their Elans and in comparison we were slow on the straights. Racing Fabrications of Bury St. Edmunds rebuilt the 1800cc twin-cam engine in a new block and immediately found us 20bhp.

"Soon afterwards I had probably the two most significant races with the first car, both at Thruxton. A bleed nipple got knocked off the rear brakes in practice for the first one and we started from the back of the grid with a 10sec penalty after one lap in the morning but fought through to finish second — to a standing ovation from spectators. I was so proud of that but I still had not won a race! Next time there I started from the back again after an ignition problem but without the penalty. By the end of the second lap I was in Thomas's boot-lid and I took him coming out of the Complex but the car took off at Kimpton — it broke away very violently — and hit the armco sideways at about 125mph and decreased the 7s width by a foot. The only thing to my credit was a lap of 1m 22.98s which at the time was 3.5s under the existing lap record. I've never been within 2s of that time since . . .

Soon after its successful race debut at Silverstone Rob Cox-Allison invited AUTO-SPORT to try the latest Black Brick derivative. Having watched the combination notch up their first race win — and as an admirer of such remarkable machinery — I jumped at the opportunity. The ultra low Caterham 7 was already being unloaded by Rob and Ted Williams when I arrived in Sussex although the weather was cold and miserable. Thank heavens the rain held off.

Without its bodywork — integral nose-cone/spoiler, smoothly contoured front wings, stubby tail and Gomm-fabricated vinyl-covered aluminium hood — it is easy to understand how the spindly panelled spaceframe car weighs around 9cwt for there appears to be little to it apart from the relatively large Racing Fabrications Lotus/Ford twin-cam engine which develops just over 200bhp from its 1800cc.

Getting in to an open car which barely comes up to ones waist can present problems but you need to be a trained contortionist to wriggle into Black Brick III, a task made fractionally less difficult by the tiny flip-up hatch in the roof. Once installed in the narrow cockpit all your Houdini escapology practice will be needed to re-emerge; unless you are practised. A couple of demonstrations by Rob simplified the procedure and after the owner had completed a dozen or so laps it was my turn.

The cockpit is further cramped by a substantial roll cage which stiffens the driver cell while a large Fire Eater extinguisher system takes over the 'passenger' well with ring-pull operation located by the driver's left elbow on one of the cross braces. A sparse dashboard carries the large tachometer plus gauges for oil/water temperature and oil

pressure while a knurled adjuster for the brake balance sits to the right of the tiny steering wheel. The cable-operated front anti-roll bar adjustment is mounted beside the fire-pull, just above the short lever into the intriguing Leeson gearbox. Newly developed by Rob 'Haggis' le Sueur, the 'box allows ratios to be changed within a standard Ford casing. Impressive!

Secure in the six-point Luke harness I listen carefully to Rob's final instructions before the engine is fired up on the auxiliary battery. Wait for Ted to disconnect the socket, ease the lever into first and the sinister black 7 rumbles up the pit lane. After a couple of slow laps — as much to re-acclimatise myself to the undulating track as warm the fat Avon slicks — I felt sufficiently confident to use full revs although a carburation fault with the twin 48DCOE Webers was restricting this to 7600rpm and, it was later diagnosed, sapping power by

around 30bhp. Nevertheless there was shattering performance on tap still.

The car is remarkably free from rattles and vibration which surpised me, particularly since the Goodwood surface is uneven, and once the tyres were working the 7 inspired tremendous confidence. The car is set up with just a touch of understeer which is preferable on such a fast open circuit and the steering has plenty of feel without being too heavy. On first acquaintance poor visibility out of the cockpit seems to limit ones cornering antics but with a few laps' practice it becomes easier to judge turn-in and apex points.

The suspension is naturally firm but gives a fairly comfortable ride to the driver in his padded recliner, jolts through the car being absorbed seemingly without drama due to the hubbub within the cockpit and the rorty cacophany from the engine compartment. Anti-roll bars front and rear do their job

admirably while Armstrong (front) and Spax (rear) dampers keep the corners on the deck. Rear suspension for the live axle is by a rose-jointed sliding A-frame which prevents axle tramp and makes the Cox-Allison car easily the swiftest modsports machine off the starting line.

Aided by very positive controls — and the gearchange was very smooth and slick — and phenomenal brakes (Girling four-pot calipers up front, two-pot behind) I felt really at home in the Black Brick which handled beautifully on all parts of the circuit. Remembering to brake in a straight line for the critical Woodcote and Madgwick corners, the car could be turned-in under full power providing the line was right for it is quite hard to make a major adjustment of trajectory, mid-corner, without unbalancing the chassis. I got the impression that the front end worked extremely well (with its single-seater geometry) while the back would be prone to sudden breakaway if one drove at or over the limit.

Once on the straights the twin-cam unit screamed up to maximum revs and was keen to be kept right up on the cam in the corners thanks to useful 'compromise' ratios. The fact that it was enjoyable and comparatively easy to drive was borne out by my best lap time which was just three-tenths from Rob's best at that point, in the 1m 26s bracket after about 10 laps. I was confident that I could get into the 24s inside 20 laps — a time which Rob managed by the end of the session with no previous Goodwood experience — but, never having driven a Lotus or Caterham 7 of any kind before, I contented myself with some lappery in a number of prototype road cars and Rob's own 'Road Brick!' Seventh heaven?

Track Test

The Black Brick

The car was enjoyable and comparatively easy to drive but the back could break away.

A couple of races were lost while the car was rebuilt around a new Arch Motors spaceframe, those events costing Rob the chance of the class championship. Ellis stopped racing as soon as he had clinched the class (his Elan was being protested at the time) and Cox-Allison became the man to beat in the division. "We decided that 'Black Brick' was light and fast enough in that form (with small sidepods and a front spoiler) but we wanted to go absolutely mad and build another 7 to take a Hart F2 engine for GT racing while still being eligible for modsports with the twin cam as there were only seven GT races at Donington. The first car was then sold to Mike Gidden (the former Clan and MGB driver) and had subsequently changed hands again.

"I commissioned Geoff Rumble of Dastle to build 'Black Brick II', incorporating the many innovations which Ted and I wanted such as centre-locking wheels which would be better suited to the racing running gear. Robin Smith of Chevron gave us a lot of help and Geoff started work, grafting B42 suspension onto the front of a standard Caterham chassis. We looked at it for modsports then made new engine mountings for the Hart GT installation, which was completed by Racing Fabrications and worked out the positions of the transmission and everything else. Gartrac Fabrications made us a special oil pump for the differential of the standard Ford axle — a known weak link but demanded in the modsports rules — but we didn't realise how complicated the construction would be, working two separate sets of regulations into one car. The engine ancillaries: filters, pumps etc all had to be made to fit while the large F2 exhausts had to be routed through the same channels as the twin-cam pipes. When everything was eventually shoehorned in the only difference between visible specifications was a bulge in the bonnet for the Hart.

"We actually had a situation where we raced at Donington in GT trim one day and had a modsports round at Snetterton the following afternoon so the car had to be altered overnight. The guys from Racing Fabrications worked with us at their shop and the engine change was completed in a little over two hours. There were some inherent problems though with the Hart. To take the power we had to run wide wheels — 14in wide rears — for which only M&H's 23 profile tyres were suitable. This threw the diff ratio calculations to start with and it proved difficult to set up on 20 profile front covers with the tall rears.

Black Brick II only ran twice with the F2 300bhp engine, mainly because the Donington dates often clashed with the STP fixtures, but there were other sizeable problems. It was impossible to find compromise gearing for the engine when coupled to a fixed-ratio Ford gearbox and the 'modsports' axle with 4.5:1 gears hence the Hart would be off the cam at corners through which 6000rpm could not be achieved or revving excessively in the faster bends.

"Had we been able to use a Hewland transaxle the car would have been stunningly quick". As it was Rob lapped in the 1m 16s bracket — with a huge Maurice Gomm bi-plane wing strung out the back — a couple of seconds better than with twin-cam motivation. With 600bhp per ton on tap the bigger-engined car could pull 150mph on Starkeys straight.

The pods on the car were boxed in to Rob's design purely to maximise what little downforce was available (bearing in mind that in modsports trim it could not carry a boot spoiler as there is nothing behind the cockpit). "They worked because the fibreglass used to stretch but the car weighed more than its predecessor and was not ideally suited to modsports. The huge rear tyres did not get warm for three laps so I was driving on marbles for the first part of each race. After that they were marvellous and M&H were very helpful to me. It was clear though that a multi-purpose car was not really workable".

"At that point we asked Geoff to build us an out-and-out modsports car, making it as light as possible for 1982, because although I was winning races in Black Brick II I was not always fastest — definitely not on the straights anyway — particularly when up against Rob Wells's Morgan Plus 8. My car was just a bit too heavy — at 10½cwt against Black Brick I wish I had fewer bolt-on goodies. In modsports terms our power-to-weight ratio was down. The 7's major advantages are its ability to turn-in early and its weight". The late arrival of the car at the start of the season left Pat Thomas with a big points advantage in his class which Rob could not erode, again due to the scoring system which favours fuller classes.

Black Brick III was started last August and eventually made its debut at Silverstone at the end of March by which time Rob had dominated the early STP rounds in the earlier car. It is much lighter than Black Brick II and runs on specially developed Avon A1 compound slicks of 10in and 11in width and low 20 profile. IRTS, distributors of the Avon rubber, have worked with Cox-Allison to make these tyres in modsports fittings, So successful has the new car been that every STP championship event bar one (at Mallory where an oil pipe burned through on III setting fire to the engine bay) has been won by a Brick! "Once again though we are in the invidious position that despite the overall wins we haven't got a chance of winning the overall championship because there are too few competitors in my class".

As single-minded in competition as he is in business, Cox-Allison is determined to earn outright championship spoils before too long but at least a class championship should come his way this year. "Contrary to what many people think I do not run on a vast budget", says Rob. "In fact it is rather the opposite. As no-one has bought Black Brick II yet — which would have helped finance BBIII — I have only just finished paying for the new car and have used the same set of tyres all season. If I cannot sell the other car we may have another go at GTs with it next year with Hart-power but in the meantime we will take in Donington and Castle Combe GT events with the latest one."

Black Brick I in 1980 at Oulton Park.

Rob Cox-Allison, now 36-years-old, first entered the realms of motor sport back in 1968, turning to the circuits after a successful auto-test debut in an MG Midget, "the first new one to come into Wilsons in Epsom. Ian Hull (who now races a modsports Davrian) was at the same event in the novice class. We somehow found ourselves leading the experts (!) until the last test when we were both disqualified on a technicality.

"After that I really got the motorsport bug so I joined the MG Car Club and turned up to race at Brands Hatch with a set of tyres which I bought from a chap called Frank Williams who was working from a flat in Harrow. Some more tyres came from Mike Crabtree and, as we didn't have a trailer, the car was towed from Tolworth to the circuit on a rope . . ."

The young Cox-Allison was rather 'green' about the business at the time, not realising that an earlier Spridget could be converted to 1275cc specification for racing. "I started with a brand new car then threw most of the bits away including the engine which was replaced with an experimental BMC unit — EXP 22241 — which developed around 120bhp from 1285cc capacity.

"Unfortunately it pumped oil out everywhere, usually onto the clutch, so we bored a little hole in the bellhousing which was plugged by a bit of chewing gum. A piece of string linked this to the gearchange and would pull it out as I grabbed second away from the grid!

"My first race was against John Britten, Richard Lloyd and Alain de Cadenet among others (Alain in an AC Ace) and it went fairly well. Eventually, after an incident at Brands the Midget was rebuilt by Geoff Rumble of Dastle who incorporated F3 front suspension on the car. Backing from Futurama Signs and Croydon Centre Garages was forthcoming for 1969 while a Triumph GT6 was built for the following season with sponsorship from Sid Hurrell's SAH Tuning firm. Assisted throughout by mechanic Ted Williams, Rob raced until the end of 1970 when the cost became prohibitive.

A structural engineer by profession, Cox-Allison then turned his hand to building up his own company, Design Home Centres, which specialises in custom-made fireplaces and replacement windows from outlets in Guildford and Sutton. "The basic problem in 1970 was that I was broke. I felt that I could go a lot further in racing if I had money so I resolved to concentrate on business first.

"It took 10 years to develop the company to the point where I reckoned I could afford to go motor racing again, albeit at a very limited level. I talked to Ted again and he was keen so we decided to compete in selected STP modsports races in 1980".

Black Brick II in 1981 at Mallory Park.

MILES Super 7
Behind the Wheel

There is a new Vegantune twin-cam engine and longer cockpit version. Caterham Super Seven goes, stops and handles as before

FOR A DECADE, Graham Nearn's modest Caterham factory has turned out Super 7s with the original and legendary Lotus Twin Cam engine, and more basic models with single and twin carburettor versions of the 1600 crossflow Ford Kent engine, which are still the mainstay of the domestic market. In single carburettor GT form it is now certified for Swiss, Japanese (who also take twin-cam) and most recently German markets.

Since we last had a look at a pair of Super 7s (*Autocar* 26 January 1980) there have been some important changes. Legroom was always a problem for anybody tall, and to achieve a longer cockpit model, Caterham have moved the which made the 20-year old design niggly and often expensive to look after.

Vegantune designed and manufactured a totally new cylinder head, using existing TC valves and the same combustion chamber design, but with detachable cam carriers, new camshafts and a toothed belt replacing the chain. Valve stem oil seals are incorporated. There is improved exhaust valve cooling and better oil drainage from the valve train and the VTA uses the standard 1600 Kent water pump.

Power and torque outputs equate almost exactly with the old "big valve" Twin Cam. On a couple of Dellorto 40DHLA twin choke carburettors, the VTA turns out 130 bhp at 6,000 rpm,

Above right: Put the hood up and life inside the car gets distinctly claustrophobic

Best to dress for wet weather rather than spend time dismantling the hood. Handling balance is delicate in the wet

Vegantune's twin-cam VTA engine puts out 130 bhp at 6,000 rpm, driving through a Ford gearbox and Morris Ital axle

seat bulkhead rearwards by approximately 2 in. This has the additional advantage of bringing the structure that forms the seat back into line with the upper and lower chassis tubes at a point of triangulation, which benefits the stiffness of the space frame structure.

The ageing Lotus Twin Cam badly needed a revamp. Vegantune had already used their experience in coaxing the last bit of life from ageing casting and pattern equipment. There was the troublesome water pump which required cylinder head removal to change, camshaft drive chain and tensioner wear rates, and excesive oil consumption via the seal-less valve guides, all of and 115 lb.ft. torque at 5,000 rpm; a fairly "sporting" power curve. Drive goes through a Ford Escort Sport gearbox to a Leyland Ital axle, adopted to replace the previously used Escort RS2000 part. Location is typically Chapmanesque; trailing arms on top of the axle and an A bracket underneath. Concentric coil spring/damper units suspend the car and work in conjunction with double wishbone front suspension.

Prices now vary from £5,996 for the basic 1600 GT (£185 more for the long cockpit version) through £6,471 for the Sprint, to £7,476 for the Twin Cam, and these prices do not include such essentials as seat belts £29.65, heater £68.42, and roll-over bar £32.77. Also difficult to resist are the 185/70HR-13 tyres on 6 in. wide alloys which cost an extra £120, and replace the standard fitment 165SR-13 tyres on 5½ in. pressed steel wheels. A top specification car leaves little change out of £8,000, and there is still a weekend's work putting it together!

From the outside a Caterham 7 with the hood up, seems an impossibly cramped machine but has plenty of headroom.

remove the hood from its storage space behind the seats and there is enough room for overnight gear, a sandwich tin, and a thermos. Pack all that and the hood – no chance. With the car rigged for the wet, getting in through the small sidescreen opening is like trying to get into a modern day formula car – wriggle and thread legs past steering wheel, then slide backside over the cockpit side. Once installed the longer cockpit is a vast improvement for the tall driver. Those with generously proportioned hips, or larger than size nine shoes need not apply, but knees are no longer drawn up to make contact with the underside of the dash, and the wheel is now at an arms-slightly-bent distance for a 6 footer. Nothing is perfect, and if there were a chance, it would be nice to see the seat lowered an inch or two so that the tall driver no longer has the screen top edge interfering with his vision. The driver still becomes well aware

Real Performance

The journey up to MIRA had been tiresome. London traffic, with the Super 7 eager to go but frustrated, is followed by motorway with the minimally silenced induction, boomy exhaust, flapping hood, wind, and road noise blending into an unholy row.

The weather clears as we get to the A5. Suddenly the Super 7 is a different machine. You're sitting low to the ground in a little racer. It flicks through roundabouts. A series of bends at speeds leaves the mirror image of an energetically driven family car visibly diminishing at each turn of the wheel. It would take a supercar to squirt past slow moving trucks with such a complete lack of fuss. Me? I can't understand why is everybody driving so slowly. Its giant-killing acceleration becomes even more apparent when it comes to taking figures. Our 7 TC tipped MIRA scales at 10.75 cwt with a 50/50 split.

but already the brick like aerodynamics are beginning to tell. It takes another 10 sec for the car to reach 100 mph, and no matter how hard we tried we could not persuade it to better a mean maximum of 106 mph. No car I can think of gets to the legal limit so fast, yet cannot top 110 mph.

Experience of the 1600 Sprint engined version was limited to a few miles, but like the single carburettor Kent 7 tested three years ago, it felt very nearly as quick though the gears as the VTA car, and perhaps even more responsive at low to middle rpm.

The test track gave the opportunity to discover – or rediscover – what delightful manners it has. There is some cornering roll but sitting so low, the driver does not sense much. On dry roads it is virtually impossible to unstick the rear end, except in second gear with power. On the road or track all the driver is likely to encounter is a progressive build up to

required on small angles of lock, leaves one with the impression of being close to a front wheel slide, when there is still grip to be had.

Svelt ride would not be expected, but compared with the last 7s we drove, this newly-rebuilt car seemed to achieve its live wire handling, at the expense of a lot of hard, fidgety movement over poorly repaired urban roads. Pushed hard over bumpy B roads, ride is best

PERFORMANCE

Standing ¼-mile: 15.0 sec 88 mph
Standing kilometre: 29.0 sec 102 mph
Maximum speed: 107 mph   **Overall mpg:** 22.2

True mph	(sec)	mph	Top	3rd	2nd
30	2.4	10-30	–	4.9	3.3
40	3.4	20-40	7.0	4.9	3.0
50	4.6	30-50	7.8	4.5	2.7
60	6.2	40-60	8.9	4.0	–
70	8.6	50-70	8.8	4.1	–
80	10.8	60-80	9.5	4.6	–
90	16.2	70-90	10.5	–	–
100	26.9	80-100	16.2	–	–

(ACCELERATION)

The 1600 Sprint engined version, although less powerful, felt rather more responsive than the VTA car at the lower end of the rev scale

Steering wheel and gearchange are perfectly positioned, but the switches remain unmarked; instrumentation is comprehensive

of the lack of shape in the seat back especially lower down in the lumbar region. Running with the hood up serves to highlight how soon the sidescreens and rear window steam up, drastically reducing visibility at junctions.

Even two up, the power to weight ratio is a healthy 190 bhp per ton. Dropping the clutch with around 4,000 rpm indicated the car shrieks off the line; to reach 60 and 80 mph in a staggering 6.2 and 10.8 sec, then on to 90 mph in 16.9 sec,

understeer unless the car is crudely handled. Back off the throttle in mid corner and there is an immediate – almost nervous – movement bringing the car into a neutral attitude. Such is the delicacy of on limit balance that wet roundabouts are an ideal and noiseless way to brush up on car control. No matter what the surface, the 7 puts the power down marvellously (hence the ability to throttle steer so easily), yet it has no limited slip differential.

In the whole handling package I would only ask for marginally more steering weight, to improve feel when conditions are slippery. At higher speeds in the wet, the car needs a delicate touch. The very small effort

described as lively. The unservoed brakes are heavy but always stop the car.

In view of previous Caterham 7 fuel consumptions in the high 20s, it came as a mild disappointment to see this one returning just over 22 mpg overall, but then it was driven hard throughout, and there was more than the usual amount of town running. Even over 273 miles, there were times when I hated it. So much would be gained by quietening the inlet system and improving the seat further. There were times when I suffered for it (the wet). But give me a Caterham Super 7, a dry road, and the world seems a rosier place.

'This is a car you'll either love or hate. If you're the kind of enthusiast willing to endure hurricane, freeze and flood in a fun car, the Westfield Seven is very appealing indeed.'

I flicked down two gears, rolled onto the brakes and drew to a halt smartly on the front row at the traffic lights. My daughter wrestled with the mini-bales of rabbit hay and straw wedged between her and the red-covered dashboard and giggled, complaining mildly that her ears were ringing. Over to the right, on the traffic island in the middle of the Farnham Bypass, an admiring group of pedestrians grinned approval – November and the hood was down.

"D'you suffer Lotus elbow?", called the most knowledgeable of them. "No" I replied, "It's the Westfield W'ist in this case...", flapping a limp hand over the side. "Good poser's car innit..."

That hadn't really occurred to me before. When Chris Smith lent me this Coventry Climax FWB-engined effective-replica of an original Series I Lotus 7, I had never dreamed it would attract so much attention. I'm not by nature a replicar fan, indeed my whole background rebels against the very thought, but when it comes to bringing fifties-style motoring squarely within the grasp of the *ordinary* enthusiast – and especially the impecunious youngster – then I believe that's something else *if*, and it's a big if, the job is nicely done.

When it is as nicely done as in Chris Smith's new Westfield Seven, then I for one am prepared to applaud the 1983 Bellini Historic Sports Car Champion's approach, wave my arms about and spread the word...

Colin Chapman described his original 7 as the "...most basic, lightest, high-performance little car – a student's car if you will – a four-wheeled motor-bike..." He unveiled it to a startled public alongside the Elite coupé at the Earls Court Motor Show of October 1957. Typically Chapman, it was based upon a sparse spaceframe, welded-up from round and square-section tube stock, with rivetted-on aluminium stiffening panels. Its independent front suspension and live-axle rear end derived from the contemporary Lotus Elite/Eleven Club thinking and the 7 was a logical extension of the old Mark 6 theme which preceded it.

Beginner's competition car

In essence the Series I was intended as a beginner's competition car in which one could learn the art of controlling a high-performance lightweight on road and track. In June 1960 it was replaced by a more refined Series II to become 'a road car also useable on circuit', and the succeeding Lotus 7s and Super 7s followed, culminating today in Caterham Cars' highly-developed and highly-entertaining fun machines.

What Chris Smith set out to do less than two years ago, when he founded Westfield Sports Cars Ltd to produce a look-alike enveloping-bodied Lotus 11 replicar, was to bring that type of motoring much

WILD WEST

Doug Nye takes to the road in Westfield's Lotus lookalike fun machine

more within reach of the man in the street – catering for the average *Autosport* or CLASSIC & SPORTSCAR reader as opposed to the high earner looking for ways to enjoy his spare cash. There were two ways to do this. One was to slap together a cut-price rolling accident looking for a likely place to happen. The other was offer a low-labour kit, to trim profit margins with a realistic pricing policy, keep overheads low and pull together a dedicated and capable workforce willing to get their heads down and beaver, hard. As an example, their welder worked regular 60-hour weeks throughout the past year!

Smith is a pretty blunt, practical character, and he explains his value-for-money pricing policy with the

Primitive – the internals of a Westfield Seven shell

line: "I want to sell 'em – not collect 'em..."

He thought he might, just, be able to sell a couple of dozen Westfield 11s over two or three years. In fact within the first year production has already exceeded 105 and orders are still rolling in. The original product has been extensively developed and improved and an eager distribution chain in the USA is already into repeat orders.

Better term than replica

Now a separate company, Westfield Seven Ltd, has been set up to handle the latest lookalike – and that's a better term than replica, for both the Eleven and the Seven are obviously different animals from the Lotus prototypes upon close inspection. An impressive feature of both Westfield models is the rigidity of their tubular spaceframe chassis. For simplicity both are welded-up from square-section stock, and while neither Lotus featured centreline framing around the transmission tunnel both Westfields have it.

Both are sold in kit form, the idea being that you invest in a rusted-out Spridget, buy the kit and then assemble it to use reconditioned engine, gearbox, braking system, axle and so on, cannibalised from the Sprite or Midget. Smith would prefer not to become involved in total assembly to sell finished cars, but it can be arranged. He does provide a service to perform any small specialist operations the kit builder might find problematic, and in addition the Eleven is available in various degrees of kit-completion. That does not apply to the Seven, however, the new kit for which is available in one specification only, priced at £2750 plus VAT. In theory, with a £2-300 outlay on a scrap Spridget you can put your self-built fun car on the road for something the right side of £3500-£3750. And there's not a lot of worthwhile choice available when it comes to performance cars around that mark.

The basic kit is not as comprehensive as one might expect of something like the Caterham Seven, which includes all mechanical parts, and it takes in the following items: Aluminium-panelled epoxy-powder coated chassis frame in grey or black finish with bright panelling, ready-fitted with scuttle, bonnet, dash and glass-fibre nose cone; self-coloured glass-fibre wings with all necessary brackets; laminated windscreen with two side brackets; hood and hoodframe; five-gallon aluminium fuel tank; four front suspension wishbones; four rear trailing arms; one rear Panhard rod with all relevant suspension bushes; two Panhard rod location brackets for welding onto the Spridget back axle (the company will do this for the customer if he brings the axle in, or will supply part-exchange overseas); a pair of rear wheel spacers to give chassis clearance; steering wheel and column including UJs; complete wiring loom; two Lotus 7 Series I-style Butler tractor

headlamps; two Austin A35 side-lights; four indicator lamps; upholstered cockpit seat back and two squabs; four adjustable Spax dampers and coil-springs, and an original-style exhaust manifold and silencer – the silencer actually being a Peugeot estate rear box...

This standard Seven kit is jigged entirely for Spridget parts, but a special-engined alternative for rather more than twice the kit price would be 1460cc Coventry Climax FWB-engined like the prototype car loaned to me for test.

Before describing that device, I should explain the fundamental differences between the Westfield Seven and the Lotus prototype on which it is based, for while it retains the low-sprung pert looks of the 1957 original it embodies numerous improvements.

For a start it is 3ins longer to give more cockpit room, though the nose, bonnet and scuttle all fit an original Series I. The cockpit shoulder room is also 1in greater than an original 'S1', 39ins instead of 38. The Westfield has that hefty tunnel framing for added rigidity in all planes. Where the Lotus rear axle was located by an A-frame beneath the diff-casing and twin trailing arms, the Westfield has four trailing arms and a lateral Panhard rod. This is because the original-style A-arm tended to twist the axle casing and could snap off the lug under the diff. This caused oil leaks which proved a classic 7 ailment.

The Lotus' front suspension used a front-mounted, high anti-roll bar sweeping back to couple-up with lateral links forming the top wishbones. The Westfield has no anti-roll bar, but proper wishbones. The Lotus' original rear coil-springs had axial-pin top location. This pin tended to rust-up, locking-on the fixing nuts. The Westfield's Spax dampers locate on a horizontal through-bolt fixing instead. Its Midget-derived handbrake rising from the passenger side of the transmission tunnel is also more efficient than the original under-dash device. Whereas the Lotus drew its component parts from a variety of off-the-shelf sources, the Westfield uses just one, the Austin-Healey Sprite/MG Midget range.

So what's it like?

Dependent on your outlook, this is a car you'll either love or hate. You'll know the moment you see the photos here whether it attracts you or not, and that means whether you are the kind of enthusiast willing to endure hurricane, freeze and flood in a fun car – or want more civilisation for your money. If this kind of car appeals at all, then Westfield's Seven 'Series I look-alike' is very appealing indeed.

The test car had an extra attraction for me as it was fitted with a 1460cc Coventry Climax FWB engine. This 4-cylinder sohc all-alloy unit is the kind upon which Lotus and Cooper built their reputation in sports and Formula 2 racing in the late 'fifties. It's entirely in keeping with the Seven, and makes it a mouth-watering cut above the Spridget-engined basic model. That also makes it more expensive, with the engine costing more than the rest of the car.

Probably become his test chassis

Tony Mantle of Climax Engine Services built and owned 'my' FWB, and this particular Westfield Seven will probably become his test chassis. He is a one-man band who maintains and services all the best Climax engines, including that used in Nigel Sheffield's Lotus 17 which Chris Smith drove to the Bellini Championship this past season for Sheffield Garner Ltd, the Ford main agents from Diss, Norfolk.

There is an ulterior motive for the Seven-Climax, in that if sufficient demand can be created for Climax-engined variants it could allow a fair-sized production batch of suitable units to be set up, in turn minimising their individual cost. This could be a two-edged sword, however, for Tony works alone, has built around 20 engines in the past year and finds that workload sufficient. He'd have to take on and train staff to handle more, so he's more inclined to keep unit price quite high and supply a restricted demand. As things stand at the moment he's quoting "not less than £3000" for an FWB engine similar to the one in the Seven test car. On balance I have to say that seems worthwhile, for around £6500 you have a near-genuine throw-back to 'fifties

Evocative – the Westfield Seven has all the right looks

Delectable – two Westfield Lotus 11 lookalikes line up

motoring, with all the right looks, sensations, sounds ... and drawbacks. And that's half the fun.

In Seven trim the FWB breathes through twin SU 1½-inch carburettors and with a compression ratio around 9.5:1 and a mild road-going camshaft is believed to give some 85bhp ... plus considerable mid-range torque. It drives via a standard Spridget gearbox with that notchy but surprisingly rapid change, and non-synchro first gear. For competition, bottom gear proved notoriously weak in this 'box, but I didn't know that until too late ...

The Seven cockpit is surprisingly roomy, despite that square-edged panelled-in transmission tunnel with its extra longitudinal frame tubes. I'm around 5ft 11ins tall and my feet could barely reach the pedals. It's better to have too-long a cockpit and cushion short drivers forward, than to have one too short and cramp taller men. I put the passenger seat squab behind my back which proved more comfortable than it sounds, and it did the trick.

Finish on the Westfield is generally very good, though one or two ragged corners will have to be improved on the aluminium scuttle panelling, and the glass-fibre wing mouldings showed minor imperfections. Smith's Elevens are already onto their third set of ever-improving body moulds, and I would expect Seven development to follow suit. He acts upon criticism.

Access with the well-made heavy-gauge hood erected is like making love to the circus fat lady.

Where d'you begin? The answer is either to give up before you start, furl the hood and tuck it away in the unfloored space behind the cockpit, above the fuel tank, or to step in head first, bring in the trailing foot thereafter, turn around with your head bulging-out the hood, and then slither legs down into the footwell. From outside it looks hilarious, with the hood stretching and heaving in all directions, wife leaning helpless with laughter against the garage door. I took the hood down, and the weatherman smiled upon us with a spell of mild, dry weather.

The Climax engine starts easily with a deafening blast from the out-turned side exhaust, blowing-up dead leaves three or four yards away.

The Westfield Seven inherits the stiffness and fine ride quality of its Eleven predecessor. Even at speed on quite rough country roads only those tall-bracketed tractor headlights shimmy noticeably, and the chassis/body structure proves remarkably rigid. It also runs arrow-straight hands-off in those conditions, while the soft-sprung/stiff-damped suspension with low tyre pressures soak up ridges and bumps remarkably well.

In finest Lotus tradition

Steering is high-geared and direct in the finest Lotus tradition. With the wheels in sight you can aim the car very accurately indeed. Brakes which are perhaps no more than adequate on the standard Spridget are quite powerful without being fierce and prone to grabbing in the lightweight Seven. In normal driving, off the mark acceleration was certainly vivid, the tacho needle whacking round to the 6000rpm 'caution' mark most impressively through the gears. I didn't manage to take proper times but 0-60 *felt* like something in the 7secs bracket.

To preserve original looks and proportions, Chris supplied the car with 15in MGA wire wheels carrying narrow-tread 155 SR-15 tyres front and rear on 4J and 4½J rims. In this form the Seven was prone to wagging its tail, especially in roundabouts and tight corners and it was obvious the FWB gave just too much power for the contact patch available. On wider 165 SR 15s behaviour was improved. Now you could kick the tail out and within reason hold it there, the rigid frame giving a great feeling of stable security. With more grippy tyres than Kelly-Springfields perhaps it would all feel better still. . . there was more juggling to be done and I was enjoying myself heartily charging around the Hampshire byways. Eventually I decided the time had come to try some standing starts.

Tacho needle vertical, 3500rpm, seemed a reasonable place to start, so with the FWB singing lustily away I snicked-in first, checked the mirror, and popped the clutch.

An earthquake struck, the poor little Seven bounded into the air and clattered to rest, and I switched off, wondering what on earth I had done.

It was remarkable, visible testimony to the FWB's torque. The lower radius rods either side are quite short, made of 16-gauge steel tube; heavy, thick and virtually impossible to bend even in a vice. Now they had bent through some 45-degrees, the left-side tube down until it bottomed-out against the chassis lower rail and the right-side tube upwards, the axle twisting bottom forwards as those Kelly-Springfield rear tyres refused to break traction and spin! As the left-side radius rod bottomed-out on the chassis rail – and the prop-shaft UJ on the side of the transmission tunnel – the axle could rotate no further, so that weak bottom gear stripped.

I didn't feel very proud of myself, but they had asked me to test the prototype. If you can't take a joke, you shouldn't have joined. In fact a redesign is under way, and you can be sure a better car will emerge. Remember I was impressed by it as it stood.

Chris Smith has set out to bring this type of classical Lotus motoring within reach of Mr Average, and is doing the job very well. For around £3500 and the investment of some hours' sweat you can be on the road in a well-made, robust and well-thought out classical style performance car – destruction-tested by experts in this case ... Some years ago after testing a Caterham Seven – which is in a higher price bracket – I wrote that it was hard to believe so much fun could be legal. That holds true today.

Super – Climax FWB twin carb engine turns out some 85bhp

Buying A Lotus Seven

It isn't for the faint hearted, says Geoff Le Prevost

The brash but purposeful Seven was the first production car from Lotus to be designed for road use though, with a succession of ever-more-powerful engines being made available, many owners did, and still do have, other ideas. A road car it might have been, but there was little thought for creature comfort. Back in the fifties, Colin Chapman had in mind a car which would be cheap and fast. Today, alas, it is only fast.

It is unusual for *Practical Classics* to feature cars which are still available in the new-car showrooms — incredible though it seems, the car, which first appeared in 1957, lives on as the Caterham Seven. You cannot refer to the Lotus Seven without mentioning Caterham, and I went along to the factory to talk to Graham Nearn.

Caterham Car Sales have been involved with the Seven since it was introduced and, under Graham's direction in 1967, became sole concessionaires. In 1973, when Lotus was heading resolutely up-market, Caterham Cars took over the manufacturing rights and began building the then-current 'boxy' glass fibre-bodied Series IV Seven under their own name.

The Seven is said to be an easy car to work on, but with an overall height of just 3ft 1in, it could be bad for your back!

Buying A Lotus Seven

The Lotus Sevens were bodied in either aluminium or glass fibre, so no rust problems here, right? Wrong! All the Sevens, throughout the car's 26 year history, have been built around a tubular steel spaceframe and it is here that any rust will be concealed. Study the side rails closely, they trap water with the usual dire

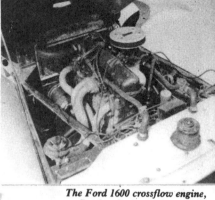

The Ford 1600 crossflow engine, as fitted to Series II, III and IV cars.

The Super Seven Sprint engine, fitted to current cars, develops 110 bhp in standard form.

Driver and passenger should be friends, or at least on shoulder-rubbing acquaintance.

Shortly after production began, Caterham Cars took a step back in the history of the car by reverting to the aluminium bodied, more rounded, Series III shape, a move which proved successful from a marketing point of view, and very, very advantageous for someone repairing a Series II or III Lotus as many of the Caterham components are suitable — nose cone and wings for instance.

If you are looking for a vehicle which is exhilarating to drive and equally at home on road or race track; if you do not mind noise, frostbite or fear, and if you are not looking for a dazzling array of instruments or somewhere to put luggage larger than a cigarette packet, then the Lotus/Caterham Seven might be worth considering.

If, on the other, you thought a sports car might be nice but you are torn between that and, say, a Morris Minor Convertible, forget it! The Seven is not for you.

What to look for

The very first thing to seek out is the chassis plate, under the bonnet. It doesn't mean that if it hasn't got one, it isn't a Lotus, but be warned, there were some 'copies'. Look for the prefix SB and four digits on cars made after 1960 (Series II on). Graham Nearn would add that many Sevens were raced and, when they became uncompetitive, were put on the road — hence no chassis plate. These cars are not necessarily bad, they just need to be carefully checked.

The Series IV not only looks different, the space-frame and suspension are different as well. The squared-off rear end of the Series IV is currently out of favour although the car sold well when new. These cars are often less expensive than other types.

consequences. Look for bubbling at the base of the side panel. The Series IV cars were prone to rot.

A particularly weak point on early cars was the rear axle casing, especially the Standard Triumph unit fitted on cars made between 1962 and 68. All the rear axles take a lot of punishment and this might result in a split developing in the diff. casing so look for a

The fearsome Lotus Holbay engine in the very rare Lotus Twin Cam SS. Only a dozen or so were made and Graham Nearn owns SS1, the motor show car.

messy unit which could be dripping oil. Caterham modify the casing by welding on a strengthening plate.

The Standard axle — from the 10/Pennant range — is not readily available but a car with a duff one can be treated to a brand new unit from a Morris Marina/Ital as fitted to current cars. Whatever the car is fitted with — any of the aforementioned or a Ford axle — the strengthening filet is a good idea. Caterham Cars will fit it for you or supply the part to weld yourself.

The suspension on Series II and III cars is similar to current; however, the Series IV

Production

Series I *October 1957 — June 1960.* 1172 c.c. 40 bhp (Ford); 948 c.c. 37 bhp (BMC); Super Seven: 1097 c.c. 75 bhp (Coventry Climax). About 242 built.

Series II *June 1960 — September 1968.* 1172 c.c. 40 bhp (Ford); 948 c.c. 37 bhp (BMC); 1098 c.c. 55 bhp (BMC); 997 c.c. 50 bhp (Ford); Super Seven: 1340 c.c. 85 bhp (Ford Cosworth); Super Seven 1500: 1498 c.c. 66 bhp (Ford); Super Seven 1500 Cosworth: 1498 c.c. 95 bhp (Ford Cosworth). About 1350 built.

Series III *September 1968 — April 1970.* 1298 c.c. 68 bhp (Ford); 1599 c.c. 84 bhp (Ford); Super Seven Twin Cam SS: 1558 c.c. 125 bhp (Lotus Holbay). About 350 built.

Series IV (Lotus) *April 1970 — March 1973.* As Series III but no Super Seven model. Lotus 115 bhp Twin Cam superceded by Big Valve. About 900 built.

Series IV (Caterham) *May 1973 — June 1974.* As Series IV but no Lotus 115 bhp Twin Cam. Only 50 built.

Series III (Caterham) *June 1974 —* 1599 c.c. 84 bhp (Ford); 1558 c.c. 125 bhp (Lotus Big Valve) 1599 c.c. 110 bhp (Ford); 1599 c.c. 130 bhp (Caterham Twin Cam). More than 1,000 built.

Information supplied by Caterham Cars.

The hood is not the most attractive feature oif these cars. The rear wing on this Series III Twin Cam SS is the same as the style fitted to the current car.

The dashboard of the Series IV car is more stylised than the other cars and the handbrake has been moved from above the passenger's lap to above the driver's knee.

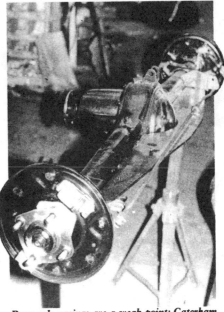

Rear axle casings are a weak point; Caterham Cars devised a strengthening plate which they fit as standard and which they can supply for your car.

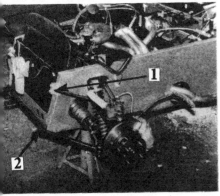

Check that the anti-roll bar bushes (arrowed 1) and the suspension bushes (arrowed 2) are sound.

Just about the only component which is not replaceable is the Series IV windscreen surround. If you have a damaged one, it can be repaired.

glass fibre car has a different set-up. Spares for all types are available. The only component which is totally unavailable is the Series IV windscreen surround. I was told that the manufacturers (not Lotus) threw away the moulds when production of the cars ceased.

On the road, the car should be well behaved and should drive properly. If the seller suggests 'The steering takes some getting used to' or 'They all bounce around like this' then beware, the car should drive as if it was on rails. Misbehaviour could be caused by worn dampers — a common fault and replacements cost £30 each — or by worn Metalastic bushes on the suspension wishbones which cost £21 per set. Check also that the antiroll bar mounting points are secure and that the bushes are good.

A spaceframe damaged in a shunt will certainly affect the handling. Make sure the car sits squarely on the road, and you might try lining up the spaceframe tubes by eye. The frames have something of a reputation for flexing, especially the Series II cars which had fewer tubes. If you have a car which was originally built with a standard 1500 Ford engine of 66 bhp but which has subsequently been given a twin cam of around 125 bhp then the frame certainly will flex.

The dozen or so Twin Cam SS cars built by Lotus had additional triangulation to stiffen the frame and the current Caterham cars have a frame which follows this pattern.

Some people are concerned that the Seven was a kit car and therefore may have been badly put together. The kit idea was devised to get around car tax. When VAT was introduced in 1973, this scheme became obsolete. Therefore, it is only the pre-'73 cars which were the real kit cars, and if they have lasted this long...

Current cars are delivered requiring some finishing but are in a far more complete state than before. This is to circumnavigate type approval laws and in these cases, it is largely a matter of making sure everything is bolted on securely. If there is going to be a problem, it

will be those antiroll bars.

Engines fitted depended on the Ford product of the day, although some early Series I and II cars boasted the 948 c.c. BMC unit of the Austin Healey Sprite. The Fords vary from the sublime sidevalve to the full-house Holbay. Engines spares are usually no problem.

What to pay

People who go to Caterham Car Sales usually know what they are looking for, having thought very hard about buying this sort of car. The most common price range is £3,000 to £3,500 for a Series II or III in fair condition, perhaps £500 less for a Series IV. "For £5,000" says Graham, "You are no longer in the restoration business."

Any Seven with an MOT will probably be offered at around £2,000 and even a really horrible car might fetch £1,750. Hopeful buyers able to stretch to £1,500 will probably not find a car other than the less popular Series IV. If you desperately need a Lotus

Buying A Lotus Seven Continued

Buying A Lotus Seven

Even with the sidescreens fitted, the wind blasts into your hair. Graham Nearn demonstrates the Caterham Seven to the editor.

Seven and if it must be cheap, then the glass fibre car must be worth a second look.

If you find such a car with a rotted out frame, and if it is at the right price, then a restoration is a good idea. The spaceframe is different to the other cars but Caterham can provide an off-the-shelf replacement for around £450 plus VAT. A new set of fibre glass (four wings and a nose cone) will set you back £113.

Prices are held up by the car's popularity and by its rarity. Lotus made about 3,000 Sevens and Caterham 1,000 more. They aren't the sort of cars which wear out and get thrown away, so where are they? Why are they so rare? The answer, says Graham, is that when the pound goes down, foreign dealers flock over here and the Seven is one of the cars they look for. Many of the Series II and III cars have disappeared overseas.

I havn't gone into the Series I cars in any detail. Recognisable by their close fitting cycle wings, they can be seen in photographs, but rarely anywhere else. The Climax engined examples are particularly rare and a nice example would top £5,000.

How Fast?

Performance from the Seven depends on the engine you choose (or can afford). The early Sevens powered by the ubiquitous 1,172 c.c. sidevalve Ford engine managed a top speed of just 81 mph and a 0-60 time of 17.8 sec. In 1963, however the tuned Ford 1500 was giving a maximum of 102 mph and 0-60 time of a staggering 7.7 sec. Fuel consumption suffered of course, dropping from around 35 to about 24 mpg. The standard 1600 crossflow produced not dissimilar figures. If you want something totally over the edge, try the 130 bhp Caterham Twin Cam — 114 mph and 0-60 in 6.2 sec!

Conclusions

The Seven was built as a fun car and its lack of interior finesse makes it a rather impractical classic. With a reasonably potent engine the car is very fast but you have to buy that performance and it does not come cheap. I couldn't live with it on an every-day basis but it would make a super summer weekend car.

The Clubs

Club Lotus is the largest club in Europe catering for Lotus enthusiasts, the secretary is Margaret Richards, PO Box 8, Dereham, Norfolk, NR19 1TF. **The Lotus Drivers Club** membership secretary can be contacted at 21 Beauchamp Avenue, Leamington Spa, Warwickshire. Owners of Climax-engined Lotus cars made between 1950 and 1960 can join the **Historic Lotus Register**. An SAE to V. Thomas, Badgerwood, School Road, Drayton, Norwich, will produce the details.

Seventh

wonder

"... a raw, spine-tingling mini-thriller; a real street racer ..." Kevin Blick drives Caterham's exhilarating Seven. Photographs by Tim Andrew

THEY'VE LENGTHENED the cockpit of the Caterham Seven now so that burly men of more than six foot can drive it. How they get in it in the first place is a different matter! This is the car with no doors: just big sidescreens that flap up and out; it's like entering a canvas Countach.

With the hood in its proper place – folded up behind the seats – it's not too tricky for the reasonably agile to clamber in and slide their legs down under the tiny steering wheel and into the long, low footwell. But make the mistake of having the hood up and getting in is as tortured a process as astronauts found entering those early, tiny space capsules – except there isn't usually a back-up crew around to help.

That sets the tone of the Caterham Seven: it's a tiny, tight-fitting machine, getting in to it is as close to the sensation of sliding down into a race car that any road car can give, and it's a thoroughly uncompromising beast that won't be adapted to suit you – *you* have to come to terms with it.

Learning to live with it is learning to love it, though. It's a raw, spine-tingling mini-thriller; a real street-racer that gives a driver the chance to peek into the exclusive, sensation-packed world of the biker.

What less should one expect

from the car that set Colin Chapman on the road to greatness and which, since Lotus moved on to bigger things, has been caringly built and sold by Caterham Cars?

After a period selling the plastic bodied Series IV Seven, Graham Nearn's company has long since gone back to the classic Series III shape, with its body of simple alloy panelling over a tubular chassis.

For the power-crazed the only viable engine option for their Seven will be the 130 horsepower Vegantune twin cam – a unit commissioned by Caterham as supplies of the original Lotus-Ford twin cam dried up. A more practical alternative, however, is the Sprint engine fitted to our test car which, while offering virtually as much performance as the twin cam, is more tractable and easier to service.

Based on the pushrod Ford 1600GT engine, which boasts a tubular exhaust system as standard, it is stripped and balanced and fitted with an uprated camshaft and a different inlet manifold. Breathing through a pair of big Weber 40DCOE twin-choke carburetters it produces a hefty 110 horsepower, and with the Seven's weight of just over 11cwt, the results are dramatic.

Slide down into the Seven, and the sensation of being in a racer is vivid even before you start to explore that power-to-

weight ratio's potential. You sit low, low down; arms and legs straight out, hands clasping the tiny wheel. Get the choice of cockpit size right when you order one – the seat doesn't move. The long cockpit model is just a bit too long for anyone marginally on the wrong side of six feet.

The simple seat hardly needs to grip you – the narrowness of the cockpit does that job, holding the driver's hips tightly between centre tunnel and body side. Your left arm lies naturally along the top of the tunnel, hand and forearm moving the few inches between wheel and stumpy gearshift. Seat belts are of the static type; pulled tight they're another help to holding you firmly in the seat, but they do take an age of fiddling to adjust between different drivers.

Look around the cockpit –

that's the word for it; it's certainly not a compartment or even a cabin – and it's either functional or crude depending on your point of view.

Certainly, it is mininal; there are no frills – not a door pocket nor a parcel shelf in sight (but who needs those in a racer?). The flat aluminium dash panel just has a simple row of Smiths dials and vintage BL-type tumbler switches. Indicators work via a two-way flip switch – no self cancelling. This is a racer's dash that concentrates on the important information and gives it simply.

Move out into traffic and you feel the vulnerability of a biker or a racer: Transits tower over you; you view tankers at hub level – and smell them, too. The pedals are heavy at first but locate the heel bar across the floor and you can improve leverage to make them much more manageable. The big, sucking Webers give the engine a distinctive huffy note but despite its state of tune it never misses a beat.

Open it up and the huffing intake roar smartly changes to a blat of exhaust howl. Stab the throttle open and the revs soar instantly in this really joyfully responsive engine as it howls round to 7,000rpm. Understandably, there's not a lot of bottom end bite but from mid-range and on it's a little rocket ship.

The short, sharp gearshift is fast enough to keep the engine in full cry and the close ratios of the Escort Sport 'box make sure the Sprint is always running hard.

Seventh wonder

After all, lightning response and acceleration are what this car is all about: it can snap to 60mph from a standstill in 6.5 seconds; respond from 50-70mph in a handful of seconds, too. There won't be many traffic light grand prix or overtaking chances that the Seven misses out on.

Beyond 80 or 90mph things to start slow down a bit; those big vibrating front wings visibly start to lift as air turbulence builds under them, dragging the car's acceleration down. It'll top 100 but needs a very long straight to extract the last few mph to its maximum.

No, this is not a car for constant high-speed motoring. Things all get just a bit too frantic. Better to ease back a little and relish the acceleration when you need it: a quick heel-and-toe on the perfectly aligned pedals, a flick of hand and wrist, and the Seven's down a gear and charging.

Enjoy it best on smooth, fast country roads where its performance and handling blend into perfect harmony. Then comes that race-car or superbike sensation, not just a simple thrill at the speed, but a concentrated pleasure of having engine, chassis, body, eye all co-ordinated and working as one.

Find that sort of curving, open road where you can enjoy the Seven through a long sequence of corners and it becomes a physically easy as well as a fun car to handle; so easy, accurate and instant are its reflexes. Taut, high geared steering means that all you need do is drop an arm, bend a wrist and be angling the car through a curve: almost as if on a 'bike, you seem to just ease your body over, drop a shoulder and the Seven is steering exactly on the line you chose, aiming out past those crocodilian headlight bulges. And with so much cornering power, too. Despite the Seven's lavish power to weight balance, Chapman's suspension genius made it grip as well as handle with the finesse of a racer.

The Seven's wheelbase is almost as long as the car; the track as wide as it could reasonably be. The result is a car which corners with virtually no body roll at all on its double wishbone front suspension and rigidly located rear axle, and which grips to neck-straining levels without the need for latest generation ultra-low profile tyres.

In fact on the standard Goodyear Grand Prix 'S' 185/70 HR 13 rubberwear the balance is beautifully precise; the Seven will signal the end of its cornering power by a gentle and building understeer. Occasionally you can feel the back end go out of line, and catch it on the rapid steering almost before it's started to move out.

The four-links and Panhard rod hold the axle tightly in line and traction is magical: power it hard out of tight bends and it will squirt down the road with just a protesting wiggle of the tail, the axle occasionally hopping on a bump.

The tail naturally slides around a lot more in wet weather and the throttle needs treating with care but, like a bike again, the wary ear will catch the warning note of revs starting to rise as grip is lost and the quick-witted will be reacting even as things are starting to happen at the rear end. Life isn't so happy on rougher roads, however. Down narrow country lanes you always have a real worry about not being seen, the car is so low, and poor surfaces jar and jolt the suspension so much it can even start to blur the vision after a few miles of endurance.

The thin, flat vinyl seat doesn't absorb much of the pain and the joggling harshness is definitely something to be avoided after a good lunch! Prolonged exposure to the noise and harsh ride can make the Seven very tiring, even though when the sidescreens are in place there is actually little buffeting from the wind. It just catches the face, head and – for some reason – the hands get very cold, too.

The Seven does have a heater, operated by a simple fan switch, so you can either be toasting or cold. It has a hood, too, of course, though that is the sort of crude affair best reserved for emergency use only (but you will be well soaked in a rainstorm by the time it is up!). Sports cars like the Seven aren't much fun in the rain with the hood up, water dripping in and the plastic windows steaming up. Better to keep the hood in the garage and get wet.

Caterham sell the Seven in the UK as a kit to step around the Type Approval regulations by including "an element of self assembly" in the car. That element comprises chiefly the minor bits and pieces to finish off the car as delivered, which has engine, transmission, body panels, suspension and wiring all in place. The competent home spanner man can add the rest in two or three days.

Bearing that in mind, and the list of near essentials which are extras to the basic price, the Seven is far from cheap. In fact its final price is up into XR3 and GTi country.

But for sheer uncompromised, unadulterated fun, that has to be a price worth paying.

Lean, graceful lines make the Seven look as good now as when it first appeared. Those pretty front wings act as an effective air brake at speed, though. The interior is stark and functional – a real street racer

PERFORMANCE

Tests carried out at the Motor Industry Research Association proving ground, Lindley.

Maximum speed	110 mph*
Acceleration through gears:	
0-30mph	2.3sec
0-40	3.4
0-50	4.7
0-60	6.5
0-70	8.3
0-80	11.0
0-90	14.8
0-100	22.9
Acceleration in fourth:	
20-40mph	6.1sec
30-50	6.9
40-60	7.7
50-70	6.7
60-80	6.5
70-90	7.8
80-100	11.0

ECONOMY

Overall consumption	26.5mpg
Test distance	530 miles
Tank capacity	7.9 gallons
Range	200-230 miles

WEIGHT

Unloaded (with fuel for 50 miles)
11.7cwt

Maximum speed run was carried out in windy conditions. On one straight, we timed the car at 114.1mph, on another the speed dropped to only 101mph. Caterham Cars claim only 105mph, which we believe to be very conservative.

A STREET-FIGHTER RACER
A look back at the Lotus Seven

BY ALLAN GIRDLER

Colin Chapman with the Series I.

This is what you got when you bought the car in a box, in this case an A Seven Series I with flathead Ford. The parts look more challenging than they were, as the really tricky stuff like wiring was already in place.

S O POWERFUL WAS the lure of the Lotus Seven for some of us, well, me at any rate, that I wanted one, longed for one, sketched example after example through endless hours of study hall, before I even knew there was such a thing.

Emphasize that. Checking the history books shows that I wanted a Lotus Seven even before Colin Chapman first decided to make such a thing.

This goes way back, to when I was a car-struck pre-teener and my indulgent dad took me to the New York Auto Show. Big stuff in those days and as a prototype car nut I grabbed up a plastic sack and filled it with all the literature I could carry. I ogled the Jaguars, the Ferraris, Siatas, MGs, show specials and . . . there it was. A polished aluminum tube, two seats, cycle fenders, just what I'd seen in those jumbled car magazines that flickered in and out of life back then. It was the perfect car, the thinly disguised racing car that I had instantly known was right as soon as the magazines told me about it.

That particular car, name withheld, never saw the light of production. Never heard of again, but for the next several years, through driver's license, a series of old Fords quickly and clumsily turned into hot rods, college and an MG TC, I had that image, that concept, in my heart.

Cut to 1959. I had driven my TC down the turnpike to the state capital and the state fairgrounds for the sports car races. Not much by modern standards but the best we had then. The local MGs and Triumphs and a few exotic Maseratis, Allards, Ferraris, home-builts and the like thundered around a landing strip and some choppy connecting roads. I sat there in the stands thinking it was all very grand and wishing I hadn't a) been

caught falsifying my age on my racing license and b) run out of money when I finally got old enough.

There it was.

Around the turn skidded a smallish car, not at all like any other car on the track. Tiny, shaped like a flattened torpedo inspired by alloy cigar box, one wheel at each corner, no doors, outside exhaust; it was the absolute realization of all those drawings and dreams.

I rushed to the paddock, bluffed my way through and found the car and its owner. I was the first person save for himself to feel this way about his car and he was happy to give me all the specs and details.

The car was, as you've surely guessed, a Lotus Seven. A Mk 1 Seven of the F variation, all of which we'll deal with in a moment.

A STREET-FIGHTER RACER

First, how the car came to be.

Two factors, no, make that three. First, throughout racing history there has persisted the idea that what we need is a formula for everyman. Budget racing, a way to equalize the cars and keep costs down and let the average enthusiast have a go on equal terms with the well-to-do or more seriously committed. We've had showroom stock, Formula Ford, Formula Vee, Formula 3 and no, now that you've brought that up, none of the formulas have done what it was hoped they'd do, but never mind that. In England, in the Fifties, this myth embodied itself as clubman racing. These cars were powered by production engines, of limited power because all English engines were creampuffs in those days. They had to have two seats and road gear and that was about it. The idea was that anybody could build one and go racing and drive home.

Second factor was the English tax system. Social engineering. There was a stiff tax on cars. Few people could afford a new car so it followed that the socialist government hit those few hard. But parts were different. Any hardworking son of the proletariat who bought parts and built a car got a nice tax break. Better, the laws were vague or loose on what were parts and what was assembly and there came into being a market for kit cars. You bought one of every part needed, all in one large box. The haulage chaps delivered the box to your driveway and you followed the instructions and bolted everything together and had your very own new car. Less tax.

Third, Colin Chapman. A self-made man who did a good job, Chapman began as a home constructor of specials and trials cars and, yes, clubman cars. The Lotus Mks 1 through 6 were torpedo-bodied, cycle-fendered. The Mk 8 was Lotus' first streamlined body, in 1954, followed by the 9, the 10, the immortal Lotus 11 and the space-frame Formula 2 Mk 12, the fiberglass-chassis Elite . . . ahead of their times and Lotus was on its way to world championships and luxury cars and all that.

But Chapman had a soft spot in his heart, just one, and it was for the sketchy sports car, the 2-seater minus doors, the car in which would-be racers of the type he used to be could have a go.

In 1957, filling the break in the model numbers, appeared the Lotus Seven.

If Chapman didn't invent the phrase Thinly Disguised Racing Car, he surely did meet the definition. The Seven was a space frame, of small round and square tubes, with the floor and driveshaft tunnel and side panels of aluminum sheet riveted to the tubes, making a stressed skin. The front suspension was right off the Formula 2 car. The whole package was barely wide enough for two people, a light press fit, in fact. There was maybe 5 in. of ground clearance and the top of the body proper was about 27 in. off the ground.

For cost reasons the rear axle was live, from a Triumph delivery van, located at the top by trailing arms and at the bottom by a wide-based A-frame, bolted to a bracket welded to the bottom of the differential housing. Worked better than it sounds.

Power at first was the venerable Ford 100E, a flathead four of nearly 1000-cc displacement. Front fenders were cycle, the rears looked more like spare tire covers and the radiator cowling/front grille was a shaped alloy hood. The complete car looked like a madman hot rodder had got hold of an old MG. I happen to think the Lotus Seven looks great, although there have been people who burst into laughter on first sight.

The Seven was a tiny car, with 88-in. wheelbase and a wet weight of 900 lb or so. The exhaust came out of a hole in the body aft of the front wheels and then to a muffler bolted to the lowest frame tube, with exit at the passenger's (assuming right-hand drive) elbow. Loud. If you can call two struts and a piece of canvas a top, the Seven had a top. The headlights were on stalks. The spare tire was strapped to the rear of the body, and to fill the fuel tank you unsnapped the top of the tonneau cover and stuck the nozzle into the filler neck just behind the seat, which was a padded piece of board and two cushions that plopped onto the bare floor. The shop manual had diagrams in case you were sissy enough to want to install a heater.

Were there many people out there who wanted a thinly disguised racing car?

No. It took two years for the first Seven to reach the central U.S. and a year or two after that for the magazines to discover there was such a thing. Lotus dealers, a brave handful, had all they could do to cope with the racing cars, the Lotus-Cortina, the Elite and then the Elan and so forth, and I heard of only two Lotus stores ever that actually took an interest. (One now sells Volvos and the other distributes motorcycle parts and if there's a lesson there I don't want to hear it.)

For the semi-historical record, there are more Seven details than can be dealt with here. The Ford-powered Seven was supplemented by versions with 1100-cc Coventry Climaxes, and by the BMC "A" series engine, which meant there was the 7F, the 7C and 7A. Later still there was a 1500 Coventry Climax option and that was the Super Seven, which should be the S7S1 because the second Super Seven was different altogether.

Demand was brisk at home, though, and in 1960 there came the Seven Series Two, with BMC A power or the new 105E Ford, the one that became the basis for the Lotus twincam engine and the Cosworth-Ford GP V-8. The second series had the engine moved farther forward, less oversteer at speed, and the alloy fenders and radiator shell became fiberglass. Easier to fix and to make. The body proper and its panels now had no compound curves.

Before I forget, just because I carry these obscure facts around and don't get to use them often, in the U.S. the SCCA required doors on production sports cars, so along with the side curtains and top, you could get two small flaps that snapped to the sides of the car. And cycle fenders were outlawed so Colin and clever crew whipped out some clamshell style fronts, of fiberglass. Sevens with them were known as the Seven America; that is, a Lotus 7A is not necessarily a Seven America. To further obscure the details, the clamshell fenders worked so well they were simply adapted for the home market too, so not all Seven Americas came to the States.

The fender thing illustrates what actually was the soul of the car and its owners. For reasons never made public, the SCCA or perhaps the people who were in charge at the time didn't like the Seven. They liked the Super Seven even less.

The second Super Seven appeared when Chapman and Cosworth did a deal for souped-up 1500-cc Ford engines. They came with hot cam, flowed head and two Weber carburetors and the car dealt with the extra speed by getting real magnesium wheels and the disc front brakes from the Triumph Spitfire (The suspension bits already were Triumph, see, so it was an easy swap.)

This happened just about the time the SCCA was changing from displacement classes to performance classes and the rules allowed optional equipment. It was a great opportunity and instantly every factory with a model in the listing for production cars discovered gear sets, cylinder heads, big carbs, oil coolers, all manner of stuff never seen on the showroom floor.

This was okay. What wasn't okay was the Super Seven, which really did come with all the good parts, stock. The SCCA declared the car contrary to the "spirit" (read, they met the letter)

A STREET-FIGHTER RACER

of the regulations. Chapman had to offer detuned engines, the 1340-cc 109E with twin carbs or the 1500 with one Weber on a manifold devised for the occasion.

Why the SCCA really did it, I believe, was because the Super Seven was embarrassingly fast. On a tight course the Lotus could whip all the other production cars, not just in class. The rules called for big fast cars, AP; slower big cars, BP; quick small cars, CP, and there was the Super Seven, classified CP and often beating the A and B cars. Small comfort that the car was a tiny barn door and had a top speed of 110 on the best of calm days.

Back then there was a market for genuine, open production sports cars and the SCCA liked it when major brands won titles. Said brands advertised heavily and I think it no coincidence that each big factory had a car in a class that it could win.

The irony, other than having the factories using their clout to win amateur events, I mean, was that no other sports car more closely matched the ideal of the sporting driver, the drive-it, race-it, drive-home crowd.

The SCCA missed this because they didn't believe it. Here was this fragile projectile. No bumpers, fenders so thin a small girl could break one if she leaned on it—my neighbor's daughter, age 5, did just that—a ride like a hay wagon, noise enough to make your ears ring. No heater, no defroster, never mind a radio. No trunk. No luggage space, no fuel gauge, no insulation. You had to always carry a quarter, because checking the oil level meant you removed the hood, putting it in a safe place because it was aluminum, then used the coin to spin the ol' Dzus fasteners and pulled off the radiator cowling, *then* asked for a rag so you could examine the dipstick. Honest. When they moved the engine forward for the Series 2, they forgot where the dipstick was.

Inclement weather brought out the top; two struts and some canvas. Remember the Porsche Speedster? The Seven with top in place made the Speedster look like an observation tower. Already you were lower than a truck's axle. With top, you couldn't even look up, much less out or back. The side curtains hinged on little posts on the windshield, then were kept in place, loosely, with snaps and straps. Leaping into a Seven in normal trim, that is, top down, allowed one a certain flair. With top up, climbing in meant you thrust left leg into aperture, two feet wide and one high, then hopped on right foot until you could grasp the steering wheel and duck your head into the cockpit. Swivel the backside, let go the wheel and you fell, literally, into place. Then all you had to do was lean left and drag your right foot inside, up and then down the slot between wheel rim and body. Like getting into a golf bag, I wrote once.

Not a car for normal people. One day I gave a ride home to the wife of a friend. A fairly nice day, too, and I even let her wear my jacket. Further, her husband was a car nut and she was acquainted with odd machines.

"Very interesting," she said as she clambered over the side at ride's end. "I used to think I wanted one of these."

Considering the above, even I can see why the SCCA didn't believe anybody actually bought a Lotus Seven to drive around, and by extension why the Super Seven was considered too much for production status.

But it wasn't. Instead, the Seven, no matter which engine, was the last refuge for people who didn't want to trailer to the races, weren't interested in getting sponsorship, preferred the challenge of building a car nobody else believed in, and sometimes all of the above.

There was one man in Oklahoma, who got his Seven a couple of days before there was a hillclimb . . . in Pennsylvania. What fun, he thought, so he drove the 1000 miles, ran in the hillclimb and took 1st in class or 2nd overall or something impressive like that, then drove home. The gearbox lost 2nd or 3rd, I forget which, but it didn't bother him much. We were in it for the challenge.

We were also loosely wrapped. Relics of an earlier time. The first sports cars were all like the Seven: spartan, stark, stiff, demanding and appealing only to those who liked to drive all the time. As the market grew, it widened and the cars became more normal, as it were, to suit the people who enjoyed driving—but not that much. And the production rules were relaxed, to allow what amounted to full race engines and suspension and modified bodywork, all of which made it more and more difficult to drive what you raced. The MGs, Porsches, Corvettes, etc, became either road or track, while the Seven, which as we've seen arrived from the factory already as modified as it could be, still was legally equipped for double duty.

Oh. Nearly forgot to shatter a legend. Recall that in England the tax laws created the kit car, the big box with all the parts.

Part of the outsider's view of the Seven was that they came like that here. Mostly, they didn't. The import duty on parts was higher than the duty on cars, oddly enough, so the money that could be saved by not bolting the parts together at the plant was lost at the customs shed. Some dealers did bring the cars in unassembled, but not many.

(There also was a small business in the boxes. Yes. You could buy the box, prop it in the corner of your garage and then tell your gullible neighbors that you'd built the car yourself. Although to be fair, while I did see an ad for the boxes, I never actually met anybody who'd bought one.)

Back to factual history. We drove Sevens and raced them. Several of the more talented owners won national championships. The rest of us battled the factory teams and had a good time doing so.

The Safety Act of 1966, the federal laws that required all cars to prove their innocence or be found guilty, took effect in 1968. Cars built after January 1 of that year had to be certified or they couldn't be imported.

Coincident with that, Lotus introduced the Series 3 Seven. There were marked improvements, like you could get the Twincam 1600 engine and the spindly Triumph differential was replaced by a sturdier unit from the Ford Escort, and the top even had rear side windows. The exhaust had a pipe leading to the rear, instead of your offside ear, and the filler cap was accessible from the outside. Remarkable.

Also illegal. The cars were built on a schedule of one or two per week, which meant the economics were impossible. The Series 3s were not certified for U.S. sale. Determined people did bring them in, but this is not the place to tell you how. One such man offered his Twincam Series 3 for test, we tested it, and the feds came down on him hard. How were we to know they read the magazines?

The magazines. The Seven always got a good press. Sometimes the facts were muffed some, but that was because usually the test car was borrowed from a private owner, there being no need for the importer to bother with the press, and the owners didn't always know what they had. And there were some odd parts. The first test I ever read had a Series 2 fitted out with the wheels from the Spitfire, genuine wire wheels. Looked nice.

CONTINUED ON PAGE 137

From my racing album, Warbonnet Raceway, Oklahoma. As you can tell from the expressions, I had been blocking #17 and he's just got past. My knuckles, could you but see them, are white on the wheel.

PHOTO FROM AUTHOR'S COLLECTION

SEVENTH
HEAVEN

**The Colin Chapman-designed Lotus 7
is alive and well in Caterham — the Super
Sprint has blistering performance**

ANDREW YEADON

Detail chassis work and a more highly tuned version of the Ford Kent-series crossflow block are the major modifications to Caterham Cars' most recent version of the Colin Chapman-designed Lotus 7.

On the outside there is little difference between this and the road test car of 1961. The wheel arches have grown in size to accommodate the wider rim and tyre combinations needed to harness the copious amounts of power, which has steadily increased over the years. In its latest 135bhp (at 6000rpm) form, the 1700cc Super Sprint has a creditable power to weight ratio of around 225bhp/ton — compared to the original car's 89bhp/ton when tested back in 1957 with Ford 100E side-valve power.

There is only a handful of supercars that can match the blistering acceleration the Super Seven provided. A 0-60mph time below 6secs is in Porsche territory, yet this little projectile — costing less than a third of the price of a new 911 Carrera — is capable of such a time, and it carries on impressing, until aerodynamics take over.

Caterham developed this special version of the ubiquitous Kent engine following delivery problems with the Vegantune VTA twin-cam unit, which it has now dropped as an engine option. Instead, Caterham has assembled a simpler, yet no less effective, conversion of the twin cam and an engine that produces only 15bhp less than the Ford BDR engine. This is still an option but at around £2000 more.

Caterham has achieved the high power output by using tried and tested tuning methods. First the block is bored out to 1691cc, a high lift but short duration cam is installed, the flat top head gets its ports fully flowed, heavy duty valves and springs are fitted, along with the customary twin 40DCOE Weber set-up equipped with 32mm chokes.

Though not an obvious modification, internal dimensions ▶

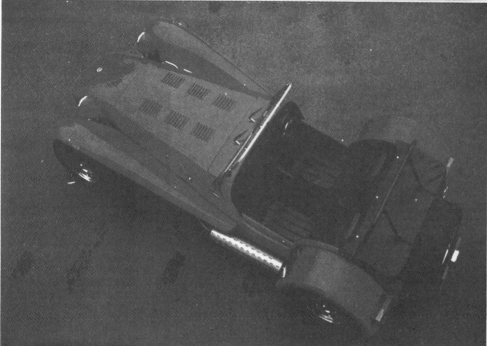

◀ of the car have been increased to produce this 'long cockpit' version. This is achieved by relocating the chassis cross-members under the seats, together with the bulkhead, further towards the rear of the car. The 2.25in increase is made primarily to improve the stiffness of the chassis which is now 35 per cent improved in torsional stiffness, and 50 per cent better in beam stiffness, according to Caterham. The useful spin-off of increased interior space now means that taller drivers are more easily accommodated.

PERFORMANCE

One hundred and thirty-five isn't a spectacular number of horsepower (even if it's not bad for a 1691cc pushrod all-iron engine), but stick that lot in a car weighing only a little over half-a-ton at the kerb, and you have spectacular acceleration. Certainly, making this masterpiece of lightweight motor car carry the tiresomely necessary weight of a driver, 50lb of test gear plus — even in these days of automatic acceleration and speed recording — our traditional test observer, adds an extra 414lb, but the laden power-to-weight ratio is still a rousing 188bhp per ton.

The water temperature gauge is showing midway between its open road running 90deg C and the 100-odd deg it reaches in traffic. The engine is ticking over rather fast but evenly, at 1100 rpm. You extend your left foot to open the clutch — it needs a

TECHNICAL FOCUS

It is perhaps hard to believe that the Lotus Seven dates back to 1957. It was first offered with the Ford side-valve 1172cc engine which gave acceleration to 60mph in 17.8secs and a mean top speed of 76mph. There was a Coventry Climax engine option for the more performance-minded.

Lotus continually slotted in current Ford power units as they became available, working through the 997cc overhead valve units to the more potent 1340cc and 1500cc versions. The 1340cc option gave commendably good performance; 0-60mph in 7.6secs and a mean top speed of 103mph when tested in 1961. The Kent 1599cc unit was to follow and has remained in production since.

When Lotus talked about dropping the Seven in 1967, one of its agents with whom it had built close ties, Caterham Cars of Surrey, stepped in. It had been selling the little two seaters since 1959 and finalised a deal for sole production rights. Caterham bought everything that remained from Lotus: jigs, body moulds, chassis and spares, then set about re-manufacturing the Series 3 model, as this was the one most loved by enthusiasts. It carried on with the Ford Kent engine, but also decided

to offer the Lotus twin cam version with 126bhp on tap, to give the car a new lease of life. Acceleration from 0-60mph dropped to 6.2secs and top speed went up to 114mph.

More recent changes have resulted in Caterham offering the Kent unit in various stages of tune right through from 85bhp of the standard GT engine to 110bhp for the Sprint, 135bhp for the Super Sprint and 150bhp for the Cosworth-designed BDR engine with its twin cam, four-valve head arrangement for the Kent block.

Under the skin, the car has changed very little in terms of layout and still retains the independent wishbone/coil over shock absorbers front suspension, and live rear axle arrangement, though there have been changes in springrates which were increased in 1982/3 from 55lb/sq in to 75lb/sq in to help prevent pitching.

A change in front brake pad material was also made at this time to help give more even braking without excessive front wheel locking, while more recent changes have resulted in a more efficient lightweight radiator being installed, along with Caterham's own design of steering rack, rather than the previous Spitfire unit.

heavy-ish 46lb shove and, like the gearchange, steering, brakes and suspension, it has little travel. It is a relief to work as there's no easily-found place to rest your clutch foot. You nudge the stub

of a gearlever under its plain ball knob into first, rev the engine to about 3800 rpm, then let go.

With that sort of restraint, the wheelspin is kept down to a minimum, which gives the best

starts. Our Leitz-Datron Correvit opto-electronic test gear records every decimal speed, and helps one analyse starts as well. On one particularly effective run, the Super Sprint reached 10mph from rest in 0.33sec, 20mph in 1.34sec and 30mph in 1.97sec; the corresponding mean times of best runs in each direction were not far behind — 0.50, 1.41 and 2secs respectively. The engine's spread of power is surprisingly good, considering its rorty character, and one can certainly let it get on with the job unaided by wheel or clutch slip from comparatively low rpm.

And, get on with it, it does — and how. Slash the lever back into second at 6500rpm and 36mph — first is quite a high ratio — revs dropping to 3900rpm, and that just takes you to 60mph in 5.6secs before the not-so-easy cross-gate shift into third, begun at 4600rpm. Seventy is passed in 8.2secs, 80 in 10, and the final easy change into top at 85mph drops the revs to the same 4600. Ninety is still stunningly quickly done, at 13.9secs and 100 in 19.9secs.

All of which is accompanied by the tremendous bark of the intakes and exhaust, dominating everything else, so that you always seem to be going very fast. In fact, as the clock shows, the built-in headwinds of the Super Sprint's spreading wings, separate headlamps, near open wheels, naked suspension, and uncompromisingly bluff profile have started to overcome that power from 90mph onward. There are 3.9secs between 80 and 90, nearly twice as long — 6secs — between 90 and 100, and another doubling — 13.6secs — for the 100-110 interval.

The Caterham's time with us coincided with the recent bout of unsettled weather, and we had to settle for a dry but quite windy day — 7-14mph. It was nearer the upper end of that bracket for the maximum speed laps, so that the fact that the car slightly exceeded its maker's claimed top whack by doing 111mph mean is impressive, with a best speed of 116mph.

One further performance detail underlines just how anti-aerodynamic this acceleration machine is. We always test convertibles with their hoods up, since the discontinuity of the upper works of an open car is considerably eased with the hood

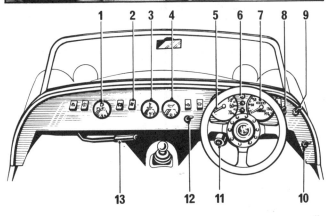

1 Fuel contents gauge, 2 Ancillary switchgear, 3 Water temperature gauge, 4 Oil pressure, 5 Tachometer, 6 Warning lights, 7 Speedometer, 8 Headlight switch, 9 Horn, 10 Headlight flasher, 11 Ignition switch, 12 Indicator switch, 13 Handbrake.

From top: The 7 has been developed continually since 1957 when it was launched. The 1700 is the most up-to-date engine but other, less powerful, versions are still available. Although the seats are now adjustable, anyone over 6ft 2ins will have a problem finding a comfortable driving position. Footwell space is also cramped for large feet. Instruments are large and well laid out, in character with the car, but switches can be confusing in the dark

if raucously frantic all the way to 6500rpm and beyond), we were pleasantly surprised how, with a little care, one could pull away from below tickover speed — an academic exercise in this sort of car, but remarkable all the same. This makes it easy to amble relatively unobtrusively through towns and villages, or past persons in blue uniforms.

ECONOMY

The Super Sprint is not your economy ideal, in spite of its lightness and generous power to weight ratio. Perhaps something appreciably better than our overall 23.5mpg could be obtained with gentle driving — we did see 28.1mpg on one long run, but anything much above this would mean total misuse of the car.

The eight-gallon tank provides one of the few really unacceptable aspects of the car in its appallingly restricted filler which, because of the unhappily flattening flexible pipe which turns the horizontal entry pipe down into the tank, will not under any circumstances take anything more than about one third of full flow delivery. The makers are aware of the problem and plan to correct it.

REFINEMENT

What refinement? To be frank, the Super Sprint has none. Engine noise dominates of course and, while it is fun in small doses, one cannot help wishing for rather more exhaust muffling on long trips; ear plugs are a good idea. At low speed, up to 40mph, you hear some back axle whine, particularly when the hood is up. The back of the test car's bonnet rattled when trying to lift against slackly set fastenings. Wind noise open or closed is prodigious.

With the hood down and sidescreens off — generally the only way to run the car, as vision is so very much better — the buffeting above 80mph is considerable. It is, of course, a four-wheeled motorcycle, and you dress accordingly.

ROAD BEHAVIOUR

What one cannot help thinking of as a *Lotus* Seven should be provided to car testers as part of standard equipment, as a reference, a reminder after months of testing other cars, of what good steering really is.

To be fair to Caterham which, by taking over Seven production after Lotus gave it up, saved the car for a later generation, the undeniable amount of good development work done should be recognised by always using the correct name today. This applies as much as anywhere else when talking about the Super Sprint's steering which, like all current Caterham Sevens, has a special rack developed by Caterham, making it higher geared. The lock is still a little wide for such a short wheelbase (88ins), at 33ft 5ins left and 37ft 10ins right, but 2.3 turns of that tiny thick-rimmed 11½ins diameter steering wheel is magically right for the car.

It is of course light, yet never twitchy or uneasy in spite of having marvellous response; this is *so* refreshing after the number of examples of wandery, overresponsive front-drive steering we have encountered lately. It is superbly accurate, allied to ideally relaxing dead-stick straight stability on smooth roads, which is only slightly deflected on bumpy ones — just enough to add to the already excellent feel of exactly what the front wheels are doing.

Another benefit of the drive layout is what is effectively when laden a perfectly balanced weight distribution. This is a major extra reason for the car's nimbleness. You don't steer it consciously — it's nearer a good motorbike than a car in the way you hardly move the wheel through a fast set of S-bends.

Power is there, of course, to blend with the steering in the right ways. Power in a bend initially tends to neutralise the small amount of natural understeer present, but with a pleasurable excess, especially at lower speeds and gears, the tail can be steered out with the right foot ▶

erected. You can prove this on nearly all convertibles by measuring the maximum speed with and without the top (and sidescreens); the difference for most is around 5 per cent — that is, slower when open.

On the Super Sprint, with hood and sidescreens removed, the mean and best speeds each dropped by only 1 mph, which rather confirms what one suspects, that most of the drag is generated in the front and that the airflow aft of the screen is too disturbed thereafter to notice the benefit of the hood as much as it does in other convertibles.

The engine starts easily if a little noisily with three or four prods of the throttle pedal, to provoke the accelerator pumps of the Webers. In gentle running, what Caterham Car Sales says is mildly weak carburettor jetting, provokes an occasional spit back in the half-outside air cleaners, and there is some overrun popping when hot. Considering how, when accelerated in anger from a low speed, the power does not start to come in until 3000rpm, and not truly strongly until 4000rpm (whereafter it is evenly

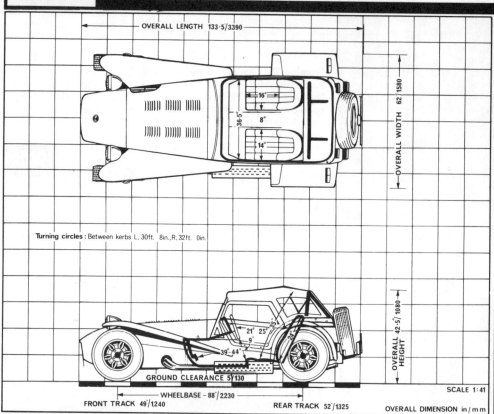

OVERALL LENGTH 133·5/3390

OVERALL WIDTH 62″/1580

36·5″ · 16″ · 8″ · 14″

Turning circles : Between kerbs L, 30ft. 8in., R, 32ft. 0in.

21° 25° · 9° · 39°-44° · OVERALL HEIGHT 42·5″/1080

GROUND CLEARANCE 5″/130

WHEELBASE – 88″/2230 · SCALE 1:41

FRONT TRACK 49″/1240 · REAR TRACK 52″/1325 · OVERALL DIMENSION in/mm

COSTS

Prices
Basic	£6180.00
Special Car Tax	£517.00
VAT	£927.00
Total (in GB)	**£7624.00**
Licence	£100.00
Delivery charge (London)	£35.00
Number plates	£10.00
Total on the Road	**£7769.00**
(excluding insurance)	
Insurance group	6

EXTRAS (inc VAT)
*Electronic ignition	£49.22
*185/70R 13in tyres	£132.25
*Seat belts	£33.10
*Individual adjustable seats	£145.00
*Leather upholstery	£60.00
*Alloy wheels	£115.00
*Halogen headlights	£28.06
*Locking fuel cap	£8.70
*Passenger door mirror	£7.48
*Rollover bar	£37.37
*Fitted to test car	
Total as tested	
on the road	**£8385·18**

SERVICE & PARTS

Interval
Change	3000	6000	12000
Engine oil	Yes	Yes	Yes
Oil filter	No	Yes	Yes
Gearbox oil	No	No	No
Spark plugs	No	No	Yes
Air cleaner	No	No	Yes
Total cost	£51.15	£96.38	£146.78

(Assuming labour at £14.35 an hour inc VAT)

PARTS COST (inc VAT)
Brake pads (2 wheels) front	£11.03
Brake shoes (2 wheels) rear	£10.74
Exhaust complete	£78.49
Tyre—each (typical)	£74.75
Windscreen	£32.00
Headlamp unit	£5.08
Front wing	£29.83

EQUIPMENT
Ammeter/Voltmeter	N/A
Automatic	N/A
Cruise control	N/A
Economy gauge	N/A
Five speed	N/A
Limited slip differential	£333.50
Power steering	N/A
Rev counter	●
Steering wheel rake adjust	To order
Steering wheel reach adjust	To order
Headrests front/rear	N/A
Heated seats	N/A
Height adjustment	To order
Lumbar adjustment	N/A
Seat back recline	N/A
Seat cushion tilt	N/A
Seat tilt	N/A
Door mirror remote control	N/A
Heated rear window	N/A
Interior adjustable headlamps	N/A
Tinted glass	N/A
Headlamp w/w	N/A
Low profile tyres (185 60HR14)	£299.00
Cigar lighter	N/A
Clock	N/A
Fog lamps	N/A
Internal boot release	N/A
Luggage cover	●
Metallic paint	To order

● Standard N/A Not applicable

WARRANTY
6 months/6000 miles parts warranty

PRODUCED AND SOLD BY:
Caterham Cars Ltd
Town End, Caterham Hill, Surrey

SPECIFICATION

ENGINE
Longways front, rear-wheel drive. Head/block cast iron. 4 cylinders in line, bored block, 5 main bearings. Water cooled, electric fan.
Bore 83.27mm (3.28in), **stroke** 77.62mm (3.06in), **capacity** 1691cc (103 cu in).
Valve gear ohv, 2 valves per cylinder, chain camshaft drive. **Compression ratio** 10.5 to 1. Breakerless ignition, twin Weber 40 DCOE side draught carburettors.
Max power 135bhp (PS-DIN) (100.6kW ISO) at 6000rpm. **Max torque** 122 lb ft at 4500rpm.

TRANSMISSION
4-speed manual. Clutch 7½in dia.
Gear	Ratio	mph/1000rpm
4th	1.0	18.56
3rd	1.418	13.09
2nd	1.995	9.30
1st	3.337	5.56

Final drive: Hypoid bevel, ratio 3.636.

SUSPENSION
Front, independent, double wishbone, coil springs, combined with telescopic dampers, anti-roll bar.
Rear suspension, live axle, A-bracket, trailing arms, coil springs combined with telescopic dampers.

STEERING
Rack and pinion. Steering wheel diameter 11.5in, 2.3 turns lock to lock.

BRAKES
Dual circuits, split front/rear. **Front** 9in (203mm) dia discs. **Rear** 8in (228.6mm) dia drums. Handbrake, side lever acting on rear drums.

WHEELS
Aluminium alloy, 6in rims. Radial tubeless tyres (Goodyear NCT on test car), size 185/70HR13, pressures F20 R20 psi (normal driving).

EQUIPMENT
Battery 12V, 40Ah. Alternator 35A. Headlamps 55/60W. Reversing lamp standard. 8 electric fuses. 2-speed screen wipers. Electric screen washer. Water valve interior heater; air conditioning N/A. Leather seats. Carpet floor covering. Scissor jack; 2 jacking points each side. Laminated windscreen.

PERFORMANCE

MAXIMUM SPEEDS
Gear	mph	kph	rpm
Top (Mean)	111	179	6000
(Best)	116	187	6250
3rd	85	137	6500
2nd	60	97	6500
1st	36	58	6500

ACCELERATION
FROM REST
True mph	Time (sec)	Speedo mph
30	2.0	34
40	3.0	44
50	4.2	54
60	5.6	64
70	8.2	74
80	10.0	83
90	13.9	93
100	19.9	103
110	33.6	113

Standing ¼-mile: 14.6sec, 95mph
Standing km: 27.7sec, 107mph

TEST CONDITIONS
Wind:	7-14mph
Temperature:	15deg C (59deg F)
Barometer:	29.76in Hg (1009mbar)
Humidity:	85 per cent
Surface:	dry asphalt and concrete
Test distance:	727 miles

Figures taken at 8750 miles by our own staff at the General Motors proving ground at Millbrook.
All *Autocar* test results are subject to world copyright and may not be reproduced in whole or part without the Editor's written permission.

IN EACH GEAR
mph	Top	3rd	2nd
10-30	10.3	5.8	3.5
20-40	7.6	4.7	2.6
30-50	7.1	4.0	2.4
40-60	7.1	3.5	2.6
50-70	6.7	3.6	—
60-80	6.5	4.2	—
70-90	7.5	—	—
80-100	10.3	—	—

CONSUMPTION
FUEL Overall mpg: 23.5 (12.0 litres/100km) 5.17mpl
mph	mpg	mpl	mph	mpg	mpl
30	46.6	10.25	70	28.3	6.23
40	38.0	8.36	80	24.6	5.41
50	33.3	7.32	90	21.2	4.66
60	31.2	6.86	100	17.2	3.78

Autocar formula: Hard 21.2mpg
Driving Average 25.9mpg
and conditions Gentle 30.6mpg
Grade of fuel: Premium, 4-star (97 RM)
Fuel tank: 8.0 Imp galls (36.4 litres)
Mileage recorder: 3.6 per cent long
Oil: (SAE 10W/40) 650 miles/litre

BRAKING
Fade (from 95mph in neutral)
Pedal load for 0.5g stops in lb
start/end		start/end	
1	45-40	6	70-80
2	50-50	7	70-100
3	50-45	8	85-100
4	50-45	9	70-100
5	70-65	10	70-100

Response (from 30mph in neutral)
Load	g	Distance
40lb	0.30	100ft
80lb	0.65	46ft
100lb	0.85	35ft
120lb	1.00	30ft
140lb	1.05	28.7ft
Handbrake	0.40	75ft

Max gradient: 1 in 3
CLUTCH Pedal 46lb; Travel 4¾in

WEIGHT
Kerb 10.7cwt/1196lb/543kg
(Distribution F/R, 51.1/48.9)
Test 14.4cwt/1610lb/730kg
Max payload 508lb/230kg

THE OPPOSITION

FIAT X1/9 VS £7500

A worthy contender in this class, offering an acceptable combination of ride, comfort and performance in a chassis which offers all the handling virtues normally associated with the excellent weight distribution of a mid-engined layout. Fiat broke ground with the X1/9, proving that it is possible to build a car of this sort using the corporate parts bin.

Tested	13 March 1985
ENGINE	1498cc
Max Power	85bhp at 6000rpm
Torque	87lb/ft at 3200rpm
Gearing	18.25mph/1000rpm
WARRANTY	12/UL, 6 Anti-rust
Insurance Group	O/A
Automatic	N/A
5-Speed	●
Radio	N/A
Sunroof	Targa top
WEIGHT	2010lb

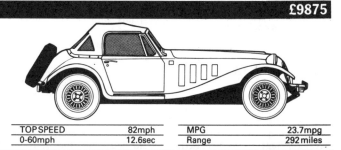

TOP SPEED	110mph	MPG	26.8mpg
0-60mph	10.8sec	Range	288 miles

MORGAN 4/4 1600 TC 2-SEATER £9518

The 1.6-litre Fiat twin cam engine, fed by a single Weber carburettor replaces the previous Ford CVH unit in the restructured Morgan range. The on-paper figures suggest good performance, coupled with particularly good economy. The Morgan is one of the few totally hand-crafted traditional-style sports cars and has changed very little since its introduction.

Tested	N/A
ENGINE	1585cc
Max Power	98bhp at 6000rpm
Torque	93.6lb/ft at 4000rpm
Gearing	22.1mph/1000rpm
WARRANTY	12/12,000
Insurance Group	5
Automatic	N/A
5-Speed	●
Radio	D/O
Sunroof	Convertible
*WEIGHT	1624lb

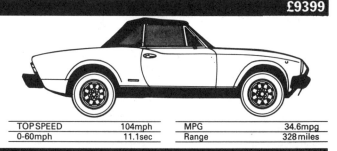

*TOP SPEED	115mph	*MPG	32mpg
*0-60mph	8.0sec	Range	400 miles

PANTHER KALLISTA 1.6L £9875

A similar concept to Caterham's Super 7, but with added refinement, the Panther Kallista is aimed at the driver who wants to recapture the days of vintage-style, wind-in-the-hair motoring. Build quality of the Korean-bodied, UK-assembled Kallista is excellent, as is serviceability, thanks to the straightforward front engine, rear drive layout.

Tested	19 June 1985
ENGINE	1597cc
Max Power	96bhp at 6000rpm
Torque	98lb/ft at 4000rpm
Gearing	22.0mph/1000rpm
WARRANTY	12/UL
Insurance Group	O/A
Automatic	N/A
5-Speed	●
Radio	●
Sunroof	Convertible
WEIGHT	1984lb

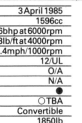

TOP SPEED	82mph	MPG	23.7mpg
0-60mph	12.6sec	Range	292 miles

PININFARINA SPYDER EUROPA £9399

It was originally built by Fiat as the Sport Spyder, but is now assembled by Pininfarina using similar Fiat mechanicals including the old 124 floorpan. Otherwise this traditional sportscar, which is now badged as the Spyder Europa, looks almost identical to the original car of the late sixties. A 2-litre fuel-injected engine allows adequate performance.

Tested	N/A
ENGINE	1995cc
Max Power	122bhp at 5300rpm
Torque	127lb/ft at 3500rpm
Gearing	19.4mph/1000rpm
WARRANTY	12/UL, 6 Anti-rust
Insurance Group	7+
Automatic	N/A
5-Speed	●
Radio	D.O.
Sunroof	Convertible
WEIGHT	2296lb

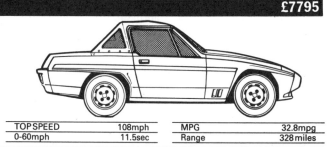

TOP SPEED	104mph	MPG	34.6mpg
0-60mph	11.1sec	Range	328 miles

RELIANT SS1 £7795

A good attempt at providing an up-to-date equivalent of the much-loved MGs and TRs, this little two-seater offers modern looks with Michelotti styling, potentially reliable Ford 1600 CVH power and thoroughly conventional layout. Strength comes from fabricated steel chassis carrying new-era damage-resistant plastic panels. Performance is not exciting.

Tested	3 April 1985
ENGINE	1596cc
Max Power	96bhp at 6000rpm
Torque	98lb/ft at 4000rpm
Gearing	20.4mph/1000rpm
WARRANTY	12/UL
Insurance Group	O/A
Automatic	N/A
5-Speed	●
Radio	○ TBA
Sunroof	Convertible
WEIGHT	1850lb

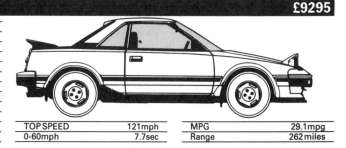

TOP SPEED	108mph	MPG	32.8mpg
0-60mph	11.5sec	Range	328 miles

TOYOTA MR2 £9295

The all-new MR2 is a most civilised sports two-seater that offers excellent performance from its twin cam 16-valve engine, combined with outstanding economy, courtesy of the efficient fuel-injection and four-valve head arrangement. Good handling, thanks to the mid-engined configuration and a high equipment level are other major attributes.

Tested	13 March 1985
ENGINE	1587cc
Max Power	121.9bhp at 6600rpm
Torque	104.8lb/ft at 5000rpm
Gearing	18.6mph/1000rpm
WARRANTY	12/UL
Insurance Group	7
Automatic	N/A
5-Speed	●
Radio	●
Sunroof (manual)	●
WEIGHT	2319lb

TOP SPEED	121mph	MPG	29.1mpg
0-60mph	7.7sec	Range	262 miles

● Standard ○ Optional at extra cost † Optional choice at no extra cost N/A Not applicable DO Dealer Option * Manufacturer's figures ** European Legislative Average

Above: Caterham has light but extremely precise steering response. Ride is not a forté but is considerably improved from the previous model. Understeer is the predominant characteristic but the tail can easily be kicked out with the application of just a little throttle

◄ as you wish. In a long, constant radius bend, driven on its limit one-up, this is certainly true on right handers, but the absence on the test car of a limited slip differential — a worthwhile optional extra — meant that on left-hand turns, the weight of the driver on the outside increased the slight roll enough to allow the inside wheel to spin, so that one just understeered. The not-too-happy front-to-unsprung weight ratio of the live rear axle is only occasionally obvious in the odd small bump-skip on an uneven corner. The test car suffered slightly from a hint of corkscrew motion on bumpy roads, agreed by the makers to be caused by unmatched dampers.

Ride is not the Super Sprint's forté, but we felt that it wasn't as bad as before. Considering the character, it rides well enough, firmly but not really uncomfortably. The brakes are a delight — heavy certainly, very much so, but in this sort of car one doesn't mind, since the ability to control the car's exceptionally good maximum braking is improved. Brake balance is superb, and the good weight distribution means that the awkwardly-placed handbrake is capable of giving 0.4g, which is at least one third better than usual.

AT THE WHEEL

For the first time in a 'Seven, there are adjustable seats. The back rests remain fixed as before, but there is fore and aft movement of the seat base.

Anyone over 6ft 2ins, howev- er, is still likely to experience problems, although it must be said that Caterham will custom-build a car to the buyer's specification. Tall drivers can opt for a fixed seat, set an inch or so further back, plus a modified pedal box with shorter clutch, brake and accelerator pedals.

The transmission tunnel has shed 1in of its width to give a slight increase in the two tub-like areas but space in the footwells remains painfully small for size 10 wearers, as one foot often interferes with the other. There is no place to rest one's left foot when not in use, but the spirited performance — requiring constant use of the gears — means that one's foot is rarely off the clutch in any case.

Instrumentation is in character with the sporting nature of the Super Sprint; a large tachometer and speedometer occupy prime positions and are clearly visible even through the minuscule 11½ins diameter leather-bound three-spoke wheel. Mounted along the length of the dashboard are the ancillary rocker switches, broken by fuel contents, water temperature and oil pressure gauges. The flick switches to the right of the wheel are a little confusing at first as they are unmarked. The indicators are controlled by another flick switch to the left of the wheel, a somewhat basic non-self cancelling type but nevertheless one which we didn't mind too much as it is close to hand.

The driver peers through a tiny windscreen, equipped with dinky little windscreen wipers. These work effectively enough, though the washers seemed to have a mind of their own; cornering quickly causes them to come into operation which is not always desirable.

Seat belts are of the static type and especially welcome with the hood down to help overcome the exposed vulnerable feeling which some drivers experienced when travelling at speed.

CONVENIENCE

Quite clearly, the Caterham is a fair weather machine and one, given the choice, that would only come out of the garage on a clear sunny day.

The hood fits snugly enough, but is so low — following the line of the screen and barely rising above it — that entry and exit for even moderately proportioned users can be painful, due to the limited amount of space. The cloth doors hinge up and over the screen exposing the shallow slot through which one must climb. The fact that the car sits so close to the ground makes entry even more awkward.

The driver's side door mirror fell off during the period of our loan; it broke away from its ball-type adjustable pivot and illustrates just how much vibration the car and driver are subject to. With this gone, rear visibility is extremely limited with the hood raised. A small rear view mirror and passenger door mirror are provided, but making out shapes through the plastic windows is none too easy.

Erecting and folding the hood is a straightforward affair that need not take more than a couple of minutes, but we found the press stud fastening at the top of the screen would occasionally pop loose when travelling at speed, allowing in a rush of air.

Only the tiny space behind the thinly padded seats can be used to stow anything, including the hood. So luggage needs to be of a bare minimum and preferably of the squashable variety.

The car has a very efficient heater and two speed fan. If anything, the car gets too stuffy with the hood raised, as hot air is still emitted even with it switched off. There are no fresh air vents, so one has to rely on the various draughts round the doors to provide refreshment.

Engine accessibility is nothing short of fantastic. Release the four bonnet catches and the long, lightweight engine cover comes off to reveal all engine consumables. In addition, if the four Dzus fasteners that hold the nose cone in position are undone, the whole of the front of the car is exposed.

SAFETY

The safety aspect is not an obvious strong point on a car built with performance and handling as the prime objectives. Caterham, however, has made a conscious effort to fall in line with current safety legislation, even though the car is exempt from type approval, by nature of construction.

On the outside, detail changes include recessing the spare wheel fixing, changing hood fixing studs and removing the wing-mounted side lights to rid the shape of sharp protrusions.

Inside, the seat belt anchorage points have been tested to meet EEC seat belt anchorage legislation and are significantly different to those on the early Lotus cars. All interior controls are laid out within easy reach and Caterham deliberately avoided using a servo on the circuit brake system — with failure warning light — to ensure that they are not easily locked up in an emergency.

A roll-over bar is offered as an option but we would have thought it a mandatory piece of equipment on such a car. Any vehicle that weighs as little as the Super Sprint is at an obvious disadvantage to most other cars on the road and the light flimsy shell is not known for its impact-absorbing qualities.

VERDICT

The fact that Caterham has full order books suggest that the Chapman concept still has tremendous appeal 28 years on.

For those on a budget, the Caterham offers the sort of excitement normally reserved for expensive supercars; affordable performance, albeit in a no-compromise package that is more akin to a current racing car. Those looking for the creature comforts of today's family car would of course be disappointed by the cramped twin coffin-like cockpit arrangement, constant exhaust and induction roar and limited weather protection, but then a Caterham owner would be disappointed by the family car's lack of performance.

The Caterham is an enthusiast's car: we know of no other that comes close to offering the sort of buzz the 1700 Super Sprint has to offer for the price.

SEVEN
DEADLY SPINS

PHOTOGRAPHY BY MAURICE ROWE

A530 FPJ

GASP at the Seven's power!
THRILL to the sound of the engine!
SCREAM as it whips round bends!

It's 'X' rated Fifties fun as the Caterham Seven duels with a Peugeot 205 GTI on a treacherously slippery Harewood hillclimb course in Yorkshire. Richard Bremner reports

CAN MOTORING be a vice? Drive a Caterham Seven, and you begin to believe it. It's fast and dirty, loud and thirsty and gives you that "morning after the night before" feeling. You won't be able to get enough of it, either.

A Seven is equipped to provide a heavy dose of entertainment. It has a powerful engine (anything up to 150 bhp), rear-wheel drive and space for two maniacs. And it weighs half as much as a Volvo 360. Geoff

Capes could overturn a Caterham with one hand.

Rev a Seven up, release the clutch and it's like letting a wasp out of a jam-jar. The engine grunts, spits, and sends the car snaking forward, tyres fighting

for grip, driver sawing at the wheel. Caterhams have an aversion to parallel lines. They are at their best on winding, twisting roads, preferably empty ones.

And since vice is best practised in private, we thought we'd take the Caterham to a hillclimb, where there would be no police, no pedestrians and no obstacles approaching in the opposite direction. Finding a hillclimb open at this time of year is not easy. Some are shut because they double as farm tracks for dung-clad Land Rovers, while others become breeding grounds for pheasants. Still more are closed because their owners don't wish to be disturbed by the sound of Nikolaus Otto's invention in full flight.

But Harewood hillclimb, near Leeds, was open, just (our thanks to the directors who allowed us on it, and the lady whose farm has the misfortune to straddle the track), for a few hours of raw entertainment.

And raw it certainly was. The Seven is a windy experience with the hood off (doors too; it's easier to see when you're travelling sideways); the airstream chills the right side of your face and the front wheels fling dirt at it. Just 10 minutes on a muddy road will have a Caterham driver looking as if he has returned from army manoeuvres. But a Seven pilot gets his just deserts (especially if he drives with his mouth open) for such hardship, in the form of enormous exhilaration.

So if the Seven is such fun, why pit a Peugeot 205 GTI against it? After all, one might as well compare a sculler with a speedboat. Yet, apart from having four wheels and an engine in common, these cars were conceived with the same goal in mind: providing entertainment. The question is, can a modern, efficient but nevertheless engaging hot hatch prove anywhere near as diverting as a Seven? We thought it was worth finding out.

How do you measure entertainment? Is it really possible to derive any pleasure from driving a machine that builds a mud pack on your face and could double as training apparatus for budding Houdinis? Yes. Because, like sex, the Seven provides a rich sensory experience. It accelerates like a catapulted missile. It corners like a roller coaster. And it sounds as exciting as a rock concert.

But it's a difficult car to master, especially on a hillclimb. Not that it is difficult to drive — the Caterham has a supremely smooth power train (no snatch, shudder or judder) and a stubby gearlever that moves with the ease and precision of Torvill and Dean — it's just that one's progress can suffer from a surfeit of power.

Take one of Harewood's long sweeping bends. The Seven will dive in with enthusiasm and can be held, tail drifting slightly, until the corner's end. But only if the accelerator is depressed by precisely the right amount. So potent is the engine, and so sensitive the throttle, that it is very easy to precipitate a swift and unexpected change of scenery. Achieving the right balance is the crucial thing.

Negotiating the hill's tighter turns demands still greater circumspection. It's no good entering on a trailing throttle and then stamping on it after turning the wheel, because the Seven will go straight on, rapidly changing the view ahead from grey tarmac to green grass. Instead, the power must be fed in more gently, allowing the front tyres to maintain their hold so that the rear can be pushed out.

In fact, after several runs (and a few trips to investigate Harewood's flora and fauna) it became apparent that the quickest method was to drive as neatly as possible, with the tail kept in check on the tight bends and sliding gently on the faster ones.

Not that this was easy. The temptation to use the Caterham's power was simply too great.

As much as anything, it's the *noise* that prompts an enthusiastic extension of the right foot —at 3000 revs it sounds like a Spitfire (Battle of Britain variety) and at 5000 you're being chased by a whole squadron. Release the accelerator, and the exhaust mimics a popcorn machine. But performance is what makes the Seven memorable — it accelerates as though it had taken steroids. In 1700 Supersprint tune, it will reach 60 mph in 5.5 sec, 80 mph in 9.5 sec and 100 mph in 18.9 sec. In fourth gear it will do 20-40 mph, 70-90 mph and all increments between in under eight seconds. And 30-50 in fourth takes only 6.6. The only disappointing performance statistic is top speed, which we estimate (we were unable to obtain a figure) to be only 115 mph, because the Seven has the aerodynamic properties of a pot plant — ie none.

With such staggering sprinting ability it soon became apparent that fully depressing the Sev-

Top, middle left and above: Sometimes you get it right…and sometimes you don't. Above right: Peugeot steams ahead. Right: A pair of massive Webers. There's an engine somewhere in there too

en's throttle was tantamount to suicide on Harewood's short straights; though the brakes are progressive (but heavy, owing to the lack of servo, unnecessary on a car so light) and powerful, it was easy to lock the wheels on a track which was damp and muddy. Delicacy was the key.

And it was not difficult to determine where the Caterham's limits were, because it transmits so much feel. Much of this is channelled directly into the driver's spine, because the seats barely caress his thighs, let alone support them, and matters aren't helped by the proximity of the rear axle to one's posterior either. Which makes it unfortunate that the Caterham rides rather firmly

and restlessly. Still, on a bumpy road the driver is less likely to be concentrating on the state of his back than on which way the Seven will dart next; it can become quite nervous at speed when the going gets rough, though the impression that it is unstable diminishes with more miles.

In any case, what steering correction is necessary can be rapidly applied thanks to a very quick rack, which sends plenty of messages through to the tiny wheel's rim. Like the rest of the car, the steering gives the impression that there are very few rubber bushes in a Caterham — it is precise, quick-acting and free of slop.

So is the Peugeot, especially by hot hatch standards. But compared with the Caterham, it feels a shade remote, a little desensitised, as though you are wearing rubber gloves. The 205 is less dramatic on the hill. The climb actually starts on the level, rises briefly and sharply, and then flattens out before the first bend, a 90 degree left-hander.

The Peugeot leaves the start more briskly than the Seven because the surface is slippery — more weight, most of it over the driven wheels, gives it a real advantage. Setting it up for tight bends is easier than with the Caterham — enter too fast and you merely lift the throttle momentarily to tighten the car's line; indeed, it's a technique that can be used to get round that much faster. It means that unless you're travelling at a demented speed, the GTI will always stay on the track.

A short straight follows, and the Peugeot barely climbs at all; if both cars were racing, the Caterham would leave the GTI floundering here. The track turns right now, sharply at first, the bend getting faster as the car drifts out towards a substantial thicket hedge. One is hardly conscious of this when enclosed in the 205, but in the Caterham, it's more of a worry; a trip into the bushes will do more than comb your hair. Even now the hill has hardly begun, the next straight virtually flat before the pair of esses that precede a sharp right turn.

Hard braking is needed here if the car is not to enter the first ess untidily, and although just as effective, the 205's brakes are much spongier than the Caterham's, as though they were filled with blancmange instead of brake fluid. The Peugeot can be rushed through here in satisfyingly neat style, though one becomes very aware of the steering weighting up — it certainly requires more effort than the Caterham.

Out of the last turn, and the track surface changes from concrete to tarmac, a transition marked for some competing drivers by brief flight because the road has quite a kink in it here. We have to slow right down though, because this is where the farm crosses the track, and nearby lives a large family of cats . . .

Once past the farm the track really starts to climb. A long, rising left-hander follows, and it's slightly cambered too. The best line is not that obvious here, and probably isn't as crucial; as long as the bend is entered wide it can be taken very quickly, though the over-keen may see their cars topple down the other side. It is followed by Harewood's only steep straight, which runs long and hard, flanked by the hill on one side and by solid Armco on the other.

Somehow the sight of a barrier is slightly off-putting — it hides a drop that would make a stunt man smile — and it is difficult to summon the insanity necessary to press the throttle to the floor. But in the Peugeot it's a lot easier, because it is not as fast, and because it has a roof of steel, not cumulus.

We have chosen a foul day for hill climbing, and fog is actually descending on the track's last turn. It's a tight, blind, rising right-hander (mere feet from the finish) yet it turns out to be one of the easiest bends on the course. Being slower, and quite wide, it is easy to judge the amount of power necessary to send the car sliding towards the turn's outer edge; this is particularly true in the GTI because of its inherent understeer under power.

The first ascent complete, the Peugeot is climbed a few more times. It is far easier to become quicker in it than the Caterham because it is so predictable and forgiving. On the damp track it is almost certainly quicker than the Caterham. But I doubt if it would stay ahead on a dry day.

So, which is more fun, the more entertaining? Inevitably, perhaps, it has to be the Caterham. It's because it provides the biggest challenge, the greatest exhilaration and the best sensation. The Peugeot is enjoyable too, yet tame, even dull, in the face of the Seven.

But vice has its price: driving the Seven down from Harewood is no afternoon of leisure, even if it has got a good heater. Buy the Seven only as a second car; it rewards less strongly as practical transport.

A Street-Fighter Racer

CONTINUED FROM PAGE 127

Bolt right on, seeing as all the other parts like brakes and hubs were Spitfire, but the catalog doesn't show this and I've never seen another.

But in general the magazines enjoyed the Seven, reporting that it was great fun to drive, not at all practical and just the thing for those who wanted to run around in a race car with license plate.

That meant a minority, as you'd guess. No more than a handful of Series 1s ever crossed the ocean. The semi-official Lotus history says the company's component branch built 1350 Series 2 Sevens with various engines, 330 Series 3s and several hundred S4s. The Seven was very much an English car—had it been any more English it wouldn't have been a car at all, as the joke goes—so no more than a few hundred, maybe even as few as 100 came to the U.S. If half of them raced, it doesn't make for good odds. Saying that a Super Seven won a national SCCA championship in 1962 and another championship in 1978 tells you just how fierce the car was, and how dedicated were its owners.

This story makes a nice, neat full circle. They still do make Lotus Sevens. An outfit named Caterham Car Sales was the concessionaire for the model when Lotus got too big to bother. The Series 4 was more a beach buggy than disguised racer and it was allowed to disappear. But Caterham got so many requests they were given a license to keep turning out Sevens, in Series 3 form.

Which they still do, and that leads us into another tricky part.

People are funny. Fashions come and go, so roadsters, mass-produced ones anyway, came and went. But while many people change from this style car to that, there remain the inflexible few, the people who insist on just such a machine as the Seven.

These inflexible few haven't had it easy. Federal regulations make it darned hard to certify cars made in small lots. Hard in this case translates into expensive, and for some reason the people who like thinly disguised sports/racing cars have more enthusiasm than money.

There were several years during which Lotus Sevens couldn't be bought new. Asking prices for used ones escalated in proportion. You could (still can, actually) get a used Seven for several thousand dollars if you're lucky, the car is tacky and the owner needs the money. Prices get into the 5-figure bracket if the car is restored or has a pedigree or if the owner knows what he's got.

Caterham is still on our side, however. At this writing Caterham is opening a branch office so to speak, in the form of Super 7 Inc, Palm Beach, Florida. They'll be offering kit cars, rolling chassis with the hard parts already done, with prices beginning at $9988. The buyer can find his own engine or Caterham will ship a Ford 1600 from England.

Real do it yourself, this is, meaning you still must be a little odd to get involved. Case in point: my own.

But you still must be a little odd to appreciate this. My own car was sold when I finally got it completely done, right down to full competition equipment and even a top and side curtains. The Don Juan of Fiberglass is what I was and as soon as all the work was done, I gave in to a guy who'd been calling and offering cash for months.

He got the car home, and telephoned two days later.

"Geez," he said, "the ride is terrible. Beats me black and blue. The engine overheats in traffic, the rain comes in, I'm getting heat stroke, I don't dare park it where I can't see it."

"I told you all that before," I said.

"Sure is fast."

"Have a good time," I said.

Road Test:

Caterham Seven 1700 Super Sprint

IT IS astonishing to recall that the car we now call the Caterham Seven has been with us for nearly 30 years. As the Lotus Seven, it first saw the light of day two years before the Mini and was being readied for its launch at about the same time that Fangio won the 1957 German GP in his Maserati 250F. Over the years it has changed in detail but has remained essentially the same animal: a lightweight sports car with little in the way of creature comforts but which offers extraordinary performance at the price.

Lotus made four distinct types of Seven, the Series IV having a rather boxy fibreglass body which was generally felt to be less attractive than its predecessors. Lotus Components, the company which marketed the car along with Lotus' production racing cars, began to lose interest around 1967, at which point it became heavily involved in the production of FF1600 cars, but continued to supply kits to Caterham Cars on an irregular basis for the next few years, Caterham having been the country's first Lotus dealer. When the Lotus group of companies moved from Cheshunt, Herts, to Hethel, Norfolk, it underwent a re-organisation

FILTERS for the two twin Webers protrude through the bonnet, right; simple fascia, far right, works surprisingly well with essential controls near at hand.

which saw the shedding of the production racing car business and a concentration on more up-market road cars. In 1973, Caterham Cars purchased the plans, jigs, shape and goodwill of the Seven, but not the Lotus name, and thereafter the company has produced what is effectively a Lotus Super-Seven Series III.

The date of the purchase was not ideal for it more or less coincided with the three day week, the imposition of VAT on kit and

component cars, and the 1974 oil crisis. Still, the model has survived and nearly 1,000 Caterham Sevens have been produced with production currently running at around 200 p.a. with half exported as fully assembled cars mainly to Germany, Switzerland and Japan.

In the UK the Seven is marketed either as a kit or as a component car. This is a nice distinction and it is the main one which

MOTOR SPORT uses when deciding whether to accept a particular car for testing. A component car is one made from new parts and which is loosely assembled in such a way that a buyer of even limited mechanical ability can put on the road a vehicle which meets the minimum specification conceived by the manufacturer. A kit car is one which requires the customer to buy in many major components, possibly using a donor vehicle. We do not test kit cars for the simple reason that we cannot guarantee that the average home assembler can achieve anywhere near the standard of the demonstration car supplied by the maker.

In kit form, Caterham Seven prices start at £1,985 for a body/chassis unit complete with brake pipes, wiring, instruments and windscreen wipers and motor. Using secondhand or reconditioned components, it would be possible to put such a car on the road for under £5,000. Part of the attraction of taking this route is that the owner can uprate the car's specification as and when finances permit as well as making some saving in labour charges. The Seven's pedigree ensures healthy secondhand values in contrast to some other kit cars and, indeed, looking at the asking prices of secondhand Sevens, it is apparent that the car is one of the select few, along with the likes of the Morgan range, which will maintain their purchase price, or something close to it, for several years.

Over the years, the car has been refined and developed, the spaceframe has been stiffened, a long cockpit option is available as is a de Dion rear suspension set-up which is likely to become a standard feature sometime in the future. Currently, four engine options are available: three with the Ford "Kent" engine in various states of tune (84 bhp, 110 bhp and 135 bhp) and the 150 bhp Ford RS 1600 BDR. Last October, Caterham introduced the 1700 Super Sprint which uses an enlarged (1,700 cc) version of the "Kent" engine which, with its two twin-choke Webers, gives very nearly the performance of the twin cam but with a saving of over £1,800 in price and easier maintenance. It was with this car that I recently lived for around 2,000 exhilarating miles. Drive is through a four speed Escort Sport gearbox to a strengthened Morris Ital live axle.

The basic cost of this model is £8,142.00, inclusive of taxes, but the one I drove had over £1,700 worth of extras: a limited slip differential, heater, seat belts, roll-over bar, leather, adjustable seats, a Mota-Lita steering wheel, long cockpit configuration, alloy wheels and a paint job on the otherwise natural aluminium — the fibreglass wings and nose cone come in a choice of six colours.

Now the foregoing is a calm, rational, description of the car and its pedigree. But this is not a car to treat calmly and rationally. It is a car which has an

extraordinary effect on everyone who comes into contact with it. Children would whoop and wave, friends begged for a quick drive, enthusiasts would smile and give a "thumbs up" and, as for myself, I jumped at every possible excuse to drive it — and managed to find the longest possible route between two points.

Yet as I eased away from Caterham Cars, and towards lowering clouds with the hood down, I began to have my doubts. Was I getting too old for this sort of thing? How long before I'd need an osteopath? Leaving behind my trusty Golf GTi, I felt like someone who had just exchanged a comfortable house for a sleeping bag and billy can.

Within 24 hours, however, I had covered nearly 400 miles and was getting to grips with the beast. The steering, which at first appeared so heavy, had become the only steering to have — quick, precise and free of vice. Used to servo-assisted brakes, it took a little time to adjust to the heavy pedal but, within a short time, I was in harmony with it, revelling in the feel which the Caterham's system (9 inch discs, ex-Mk VI Spitfire at the front, with Ital drums at the rear) provides. "Harmony" is perhaps the word which best sums up the Seven: it's noisy to be sure, it vibrates, the ride is hard (but not harsh) but all its characteristics combine to present a unity of style. Indeed, one reason why Caterham has not pursued its experiments with turbo engines is that the quiet power of a turbo was at odds with the character of the car.

I had been advised that driving with the sidescreens in place would prevent buffeting which was sound advice as we discovered when we tried running without them, and besides, they are impossible to store in the car. Since the external mirrors are mounted on the sidescreens, I thought that vibration would render them useless, but found them perfectly adequate. The top of the screen, however, interfered badly with my

sightlines making tight right hand bends and the negotiation of roundabouts an anxious time.

Another doubt which was soon dispelled was the layout of the control switches which are either tumbler or rocker switches scattered around the dashboard apparently at random, yet it was soon clear that all the most frequently used controls were within finger reach and one could switch on the lights, indicate, operate the horn and so on without taking one's hands from the tiny steering wheel. Even the fact that the direction indicators are not self-cancelling seemed to enhance one's pleasure, giving one a sense of being at one with the vehicle. It is as perfect a layout as one could imagine.

There are no doors, of course, and when the hood is up this presents some difficulty if one is blessed with a fuller figure. I found no dignified way of entry or exit and had to insist that a passenger took his, or her, turn. Given the contortions involved, had I had a lady already in the passenger seat, the only decent thing would be to have married her. I must say I rather took against the hood. In theory it is quite easy to put up, with a built-in frame and a separate covering which is fixed with studs, after you have first removed the spare wheel which sits on the back. In practice it takes several minutes to erect single-handedly and I used it mainly to protect the seats when the car was parked outside overnight. I never could get the heater to keep the windscreen and transparent panels clear of condensation in rain on a humid day and then preferred to dress accordingly and drive with the hood down. The condensation so affected visibility that it made driving the car positively dangerous.

Another thing which I took against was the petrol tank. With a capacity of just eight gallons and an average economy (excluding performance testing) of 21 mpg, the car's theoretical range is just 168 miles but on "my" car the fuel gauge was such that it was prudent to call in for fuel every 140 miles or so. Once on the forecourt, unless you hold the pump nozzle just right, you can spend a long, long time trickling petrol into the tank for it is incredibly easy to get four star all over the back of the car. The combination of short range and slow fuelling (it takes at least twice as long as on the average car) is frustrating in the extreme and plays havoc with one's average speed on a long journey.

Luggage space is minimal. Enough basic clothing for two for a weekend can be stored at the back and in the passenger's footwell, providing it is packed in soft, slim, bags and if you don't mind the creases. The point is, though, that we are dealing with what is essentially a vehicle designed solely for driving pleasure. You have to forget practicalities, forget the crude heater and go with the car. When you do so, the rewards are immense.

Top speed is a claimed 112 mph, for the Seven has the aerodynamics of a breeze-block, and on the two mile straight at Bruntingthorpe we achieved this exactly with the hood up, recording a best one way run of 116.5 mph. Other cars claim much higher figures but the Seven achieves its maximum under the conditions which most of us can manage (ie without pounding around a banked test track or finding a stretch of deserted autobahn). With the hood down the average of two runs was 109.6 mph. Top speed is not anyway the area from which the driver extracts his pleasure from the Seven, unless you enjoy having every sense assaulted. It is the phenomenal acceleration, the sure-footed handling, the precision of the steering and the overall sense of harmony which gives so much pleasure.

The engine rasps under power, but we are not worried here about noise of any description. I feared it might bog down in town traffic but it happily coped with London traffic in the rush hour, though the hand brake, which is located under the scuttle on the passenger's side, was awkward to reach.

Acceleration is extraordinary, even if you do have to fight the car on a quick getaway. Caterham claim a 0-60 mph time of 5.8 sec but our best was six dead. We managed 0-30 mph in 2.6 sec, 30-50 mph in just 2.2 sec, 50-70 mph in 3.9 sec and 70-90 mph in 8.0 sec. This is acceleration for which you normally have to pay telephone numbers. In practice, on the road, it means that lines of slow moving traffic cease to exist and even short straights become safe places to pass.

While the combination of power and light weight gives outstanding acceleration, it can present problems. The car is distinctly twitchy in strong side winds while, in the wet, it has to be treated with the utmost respect. Nobody could call the rear end traction "limpet-like": it is fairly easy to spin the car in the dry (I hasten to add we were using a test pad) and very easy on wet surfaces. The test car was fitted with 13″ HR-rated 185/70 Goodyear NCTs and we felt that slimmer tyres would be desirable for when the back end goes in the wet, it goes quickly indeed. We found that braking in the wet left something to be desired, the car is so light that the wheels lock up very easily. You soon learn to treat the throttle and brake pedals with delicacy.

The Caterham Seven is a car in the memorable class for it changes the man who drives it. I found a whetting of the appetite for driving which is something for one who averages over 1,000 miles per week, and I also found myself being a better, more sympathetic, driver as a result of my experience of the car. It has its faults but what it gives the enthusiast driver is something beyond price. M.L.

Car: Caterham Super Seven Series III 1700 Super Sprint (long cockpit variant).
Type: 2-seater convertible, no doors.
Construction: tubular steel spaceframe, aluminium body panels, fibreglass nose-cone and wings.
Maker (and sole supplier): Caterham Car Sales and Coachworks Ltd, Seven House, Town End, Caterham Hill, Surrey, CR3 5VG.
Basic Price: £8,142.00.
Price as tested: £9,869.27.
Engine: tuned Ford "Kent" bored out to 1,699 cc (83.27 mm × 77.62 mm). Max bhp 135 at 6,000 rpm. Max torque 122 lb/ft at 3,500 rpm. Four cylinders, pushrod ohv, mounted in line, two twin-choke Weber 40DCOE carburettors.
Transmission: 4-speed manual Ford Escort Sport. Ratios: 1st, 3.34:1; 2nd, 2.0:1; 3rd, 1.42:1; 4th, 1.0:1. 8 in mechanical clutch. Final drive: 3.64:1, limited slip differential.
Front suspension: coil spring and wishbones, telescopic dampers, anti-roll bar.
Rear suspension: live axle, coil springs, telescopic dampers, A-bracket and radius rods.
Brakes: non-servo 9 in discs front, 8 in drums rear. Twin circuits, split front/rear.
Steering: rack and pinion. 2¾ turns lock to lock. Turning circle, 33 ft.
Wheels and tyres: 6J × 13 in alloy "Revolution" wheels, 185/70HR 13 Goodyear NCT tyres.
Dimensions: Wheelbase: 88.5 in; front track: 50 in; rear track: 52 in; overall length: 133 in; overall width, 62 in; overall height:(hood up) 43 in, (hood down) 41 in; ground clearance: 4.3 in; luggage capacity: 2.7 cu ft; fuel capacity: 8 galls; kerb weight: 1,124 lb.
Maximum speed (after two miles): 112 mph mean, 116.5 mph best one-way run.
Acceleration: 0-60 mph, 6.0 seconds; 0-30 mph, 2.6 seconds; 30-50 mph, 2.2 seconds; 50-70 mph, 3.9 seconds; 70-90 mph, 8.0 seconds.
Economy (excluding performance testing): 21 mpg average. Max range: 168 miles.
Insurance: Group 7.
Delivery: approx three months for "kit", approx nine months for "component" car.
Comments: Impractical as a sole car but superb as a fun vehicle for the driver who wants to be involved in his driving. In terms of acceleration, it is marginally beaten only by a handful of exotic, and expensive, cars. Impeccable pedigree and excellent resale value.

CATERHAM 7 1700 SUPER SPRINT

Motor enjoys driving the lastest version of Britain's serious fun car

The Caterham Super Seven has developed almost mystical powers in recent years. From being the most fun you could have with your clothes on, Lotus's 30-year-old minimalist design now confidently transcends the boundaries that contain conventional driving experiences to offer an altogether higher state of consciousness. Or so it would seem listening to some of the Super Seven's more obsessive advocates.

Thankfully, Caterham Car Sales, who have manufactured the Seven since 1974, take a rather more pragmatic view of their product's role in life. They call it "a light, highly efficient, ruggedly constructed car made up from tried and tested components", and go on to say that "with even the most basic engine option, the power-to-weight ratio gives tremendous acceleration". True enough, the whole may add up to more than the sum of these elements but, when you get down to it, the root appeal of the Seven lies in its raw, savage performance, its ultra-responsive handling and its endearing simplicity.

It is, and always has been, a serious fun car and that's where we start our story of the latest 1700 Super Sprint. Caterham have built around 200 Super Sprints since 1984, making it their most popular model. By no means is it the fastest roadgoing Seven – the 170 bhp twincam BDR-engined Super Seven HPC holds that honour – but it does offer the best compromise between performance and reliability and therein lies the secret of its success.

The most major of recent developments has seen the acquisition of a De Dion axle with "A" bracket and radius arms, which goes hand in glove with the use of wider, lower profile tyres. This, along with a five-speed transmission, has now been standardised across the range.

Other modifications are of the detail nature, some of which might not meet with universal approval by aficionados of the marque; items like rounded rocker switches in place of the classic flick-switches. But only tall and very selfish drivers (with short friends perhaps) will complain about the seat now being mounted on runners, particularly in the long cockpit car tested.

The Super Sprint is produced both in component form – £10,087, with trailer collection or delivery and around 15 hours of work to complete – or in true kit form with the owner supplying most of the mechanical components. It's manufactured in a little corner of Surrey and the workshops (not a factory) can handle around 20 component cars and 16 kits a month.

Certainly the beauty of the pushrod 135 bhp engine is that of relative simplicity and low cost. The Ford "Kent" engine is bored out to 1691 cc; the compression ratio is 10.5:1, with larger valves and full gas flowing, cast aluminium pistons, Caterham high-lift camshaft, Caterham-fabricated exhaust system, a balanced and lightened flywheel and competition clutch. Twin Weber 40 DCOE carburetters with K and N air filters take care of induction. Apart from a high-pressure oil pump, the engine's bottom end remains largely untouched with just the bearing shells being changed to a competition-type material.

The combination of the de Dion rear axle and Ford Sierra five-speed gearbox adds a little extra weight to the Caterham – most of it appearing over the rear wheels. Helped by superb traction from a standing start, the Seven catapults its occupants to 30 mph in just 2.2 sec before going on to reach 60 mph in 5.6 sec and 90 mph in 13.0 sec with scarcely diminished vigour.

Only at near three figure velocities, when fourth or fifth gear is selected, does the car succumb to the forces trying to arrest it. At 107.9 mph, the mean maximum speed is proof enough of the Seven's parachute-like aerodynamic qualities. The test car might have come closer to the claimed 112 mph maximum, were it not for an inexplicable loss of power sustained when running flat-out.

The pushrod Ford "Kent" engine is naturally in a high state of tune and works best in the 4000-6000 rpm range hinted at by the high revs at which the peak torque is developed. It coughs and

Super Sprint's underbonnet is dominated by a pair of K and N filtered Weber 40 DCOE carburettors

gulps in response to wide throttle openings at very low revs, but driven with sensitivity, the 1700's tractability is acceptable; it pulls uncomplainingly from 30 to 50 mph in 7.0 sec.

Bearing in mind the Caterham's phenomenal performance potential and the frequency with which we exploited it, the overall 24.5 mpg consumption is not just acceptable, it's downright abstemious.

Much of the Super Sprint's appeal lies in its straightforward simplicity of line (particularly after the abortive Series 4), with wings standing proud, round torpedo headlamps, flat windscreen, and a simple wire-mesh protected hole at the front for the radiator's air. It cares not a jot for aerodynamics, and neither should it. Items like doors are, of course, entirely superfluous to the Seven's *raison d'être*.

Functional cockpit possesses an air of stark beauty. Handbrake is awkwardly placed under scuttle on passenger's side

The driver and one intrepid passenger sit as near to the road as is feasible, on either side of the propeller shaft. The Ford five-speed gearbox intrudes into footwell space so the wearing of trainers is a prerequisite for nimble working of the closely spaced pedals. The engine is mounted as far back into the chassis as possible to aid the polar moment of inertia.

The compromise, as ever, is in the machine's favour. That does, however, mean providing a comfortable driving position, and this, with the aid of fore and aft seat adjustment, is achieved. With arms and legs very nearly straight the tiny Mota-Lita wheel is right in front, and the gear lever – no more than a threaded stub for the knob – is perfectly placed.

Thus seated the driver's right hand can be placed, palm spread, comfortably on the road, so ground-hugging is the car. Indeed, the road surface is an essential element for levering oneself into the Seven. Luggage is best kept to squashy overnight bags.

On the road is where the Seven was designed to be; but not just any road. The spitting and fluffing from the engine signals that the suburban stop-go is no place for a car which likes to clear its throat regularly. Similarly, the motorway or dual carriageway shows up the shape as unsuited for cruising at more than 80 mph. Try it and the buffeting, plus a very high level of mechanical noise and constant minute steering inputs become wearing to the driver.

But given a twisting "A" or "B" road and perhaps a sunny day, and the Super Sprint is magic. Traction is superb with the optional 185/60 HR 14 tyres both from a standing start and during dry-road cornering. Some practice is required when performance testing to ensure the smallest amount of wheelspin without the engine going off-cam at below 4000 rpm.

Such are the car's immensely quick reactions, particularly to steering inputs, that seldom can the man/machine relationship be more intimate. Every bump, ridge or mere loose chipping is felt precisely, even though minor suspension deflections are well-absorbed by the chassis. Larger road irregularities are dealt with less competently, to the point where backing-off – or avoidance – is required.

The de Dion rear suspension has certainly enhanced the

Sprint's sheer gripping ability, especially when traversing mid-corner bumps. The minus side is that with such a well-controlled pair of rear wheels, understeer can become a mite too strong. Only sharp provocation will prompt the car to move into a satisfying balanced drift.

The unservoed disc/drum braking system is well able to cope, but the firm pedal requires quite a push until the pads are thoroughly warmed.

Brickbats are almost cruel to mention in respect of such a unique and unpretentious machine. But if the car is used as everyday transport, then it must be stated that visibility with the hood and sidescreens in place is appalling. Side view is hindered by the narrow vinyl apertures being too low. Wet weather exacerbates the problem disproportionately. Road spray is also a very real dilemma when it is remembered that the driver's eyeline is little higher than a juggernaut's wheel hubs.

That, plus a lack of security and the Houdini-like contortions

necessary to get in and out makes the Seven an impractical choice of everyday transport. But that is not the point. The Super Sprint is devastatingly quick, race-car responsive through corners, gloriously raucous and always begging to be driven well and hard.

There is no molycoddling padding, no sound insulation; not a single unnecessary component or piece of ornamentation. It is a functional concoction of steel, aluminium and grp and it delivers supercar performance for hot-hatch money.

With the 309 or Golf GTi there is a fair degree of driving pleasure to be had every day. The Super Sprint cannot be so compared: it provides exhilaration – but only when time, road, and weather come together. It depends on how you wish to take your pleasure. Ⓜ

MOTOR *ROAD TEST*
CATERHAM 1700 SUPER SPRINT

PERFORMANCE

WEATHER CONDITIONS
Wind	7 mph
Temperature	55 deg F/13 deg C
Barometer	30.0 in Hg/1017 mbar
Surface	Dry tarmacadam

MAXIMUM SPEEDS
	mph
Banked circuit (4th gear)	107.9
Best ¼ mile (4th gear)	109.7
Terminal speeds:	
at ¼ mile	93
at kilometre	107
Speeds in gears (at 6000 rpm):	
1st	35
2nd	65
3rd	94

ACCELERATION FROM REST
mph	sec
0-30	2.2
0-40	3.3
0-50	4.3
0-60	5.6
0-70	7.7
0-80	9.8
0-90	13.0
0-100	18.6
Stand'g ¼	14.5

ACCELERATION IN TOP
mph	sec
20-40	12.1
30-50	10.3
40-60	10.2
50-70	14.0
60-80	16.6
70-90	16.7

ACCELERATION IN 4TH
mph	sec
20-40	7.9
30-50	7.0
40-60	7.8
50-70	7.6
60-80	6.7
70-90	7.2
80-100	9.5

FUEL CONSUMPTION
Overall	24.5 mpg
Fuel grade	97 octane
	4 star rating
Tank capacity	36.4 litres
	8 galls
Test distance	515 miles
	830 km

*Based on official fuel economy figures – 50 per cent of urban cycle, plus 25 per cent of each of 56/75 mph consumptions.

NOISE
	dBA
30 mph	79
50 mph	87
70 mph	94
Maximum†	104

†Peak noise level under full-throttle acceleration in 2nd

SPEEDOMETER (MPH)
True mph	30	40	50	60	70	80	90	100
Speedo	29	40	50	61	72	81	93	103

Distance recorder: 2.6 per cent slow

WEIGHT
	kg	cwt
Unladen weight*	578	11.4
Weight as tested	755	14.9

*No fuel

Performance tests carried out by *Motor*'s staff at the Motor Industry Research Association proving ground, Lindley, and Millbrook proving ground, near Ampthill.

Test Data: World Copyright reserved. No reproduction in whole or part without written permission.

GENERAL SPECIFICATION

ENGINE AND TRANSMISSION
1690cc, 4 in-line
Bore/stroke 83.3/77.6 mm
Power 133 bhp at 6000 rpm
Torque 122 lb at 4500 rpm
Cast iron block and head, pushrod ohv, 2 valves/cylinder
Compression ratio 10.5:1
Two Weber 40DCOE sidedraught carburetters

Overall gearing 22.2 mph/1000 rpm
Ratios 0.28, 1.00, 1.26, 1.81 and 3.36:1
Final drive 3.62:1

FRONT SUSPENSION
Double wishbones, coil springs and anti-roll bar

REAR SUSPENSION
De Dion axle, located by "A" bracket and radius arms

STEERING
Rack and pinion, 2.8 turns lock to lock

BRAKES
Discs, 23 cm dia/drums 20 cm dia

WHEELS AND TYRES
Alloy, 6×14 in (optional)/185/60 HR14 Goodyear NCT

Make: Caterham **Model:** 7 1700 Super Sprint **Country of Origin:** UK **Maker:** Caterham Car Sales and Coachworks Ltd, Seven House, Town End, Caterham Hill, Surrey CR3 5UG **Tel:** 0883 46666 **Total Price:** £10,087 **Extras** *fitted to test car: Cibie headlamps (£32), Stainless steel brake hoses (£15), Motolita steering wheel (£40), Red paintwork (£518), KN Jupiter wheels with 185/60 NCT tyres (173), Roll-over bar (£46), Tonneau cover (£79), Rear wing protectors (£26), Wind deflectors (£29), Seat belts (£36), Heater (£76), Air horns (£14), Electronic ignition (£63), Leather seats (£282), Limited-slip differential (£334), Spare wheel cover (£32), Oil cooler (£61)* **Price** *as tested:* £11,516

SECRET SEVEN

The Series 4 version of the Lotus Seven is the least loved. Except,
that is, to the man who designed it – Alan Barrett. Mark Hughes
met him and drove his newly-built S4; pictures by John Colley

A golden rule of Seven culture is that the Series 4 – 'the plastic one' – is the car *not* to buy. Although a manufacturing rate higher than any previous Seven, with nearly 600 built in two years, made the S4 popular enough in its day, it has become the forgotten Seven. It's rare to see one nowadays, and then you do it's invariably tatty. Out of all the Sevens produced by Lotus and Caterham over 30 years, the S4 is the cheapest on today's market, because no-one seems to love it.

Alan Barrett doesn't belong to this school of thought. He likes the S4 so much that last year he finished building up a brand new example – the one you see in these photographs. He positively bridles when the S4 is criticised, but this is hardly surprising – he designed it.

In hindsight, given the consensus that the S4 isn't a real Lotus Seven, as well as Caterham's success in building its S3-derived cars, it seems odd that Lotus should have produced such a major redesign. At the time, however, the logic of the move was all too clear: the decision to build an S4 stemmed from the need to make the Seven more profitable. According to Mike Warner, then newly-arrived as Chief Executive of Lotus Components, the company was losing between £100 and £110 on every S3 it made.

One of Warner's first exercise at Lotus Components (the subsidiary which manufactured the Seven as well as customer racing cars) was to think about how the Seven could make money. It had to be simpler to build than the labour-intensive manufacture of the existing Seven, and it had to be made in higher volume. A major cost of the S3 had been its hand-made tubular chassis and aluminium panelling, manufactured by Arch Motors, so consideration of alternative chassis designs was the first step. Proposals to design an S4 around an Elan chassis (at around half the cost of an S3 chassis) or a widened Formula Ford chassis were considered before the decision was taken to design an entirely new car.

Warner was also thinking about exports, for his plans to step up production (to as much as 2000 a year to make the necessary profit) required entering new overseas markets, many of which had legislation barring the S3. Rather than attempt to re-engineer the S3, he felt that a new car would be a more straightforward way of meeting those requirements. Furthermore, by 'civilising' the Seven –

giving it more comfort and weather protection – he could attract buyers who might otherwise consider an MG Midget or a Triumph Spitfire, and stand some chance of meeting his production target. Beyond this, he felt that an improved Seven would act as an 'entry-level' Lotus, enticing young buyers up to the more glamorous models in the range. It all made a lot of sense at the time.

It has been written that all this scheming was done behind Colin Chapman's back, that the first the boss knew of the car was when a finished prototype was shown to him. Although Warner and his design team had considerable autonomy at Lotus Components, Alan Barrett remembers that they weren't totally left to their own devices.

"Chapman was so in touch with every part of

Lotus," says Alan, "that a thing as big as this could never have happened without him knowing. Some days he used to wander everywhere in the factory to keep an eye on what was going on, making suggestions, altering drawings, occasionally getting very angry when he saw something he didn't like. He knew about the S4 proposal, the first saw my ideas for it when Warner, the chassis designer, Peter Lucas, and myself had a meeting with him in the boardroom to show my quarter-scale model.

"I had made this model with different front and rear wing designs on each side – on one side was my preferred treatment, with the more substantial rear wing that appeared on the final car, and on the other was a cycle-wing style similar to the old S3. Chapman didn't think my rear wing would work on the full-sized car, although he conceded that it looked all right on the model. I argued with him and he got quite shirty with me, but eventually he agreed that I could make a full-size mock-up with my rear wing style.

"I made this mock-up with the two types of wing treatment, and made a hood out of brown paper painted black. I took rather more trouble over the side of the car I wanted! For the other side I took an S3 wing from the stores and jammed it on as best I could – it would have looked better if I'd thrown it on. When I was ready, Chapman came down and looked at the mock-up. He grinned because he could see that I was playing down one side and taking trouble over the other, but he agreed that I could go ahead with what I wanted."

Along with Peter Lucas, Alan began work on the approved S4 design in March 1969. Cheapness of manufacture was uppermost in his mind, so there was never any question that the bodywork had to be glass-fibre instead of aluminium. He produced a clever structure made from two mouldings: self-coloured outer skin formed the exterior bodywork, and this was bonded to a 'bathtub' section forming the cockpit and scuttle. The whole assembly had bobbins sunk into the glass-fibre at the points where it would be bolted to the chassis. Flared front wings and a one-piece front-hinged bonnet completed the bodywork. The hood, designed specially for the car by Weathershield, was truly a design leap, introducing to the Seven the novelty of sliding perspex side windows (although the rudimentary sidescreens still

hinged on the windscreen) and much better weather protection.

Lucas's chassis was a simple spaceframe with flat steel panels spot-welded to it along the cockpit and engine bay sides, and a folded pressed steel cross-member at the front. Like the Elan, but unlike earlier Sevens, the chassis relied on the bodyshell to impart some of the car's torsional rigidity.

Mechanically, the S4 continued to use bought-in components, mainly from Ford. The top model had Lotus's superb 115bhp twin-cam engine (125bhp was available from the Holbay-tuned version also catalogued), while 1600cc and 1300cc Ford cross-flow 'Kent' engines were also installed. All models used the Corsair 3000E's four-speed gearbox and an Escort rear axle. To overcome the axle strengthening needed with the S3's A-frame rear suspension (cracked differentials were a notorious Seven problem), Lucas revised the rear suspension with a pair of Watts linkages, and a triangulated arm on the offside for lateral location. Europa double wishbones formed the front suspension, and there were coil spring/damper units all round.

"This all took place in just seven months," says Alan. "Once we were given the go-ahead, I asked for a Seven to drive, as I'd never driven one! I took a metallic blue S3 for a weekend, and after the journey home I never wanted to drive it again. I hated it that much at first. But by the time I took the car back to the factory on Monday morning I was beginning to enjoy it – it's a taste you have to acquire. Peter Lucas and I drove it as much as possible while we were developing the S4. Our first step was to build a

Alan made the car from original S4 parts – he had to make sidescreens and bonnet catches himself. The hardtop was actually a factory design but Alan has used hinged rear window instead of Perspex original. Interior is trimmed to Rolls-Royce standards and even the boot is carpeted

test chassis – just a chassis with a windscreen and roll hoop, and seat belts to stop you falling out of the thing. We often used to do a couple of hundred miles in a day around the test track at Hethel, and in between I would be working out the body.

"Peter and I were left to get on with the job on our own, which was the best way. Graham Nearn of Caterham had ideas about which way to go with the Seven, but as I wasn't getting interference from within the company I didn't see why I should put up with any from outside. If you have too many people working on a design you get a botched job."

After its launch in March 1970, the S4 was greeted very favourably by the motoring press, production climbed to a new level of 15 a week (although Warner's 2000 a year target was wildly optimistic) and a £150 profit was made on each car. Twelve months later, however, the future of Lotus Racing (the new name for the Lotus Components off-shoot) hung in the balance as Chapman assessed its viability. Unsold stocks – among them 54 three-year-old Formula Fords! – prompted the decision to stop building customer racing cars, Lotus Racing was wound down and production of the S4 was moved to the main Lotus Cars factory.

What finally killed the S4 was Chapman's growing belief that Lotus's future as a manufacturer of road cars lay in Porsche and Ferrari territory, where profit margins were much higher. As the presence of a 'kit car' in the range didn't suit that aim, the decision to axe the S4 was taken in July 1971, just 16 months after launch. Using up large chassis stocks kept the car in production until October 1972, by

Right: Engine is Lotus twin-cam rebuilt by Anglia Cars. Below right: Seven's cockpit is still spartan. Bottom: The Sevens line up. From left, S3 with Ford engine, SS with Lotus twin-cam and S4 with squarer, flatter looks

which stage nearly 600 had been built.

This was when Graham Nearn of Caterham Car Sales stepped in. Nearn had built his business around the Seven, and took a calculated risk in taking over its manufacture. Another 38 S4s were built at Caterham, largely from parts stock that had come from Lotus, but Caterham's lower level of production – only one a week – was causing problems with component suppliers used to serving much larger orders.

"The crunch came for the S4," explains Nearn, "when Weathershield wanted us to place a huge order for hoods – £50,000 was their minimum for resuming production, and that was obviously not on. It had always been in the back of my mind that the way for us to go was by developing the S3, so we built eight or nine of them out of spare parts, sent out a press release and waited for the reaction. The 'phone didn't stop ringing!

"I was quite happy about taking this course after that. The S4 had always suffered a tremendous reaction against it from the die-hard enthusiasts. I hadn't liked it that much either, although it must be said that it sold very well – it reached a slightly broader public than the S3, and the market was very buoyant at that time. But the S4 was a difficult car for us to build – fitting the bodyshell to the chassis was a task in itself.

"Being honest, I was upset that we weren't given the opportunity to assist with the S4's design. After all, it was our livelihood. As the sole distributor, we knew the Seven better than anyone. Yes, it had the advantages of more legroom and luggage space, it was more comfortable to drive and had better weather protection, but I would have preferred an uprated S3, the sort of thing we are building now."

With the closure of Lotus Racing, Alan Barrett left Hethel to set up his own company, Barrett Design, and among his early contracts was one to build S4 bodies. For a time he also manufactured Europa bodies ("Lotus found it easier to switch me on and off than cope with the ups and downs themselves"), before concentrating his energies on design. Most of his work since then has been in the racing car industry, from Formula Ford to F1, but he also

designed an Invader successor for Gilbern. A striking 2+2 coupé reminiscent of the Owen Sedanca in outline, it was at clay model stage when Gilbern closed.

Alan's deep involvement with the S4 as designer and body manufacturer meant that he accumulated many parts over the years, to the extent that he almost had a complete car. Why not finish the job?

"I had always intended to build these parts into a car, but never had the time. Then, 18 months ago, I had a purge and decided to finish it. I had to make a few bits, like the sidescreens and bonnet catches, but knowing the car intimately made all that quite easy. I used the opportunity to build in a few modifications in line with how the car might have developed in production."

The most obvious feature is its hardtop, which is actually a factory design. Twelve were made, but whether any reached the public is uncertain. Alan has changed the original perspex rear window ("it leaked") for a hinged glass one, to give a kind of hatchback arrangement. Two bolts at the rear and two windscreen clips hold the top in place, and it really does make the car very cosy inside.

Alan has taken considerable trouble over the interior, trimming it lavishly with Rover and Rolls-Royce materials – even the boot is carpeted. He has given the facia a matt black (instead of body colour)

Top: Alan with original S4 in the seventies. Note period costume. Above: Hardtop is held on by two rear bolts and two screen clips; once manoeuvred into place it makes the cockpit very snug and quiet. Below: That's what you buy a Seven for – phenomenal performance, handling that sets sports car standards

finish, fitted a slightly incongruous digital clock ("yes, that's a mistake"), altered the wiper pattern to give the driver a better view and added a windscreen demister. Placing the handbrake between the seats is a splendid idea, as production S4s always had a nasty Victor umbrella-type fly-off item.

Mechanically, Alan's S4 is little changed apart from brakes and suspension. Using Triumph Spitfire competition uprights (skimpier Herald uprights with Ford hubs were standard wear) and steel disc 5½J wheels allowed him to fit larger Triumph disc brakes at the front, although the Ford drums at the rear have been retained. Those wheels carry larger 185/70 Goodyear G800 tyres, which meant widening the rear wings by ⅝in to give clearance. A twin-cam engine rebuilt by Anglia Cars is installed.

With only half a mile on the clock when I got behind the wheel of this unregistered S4 at RAF Coltishall (a venue arranged by Alan's neighbour, Jaguar pilot John Marden), the first impression on the move was of how tight and new the car felt. Apart from being almost completely free of rattles and squeaks, the S4 feels very rigid and solid, giving really brilliant, progressive handling. Although it still has a live rear axle, the effectiveness of its location minimises some of the skittish feeling of earlier Sevens in bumpy corners – it almost feels like independent rear suspension. The ride is softer than other Sevens, but Alan's large tyres help to heighten the contrast.

The way the twin-cam begs to be revved gives stunning performance, which contemporary road tests measured as 0-60mph in the 8sec bracket and a top speed of around 110mph. A snappy gearchange and the engine's willingness have your stirring round the 'box just for the pleasure of it, although the twin-cam delivers through a broad rev range. All the normal dynamic standards have to be re-written when you drive any Seven, and the brakes and steering match the rest of the car's abilities.

When Alan's S4 stands clear of other Sevens is in its interior refinement – with the hardtop in place it's almost quiet, and all the added interior trim helps to damp road and mechanical noise. This must be the most refined Seven there is.

As the man responsible for the S4, is Alan upset by criticism of it? "No, not really. I've become used to not worrying about what people say. The S4 is regarded as the undesirable Seven, I know, but not because of how it looks, or because it's too civilised. I think it's mainly because Lotus rejected the S4 so early on that it has become under-rated."

SEVENTH HEAVEN

The Caterham Seven has long been established as the
ultimate kit-car. We tried the company's development car featuring a De Dion back axle

It's hard to imagine a car as basic as the Caterham (née Lotus) Seven going up market, but a look at the specification sheets reveals that this four-wheeled motorcycle carried a pricetag of £499 when it first appeared at the 1961 Racing Car Show while the present 1700 Supersprint version retails at £8441 fully assembled and the twin cam RS1600 BDR at £10,365. Using the Supersprint as a comparison, it means the price has increased by 94 per cent in 25 years. Externally, this space-framed chassis sports car looks little changed from its predecessor, but under the aluminium skin there have been a number of useful changes.

The 'Old Dog', as our test car is affectionately known by the Caterham staff (it started life as a 1983 chassis), in fact serves three functions: development hack, demonstrator and race car. It is also an early example of the so-called 'long cockpit' configuration introduced for the 1982 model year, but incorporates the latest modifications which include a significantly narrower transmission tunnel to give the driver and passenger more space — 5ins extra legroom for the passenger, created by relocating the battery, an adjustable rear anti-roll bar and increased steering lock to improve the turning circle. Rather less obvious is the extra front chassis crossbrace plus additional bracing at the top of the engine bay. These modifications were incorporated following torsion tests carried out at City University on a Caterham chassis. As

Caterham's *development car competes in the Caterham Cars BRSCC Roadgoing '7' Series*

a result, the tubular space frame which is the heart of the car is now 12 per cent stiffer than before.

In its role as development hack, the Old Dog was also the first Seven to have the much-discussed De Dion rear axle conversion and a five-speed gearbox. This is the close-ratio unit fitted to a number of V6-engined Fords including the Sierra and Capri. By using a spacer between the gearbox and bell-housing, it is possible to position the gearlever sufficiently far enough back on the tunnel that there is no need for the remote shifter linkage of earlier models. Finally, the installation of the De Dion back axle has allowed the rear bulkhead to be moved rearwards by a further half inch — not a terribly significant amount, but a help to taller-than-average drivers.

Under the bonnet, Old Dog is fitted with the Super Sprint version of the familiar Ford Kent overhead valve, crossflow engine. This involves taking the capacity out to 1695cc, gasflowing the cylinder head and enlarging the ports. Larger inlet and exhaust valves are fitted plus increased ratio roller rockers, cast aluminium flat-top pistons, Caterham-specification BDD camshaft (high lift, short duration profile) and a lightened and balanced flywheel. Carburation consists of a pair of Weber 45DCOE twin-choke, side-draught units fitted with K&N high performance air filters while exhaust gases exit via a tubular four-into-one manifold. In deference to the car's part-time career as a contender in the Caterham Cars-BRSCC Roadgoing Seven series, the power unit is fitted with competition-type main and big-end shell bearings, competition clutch and a high-pressure oil pump working in conjunction with a standard wet sump. In this form, the Kent engine produces 150bhp at 6500rpm with an absolute redline of 7250rpm.

The car's circuit-racing life has also called for several predictable modifications to be made to the suspension specification compared with the standard version. The front and rear coil springs, for instance, are approximately 35 per cent stiffer and they have also been shortened, thus lowering the car by approximately ¾ins all round. Dampers are Spax gas units with adjustable spring seats while the rear suspension is fitted with an

anti-roll bar which may be offered as an option on production Sevens (along with the stiffer suspension) should there be sufficient customer interest.

Caterham claims that in this form the Super Seven is quite a viable proposition as a regular weekday road car and successful weekend racer, the only requirements for the latter role being a rollover bar, harness, fire extinguisher and a set of racing slicks. And just to prove the point, Old Dog has contested four rounds in the Seven Series and achieved top-six placings each time. Jez Coates of Caterham Car Sales estimates that a Super Sprint engine of this specification will have a 10,000-mile span between rebuilds, or put another way: "You could use

There is virtually nothing to match a Seven for sheer enjoyment and exhilaration

the car daily for driving into London as well as a season of racing without the need to tear the engine down."

In the normal course of events, dual-purpose vehicles, which try to fulfil both competition and roadgoing roles, are not terribly successful since they tend to fall into the 'neither fish nor fowl' category. The modifications required for racing render the vehicle harsh, noisy and therefore ultimately tiring to drive long dis-

The 1695cc *Kent engine has been tweaked for competition use*

Transmission tunnel *is narrowed to increase interior space*

The reduced *ground clearance on our test car was noticeable*

'Old Dog' is an early example of the long cockpit format

tance, while the compromises for road use mean the car can never be prepared to the ultimate spec of one used solely for competition.

There isn't another vehicle around, though, that is quite like a Seven — its existence in this age of aerodynamic preoccupations is strictly down to the enthusiasm of the staff at Caterham Car Sales — and it actually seems to fulfil the roles of racer and road car quite successfully. This could be because the standard car is only a thinly disguised race car to begin with and therefore refinement has never been high on its list of attributes. The main differences between Old Dog and the last Caterham Super Sprint we tested (*Autocar*, 19 June 1985) are the louder exhaust note, reduced ground clearance (you need to be careful of the sump when going over large bumps) and a notably stiffer ride.

The obvious place to look for a quantifiable difference, though, had to be the performance figures. The previous Super Sprint produced a 0-60mph time of 5.6secs, a mean maximum speed of 111mph and an overall fuel consumption figure of 23.5mpg. Old Dog produced figures of 5.3 secs, 114mph and 22.9mpg — a small but useful improvement without an over-heavy penalty in fuel consumption. It must also be borne in mind that the car is fitted with a 3.92 final drive while the normal ratio is a higher 3.62-to-1.

The slightly lower overall gearing will improve acceleration, although the engine must necessarily work that

little bit harder to maintain speed. Even so, with a redline of 7250rpm — and the engine reaches that with contemptuous ease — the spread of performance is impressive.

Start-up involves the standard Weber sidedraught carburettor procedure of two pumps on the accelerator pedal and then virtually instant ignition as the Kent engine barks into life. The tuned nature of the power unit is instantly obvious from the thrummy, slightly uneven idle, but as soon as the revs build up and the clutch is dropped, the diminutive machine rockets away to a shattering mechanical cacophony. The driver's left hand then has to work the stubby gear lever very rapidly and deftly to avoid over-revving the engine.

There can be no doubt, though, that given the right circumstances — a sunny day and a twisting, leafy lane — there is virtually nothing to match a Seven for sheer enjoyment and exhilaration. The handling is as crisp as ever and the steering quick and precise. In fact, it wasn't until we took the car around the inner handling circuit at the Millbrook proving ground that we discovered a slight change in the handling balance of the latest offering from Caterham. Whereas before it was ultimately an oversteerer when cornered hard, now the Seven understeers noticeably before snapping into oversteer, and although it is controllable with the throttle and high-geared steering, a degree of care *is* required.

This increased understeer, Coates explained, is the result of the new rear

anti-roll bar. The suspension settings make the car rather easier to drive quickly, although ride quality, predictably, has suffered with indifferently surfaced roads eliciting a harsh reaction from the suspension.

As far as the two major modifications to the latest Caterham are concerned — the five-speed gearbox and the De Dion rear axle — they seem to be a success. Combined with the standard 3.62 final drive, the former endows the Seven with a rather more relaxed high-speed cruising ability while the latter seems to have improved the ride and handling, although we would need to try a car on 'standard' as opposed to 'competition' suspension settings before it would be possible to say for certain if this was the case.

Interestingly, the position of the De Dion back axle has been altered several times and at one point resulted in that version of the Seven having a slightly shorter wheelbase than the so-called 'live axle' car. In the latest form, however, the De Dion axle has been moved rearwards so both models have the same wheelbase. This will allow Caterham to offer De Dion kits to owners of earlier Sevens.

The Caterham may be something of an anachronism, but sales are better than ever with the four-wheeled rollerskate now TUV-approved and able to be sold fully built in the stringently regulated German, Swiss and Japanese markets where it is much sought after.

And in case you think the men at

Caterham are sitting on their laurels, there is a 1700 BDR Super Seven with 170-175bhp on tap to be launched at the Birmingham Motor Show. There is also the possibility of a 'Prisoner' commemorative model finished in the evocative Team Lotus colours of British Racing Green with a yellow nose and red trim.

History will record if this is the first Seven to be fitted with an electronic voice recording to remind the driver that he is not a number but a free man. ∎

Handling is crisp, *and the steering quick and precise*

CATERHAM SUPER SEVEN

Grosse Pointe—

To comprehend the praise that I am about to lavish on this peculiar automobile, you should be aware that I have always wanted to host a garden party at which the guests would be entertained by a strolling tuba player.

That would be my kind of garden party. The Caterham, in like fashion, is my kind of car. Few people in their right minds would buy one, and almost nobody can resist wanting one.

Joe Schulte, the owner of the Caterham Super Seven Series III pictured here, blames me for his good fortune. Having heard me extol the virtues of the Autokraft Mk IV, a fine Cobra reproduction [May 1986], he began to lust after roadsters, settling finally on the Caterham.

Schulte is one of several editorial, art, and advertising people who breakfast

An elemental roadster that's more fun than the seven deadly sins.

BY WILLIAM JEANES

PHOTOGRAPHY BY GUY MORRISON

This is not a reproduction or a replica; it is a lineal descendant of the Lotus Super Seven.

every Saturday at Janet's Lunch in Grosse Pointe Park to trade stories and talk about everything from cars to bird hunting. He made his Caterham compulsion known at such a gathering.

"It'll only cost about $13,000, and the factory says it only takes fifteen hours to assemble," said Schulte.

"I helped my neighbor down in Texas put a kit car together once," said Jim Ramsey, one of the breakfast regulars. "It took months, and we almost never got the electrics to act right." Ramsey's was a typical caution, but we ultimately encouraged Schulte, knowing that his money would provide no-cost entertainment for the rest of us. This support, plus prayer and meditation, convinced Schulte to order his Caterham.

The Caterham, as you may very well know, owes its existence to the late Colin Chapman. It is not, however, a reproduction or a replicar; it is a lineal descendant of the real Lotus Super Seven. In 1973, Caterham Cars, a Lotus distributor since 1959, purchased manufacturing rights for the Super Seven from Mr. Chapman. In the years since, Caterham, headed by Graham Nearn, has established itself nicely as a small coachbuilder in Surrey. Its facility cannot be called a factory, although it can build about twenty cars a month if everyone works late.

Sevens & Elans [see sidebar], the Caterham distributor for the United States, offers the Caterham as a rolling chassis or as a kit that will come to you in a crate measuring twelve feet by four feet by three feet. A smaller crate contains the axle and the transmission. Schulte chose the kit and was equipped, emotionally and physically, to deal with it. His garage contains one of those red toolboxes the size of an upright piano, an A-frame and hoist, welding equipment, and a refrigerator that's never without Miller Lite. An ideal venue in which to watch someone work.

Five engine choices for Caterham's Super Seven are listed in the company literature: Ford 1600 GT, Ford 1600 GT Sprint, Ford 1700 Super Sprint, Cos-

worth 1600 BDR Four-Valve, and Cosworth 1700 BDR Four-Valve. The horsepower ratings range from a calm 84 to a suicidal 170. Rather than run afoul of the morass of EPA and DOT regulations governing completely assembled automobiles, Sevens & Elans does not supply engines. But its genial major-domo, Chris Tchorznicki (say Chor*neet*ski, or say to hell with it and call him Chris), can be most helpful in locating a powerplant for you.

Schulte found his engine in a Lotus 61 Formula Ford racing car . . . his own. It was sent away for serious modifications [see sidebar, again]; after that, the engine completed his Caterham kit.

The car shown on these pages was built with more professional help than a less demanding and meticulous car addict would need. Schulte, when trying his best to be straight-faced honest, admits to having invested $25,000 in the car, starting from a base price of around $12,500, less engine but including everything else. The word investment, however, is accurately applied.

"If you bought the kit and didn't do as many extra things as I did, and if you don't count beer-drinking and standing-around time, I really think you could put it together in twenty hours," Schulte

says. He estimates his own hours at around forty. Again, because he wants things better than right, this estimate is likely low.

But enough of background material, you say. What is this machine like to drive?

Unless you had lived through the years I think of as the Era of Flopping Side Curtains, when men were men and sports cars spent a lot of their time acting cranky, the Caterham may not make any sense to you. It's loud, it rides about an inch off the road surface, and, with its top erected, it has the visibility of a body bag.

It is expensive, dangerous, windblown, cramped, and ungodly quick, and it has a driving position that would shame a wooden folding chair. In short, it is all the things we once loved about sports cars.

The Caterham is more fun to drive than you can imagine. Few who observe you as you move through your neighborhood at full blat know what the car is, but they love it on sight. Some Corvette and Porsche drivers, the ones with the gold chains and the recent divorces, try to act as if it isn't there at all, studiously avoiding eye contact. But most people who love cars, even the folks

The sophisticated wishbone suspension (above) is taut but never harsh, offering responses like those of a Formula Ford racing car. Lotus-Holbay dry sump engine (top right) *was* taken out of a Formula Ford car and then seriously modified. Sucking noises from the dual Webers are just part of the car's appreciable repertoire. Profile of Caterham's Super Seven (right) dates back to the beginning of the Lotus motorsport dynasty and remains true to the original functional minimalism.

forced by the impedimenta of family and children into Ford Country Squires, are enchanted by the Caterham. The most enthusiastic and sincere questioner I encountered was a K-car driver well past 65—proof, if you need it, that driving the Caterham around town is like walking through the park with a friendly puppy.

Driving the Caterham vigorously, on the other hand, offers the excitement of riding a spirited horse. For all the right reasons, it's just like driving a Formula Ford on the street, but with marginally greater creature comforts. A well-located short-throw shifter atop the driveshaft tunnel controls the Ford-built four-speed transmission through a short and unusu-

ally positive mechanical linkage. This and the quick-ratio steering give all the racing-car feel that most of us can stand.

Gearchanging is made even easier by the positioning of the driver's left foot, which rests on the clutch pedal for the compelling reason that no room exists for it elsewhere. The space allotted for your feet is filled with the three operating pedals, with the result that your feet never touch the fire wall. The clutch's return spring is strong enough to permit its being used as a dead pedal, however.

At speed, the Caterham makes truly worthwhile noises. There's a constant sucking sound from the Webers, a sensational exhaust note, and a small squeak or two from the taut but never harsh suspension. If you did no more than sit at a traffic light blipping the throttle, your day wouldn't be entirely wasted.

The real fun comes on twisty roads at speeds below 70 mph, which removes buffeting from the equation. Here, turning right and left with the surety of a monorail, you are conscious of the road surface, which is speeding by within arm's reach, and of an overpowering sense of speed. You also feel in command, remarkable in that much of your

Unless you are British, the Caterham is a fair-weather friend.

time can be spent observing your reflection in other people's hubcaps. An ounce of prevention has been added to the low profile by the fitting of a dry sump lubrication system, thus raising the car's ground clearance.

The 1640cc engine in Schulte's car has 123 horses available to tow a wet weight of 1220 pounds. *That* is a favorable power-to-weight ratio—about 9.9:1. A Mustang GT, by comparison, has 225 bhp and weighs over 2900 pounds, for a ratio of 12.9 pounds per horsepower. The Caterham will move from 0 to 60 mph in under six seconds and, in so doing, will make you feel exactly as if you're being hauled up on water skis by a boat with all the power in the world.

The Weber carburetors do require frequent throat clearings in stop-and-go traffic, and the fuel economy falls from over 20 mpg to well under that in city driving. But those drawbacks, plus the constant fear of being flattened by a bus, are the only real reasons not to use the Caterham as everyday transportation.

My constant association with power-assisted brakes made the Caterham's un-boosted four-disc braking system seem pedal-heavy, when in fact it takes no serious effort to rein the car to a stop from highway speeds. If you were to drive down the face of Hoover Dam with your foot on the pedal, the brakes *might* fade, but I doubt it.

The Caterham's body shape exhibits an open contempt for airflow management, moving through the atmosphere with the aerodynamic efficiency of a forklift. This results in a terminal velocity somewhere in the 105- to 110-mph range, at which speeds the occupants will sustain buffeting severe enough to

cause deep bruises. With the top down, most drivers will reach their limits of physical endurance about the time the car reaches 75 mph.

And there's nothing wrong with that. The Caterham never claimed to be a turnpike cruiser, and even if it could roll along the Interstate at high speeds, the speed would be wasted. The Caterham, you see, isn't about top speed; it's about acceleration and handling. That, and outrageousness.

Among this Caterham's more outrageous features is an interior done in closely woven Wilton wool carpets and matching soft tan leather seats. This is excess beyond the wretched, the sort of extravagance that separates gentlemen from charlatans and coxcombs.

A small-diameter Smiths tachometer and a companion speedometer stare at you from the leather-covered dashboard, marginally visible through the tiny, thick, black leather Motolita steering wheel. Other instruments include an ammeter as well as water temperature, oil pressure, and fuel gauges. Toggle switches sound the horn and dip the headlights, and rocker switches operate the wipers, washers, lights, backup lights, emergency flasher, and brake fluid level check. There's even a turn indicator toggle—which must be returned to the off position manually after executing the maneuver. Other touches are four-point Sabelt competition seatbelts and a locking gas cap. This last device, on a car that itself cannot be made safe from prowlers, is entirely in keeping with the Caterham spirit.

Getting into the Caterham when its top is down is relatively easy for most primates, including veterans of the MG TF and the Austin-Healey Sprite. Although it is true that a chain hoist would be enormously helpful, a little practice will teach you to grasp the roll bar and the side of the body, lift both feet from the ground, and slide them into the space under the steering wheel. This sounds much easier than it actually is. With the top up, it becomes much worse. Only one man, a professional contortionist, is known to have successfully entered the Caterham when its top was up.

Helping the space problem a bit,

Schulte ordered his Caterham with the optional long cockpit, which added two inches of legroom and made matters easier for large persons. The long cockpit is now standard for the series.

Beneath the archaic exterior lies a tubular space frame and suspension that are truly rudimentary. The newest Caterhams, now available with an optional de Dion semi-independent rear end, have the same basic suspension design that appeared on the Lotus Seven Series I racing car in 1957. (The production versions, including this one, all offered only live axles at the rear until recently. Schulte's is the last live-axle Super Seven.) The front suspension incorporates double wishbones, coil springs, and an anti-roll bar. The live-axle rear, like the front, uses adjustable Spax gas shock absorbers with adjustable coil springs.

Unless you are British—a race of motorists who enjoy breaking up the monotony of driving with hypothermia and pneumonia—the Caterham is a fair-weather friend, drafty in winter and top-less in summer. You could stow the top in the small boot for a trip, but the side curtains would have to be either strapped to the tiny luggage rack—in lieu of luggage—or placed in your passenger's lap. A chase vehicle is a third possibility.

According to Chris Tchorznicki, a new-design folding side curtain is on the way. That plus a new fuel tank that expands the "trunk" may allow side curtains to accompany their owner on excursions.

The Caterham, in sum, makes very little sense for the average citizen. Which is precisely what its creator doubtless intended. It has the single-minded utility of an elephant gun and the irresistible attraction of free champagne. The Caterham is a car to which the young instinctively relate, and in which the old see vestiges of their youth. And with good reason. With the sun beating down on you, the wind whipping your face, the sound of a powerful exhaust note, and the peripheral awareness of pavement rocketing past, you either grow suddenly older or abruptly younger.

And you grow very happy.

Because what you are driving is more a state of mind than a car, and more dream than reality. Pair the Caterham with a strolling tuba player, and you can melt the heart of the devil himself. ●

BUILDING THE CATERHAM

. . . with a little help from his friends.

Caterham Cars is represented in the United States by Sevens & Elans of Cambridge, Massachusetts (617–497–7777). The firm, headed by Christopher Tchorznicki, sells a dozen or so Super Sevens each year. All Caterhams come to this country in kit form and are subject to import duty and brokerage fees. Even so, a rolling chassis less engine will cost only about $13,500 delivered.

Joe Schulte, owner of the Caterham shown on these pages, bought the long-cockpit version, with fourteen-inch wheels and Goodyear NCT 60-series tires. Schulte removed the engine from his Lotus 61 Formula Ford racing car and shipped the 1600cc unit off to Vanguard Engines in Medina, Ohio, where Jerry Mong put his considerable talents at Schulte's disposal.

Mong, who was the late Jim Trueman's engine man once upon a time, and who built the highly successful Bobsy sports-racing cars in the late 1960s and early 1970s, bored the engine out to 1640cc, line-bored it, fitted dual Weber DCOE 40s, and supplied a tractable camshaft. The result was a 123-bhp engine with a flat, satisfying power band that goes from 3200 to 6000 rpm with nary a fit nor a start. (Jerry Mong receives serious inquiries only, at 216–725–4350.)

As he assembled the Super Seven in his Grosse Pointe garage, Joe took a number of suspension components and the roll bar to Yee Collision in East Detroit (313–771–0210), where his friend

Stan Yee, a longtime racing driver and builder of short-track stock cars, did chrome plating and epoxy painting of the bits. None of this was necessary for utility but was deemed essential by Schulte for beauty.

More visual horsepower was added by Murph Mayberry at his vintage car restoration and maintenance facility in Lime Rock, Connecticut (203–435–9703). Murph, once the crew chief on the Smothers Brothers Formula 5000 team, bills his business, Car Care Company, as "the best damned garage in town," although it's unconnected to the legendary Smokey Yunick's place in Daytona Beach. It is also the only garage in the hamlet of Lime Rock.

Murph's contribution centered around making the fiberglass and aluminum body look absolutely stunning, and plumbing the car's dry sump lubrication system. Murph also performed the final alignment and readying of the car for actual use on the street.

Schulte's only other significant on-site help came from his friend George "the Fabricator" Blake, whose tool and die business provided such wonders as a remote oil-filter mount made of 6061 aluminum instead of the usual pot metal.

The Janet's Lunch breakfast club's contributions were largely limited to drinking up all the Miller Lite and poking around in dozens of plastic bags containing the Caterham's add-on pieces, with the exception of actual work performed by Jim Ramsey and Frank Kropscott.

"I can't overstate the help I got from Chris Tchorznicki at Sevens & Elans," says Schulte. "I'd heard all the horror stories about how nobody who sells you a kit car ever wants to hear from you once your check clears. Chris is different. If you don't call him, he calls you to see how it's going. No question was too dumb, and no request for help was too big."   —WJ

Morgan uses Rover's 1994cc twin-cam 16-valve M16 engine delivering 138 silky bhp. Caterham achieves amazing 135bhp from Ford pushrod 1597cc engine

DUEL!

Superficially the Caterham Seven and Morgan Plus 4 have much in common. Throwbacks to a past era, both have quirky, appealing, unaerodynamic and distinctive shapes. Both are hand-built by small-scale manufacturers whose production levels today are higher than ever before, yet waiting lists — nine months for the Caterham, several years for the Morgan — show that demand is unabated. Both defy marketing logic to provide a very different driving experience as minimal two-seater sports cars offering few concessions to practicality.

The comparisons, however, cannot be taken too far. For all their similarity, these two revised versions of existing cars are at opposite ends of an anachronistic branch of motoring. Whereas the Caterham has been continually developed to remain at the sharp end of modern dynamics standards, the Morgan clings stubbornly to its traditional qualities. The Caterham can be measured against the best current performance machinery, but the Morgan is unashamedly vintage in character, its maker resisting any temptation to tamper with a proven formula.

Graham Nearn and his staff at Caterham recognise that the Seven's appeal centres on exhilarating performance and the class of chassis. Taking the best hot hatches as their yardstick, they are determined to keep the Seven's acceleration, handling and roadholding abilities ahead of all non-exotic opposition. This aim has seen a package of improvements for 1988 — the car, tested here in 1700 Super Sprint form, has not been so intensively re-engineered for years.

Braking and suspension are the main areas of change. Disc brakes appear at the rear of the Seven for the first time. These 9ins discs — the same size as those at the front — carry Sierra Cosworth calipers and asbestos-free pads. There is a significant reduction in unsprung weight at the rear and the car continues without servo assistance.

After Lotus borrowed a Seven during its M100 development programme, the trade-off for Caterham was advice on a batch of front suspension changes. Caster, camber, toe-in, spring rate and bump steer alterations have given more bite to the front wheels. Interestingly, after years of progress towards eliminating bump steer, Lotus suggested that more should be introduced to improve stability on poor roads. Work continues on stiffer spring rates, but the test car had springs of double the normal stiffness.

The pedal box has been redesigned for the first time in 30 years to eliminate the old Seven problem of the driver's feet getting damp when it rains: water used to seep down through the bonnet louvres. Although the car's traditional stove-enamelled spaceframe withstands corrosion well, the entire chassis is now coated with epoxy powder. The Seven's cooling now features a larger radiator with a cowl for the electric fan. A detachable rear window for the hood will be available soon.

Otherwise the Seven recipe is much the same as Colin Chapman's original 1957 concept. The car looks eccentric with its skimpy aluminium bodywork, glass-fibre wings and bug-eyed headlamps. Its suspension is a sophisticated mix of double wishbone front and De Dion rear, with telescopic dampers and coil springs all round. At around 10cwt it is incredibly light and the 135bhp punched out by its Caterham-modified 1698cc Ford ohv 'Kent' engine gives a formidable power to weight ratio.

Morgan also has something new to offer in the car pitched here against the Seven. The Plus 4 is the most powerful four-cylinder car Morgan has ever made. For the last two years, Ford's 1597cc ohv engine has been used in all four-cylinder cars since the Fiat twin-cam unit was phased out two years ago after a production run of 126 owing to servicing difficulties.

After examining many engine options, Morgan chose Rover's 1994cc, twin-cam, 16-valve M16 unit, complete with multi-point fuel injection. The engine itself is unaltered from the 138bhp form in which it is used in Rover's 820 range, but a new transmission backplate has been added so that the Plus 8's end-on gearbox, driving a Salisbury rear axle, can be used.

Apart from its new engine, the Plus 4 is substantially unaltered from traditional Morgan specification. The powder-coated steel chassis frame — galvanised steel is optional — retains two-deep longitudinal sections with five boxed or tubular crossmembers. On to this base is mounted an ash frame to support hand-beaten steel or aluminium bodywork. In the time-honoured way, the ash frame is entirely cut and screwed/glued together by hand, but a recent innovation is a 40-minute dip in Cuprinol. The whole structure is strong, but not very torsionally rigid. Indeed, Morgan owners can sense the handling feel change slightly with the weather, since a prolonged dry spell causes the ash frame to stiffen.

This craftsmanship and the car's aggressively traditional appearance are the key to its enduring appeal. Back in the early '60s Morgan put a toe in the water of modernity by designing a sleek coupé, the Plus 4 Plus, but it flopped completely. Ever since, Peter Morgan has learned his lesson and steadfastly maintained Morgan's traditional values. If it doesn't look like a Morgan, the customers say, it's not a Morgan.

Morgans must look like the '30s sports cars that they continue to be in essence under the surface. They have a few concessions to modern requirements, like indicators and windscreen washers, but otherwise they are full-blooded nostalgia machines, all the way from the chrome-plated brass radiator grille to the raked rear quarters. Many replicas attempt

Morgan is arm and elbow car. You have to grasp the wheel and will it through corners. Tyres provide enough grip to allow Morgan some poise but it's unsettled by slightest bumps

to imitate the charisma of a Morgan, but none carry it off as well as the real thing.

With traditional looks you also receive a fair dose of archaic specification. The suspension is truly primitive, with leaf springs and lever type hydraulic dampers controlling the live rear axle. Front suspension is a sliding pillar independent system which looked old-fashioned in the '30s. Brakes are discs at the front and drums at the rear. But the steering is rack and pinion.

The stark differences between Caterham and Morgan are brought home as soon as you sit in the Seven. You need to be agile to prise yourself into its tiny black cockpit, but once you have slipped your legs down into the narrow footwell everything feels comfortable, tight and cosy. The adjustable vinyl seats, hug your body perfectly if you are of average height and build and the optional Motolita leather-rimmed steering wheel sits nicely in the hands. The hollow in the newly-designed sidescreens give an amazing amount of elbow room compared with Sevens of old. If you ignore the equally minimal passenger space on the other side of the high transmission tunnel, this feels exactly like a little single seater racing car.

The facia is merely a flat panel of vinyl-covered metal, with dials and switches neatly arranged across its full width. A 7000rpm rev counter with no red line marked, and 110mph speedometer are just visible through the steering wheel if you lower your head and keep your hands out of the way. In front of the passenger seat are small gauges for fuel, water ▶

Tremendous chassis makes cornering the Caterham very rewarding. You never feel it's going to let go. Corners require just a subtle flick of the wrists and bootful of power

Seven remains close to Colin Chapman's original concept: it has skimpy aluminium bodywork, glass-fibre wings. Very light, it has formidable power to weight ratio

temperature and oil pressure. A toggle switch sprouting from the facia by your left hand looks a primitive means of operating the indicators but works well, and similar switches take care of the horn and headlamp flashing — there are no conventional column stalks. The rest of the switches are rockers and include one to operate the optional heated windscreen: the familiar Seven winter problem of seeing through misted glass has been eliminated.

The Morgan's interior is far more plush, although less convenient. Since the cars are hand-made, almost any combination of trim colours and materials can be requested — 33 are available in leather. The test car had red leather with blue piping and a coloured facia instead of optional burr ash or walnut. It feels nice to sit in, far more spacious and upright than the Seven, and not so uncompromisingly designed for driving efficiency. The seats, although very comfortable, provide woefully little side support on the backrests, while the column stalks for indicators, horn and wipers are uncomfortably close to the dash. The three-spoke steering wheel feels twice as large as the Seven's, but the size is right for the steering weight. The view through the windscreen, swept by three stubby wipers, is just as evocative as the Seven's, and you sit equally low in both cars.

Large dials for speed (calibrated in white on black to 140mph) and revs (to 7000rpm, with no red line) sit directly in front of you. In spite of the steering wheel's size, their top sectors are obscured. A large rectangular panel in the centre contains rocker switches and gauges for fuel, water temperature, oil pressure and volts. The gearlever is tucked away under the facia and to its left is a fly-off handbrake.

If the interiors don't convince you of the Caterham's chalk to the Morgan's cheese, the performance of the Seven certainly does — from the very first time you ease up the light clutch and open up the accelerator. The Super Sprint engine whips the car forward with a

The car whips forward with a force unbelievable from a Cortina engine, no matter how modified

force unbelieveable from a Cortina engine, no matter how heavily modified and balanced. Response is instant and electrifying. The Seven catapults itself up the rev range in an instant through the first three gears, recording spectacular figures as it goes — 0-60mph takes just 5.3secs.

You are so low to the ground, so exposed to the elements, that this incredible acceleration feels subjectively even faster than the figures suggest. For all the world you could be sitting in the fastest object on four wheels as you open up down a quiet lane. The wind knocks your head about, the twin Weber 40DCOEs snort eagerly and the exhaust crackles like machine-gun fire as speed builds. The raw edge of exhilaration of most performance cars becomes blunted with familiarity, but the Seven's slingshot progress remains just as vivid to the senses a thousand times later. In a perfect driving environment, such as we found in the Cotswolds on a sunny spring day, you never tire of this car.

The engine is very flexible, but from 3000rpm to the 7000rpm limit it really lights up, quickly asking for another split-second pull of the short, delightfully snappy gear-change. It does not move quite so forcefully through fourth and fifth gears as the wind starts to create an invisible wall, but at 90mph the car feels quite fast enough. With sidescreens removed, the windscreen's protection is minimal: you have to squint to keep grit out of your eyes and the wind flares your nostrils. But then one of the greatest joys of the Seven is that you can experience its gutsy performance at useable speeds.

Measured against the Caterham, the Morgan's performance feels civilised and almost gentile, although this too is a quick car. A severe misfire above 4500rpm prevented us from taking figures, but Charles Morgan reckons that the Plus 4 should just nudge into the 6secs bracket for 0-60mph.

Undoubtedly the V8-engined Plus 8 would

Apart from the engine, little has changed on the Plus 4. In the early '60s a sleek coupé was designed but it was a total flop. Morgans really are like '30s sports cars

be a far closer match for the Caterham's acceleration.

The Rover M16 engine is a lusty performer, although it needs to be revved hard beyond 4500rpm to deliver its best. Acceleration is reasonable up to this point where maximum torque of 130lb ft is developed, but there is a subtle increase of urge beyond it. At lower engine speeds the Morgan emits none of the tingling sounds of the Caterham, the gentle whine of 16 valves dominating this engine's character. But higher up the scale a transmission harshness — we assume it is a result of the Plus 8 gearbox, since none is present on the Rover saloon — begins to intrude and spoil the smooth installation. Towards its 6500rpm limit it sounds distinctly breathless, even though this is where its strongest performance is delivered.

The Morgan's gearchange works pleasantly and firmly, but does not have the Caterham's trigger-like quality. In fourth and fifth, the car feels far more long-legged and high-speed progress is more refined, although with these cars we are talking comparatively. You could travel further in greater comfort in the Morgan since it cruises more readily and protects you just a little more thoroughly from the elements when the hood is down. But its acceleration is nowhere near as thrilling as the Caterham, or indeed the Plus 8.

Cornering quickly in the Caterham is just as rewarding as stamping on its throttle thanks to its fine chassis. The test car was fitted with optional 185/60R14 tyres on 6J alloy rims and adhesion is tremendous: you never feel that the car is about to let go. With such a quick steering ratio and tiny wheel, darting into corners requires just a subtle flick of the wrists and then a bootful of power to balance the car through. This is classic rear-wheel drive poise and only the most single-minded provocation upsets rear end grip. The car is light to control, utterly faithful to sensitive commands and immensely fast on a twisty road.

The Plus 4 is also quick. It can get from 0.60mph in less than 8 secs

Although you sit close to the rear axle line, the Caterham's ride quality is a surprise. You feel every ripple, of course, but the springing and damping efficiently round the bumps to eliminate any jarring. You feel deliciously in contact with the road at all times, which inspires great confidence in the Seven's tremendous cornering power.

On smooth roads the Morgan also has capable handling, but it is entirely different in character. This is an arm and elbow car, with much slower and heavier steering giving little self-centring effect. You have to grasp the wheel and will the car through corners, using the power far more deliberately to counter initial understeer. Grip from the 195/60R15 tyres is good enough to allow the Morgan to take corners with fair poise and speed, but the slightest bumps are very unsettling.

This is where the Morgan's primitive design sets it into a past era most persuasively. The steering kicks and the live axle rear end crashes up and down when the road surface breaks up, destroying all the handling pleasure which the car can provide on a smooth road. This is never dangerous because the back wheels sort themselves out happily enough when they meet the road again, but this bouncy, twitchy progress, accompanied by old-fashioned chassis flex, makes the Morgan an effort to drive on imperfect roads. A good A-road is its favourite environment, whereas the Caterham loves nothing better than the most sinuous, bumpy B-road. Right-handers are much easier to manage in the Morgan because the mirror's position, bang in the middle of the windscreen, completely obscures your view through left-handers. Both cars have good brakes, although the Caterham'a all-round discs win on bite and efficiency, while the Morgan on the other hand asks for more pedal pressure to operate its front discs and rear drums.

The cars, both fun machines, are contrasting and totally impractical ways to enjoy performance of rare character. You revel in the

battering of the wind, the rush of the tarmac inches from your backside and the feeling of wearing the cars, rather than sitting in them. But each is different. There is the thoroughness of the Caterham's engineering for uncompromised ability. But the Morgan has a simpler appeal which wallows in pure nostalgia. The Seven is a driver's car, but the Morgan suits a gentler traveller. Both have strong merits, vivid personalities and offer an evocative driving experience, but the Caterham is much the better car . . . and cheaper by £3000. ∎

HOW THEY COMPARE

Morgan's interior is plush red leather with blue piping. More spacious than Seven but seats give little side support. Column stalks too close to dash. Wheel obscures tops of dials. Gear lever is under facia. Steering is slow and heavy, but handling is capable and grip good

DRIVETRAIN	CATERHAM	MORGAN
Cylinders	4	4
Capacity	1690cc	1994
Bore/stroke (mm)	83.3/77.6	84.5/89.0
Head/block	cast iron/cast iron	al alloy/cast iron
Valve gear	2 per cyl	4 per cyl
Valve operation	push rod	DOHC
Compression ratio	9.7:1	10.0:1
Induction	2 Weber 40	Lucas multi-point
Power/rpm	DCOE	fuel injection
Torque/rpm	twin choke carbs	
Gearbox	135bhp/6000	138bhp/6000
Drive	122lb ft/4500	131lb ft/4500
Final drive ratio	5-speed	5-speed
Mph/1000rpm top	De Dion rear	live axle rear
Tyres	3.92:1	3.73:1
	20.3	24.4
	185/60 HR 14	195/60 R15

DIMENSIONS		
Length (ins)	133.0	156.0
Width (ins)	62.0	63.0
Height (ins)	44.0	52.0
Wheelbase (ins)	88.5	98.0
Track f/r (ins)	50/52.5	53/54
Kerb weight (lb)	130g	2042
Distribution f/r (%)	49/51	57/43

PRICES		
Total in GB	£10,691	£13,500

FUEL CONSUMPTION		
Overall mpg	19.3	—
Fuel tank (gals)	8.0	12.5

TOP SPEED		
Mean	114	109

ACCELERATION (secs)		
0-30 mph	1.9	2.7
0-40	3.0	4.3
0-50	4.1	5.6
0-60	5.3	7.7
0-70	7.6	10.5
0-80	9.7	13.6
0-90	12.5	18.0
0-100	17.0	26.1
Standing ¼mile	14.6/95mph	15.2/86
Standing km	27.6/111mph	29.0/104

In each gear — CATERHAM				
mph	top	4th	3rd	2nd
10-30	—	—	6.1	3.9
20-40	10.5	8.2	5.3	3.2
30-50	9.9	6.4	4.6	2.8
40-60	8.6	5.7	4.3	2.9
50-70	8.8	6.2	4.3	—
60-80	11.4	6.0	6.0	—
70-90	15.1	7.2	7.2	—
80-100	22.6	10.8	10.8	—

In each gear — MORGAN				
mph	top	4th	3rd	2nd
10-30	—	9.8	6.0	3.5
20-40	13.4	8.3	4.9	3.3
30-50	11.2	7.2	4.8	3.3
40-60	10.9	7.3	5.1	3.6
50-70	12.2	8.1	5.2	—
60-80	14.6	9.5	5.7	—
70-90	25.0	10.9	7.9	—
80-100	—	13.0	—	—

Seven feels like a single seater. Seats adjust and fit well. Facia is just a flat panel with dials and switches across its width. There are no column stalks. Toggle switch operates the indicators. The 1988 1700 Super Sprint has very much improved suspension and handling

Seven's heaven

Revisiting an old friend, we found it hadn't aged at all.

by Barry Lake

photography by Kent Mears

Think back 30 years — to early 1958. Australia's family car was the FE Holden, about to be replaced by the facelifted FC. Ford was still selling the Consul and Zephyr, with the first Australian Falcon still more than two years away. The most common sports cars were MGAs and Austin-Healeys, with the basic little bug-eyed Austin-Healey Sprite about to be released on our market. All were quite primitive cars by today's standards.

Over in England, a rapidly developing racing and road car designer named Colin

Chapman had just released perhaps the most simple of all post-war car designs: the Lotus Seven. Little more than the basic engine, transmission and wheels, tied together by a very light tubular steel frame and clothed with the barest minimum of aluminium and glass fibre panels, the Seven was designed to carry one or two people for daily commuting plus, because of its light weight and good handling, being able to double as a competitive hillclimber or club circuit racer at weekends.

Creature comforts were of secondary importance. There was no heater, although it did have a simple hood and side-curtains to keep most of the rain out. There was no seat adjustment — in fact there weren't actually any seats: the passengers sat on and leaned against lightly-padded cushions on the floor and against the rear bulkhead panel. Its saving grace was that it performed well and out-cornered most cars on the road. But that was three decades ago. How does the car stand up 30 years on?

Spartan interior, neat engine bay, and contrasting styling.

Since the Seven was a mainstay of the Lotus company from the 1950s, it seemed like a good idea to bring one along when we did photographs and performance testing of the latest Lotus Esprit Turbo. The idea was to show how far Lotus Cars, the company, had progressed in 30 years, and to emphasise the fact that Lotus is no longer merely a supplier of budget performance cars but is now a producer of true supercars.

Lotus Cars in 1988 is aiming directly at the recognised supercar manufacturers — particularly the likes of Ferrari and Lamborghini. And the new Esprit is a fine example of how far Lotus has come in this quest. The quality of build, the superb surface finish of the glass fibre body and the detailed design and workmanship in this latest car — not to mention its super performance — put it squarely on course for its title challenge. Perhaps it isn't quite a Ferrari-beater yet — not in all areas, anyway — but the gauntlet is down, and future models from Lotus will be well worth watching.

The Seven was designed and shown to the public in 1957, first got into its sales stride in 1958, and found its own niche in the market over the next eight years. But it almost went out of production in 1966 when Lotus Cars had already begun its move into the world of more up-market cars. The company felt it no longer needed such a car, but Graham Nearn of Caterham Cars saved it by talking Lotus into continuing to build the car. Nearn placed an order for 20 cars immediately just to make sure, and took on the sole distributorship for the Lotus Seven and Super Seven.

It was Nearn who came to the car's rescue again when Lotus really had to give it the chop in 1973 to make way for bigger and better things. He bought the rights to the design and to the name Seven, although the Lotus title had to be dropped and was replaced by Caterham.

I read of the first Lotus Seven as a schoolboy when it first appeared in the British motoring magazines, and was testing my first racing car at Warwick Farm on the same day in 1961 that Edward du Cros had his first drive in a BMC-powered white Lotus Seven. It was the first I had ever seen and the first, I think, in this country.

I raced against Sevens in all-comers races over the next few years, considered buying one of the larger-engined Super Sevens when they first appeared about three years later (but had no hope of raising enough money), and in 1969 worked on Sevens as a mechanic for Geoghegans when they were the Australian Lotus importers. I helped assemble the last Super

Seven they ever imported and did repairs, services, and high-speed test drives on at least a couple of dozen examples. You could say I knew the cars well.

My memories of Lotus Sevens and Super Sevens were of flexing chassis and lots of rattles, mostly from loose rivets in the aluminium side panels; of a variety of different engine/gearbox combinations; of so many owners' individual modifications that no two were alike; of fearsome rear axle tramp on hard standing-start acceleration runs; and of that final car having so many bits and pieces missing from its kit that ex-McLaren F1 and CanAm mechanic and ace fabricator Wally Willmott was kept busy making parts for weeks.

But most of all I remembered sensational acceleration, performance and handling that — on public roads — seemed to know no limits. Only on the race circuit could the car be forced to lose its handling manners, and then only in the form of increasing understeer. A driver has to be pretty foolhardy to get into real trouble in one of these cars; they just don't have any real vices.

Doug Macarthur's Lotus Seven Series 3 is powered by a relatively mild 1.3-litre Ford engine producing 82 kW (110 bhp). It isn't the most powerful Seven I have driven but, combined with its light weight, has enough poke to sprint through the

standing-start 400 metres in similar times to the likes of Mazda RX-7 Turbo, Holden Commodore Turbo, and is quite close to the times of the red Holden VL Group A Commodores. A time of 15.9 seconds for the two-way average isn't shabby at all.

Macarthur, we should explain, is a more than respectable racing driver from way back. He started with a bug-eyed Sprite in 1963, and then progressed to a Mark 2a version with which he held a class lap record at Catalina circuit at Katoomba.

Doug went to the UK for an extended holiday, and while there bought a lightweight Lotus Elan that he raced in England a few times and then brought back to Australia.

In 1971 and 1972, Doug raced a Rennmax sports/racing car, first with a BMW engine, later with a Repco V8. After a three-year break, he came back in 1975 and 1976 with a Lola T360 Hart Formula 2 car, retired again, and came back for 1982 and 1983 with a Ralt RT4 Formula Pacific car. His last race was the Australian GP at Calder in November 1983, where he qualified 14th but broke a driveshaft and retired.

Nowadays, Doug contents himself by taking the Seven out for an occasional punt through his favourite series of corners, and occasionally thinks about the idea of getting into of racing again . . .

Side curtains are used on the road to avoid wind buffeting in full open trim.

It is easy to see why he enjoys the Seven so much. This is a beautiful example of the model. The chasis is stiffer than the early models and there are no rattles, no loose panels. The steering feels precise and light, the pedals and the gear-shift lever are also light and smooth to operate and the axle doesn't tramp during fast take-offs. The pedals are nicely placed for heel-and-toe gear changes, and footwell space is not as limited as I remembered.

Doug's Seven is a joy to drive. It can do incredibly fast lap times without even squealing the tyres, and showed its race circuit breeding by chasing the Esprit through the tight bits while being more composed than the later car. This is despite the fact the Seven has only a docile 1.3-litre engine, a normal wide-ratio Ford Escort gearbox, and 78-series Avon tyres that have been on the car for years. The Esprit is designed for fast open roads and European motorways, so it is not as comfortable on a short, tight, race circuit. But its superb turbo power rockets it down the short straight at incredible speed. There, the Seven, with its limited power and un-aerodynamic styling, struggles to reach 175 km/h, while the Esprit is capable of 247 km/h, given a long enough straight.

But the Esprit is a tricky car to corner really fast, and as we loathe to scrub out the tyres on a car for which a potential owner was anxiously waiting, we did only a handful of laps. This is a car that would require quite a lot of laps before the best could be drawn from it.

The Esprit was capable of 54-second laps, maybe better with a real ace at the wheel and the tyre pressures adjusted accordingly, but the Seven was remarkably quick at 55.9 seconds. That ranks the square-rigger with the likes of the Mazda RX-7 Turbo, and faster than the red VL Group A Commodore. In fact, it is only tenths slower than the HSV Group A . . . and it is by far the easiest car we have ever driven at that pace.

On the circuit, the ride of the Seven is superb. On the open road, bumps and pot-holes can jar it, but it is still better than my memories of older examples. Driving with the top off and no side curtains, the wind buffets the occupants, pumps up the lungs so it is hard to breathe, and makes it hard to see. Doug usually drives with the two side curtains attached (but with the top still down) and this puts an end to the buffeting.

It is a sweet little car, this Seven; far better than any I have driven before, and it has rekindled my interest in buying or restoring one — a dream I have had for about as long as the Lotus Seven has existed. □

LOTUS SEVEN S3
1.3-litre, four-speed manual

ENGINE
Location	Front
Cylinders	Four in-line
Bore × stroke	80.9 × 62.9mm
Capacity	1297 cm³
Induction	Two, dual-throat, side-draught carburettors
Compression ratio	9.2 to 1
Fuel pump	Mechanical
Valve gear	Push-rod operated ohv, two valves/cyl
Claimed power	82.0 kW at 6000 rpm
Claimed torque	135.0 Nm at 5000 rpm
Maximum recommended engine speed	6500 rpm
Specific power output	63.2 kW/litre

TRANSMISSION
Type	Four-speed manual
Driving wheels	Rear
Clutch	Single, dry plate

Gearbox ratios

Gear ratio		km/h 1000 rpm	Max Speed	At (rpm)
First	3.656	7.7	50	6500
Second	2.185	12.8	83	6500
Third	1.425	19.7	128	6500
Fourth	1.000	28.0	175	6250
Final-Drive Ratio				3.890 to 1

SUSPENSION
Front	Independent by unequal-length upper and lower arms, with coil springs and anti-roll bar
Rear	Live axle located by four trailing arms and Panhard rod, with coil springs
Wheels	Alloy, 5.0J × 13
Tyres	Avon Turbosteel 165/78 SR13

BRAKES
Front	244mm discs
Rear	228mm drums

STEERING
Type	Rack and pinion
Turns, lock to lock	3.5
Ratio	16.5 to 1
Turning circle	9.1 metres

DIMENSIONS AND WEIGHT
Wheelbase	2260mm
Front Track	1245mm
Rear track	1321mm
Overall length	3378mm
Overall width	1549mm
Overall height (to top of windscreen 940mm) to top of hood	1111mm
Ground clearance	152mm
Kerb weight	553kg
Weight to power	6.7kg/kW

CAPACITIES AND EQUIPMENT
Fuel tank	41.1 litres
Cooling system	5.7 litres
Engine oil system	3.7 litres
Battery	12V 35AH
Alternator	40 amps

CHECKLIST
Alloy wheels	yes
Adjustable steering	no
Air-conditioning	no
Central door locking	no
Cruise control	no
Power steering	no
Power windows	no
Radio	no
Tape player	no
Compact disc player	no
Rear-window wiper	no
Remote outside mirror adjustment	no
Sun roof	no
Tachometer	yes
Trip computer	no

FUEL CONSUMPTION
Average for test	12.6 litres/100km
Best recorded	12.0 litres/100km
Worst recorded	14.8 litres/100km

ACCELERATION
0–60 km/h	3.81 seconds
0–80 km/h	5.60 seconds
0–100 km/h	7.89 seconds
0–110 km/h	9.41 seconds
0–120 km/h	10.72 seconds
0–130 km/h	13.40 seconds
0–140 km/h	16.33 seconds
0–150 km/h	20.82 seconds
0–160 km/h	27.60 seconds
Standing 400m	15.91 seconds
Terminal speed	138.6 km/h

The above are averages of runs in opposite directions

Standing 400m, best	15.82 seconds
Terminal speed, best	139.4 km/h

Figures by Datron Correvit L3 digital electronic timing equipment

LIST PRICE	not applicable
PRICE AS TESTED	approx $15,000

Includes options: (none)

DAY TWO, and the rain is both icy and horizontal. As yours truly attempted for the umpteenth time to squeeze a six foot frame into a glass fibre and aluminium pothole without hooking a jean leg on to the horn switch and frightening the sheep, I could not get the thought from my mind. Why would anyone actually *pay* for this kind of privation? Maybe it should be some kind of character-building, essential part of motoring adolescence, so we can grow up to appreciate the finer things of driving, like visibility, tranquillity and practicability. Pubescence is the acquisition of a hot hatch.

Next time someone drags out the old chestnut about motoring writers having a permanent holiday driving smart cars though, at least I have the perfect answer.

Up till then I hadn't really experienced the Seventh sense. We've all read the analogies about motorbiking, and if you hanker after a GPZXL double intercooler multi everything but are frightened of falling off, you'll buy a Seven. But having suffered Sevening, sorry, experienced it, I can see that the analogy isn't really appropriate at all. After two days in the worst condtions imaginable I'd certainly have parked the bike, but dammit, I was actually beginning to enjoy the Seven experience. It's all a question of adjusting my philosophy and there was honestly no point in slagging the car for what it *didn't* have. I knew that just by looking at it. Its virtues are purely tactile and naturally you have to experience them to find out. That said, a sunny day would have enhanced the experience . . .

There's no doubt whatsover that the Seven is a *serious* fun car. Its appeal lies in the uncompromisingly *intimate* relationship that arises between the driver and the road, once you wriggle behind the wheel, and the absolute immediacy with which it goes, stops, corners – does anything in fact. Our 911 camera car may have been quicker on a clear road, but Seven gets you closer to the action. You couldn't help noticing the reaction of others to its shape either. Love it or loathe it, the lawn mower styling is now a shape indelibly written in the pages of British sports car history.

So it was that we found ourselves on a Welsh hillside in the pouring rain, with two variations on the Seven theme. The original is of course the Caterham. Original because it is derived from the real '60s article, although it's significant that Caterham now seems a more logical prefix than Lotus. Caterham purchased the rights and tooling from Lotus in 1974, and the model had been steadily refined and improved since then. It must indeed have been basic in those days.

The best seller in a one model range offering a variety of engines, rear suspension options and states of assembly, is the 1700cc Super Sprint version and this is powered by a slightly overbored version of the Kent crossflow Cortina engine. Fitted with gas-flowed head, special pistons, cam and twin Webers, it develops 133bhp with accompanying stentorian snoring noises from the carburettor throats to match the Escort rally car rasp from behind. Torque peaks at 4,500rpm, where 122lb ft is available.

In this form, it costs £9,489 including VAT and car tax and there's about 20 hours of work to finish it, because in order to avoid type approval the car has to be sold in component form. Avoiding the bureaucrats is significant, because not only would type approval be prohibitively expensive, it would inevitably require sanitisation of the machinery until it ceased to conform to its raw, minimalist concept.

Transformation from component to mobility primarily involves insertion of the engine and gearbox into a fully trimmed, panelled and wired chassis, and is unlikely to present any major problem to anyone possessed of the ability to use a 14mm ring spanner and screwdriver.

The interloper is the Westfield. There's no doubt that it *looks* like a Seven, and yet this is a completely new car. Litigation has even arisen over previous versions, because Caterham felt that other constructors – not only Westfield – had aped the styling of the car for which they had parted with good money to Colin Chapman, in exchange for *exclusive* rights. Arguing about the styling of the Seven seems to me a bit like Dennis Hopper suing for his part in the script in *Easy Rider*, but nevertheless, every panel on the latest Westfield has been altered, the chassis design had been revised, the name Seven had been changed to SE and honour is deemed satisfied. Judge for yourself whether it looks radically different.

If the Super Sprint is the final evolution of the clubmans racer concept begun by Chapman in 1957, then the Westfield is unashamedly bargain basement Sevening. The demonstrator was fitted with a lightly tweaked 1600cc crossflow Ford developing about 105bhp, and four-speed Escort gearbox. This car also bore an SE-1 suffix in deference to recently introduced, fully independent, twin wishbone rear suspension.

Westfields are available only as kits, and the customer must supply an engine, gearbox, wheels and sundries such as Escort differential, steering rack, radiator and pedal box. In its most complete form, the Westfield kit will set you back about £2,500 plus VAT, and then there's the engine and transmission and some breaker's yard bits. How you want the finished article obviously affects the total, but the demonstrator was insured for £5,500 which gives you some idea.

It's worth mentioning here that Cater-

Or two Sevens . . . Caterham's Seven and Westfield's SE may be similar in concept, but are a long way apart in terms of price and execution. Mark Hales investigated the seventh sensation.

ham will also sell you a lower spec kitform car. The customer supplies engine, gearbox, and rear axle from a Marina rather than the Super Sprint's De Dion rear end, and parts with £4,323 plus the VAT. Both companies reckon that a full kit form car takes about 120 hours to nail together.

Now, even if you think the two cars look similar, they don't really compare. They represent opposite ends of the Seven

market and we didn't really intend to discover which was the better, rather to investigate the Seven obsession from two differing viewpoints.

Within minutes of climbing in, it became apparent that the specification of the motive hardware affects the character of the whole car, and not just from the performance angle. The Caterham's five-speed Sierra 'box has a shift which moves fore and aft in conventional style, whereas the Westfield's four-speed change moves more in a vertical plane, with a cranked lever. This may sound like a nitpick of the smallest proportion, but it's amazing how mistakenly finding the reverse gate on the four-speeder for the 10th time can affect your perception of the car. Five gears allow an overdrive top as well, and the Westfield's cruising was further hampered by a short final drive which had the Ford howling at some 5,000rpm in exchange for only 75mph. The resolution is another £50 spent at Jim's car dismantlers, but you begin to see the difference. Caterham make the decision for you, and that's part of what you pay for.

Both cars go like the proverbial. It's not the sustained outpouring of power pulling hard against tall gears stuff that you find in bigger brethren. More like a blur of hand on gearlever shifting at 30, 60 and 90mph, when 6,000rpm is showing on the Super Sprint's tacho. Even if that instrument packed up, the mechanical noise would suggest an upchange and no sooner have you banged the stumpy lever, devoid of the leverage it enjoyed in its original location, than it's time to hit it again. Once installed in either car the sheer pleasure of playing hooligan tunes up the gearbox encourages you to slow down just so you can rasp up the ratios again.

Our sister *Motor*'s performance figures for the Super Sprint showed a startling 60mph in just 5.6sec, while 30mph took a mere 2.2sec. Thereafter, sail-like aerodynamics start to take their toll, and although 90mph is reached in 13sec, the next 10mph takes nearly six seconds more. Top speed is almost academic at around 110mph because nobody would seriously cruise at that because of the wind and exhaust noise, let alone the laws of the land. Better take the B roads and play tunes past all those lorries.

Electrifying they certainly are, Caterham more so than Westfield, simply because the engine was more powerful and the gears longer. Less happy though is the aforementioned noise factor. Caterhams have the side-mounted silencer, but at least the exit is behind you. The Westfield's tailpipe finishes just ahead of the passenger mudguard . . .

So they go like Hades, but what about the twisty bits? I was expecting all the straightline alacrity that 130bhp in 12cwt

should produce, but was absolutely convinced that both cars would have the kind of ride that demands avoidance of discarded dog ends. They don't. Although both are still available with beam axles at the rear, the quest for better ride has seen the evolution of a De Dion rear end on the Caterham (built round a Sierra differential), and a fully independent setup on the Westfield. The latter is more akin to a single seater racing car and employs an Escort final drive housed within a specially cast, Elan-like, alloy casting. Cast aluminium uprights are suspended on fabricated wishbones and there are double jointed half shafts driving through Escort front drive hubs. The Caterham has an A-bracket supporting the De Dion tube with short radius rods locating the beam fore and aft.

Both systems are effective in providing excellent traction and preserving the occupant's lunch. In fact the revelation is simply amazing, and was the biggest single surprise of the whole two days. The ride of both was actually better at low speeds than that of the 911CS.

At the front, the Westfield has double wishbones again and borrows Cortina uprights and discs, while the Caterham uses Triumph Vitesse uprights and brakes and suspends them by double wishbones, the top one incorporating the anti roll bar. Arresting such a light mass proved no problem for either braking system and neither car uses a servo, although the Caterham in particular needed a firm push on the pedal. Since the test car was made Caterham have replaced the rear drums by discs, and this should also guard against the increase in pedal travel which crept in during our test.

There's never been any argument about the handling responses of these cars. Now that the average bump won't send them leaping three feet to one side, once you become accustomed to the car's dimensions and the proximity of the ground, the confidence that the chassis imparts is uncanny. Understeer going to neutral as the right foot becomes heavier, is the order of the day, but the feeling of being at one with the machine is something you won't find anywhere else outside the racetrack. The wheel becomes an extension of the arms and the slightest movement is translated immediately. In return, every ripple and crack in the road is fed back, but it arrives as feel not fight and you would need to be crass indeed not to sense impending loss of grip at the tyres. Once the command is given, there's no wait for the car's mass to settle at either end; it seems to swivel from a point beneath the driver's seat. And then because the shoulders are firmly clamped by transmission tunnel and cockpit side – more so in the Caterham than Westfield – the feeling of being *part* of the chassis is even stronger.

Even on soaking wet roads, grip is astonishing from 185 section rubber (14in on the Sprint, 13in on the SE), and apart from common sense, the biggest deterrent to researching the limits of these cars is the fact that you sit somewhere below the axle line of the average truck. Looking ahead up the road is difficult from a worm's eye view and the impression that a Volvo F18's Michelin could leave tracks over your head becomes even stronger in heavy traffic.

Of the two, the Caterham's steering has considerably more feel, and the scuttle is higher so the wheel is well clear of the thighs. The Westfield feels less intimate perhaps, partly because of steering which is so very light, and partly because the cockpit sides and transmission tunnel are lower giving a more perched on, rather than cocooned in, sensation. Once in the cars, legroom is surprisingly not a problem even for drivers over six feet tall. I didn't even need the rearmost of the Caterham's seat adjustments.

Dynamically there's little to choose in ride quality or outright grip between the two, but the Caterham as befits its price and the length of time for which the car has been in production, feels better integrated and classier. It also boasts better, adjustable seats, better belts and superior weather equipment, and has an air of confidence which you'd expect from the real thing. There's little to choose as regards basic quality of construction – both cars are nicely made.

Having started out by saying we didn't intend to make this a comparison, it's hardly fair to finish with one. It's extremely unlikely that anybody would make the decision to go Sevening between a Westfield and a Caterham. The Caterham's status is not under threat from Westfield and the SE emerged as a cheap, fun little car in the style of the real thing. In reality it's probably little different from a mid '60s Seven. Once we'd driven it though, we felt happy to mention it in the same breath as the Caterham simply because its basic chassis is so good, and it's well constructed. The fact it costs half as much seems ample compensation for what amounts to a lack of the other's class.

Few would consider using even the real thing as daily transport. Vision and ventilation with the hood up are hopeless, and ingress to the cockpit provides a ready comic performance for passing shoppers. But these cars never had any pretensions to practicality. The Caterham is the very embodiment of a *sports* car. It is raw, race-precise performance and you will never be allowed to forget that. It is strictly for the joy of driving when there's no particular place to go.

Me, I'll reserve anything that has that kind of capability for when I'm wearing a suit and helmet . . .

Caterham Super 7

Assembly instructions included. Just add power.

BY WILLIAM JEANES

• Let heaven and nature sing the praises of this brand-new 31-year-old car. A car that not only looks like something from another time, but acts like it. A roadster fitted with all the comfort and convenience items you'd find on an anvil. A rolling anachronism so utterly impractical that it's guaranteed to bring a broad smile to the face of every string-back forever mired in the swamp of sports-car nostalgia.

It's all that and one wonderful thing more: it runs like a pit bull on industrial-strength amphetamines.

What we have here is a Caterham Super 7, and it is the genuine, copyrighted, signed-sealed-and-delivered successor to the Lotus 7 brought to life by Colin Chapman in 1957.

What's more, you can build this car yourself. You can also sit on the floor of your garage and beat on your toes with a torque wrench, depending upon what you consider to be fun. Or, better yet, you can take the coward's way out and order a rolling chassis, which the U.S. importer—Sevens & Elans, of Cambridge, Massachusetts (617–497–7777)—will send your way for a hefty premium (price on application) over the $15,495 cost of the kit.

And then you can buy an engine, which

should be one of five Ford four-bangers, ranging from the 83-hp 1600 GT ($2275) to the 168-hp Cosworth BDR RS 1700 Twincam ($8990). On the day you blat your way out of your garage and onto the street, you'll have spent somewhere between $20,000 and $30,000 for your Caterham.

Is this car worth that kind of money? You bet your Whitworth nuts and bolts it is. Hell, if you can fit into one of these things, you could spend $40,000 and still feel as if you're getting the right amount of fun for your money. And one more thing: Chris Tchórznicki, head of Sevens & Elans, won't go south on you in the event you have an assembly or warranty problem. He's there if you need help.

Our test Caterham held 133 horsepower under its long, polished-aluminum hood. Its Ford 1700 Super Sprint engine, one of the five recommended engine choices, took our tester from 0 to 60 mph in a tick under six seconds, a testimony to the car's combination of light weight (1339 pounds) and muscular horsepower.

The five-speed gearbox is operated with, literally, a flick of the wrist and has as positive a shifter action as you will ever experience. The acceleration, as noted, will suck the breath out of the most jaded driver as the Caterham speeds through the standing quarter-mile in 14.4 seconds, reaching a speed of 90 mph.

Caterham Car Sales and Coachworks, Ltd., of Surrey, England, now fits each of its Series III cars with a de Dion rear suspension, replacing the live axle that was a Lotus 7 fixture since most of us were children. This improvement, combined with the control-arm-and-coil-spring front suspension, adjustable shock absorbers, and the car's almost subterranean center of

gravity, produces handling that is as positive and predictable as you're likely to find. Our car had Goodyear NCT 185/55-14 low-profile tires mounted on five-spoke Revolution alloy wheels and, thus equipped, turned in a show-stopping 0.90 g on the skidpad.

On the street, cornering in the Caterham is flat, quick, and more exciting than night sky diving. The brakes on our car were unassisted front discs and rear drums, and they hauled the Caterham to a stop with commendable competence. To make a good braking system even better, Caterhams from now on will get disc brakes on the rear wheels as well.

Another change in the offing concerns the car's side curtains. The new ones will fold, meaning that you might actually be able to take the top and the side curtains along on a trip, an act impossible with the current storage space and nonfolding curtains. The new side curtains are reputed to be water-resistant.

The side curtains, now and in the future, work in concert with a top that one erects in the fond hope that it will fend off at least some of the elements. This is, all things considered, something of a forlorn hope by modern standards. By sports-car standards of yesteryear, however, the top works reasonably well. In the case of large

drivers, it works best if the driver enters the car first and has a group of friends install the top once he is firmly in place.

The driving position is cramped but workable for a driver well over six feet tall, and is helped along by a cockpit that's been lengthened slightly over the original and adjustable pedals that also serve—necessarily—as footrests. The thick, leather-wrapped steering wheel is small but ef-

fective, and the seats are firmly padded and adjustable fore-and-aft. In every way, however, the Caterham remains a throwback to the days when real drivers wore leather helmets and the idea of glass side windows in a roadster ranked right up there with programs aimed at the dissolution of the British Empire.

But the impracticality of this car must not be allowed in any way to diminish its attractiveness. Remember that the Lotus 7 came into being as a racing car. That considered, the current Caterham is civilized indeed. And although it is—or can be—a car built from a kit, the end result is not what we would call a kit car. What you wind up with is a racing car that you can drive on the street and on winding country roads, grinning as you go.

As you drive, top down, you're regaled with a deep exhaust note, the feel of wind on your face, and a certain amount of buffeting once you exceed 65 or 70 mph. In addition, you find yourself the object of admiring, envious looks from just about every driver and pedestrian who sees you. That's because you appear to be having fun in this strange device.

And, if you deserve designation as a car enthusiast, that's what you're doing. ●

Vehicle type: front-engine, rear-wheel-drive, 2-passenger, 2-door roadster
Price as tested: $25,000 (estimated) (kit: $15,495)
Engine type: 4-in-line, iron block and head, 2x2-bbl Weber 40DCOE carburetors

Displacement	103 cu in, 1691cc
Power (SAE net)	133 bhp @ 6000 rpm
Transmission	5-speed
Wheelbase	88.5 in
Length	133.0 in
Width	62.8 in
Height	43.1 in
Curb weight	1339 lb
Zero to 60 mph	5.9 sec
Zero to 100 mph	26.5 sec
Standing ¼-mile	14.4 sec @ 90 mph
Top speed	107 mph
Braking, 70–0 mph	187 ft
Roadholding, 300-ft-dia skidpad	0.90 g
C/D observed fuel economy	19 mpg

olin Chapman might well have smiled. It's 15 years since he axed the Lotus Seven because the coarse, crude little sports car didn't fit in with his lofty plans for the future; and yet here we are, with the simple two-seater Seven not only alive and prospering (more so than some of its ambitious Lotus successors, the cynical may say), but surrounded now by a small crop of imitators.

Such imitation, they say, is the sincerest form of flattery. Graham Nearn, who has kept the Seven alive ever since Chapman showed it the door, would not agree – and has argued as much in various court actions. But are these Seven look-alikes merely artful plagiarists or do they offer something that the original does not?

To discover the answer, we took the newest, a Westfield SEi, tucked it nervously onto Sealink's flagship St Nicholas (among intercontinental heavyweights which made it look even more worryingly Lilliputian) and headed from Harwich to the Hook of Holland to meet a long established, Dutch-built Seven spin-off, the Donkervoort S8AT.

All three may *look* like the Lotus Seven, but they are really echoes of the late Colin Chapman's original. We sent **Kevin Blick** to Holland with the lookalikes: a Westfield SE meets both the Dutch Donkervoort D8 and a Caterham Seven, the Lotus's direct descendant. Are they really rivals, or just fun cars linked only by looks and homage paid to the vision of the man who created the Lotus ideal?

TRIPLE

ECHO

Meeting us there, too, was a real Caterham Seven, owned – and built – by Dutch Lotus enthusiast, Paul Derkse.

The aim was a comparison between the three; but not, it must be stressed right away, a road-test style comparison.

They may look approximately alike and may appear to be constructed alike, too – but, in reality, they differ widely in both price and performance. In simple terms, if the Caterham is the stepping-off point, one could say that the Westfield has dropped down a couple of rungs to become a more affordable 'fun car'; and the Donkervoort has jumped up a few, refining and improving on the Seven's concept but becoming much more costly in the process.

To the untutored passer-by, the three would still look much the same: tiny, stark and low, with frog-eye headlights, flat screens and flowing wings. They are the inheritors of that classic British sports car shape, handed down from 1930s favourites like the T-Type MG and Singer Le Mans and still, of course, preserved in aspic by Morgan.

That said, there are numerous differences – some of them enforced by Nearn's determination that the Caterham must

not be copied too closely. You can spot subtle variations in nose design, wing shapes, light positions, screen rake and so on, though none is enough to divorce any of the pretenders from the essential character of Chapman's original.

The same could be said of their construction. Chapman built the Seven around a simple but rigid multi-tube chassis from which could be hung as many bought-in components as possible and around which would be wrapped minimalist bodywork.

It wasn't a new idea even then, but it's no less satisfactory today, still being the preferred construction method for most kit and small scale manufacturers, including both Westfield and Donkervoort. But once past this point, the subtle differences once again begin to show.

ORIGINALITY – THE KEY

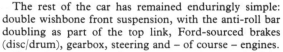

Originality has been Caterham's keynote ever since Graham Nearn's deal with Chapman in 1973 which turned the Lotus Super Seven into the Caterham Super Seven.

He wanted to build the Seven as Chapman devised it – soon reverting back to the original aluminium body panels from the ill-fitting glassfibre clothes it wore in the last days at Lotus as the little loved S4; these days, only the wings, nose and bonnet of the Seven are in glasfibre.

Other significant changes to the Seven's essential design have been made only when forced. The 'long cockpit' Seven squeezed a couple of extra inches of passenger space into the car's compact overall dimensions; Chapman, not the tallest of men, probably designed his early cars around himself, but the long cockpit Seven allowed even six-footers to experience Seven-style motoring in reasonable comfort (if that's an appropriate word) for the first time.

Then, more recently, the drying up of suitable Ford rear axle supplies forced a change to de Dion rear suspension. This, you could fairly say, is the nearest a car can be to remaining live-axled without actually possessing said unit.

The rest of the car has remained enduringly simple: double wishbone front suspension, with the anti-roll bar doubling as part of the top link, Ford-sourced brakes (disc/drum), gearbox, steering and – of course – engines.

These last are personal preference – as is so much of the rest of cars like these, whose detail specification can be tailored to fit taste and wallet.

A common choice is the 135bhp Super Sprint 1700, while the brave opt for a 170bhp Cosworth BDG. Derkse's car had neither, though it will have a Cosworth in the near future. Presently, it runs on a Lotus-Ford twin-cam pinched from an Elan Plus 2S that he's restoring, but it's also one of the Seven's former engine choices.

This is Derkse's third self-built Seven, built to his own taste – and beautifully too. Its standard of finish wouldn't disgrace any factory made model; but his choice of massive 225/50VR15 Yokohama tyres, instead of the stock 185/60s, didn't please everyone, even if they were on handsome Revolution wheels.

Joop Donkervoort began *his* involvement with the Seven as importer into Holland. However, his ideas and Nearn's soon diverged: he wanted to modify and improve the Seven so that it could be sold as a car rather than a kit. They went their separate ways and Donkervoort thereafter called his Super Seven a Super Eight.

First step was a re-drawn chassis capable of withstanding impact testing, with fuel tankage repositioned ahead of the rear axle (from behind) and giving more room inside, especially for the driver since it was designed with a 4cm offset in the centre tunnel positioning. This is a major reason for the car not being sold in the UK – sitting on the right, a driver would have to suffer the small well.

Similar looking tails hide different suspensions. The Donkervoort, left, has a triangular top wishbone with transverse and trailing links below. Caterham, centre, use a de Dion axle and Westfield double-wishbones

Like the Seven, the Eight uses aluminium body skinning and grp add-ons. The first D8s were live-axled but, like Caterham, Donkervoort has had to go all-independent in the D8A. His choice was not a de Dion axle but a fully independent system, using a triangular top wishbone, two long parallel transverse bottom links, a trailing link and progressive rate coil spring/damper unit at each side, and set up to create stabilising toe-in under braking and toe-out on acceleration.

Up front are Caterham-style double wishbones, too, incorporating the anti-roll bar in the top link. Front brakes are ventilated discs, while the rears are drums. There's no servo but – unusually – there is an adjustable balance bar to alter front/rear braking bias. Again, brakes, steering, gears and so on come via Ford.

The engine is Ford as well, but quite different from Caterham's choice. Emi-

THEY ARE INHERITORS OF THE CLASSIC BRITISH SPORTS CAR SHAPE THAT HAS BEEN HANDED DOWN FROM 1930s FAVOURITES LIKE THE T-TYPE MG AND SINGER LE MANS AND, OF COURSE, STILL PRESERVED IN ASPIC BY MORGAN

ssions certification is a necessity if you want to sell road-ready cars, so under the lift-off bonnet is a fuel-injected Pinto unit (with Donkervoort's own manifolding). But as Ford only offer a 100bhp version with catalyst equipment, Donkervoort has developed his own 117bhp variant, as well as a much more exciting 170bhp turbocharged unit for the D8AT which uses Garrett's T3 turbo blowing to 0.7bar (10.2psi), lower compression Cosworth pistons and con-rods, and intercooling. This has a three-way catalyst and all the ancilliary equipment needed to gain full emission certification up to US83, US85 and US87 standards.

ATTENDING TO DETAIL

There's a lot of nice, unseen detailing, too. For instance, air is drawn into the heater chamber from scuttle louvres, then ducted along the transmission tunnel (cooling the gearbox en route) and exits via the low pressure area under the tail. Tucked under here, too, are the silencer and catalyst, where they will form part of the deformable crush-structure in the event of a rear impact.

Chris Smith's first Westfields sailed rather too close to the Caterham for Graham Nearn's liking and writs flew. As a result, the differences are now more apparent: the biggest is that the Westfield uses glassfibre rather than aluminium bodywork. Being self-coloured, this obviates the need for painting and so makes life easier and cheaper for the home assembler – and the Westfield is aimed principally at the home handyman. It's an unabashed kit car; most UK customers buy the basics and search out the rest from breakers' yards. To make that easy, it takes the usual permutation of Ford parts, including, in the SE version, the Ford rear axle of which there are still many mouldering in the long grass.

The SEi is the more up-market, all-independently sprung model, with Westfield's own double-wishbone rear end to match the similar system at the front where, interestingly, there's no anti-roll bar at all.

The SEi also now benefits from a stretched driving compartment – three inches roomier all round, inside the same overall dimensions, and the revised chassis can now also carry Ford's Pinto engine. Ours, though, had a 'Japanese spec' 1.6 CVH with two twin-choke Webers and free-flow exhaust manifolding that produced around 100bhp.

Comparing prices of the three is tricky since two can be bought in varying degrees of kitness. Our Westfield, featuring costly, Japanese-market extras like rear disc brakes, would be around £8500 sans taxes – but you could buy a basic kit for well under £3000. Likewise, a Caterham could cost £13,000 or more on the road – or half that for a DIY job. If you wanted a left-hand-drive Donkervoort, however, you'd be talking about £16,000 to £20,000 less taxes; and there's no saving because it only comes complete.

Whichever way you add up the sums, the Westfield is cheapest by a big enough margin to make you stop and think before going elsewhere.

Of course, the difference in power and performance of these three is obvious straightaway, too. And yet, on the other hand, it's much less obvious than you might think.

POWER WITHOUT WEIGHT

All three are exceptionally light, so all have the sort of power-to-weight ratios that get you grinning from ear to ear and leave hot hatchbacks floundering.

The Westfield is lightest of all – a full 396lb less than the Donkervoort – which does a lot to offset its horsepower handicap. The Ford CVH engine is not the smoothest or best-revving power unit around (it certainly wouldn't be our first choice for a sports car engine) but the important thing is that the Westfield has still got exactly the right sort of performance and makes just the sort of noises that a Seven customer would want.

We timed it under less than perfect conditions at 7.6 seconds to 60mph, and that's certainly quick enough to see off your average hot hatch. And there's the sort of punchy, instant response to the throttle that can make even a modest performer feel rapid.

After 80mph, acceleration tails off pretty rapidly as the little engine struggles against the air brake effect of those

BUT, WHEN YOU'RE KNEE-HIGH TO A JUGGERNAUT'S WHEELNUT, THE SPRAY COMES IN EVERYWHERE: OVER THE TOP, AROUND THE SIDES, UNDER THE SCREEN (YES UNDER) AND ROUND THE SIDESCREENS

huge front wings. With this engine, you'd be lucky to see much more than 100mph.

But so what? – it's primarily a little sprinter and, above all, there's the noise. The exhaust exits in front of the rear wing through a box that's recognisable as a silencer, though it doesn't seem to function as such. The Westfield's engine note barks its enthusiasm at a volume that has passers-by tut-tutting with disgust. By turns it can be amusing, enjoyable, embarrassing or tiring for the driver.

The Westfield's performance is 100 per cent faithful to the Seven philosophy. Acceleration and response are everything; top speed almost an irrelevance. And the noise is as much a part of the experience as the performance itself.

Derkse's Seven was even more responsive, a handy bit more lively, and a decibel or two quieter than the Westfield.

The Donkervoort was quite a different machine. For a start, having to pass noise tests and being a turbo, it was a whole lot quieter – the exhaust had a pleasant rasp rather than a cacophonous roar. Parents didn't drag children to safety as you approached. . .

And it was a whole lot quicker as well. Again under far from ideal conditions, we timed it at 5.7 seconds to 60mph – a few tenths could certainly have come off that had we been able to manage more than a single run each way. Now that's not a lot quicker than a 135bhp Caterham Super Sprint Seven, but the D8's horses show beyond 60mph: it just doesn't slow down. It charges past 100mph in less than 18 seconds (that's more than ten quicker than the Westfield) and still keeps on running. Donkervoort claims a 130mph maximum and he's probably not wrong

– we were over 120mph and still accelerating. This gives the D8AT a stratum of performance missing in the other pair: where they are running noisily flat out at around 100mph, it still has a final punch to deliver.

MISSING RAGTOP SPIRIT

Yet quick as it is, the engine is arguably the Donkervoort's weak link. A turbo, however good – and this one is good, with little lag – just doesn't seem right in a ragtop. You long for that snap of instant throttle response – you even long for the rasp of exhaust. The D8's gearbox can't match the slickness of the others, either. Its Sierra shift is just that annoying bit slower and more baulky than the lightning changes of the others.

The real surprise of this comparison, however, was to discover just how differently three such apparently similar machines could handle. A local kart-cum-sprint circuit gave us the chance to find out: rarely on ordinary roads would you dare exploit the outer limits of these near-racers.

The Caterham sets an impressive standard to measure the others by. Its responses are legendary; the steering is high-geared, sharp and quick; the cornering roll-free and the sheer agility of the little car quite staggering. It begs to be flung down the nearest country lanes.

But, like a racehorse, it's also highly strung and will dart around nervously unless steered with a firm hand. The ride is better in these de Dion days but still rates as 'firm' by regular saloon standards. Unfortunately, Derkse's car was not like other Sevens we'd driven. The inherent nervousness was exaggerated and, in the wet after a sudden storm, the car aquaplaned horribly and frighteningly. Put all that down, almost certainly, to those chunky tyres. The Seven was designed around narrow rims and will only cope with wide ones on dry, smooth surfacecs – but then Derkse normally only drives his in the dry, and Holland's roads are pretty smooth. . . Even so, it was a lesson in how easy it can be to mess up a car's handling and roadholding.

At first the Westfield feels very much like a Caterham. The steering is quick and sharp, the cornering is equally roll-free and the chassis's responses feel sharp and alert.

It's good – but it isn't quite as good. The car doesn't respond so nimbly to steering which is heavy rather than crisp; so the Westfield just loses that edge of agility and chuckability which makes the Seven such a thriller. On the other hand, it's much less nervous, having excellent straight line stability.

Corner it really hard and you'll expose a few rear end limitations. Once the tail breaks away – and it will, of course, as you'd expect (hope, even) – the car is hard to hold

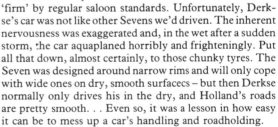

in a smooth slide, tending to come back abruptly and with a hard-to-catch wriggle of its rear. You've got to be trying some to find this out, though: grip until that point is prodigious and more than enough for the quickest road driving.

Very good, too, is the Westfield's ride quality. It's surprisingly supple, even over relatively poor roads, and has a clear edge over the Caterham, though really bad surfaces can set it squirming in a style that suggests the chassis hasn't quite got a Caterham's rigidity.

The outstanding car of the trio, however, is the Donkervoort. Indeed, it might almost be too good for its own good. Compare it with the Caterham and you'll think it lacks the hyper-active agility. Compare it with the Westfield and you'll find it lacks the red-blooded, sometimes slightly scary, appeal of a traditional, tail-swinging roadster. But compare it with something like, say, a TVR and you'll start to take Donkervoort's claims seriously.

His Eight does not handle like a Seven, and he says it was never meant to. It handles like a well-sorted, modern sports car. The steering is lighter and lower geared than the Caterham's but the D8's responses are just as pin-sharp. At the same time, it hasn't the Seven's darty, nervous feel – which might make it seem a little too easy to manage for some Seven fans.

But there's no denying the D8's superb handling and remarkable grip. It is very neutrally balanced and pushing the tail out of shape is not easy, even though you have 170bhp available to make it slide. Of course, it will power oversteer – and quickly once the turbo-boosted torque has started wrenching at those Yokohamas in a tight turn – but the car can then be held in the sort of foot-down oversteering slide that enthusiasts revel in.

Ride is equally impressive. The Westfield only feels smooth until you drive the Donkervoort, with its remarkably supple, stable and exceptionally taut feeling.

A MATTER OF CHOICE

The differences in cockpit layouts are as much to do with price as anything else. You pays your money and you takes your choice, between the clearly rather basic Westfield, with its cheap carpets and rough edges, and the smart Donkervoort, with its careful detailing and neat finish.

The dash in each is a simple flat panel – but well instrumented with a line of speedo and tacho, oil pressure, fuel and water temperature dials (plus turbo boost and oil temperature in the D8). The fuel gauge is furthest away in each – as a result we ran out *twice* in the Westfield, not spotting how quickly its tiny, six-gallon tank emptied.

A line of Austin-Rover-type flip switches works the lights, heater fan, wipers and so on. Only Donkervoort tries to provide a stalk control to work the indicators and that's a pretend one sprouting from the dash. It doesn't self-cancel and nor do the flip switches in the others, so you tend to leave a flasher winking for miles.

If you know the idiosyncracies of a Caterham, you'll probably recognise the D8's bigger seats, better sidescreens, sensibly placed handbrake (on the tunnel, not way over under the passenger side dash) and, most of all, a hood that latches easily into place.

In the Caterham, erecting the hood is nail-breaking, hard labour. The Donkervoort substitutes a simple screen-rail clip for the Seven's fiddly but traditional press buttons and the result is a top that will have you waterproof within a couple of minutes.

Westfield didn't send us a hood so we just got wet – very wet. True, the rain does actually go over your head when you're going quickly but, when you're knee-high to a juggernaut's wheelnut, the spray comes in everywhere: over the top, round the sides, under the screen (yes *under*) and around the sidescreens.

Those sidescreens are annoying in the dry as well. At anything over 60mph, they start to be blown in on you by the side force of the wind, pushing uncomfortably hard against your shoulder.

The Caterham's seating seems unnecessarily 'traditional' too. A one-piece backrest spanning the car and separate cushions provide little support and give no adjustment – you tailor your body to the car.

The others are more conventional, with separate fore-aft sliding seats. The Westfield's (remember its price) are simple flat jobs; the Donkervoort's costly, but grippy, buckets. In all of them, you sit down low, legs stretched out to small pedals; arms almost at full length and hands gripping a tiny leather-rimmed wheel.

Suprisingly, given their claimed extra space over the Caterham, neither substitute could offer a perfect footwell (the Seven's, of course, is very definitely cramped).

The Westfield's footwell was almost as tight a fit – certainly there was nowhere to rest the clutch foot, apart from the pedal itself – while in the Donkervoort, there was sufficient space but heel-and-toe shifts were impossible, which is a serious shortcoming in a sports car.

THE BIG QUESTION

Which is best? That's impossible to say. The Donkervoort is quite clearly a fully-built car and the others, just as clearly, are kits. The Dutch car is beautifully built and carefully detailed. Things have been made to work properly on it (the hood for example) that have been left as after-thoughts on the others.

You are paying for its crash-test certified structural integrity and low emissions engine, too. Consider it as a TVR or Morgan substitute and all that might well seem worthwhile – dynamically, it is the match of almost anything at its price.

But you can't get away from the fact that it looks like a Seven and, therefore, it's going to appeal to Seven enthusiasts. Maybe they would prefer something with a few more ragged edges; a bit more of the Lotus soul left in, rather than engineered out.

The Westfield is certainly full of soul and a few raw edges, too. After only a week, it was starting to look a bit shabby – carpets coming unstuck and the like. It's not a Seven, either: the handling isn't as exact and the glassfibre body isn't a patch on genuine aluminium. But it's got the soul of a Seven and, at the price, has to be a bargain.

However, it is very hard not to be persuaded that the original is still the best of them all. The Caterham does have a few flaws that ought to be ironed out – claiming 'originality' as the reason for not doing so smacks of an excuse, rather than a reason – but the handling is magical, the looks are terrific and it is, of course, the genuine article.

TRIPLE ECHO

CATERHAM CARS – CUSTODIANS OF THE LEGEND

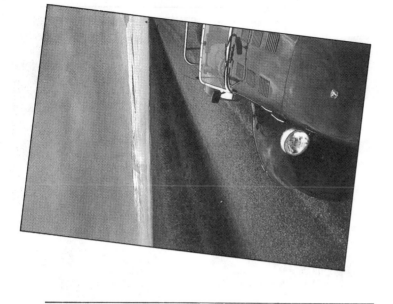

With the original Lotus Seven of 1957, Lotus offered a road car with performance and response in the same league as their world-beating racing cars. Throughout its life the Seven has been developed and improved in numerous ways yet the overall appearance of this classic design remains very much as it was conceived by Colin Chapman. Never has the rate of sympathetic development and improvement of the Seven been more rapid than under Caterham Cars whose association with Seven goes right back to 1959 and who took over manufacture from Lotus in 1973.

manners than previous Sevens, enabling full and safe use to be made of the performance offered by the range of tremendously powerful engines now available.

Colin Chapman's concept

Today's Seven remains true to Colin Chapman's concept of a light, highly efficient, ruggedly constructed car made up from tried and tested components. With even the most basic engine option, the power-to-weight ratio of a Seven gives tremendous acceleration. Coupled with superb road-holding and response this gives sporting motoring in its truest sense. With the more powerful engine options, the latest suspension design and modern tyres, a Seven has

breathtaking acceleration and handling that place it well towards the top of the supercar league.

The Seven is sold in forms to suit many tastes and pockets. From the most basic kit to the fully equipped component car with 16-valve Cosworth engine, there is a Seven for everybody.

Caterham's team of enthusiastic development engineers have seen to it that today's Seven has a chassis that is stiffer than ever, offers increased leg room, improved instrumentation, better weather-proofing and better braking. The current car has even better road

Government required the Seven to be subjected to stringent safety tests for TUV certification before it could be offered on the German market. Needless to say, the Seven passed all these tests with flying colours and achieved this envied qualification.

Caterham Cars is a Founder Member of the Society of Motor Manufacturers and Traders Specialist Car

In West Germany, Switzerland and Japan the Seven is supplied in ready-to-run form. In the U.K. it is available in two forms. The complete component car requiring straightforward final assembly comes with a Certificate of Newness which gains normal new car registration plates.

The Seven is also available in basic kit form for the customer to source secondary items such as engine, gearbox and axle separately, if desired. A kit-built Seven is not liable for car tax and gains a 'Q' suffix on the registration plates.

Seven sells right round the world from America to Japan. The German

ENGINE – FORD 1600 GT

Number of cylinders:	4 in line	
Firing order:	1.2.4.3	
Bore:	3.188in	80.98mm
Stroke:	3.056in	77.62mm
Swept volume:	97.6in³	1599cm³
Compression ratio:	9.0:1	
Valve clearance (hot) inlet:	.010in	0.25mm
Valve clearance (hot) exhaust:	.022in	0.56mm
Maximum power (DIN):	84PS	61.8KW
at:	5500 rev/min	
Maximum torque:	91.8lbf.ft	12.7mkg
at:	3500 rev/min	
Fuel octane requirement:	97 octane	
Valve arrangement:	o.h.v.	
Camshaft:	1, in cylinder block	
Carburation:	1, two choke downdraught. Weber 32 DGAV	
Spark plugs:	Motorcraft AGR 12	

ENGINE – 1600 GT SPRINT

Number of cylinders:	4 in line	
Firing order:	1.2.4.3	
Bore:	3.188in	80.98mm
Stroke:	3.056in	77.62mm
Swept volume:	97.6in³	1599cm³
Compression ratio:	9.0:1	
Valve clearance inlet:	.020in	0.50mm
Valve clearance exhaust:	.022in	0.56mm
Maximum power (DIN):	110PS	80.9 KW
at:	6000 rev/min	
Maximum torque:	105.5lbf.ft	14.6 mkg
at:	4800 rev/min	
Fuel octane requirement:	97 octane	
Valve arrangement:	o.h.v	
Camshaft:	1, in cylinder block	
Carburation:	2, twin choke side-draught, Weber 40DCOE	
Spark plugs:	NGK BP7ES	

ENGINE – 1700 SUPER SPRINT

Number of cylinders	4 in line	
Firing order:	1.2.4.3	
Bore:	3.28in	83.27mm
Stroke:	3.056in	77.62mm
Swept volume:	103.1in³	1690cm³
Compression ratio:	10.5:1	
Valve clearance inlet:	.022in	0.56mm
Valve clearance exhaust:	.024in	0.61mm
Maximum power (DIN):	135PS	99 KW
at:	6000 rev/min	
Maximum torque:	122lbf.ft	16.8mkg
at:	4500 rev/min	
Fuel octane requirement:	97 octane	
Valve arrangement:	o.h.v.	
Camshaft:	1, in cylinder block	
Carburation:	2, two choke side draught. Weber 40 DCOE	
Spark plugs:	NGK B8ECS	

WORKS:
KENNET ROAD,
CRAYFORD,
DARTFORD,
KENT DA1 4QN
Tel: (0322) 59122 (Parts)
(0322) 59125 (Service)
Fax: (0322) 524278

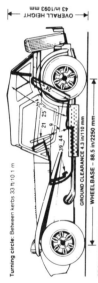

Turning circle: Between kerbs 33 ft/10.1 m
OVERALL HEIGHT 43 in/1093 mm
OVERALL WIDTH 62 in/1580 mm
GROUND CLEARANCE 4.3 in/110 mm
WHEELBASE – 88.5 in/2250 mm
REAR TRACK 52 in/1320 mm
FRONT TRACK 50 in/1270 mm
OVERALL LENGTH 133 in/3380 mm

WHEELS AND TYRES

Standard – Wheels:	5½ J × 13 steel	
Tyres:	165 R 13	
Optional – Wheels:	6 J × 14 aluminium alloy	
Tyres:	185/60 HR 14	

ELECTRICAL

12v, negative earth

Alternator output:	45amp.
Battery capacity	40ah.

WEIGHTS

Kerb Weight	580kg	1279lbf
Maximum weight:	820kg	1808lbf

FLUID CAPACITIES

Fuel tank:	8 gall	36.4 litres
Engine oil (inc. filter):	6.4 pints	3.6 litres
Gearbox oil:	3.3 pints	1.9 litres
Rear axle oil:	1.6 pints	0.9 litres
Cooling system:	9 pints	5.1 litres
(With Heater):	10 pints	5.7 litres

PERFORMANCE

	0-60 M/h	Maximum Speed	
1600 GT	7.6sec	100m/h	161km/h
1600 Sprint	6.5sec	105m/h	169km/h
1700 Supersprint	5.6sec	112m/h	180km/h
1600 BDR 4 Valve	5.3sec	115m/h	185km/h
1700 BDR 4 Valve	4.9sec	120m/h	193km/h

Road speed per 1000 rev/min. in 5th Gear: 20.2m/h 32.5 km/h (all models)

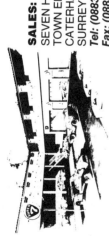

SALES:
SEVEN HOUSE,
TOWN END,
CATERHAM HILL,
SURREY CR3 5UG
Tel: (0883) 46666
Fax: (0883) 49086

SPECIFICATION SHEET
SUPER SEVEN

VEHICLE TYPE
2 seater, convertible sports car, no doors.

CONSTRUCTION
Tubular steel space frame
Aluminium panels.
Glass-fibre reinforced plastic nose-cone and wings.

MANUAL TRANSMISSION

Forward speeds:	5
Ratios – 5th	0.82:1
4th	1.0 :1
3rd	1.26:1
2nd	1.81:1
1st	3.36:1
Reverse:	3.87:1
Clutch actuation:	mechanical
Clutch diameter:	7.5in
Final drive ratio:	3.92:1

BRAKES
Two circuits, split front/rear, with system warning of low fluid level.

Front – Disc Dia:	9in	229mm
Pad Area:	14.7in²	9500mm²
Swept Area:	149in²	96700mm²
Rear – Disc Dia:	9in	229mm
Pad Area:	14in²	9030mm²
Swept Area:	149in²	96700mm²

Parking brake operating on rear wheels, actuated by hand lever. 190mm

STEERING

Mechanism:	rack and pinion
Turns lock-to-lock:	2.75

SUSPENSION

Front: independent	—	wishbones and anti-roll bar
springs	—	coil
dampers	—	telescopic
Rear: De Dion	—	"A" bracket and radius arms
springs	—	coil
dampers	—	telescopic

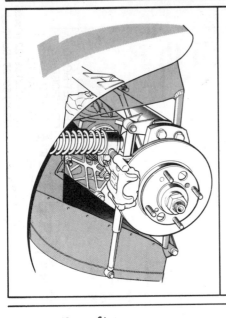

Among the most significant achievements of Caterham's development engineers has been the reintroduction of the option of De Dion rear suspension incorporating disc brakes.

The De Dion System was used on several of the first Sevens back in 1957 and was employed with particular success on the Lotus Eleven Le Mans cars. De Dion suspension is a semi-independent system with a separate differential unit mounted on the chassis. With its lower unsprung weight, the system offers the major benefits of improved ride quality and even better handling.

With its race-bred Lotus heritage it is hardly surprising that Sevens are popular race cars. Britain has a national race series just for Sevens and the car is suitable for many other forms of motor sport too. As a truly road-going racer, the Seven is an ideal way to go motor racing for the budget-minded enthusiast. In road-going form, a Seven is still capable of humbling the might of Porsche and Ferrari.

The Seven is a car for individualists, built for drivers tired of the increasing restriction and conformity of modern motoring. It is a car for people who love driving.

Manufacturers Code of Practice. To meet the standards of the Code the Seven has been subjected to a 91 point two-day inspection including an overall design analysis and safety test. The seat-belt anchorages are tested to National Type approval standards. Membership of the Code also means that Caterham Cars warrants each kit for 12 months and provides an approved assembly guide.